Fly Fishing the Inland Oceans

An Angler's Guide to Finding and Catching Fish in the Great Lakes

Jerry Darkes

HEADWATER
BOOKS

STACKPOLE
BOOKS

Copyright © 2013 by Stackpole Books

Published by
STACKPOLE BOOKS
5067 Ritter Road
Mechanicsburg, PA 17055
www.stackpolebooks.com

Printed in the United States

First edition

10 9 8 7 6 5 4 3 2 1

Library of Congress Cataloging-in-Publication Data

Darkes, Jerry.
 Fly fishing the inland oceans : an angler's guide to finding and catching fish in the Great Lakes / Jerry Darkes.
    pages cm
 Includes index.
 ISBN-13: 978-0-8117-0931-6 (pbk.)
 ISBN-10: 0-8117-0931-0 (pbk.)
 1. Fly fishing—Great Lakes (North America) I. Title.
 SH462.D37 2013
 799.12'4—dc23
                          2012047780

Contents

chapter 5

chapter 6

chapter 7

chapter 8

Foreword

Bob Linsenman

The front page of the Michigan personal income tax form has a small box in the upper right-hand corner. Individuals are instructed to place a check mark in this box if more than a certain percentage of their income comes from "seafaring or fishing." That little box says a lot about the direct and critical impact of the Great Lakes on the economy of a state with more than eight million citizens. Of course, these magnificent inland seas are central to the health and well-being of all of the United States and Canada, but they are particularly vital to the lands within the Great Lakes Basin.

I am a native Michigander and have lived in the northern Lower Peninsula for most of my years. As a kid growing up with a fly rod and ready access to great fishing water, I quickly came to appreciate the fact that living in the basin was a pretty sweet deal; all the small ponds and lakes had bass, pike, and panfish, and all the creeks and rivers seemed to hold trout. But as I grew older, I began to wonder about the "big lakes."

My first fish from the big water was a fine perch from Lake Huron, caught in front of my uncle and aunt's cottage on the beach near Port Sanilac in 1953. I was 10 years old. A few minutes later, flushed with success, I cast the small streamer my father had given me as far as I could and began to retrieve. A hard strike shocked me, but I was able to hang on long enough to land a smallmouth of about 14 inches. In my mind, my career path for the future was settled. I would hang out along sandy beaches on the Great Lakes shorelines and catch fish on flies. It did not work out exactly to objective of that early plan, but I came close—almost.

A few years later, I waded into the Lake Superior surf at the mouth of the Two Hearted River in late October and managed by dumb luck to catch a fabulous 6-pound steelhead hen on a streamer purchased from a nearby Newberry Sporting Goods store.

So far, so good. Now, where to fish next? What flies? What gear? When?

The Great Lakes area is huge. A quick look at the introductory chapter of this book will begin to give you some idea of the wonderfully extensive and diverse angling opportunities from western Lake Superior to eastern Lake Ontario. The core content of the book provides tools to develop specific road maps for successful fly-fishing trips throughout the region.

Reading through *Fly Fishing the Inland Oceans*, I made mental notes on waters fished and compared my experiences with Darkes's observations and suggestions—and found near complete agreement. More particularly noted were the places I have not yet fished, because they are now going onto my personal fly-fishing "bucket list." I have caught some great bass and pike (but no muskie as yet) on flies in Lake St. Clair. Lake Huron's coves and bays have been kind with steelhead and small-mouth. Lake Michigan, specifically near Traverse City, has generously offered chinook salmon, steelhead, and smallmouth. Lake Superior produced one of my favorite angling memories. At the top of the greatest of all lakes, near east of Nipigon, Ontario, I waded into the shallow bay near the mouth of the Jackpine River. My good friend Scott Smith, of the Thunder Bay Police Department, walked the beach and entered the crystal-clear water of the big flat a bit west of my location. It was dawn and our flat was dead calm. The sun's first beams glanced off the water and warmed the September morning. If the temperature (and clothing) had been a bit warmer, and the flora a bit different (palms instead of pines and cedar), one might think they were wading a bonefish-flat in pristine Bahamian backcountry. It was truly fabulous—but those tracks we had crossed on the beach belonged to a moose, and a cool breeze brought me back to the moment.

Scott had recommended both Lefty's Deceivers and Clouser Minnows in red and white, blue and white, and olive and white. I tied an olive-and-white Deceiver to the leader and cast toward a suspicious commotion, almost a swirl of water, about 40 feet away. It was indeed a fish-made swirl, probably a feed, and the lake trout ate my fly on the second strip. It was about five pounds and lovely, my first laker on a fly. We each caught a few more fish that magical morning. Mine were all lakers but, as I recall, Scott managed to touch a coaster brook trout of nearly 20 inches.

Since that golden moment in time, I have fly-fished many bays, coves, and a few reaches of big, open water on both the Canadian and American sides of the border. I remember wading into a small, sheltered anchorage near the mouth of the Bighead River on the Bruce Peninsula in Ontario with John Valk, of Grindstone Angling. We had been catching vibrant, wild steelhead in the river and decided that an evening with Lake Huron's healing water lapping at our waders might rejuvenate old bones. We caught fish on streamers without fighting current or slippery rocks or clay. We laughed like boys. Lake Huron always delivers.

As I read this book, these memories and more came flooding back in waves. More importantly, desires to fish new locations for new species with different techniques turned from temptations to intense yearnings. *Fly Fishing the Inland Oceans* gives full value for hard-earned dollars—an angling tool as valid as a good reel or rod. You can pick your favorite fish and then a piece of water (perhaps one close to home for a starter, or one more remote and tempting), and mesh these with a favored approach or technique, and go smile! Jerry's book is the great tempter, combined with a fine set of planning tools to ensure an antidote for any fever.

Let's say your in-laws live in Detroit and you are committed to a one-week visit in midsummer. Some folks could become mightily distressed at such a prospect, but a fly angler with this book and a little planning can turn the whole deal into a great adventure—with smallmouth, pike, maybe even muskie—on Lake St. Clair. Aunt Minnie in Duluth? Grandpa Bobby in Erie? Business trip to Milwaukee or Cleveland? It doesn't matter where, if the destination venue is within any reasonable commute by automobile. This book can make a seemingly ordinary trip into a rewarding event that will further an appreciation for the resource.

As an example, I read and made notes on the piece on brown trout, matched it to my existing equipment, and marked this with the nearest lake. I affirmed that bruiser brown tout can be caught in Tawas Bay of Lake Huron on Deceiver type streamers from October through December, and again from ice-out through May. My favorite rod—a 9-foot, 8-weight Scott saltwater model with oversize guides—and a matching Ross reel would be the right combination for this fishery. Excellent.

With a growth in overall appreciation comes full comprehension of the true value of the Great Lakes. This appreciation develops further with rewarding experience—angling success. And the appreciation merges into awareness of the requirement to preserve and protect. The lakes are mighty and robust, but they are also fragile in the extreme. The days of raw pollutants and rivers on fire are hopefully forever behind us, but new and dangerous threats—to the lakes and to the entire surrounding basin environment—continue. We as anglers must take a leadership position in the role of vigilant protectors by staying informed and by being vocal and demanding. Join a local organization and be as active as you can be; the world is run by the people who show up at meetings. The health of these lakes is not a trivial side issue to be entrusted to politicians. Get involved. Be a champion.

I have been fly fishing for more than 60 years, and even though the cold seeps in more quickly now, and the snow seems deeper and lasts longer, I simply can't imagine living anywhere but near these glorious sweetwater oceans.

chapter 1

The Final Frontier:
An Introduction to the
Great Lakes

The Great Lakes were created by a series of advancing and retreating ice sheets over a period of 500,000 years. The lakes as we see them today were formed at the end of the Pleistocene period, roughly 12,000 years ago, as ice-carved depressions filled with meltwater from retreating glaciers. They are connected by a series of narrow waterways, and water flows from Lake Superior down to outlets at the St. Lawrence River and Chicago Sanitary and Ship Canal. From Duluth-Superior Harbor to the start of the St. Lawrence River, the Great Lakes stretch 1,160 miles from west to east, with a total shoreline of 11,000 miles—longer than the lengths of the East and West Coasts of the United States combined. From north to south, the lakes span several climate zones: the southernmost point of the lakes, near Sandusky, Ohio, is in the temperate zone, while the northernmost point, in Nipigon Bay, Canada, reaches into the northern boreal (coniferous) forest.

A view of the Cleveland, Ohio, harbor area. Harbor and breakwall areas associated with larger cities attract a wide variety of gamefish and provide opportunity for urban fly anglers. The Great Lakes have a number of high-quality urban fisheries.

Sunrise hits the Wisconsin shoreline. The waters of the Great Lakes are one of the final areas to be explored by fly fishers. Wisconsin has 820 miles of shoreline on the Great Lakes, second behind the state of Michigan, which has over 3,200 miles.

The shoreline of the Great Lakes was home to Native North Americans for thousands of years before the first Europeans arrived in the early 1600s and remains home to some today. Rich in furs and other natural resources, the region was contested by the French, English, and Americans for many years; the present boundaries were established at the end of the War of 1812. Today the lakes form an international boundary of nearly 1,000 miles between the United States and Canada.

The Great Lakes are large enough to create their own weather systems. They serve to moderate seasonal temperature extremes, absorbing heat and helping to cool the air in the summer. In the fall, the lakes radiate heat, creating conditions that

While trollers work the offshore waters, this angler casts off the breakwall at Ludington, Michigan. Great Lakes harbors and breakwalls give fly fishers the opportunity to target migratory fish, such as salmon and steelhead, as well as nearshore species like smallmouth bass.

With Sleeping Bear Dunes in the distance, Capt. Jon Ray casts at the mouth of Lake Michigan's Platte River. Hundreds of Great Lakes tributaries attract seasonal runs of migratory fish.

support commercial fruit orchards and vineyards at latitudes higher than their normal range. In winter, the lakes are responsible for a phenomenon unique to the region: "lake-effect" snow. Winds pick up moisture over the relatively warm lakes and deposit it as snow over colder land masses. Lake Superior's Keewanaw Peninsula and the southeast shores of Lake Erie and Lake Ontario are best known for this weather pattern.

The overall economic value of the Great Lakes in terms of shipping, transportation, recreation, tourism, and natural resources is impossible to calculate. The lakes are the largest surface area of fresh water on the planet, with 5,500 cubic miles of water and a surface area of 94,000 square miles; only the polar ice caps contain more fresh water. The Great Lakes provide drinking water for more than 40 million people. The Great Lakes Basin, including its drainage area, extends more than 295,000 square miles and is home to more than 31 million people in the United States and Canada.

Smallmouth bass are the most widely distributed of all Great Lakes sport fish. They hit flies well and are excellent fighters when hooked.

The Great Lakes contain more than 250 species of fish. Through the late 1800s and early 1900s, the area supported a thriving commercial fishery, with a peak harvest of nearly 150 million pounds. Present-day commercial harvest still exceeds 50 million pounds. In addition to the revenue they generate for commercial fishing, the Great Lakes support a thriving sport fishery that brings in more than $4 billion annually.

The area supports an amazing diversity of plant and wildlife species and ecosystems. More than two-thirds of the fish species in the Great Lakes spawn in wetlands; many also rely on nearshore vegetation for food and shelter. Like many waterways, the lakes are under constant threat from pollution and invasive species. In the Great Lakes Basin today, some 100 individual species and 31 ecosystems are listed as rare or imperiled on a global scale.

I grew up in a suburb of Cleveland, Ohio, and lived through the years of algae blooms and dead zones in Lake Erie, along with the Cuyahoga River catching fire. At

Many fly fishers are unfamiliar with the techniques needed to fish big water, so they are a rare sight along most Great Lakes shorelines. With gear anglers close by, Jim Oates rigs up for Door County, Wisconsin, smallmouths.

An introduced species, steelhead swim in all of the Great Lakes and are one of the most popular sport fish.

an early age, I started fly fishing for farm-pond bass and bluegills and Pennsylvania trout. As Lake Erie gradually got cleaned up (the Cuyahoga River fire was one of the final events that led to passage of the Clean Water Act), fish populations rebounded and I learned to fish the big lake. Eventually, my love of fly fishing and big water crossed paths.

My first fly-caught fish from Lake Erie was a white bass. That happened more than 35 years ago. Quality sinking-tip fly lines had come onto the market, and we were finally able to take a fly to depth and hold it there during the retrieve. I used some of the first quality full-sinking lines that came out. If we could get flies to them, the fish would eat them. As more anglers have taken to fly fishing, equipment has become more and more sophisticated. Modern fly lines have become precision fishing tools. Few places are off-limits to fly fishing anymore.

Saltwater fly fishing has blossomed in popularity, and fishing the freshwater Great Lakes provides a similar experience. Anglers can stalk and cast flies to spooky fish tailing on flats in crystal-clear water, walk beaches in search of large predators chasing baitfish, and look for "blitzes" where gulls are feeding on forage fish pushed to the surface by gamefish. We can cast flies to breakwalls, jetties, rock-piles, current edges, and many other kinds of fish-holding cover. Most saltwater fishing scenarios can be replicated in the Great Lakes.

As many of our more traditional fly-fishing waters have become more crowded, the Great Lakes provide a vast, unexploited opportunity to escape and explore. An angler could fish here numerous lifetimes and not go to the same spot twice. The lakes offer rare, glamorous fish as well as common species. In the last two or more decades, I have managed to fish in all five of the Great Lakes, plus Lake St. Clair, and I feel like I have barely gotten started.

I had the idea for this book in my head for many years, but only recently did I feel I had enough knowledge to undertake such a project. I have traveled and fished the lakes from Lake Ontario's Henderson Harbor in New York, west to Minnesota's Duluth-Superior Harbor in Lake Superior. I also managed a few locations in Canadian waters. Thousands of miles rolled beneath my tires in the process.

In addition, I have spent countless hours researching all the information I could find regarding Great Lakes fishing—reading guidebooks, checking web sites, talking to tackle and fly shops owners, guides, and outfitters. I discovered there is a minimal amount of information available for the fly angler. There are very few guides who focus on Great Lakes fly fishing—probably a dozen or so, total, around the lakes. All are pioneers in their own right. Everyone was honest and open in sharing their knowledge with me. They realize there is a need for a centralized source of information, or at least a starting point for anglers to work from. I see my role as organizing the information and getting it to the fly-fishing public.

There are few no-brainers in Great Lakes fly fishing, but we have more technology available to us right now than at any time in history. Depth sounders and GPS help us point exact locations. Auto pilots on boats sync with electric motors and can hold us on a spot. Satellites show lake surface temperatures and cloud cover, and radar tracks storms. The tools we have are many.

Jeff Liskay hooks a fish on Lake Erie at a nearshore reef off Lakewood, Ohio. By incorporating the latest in gear and techniques, such as new sinking lines that allow fly anglers to fish at greater depths, Great Lakes fly fishers can catch fish in areas previously considered the realm of gear anglers.

The St. Marys River, the connector between Lake Superior and Lake Huron, is one of the few places in the Great Lakes with a fly-fishing history.

Weather, in particular, is a key variable on the lakes. As with any big-water areas, wind plays a big role in success or failure. One advantage to fishing the Great Lakes is minimal tidal influence, so that variable is out of the equation most of the time.

Fly fishing takes us back to the basics. Although we may have the latest in rods and lines to assist us, our challenge still boils down to tempting a fish to eat a hook that has feather, fur, and flash attached to it. We have "devolved" back to the simplest form of sportfishing, even though we are applying it to a massive area with countless places open for exploration.

This book, a fly-fishing journey around the Great Lakes, is designed to give you the tools necessary to locate and catch fish on flies in these big waters. The locations described here in detail are representative of many more around the lakes. Every effort has been made to give accurate information about places, regulations, seasons, and boundaries, but keep in mind that changes do occur, and you may have to adapt. A little additional homework will go a long way.

Whether you look for carp on a flat in northern Lake Michigan, strip a giant streamer for muskie in Lake St. Clair, chase coaster brook trout in Lake Superior, or night-fish for Lake Erie walleye, you will be doing something that few fly fishers have experienced so far. The Great Lakes are truly fly fishing's final frontier.

chapter 2

An Angler's Look
at the Lakes

The fly-fishing opportunities in the Great Lakes are nearly endless. All factors considered—among them species diversity, accessibility, and affordability—this may be the best "unknown" fly-fishing destination on the planet. Although more pioneering anglers are beginning to explore the fly-fishing potential of the Great Lakes, the focus so far has generally been on a few select areas. There are barely a handful of fly-fishing guides working on the lakes—and not because of limited areas to fish or because they are not able to produce fish for their clients. I believe it's because there is a general lack of knowledge and exposure within the fly-fishing community of what the Great Lakes can really offer.

As fly anglers, we tend to have tunnel vision, telling ourselves, "Since no one is doing it, it must not be any good." What is really needed is more fly fishers willing to step outside the box, fly rod in hand, and willing to explore, learn, and share their experiences. In the Great Lakes, they will discover a wealth of distinct, diverse, and productive fisheries accessible to millions of people, wonderful opportunities that have been overlooked and undiscovered.

Most saltwater fly-fishing scenarios can be replicated on the Great Lakes. We can stalk fish on clear-water flats, blind-cast along the edges of weeds and structure, follow schools of predators that have pushed bait to the surface, and track the journey of migratory fish as they move to locations where they become reachable with flies. We can target species anywhere from 6 inches or so to nearly 6 feet in length, depending on the time of year and the characteristics of the individual lake.

Most of the same gear we use to chase saltwater species will serve us well on the Great Lakes. We will also find similarity in fly patterns. Some will imitate small crustaceans and baitfish, others will mimic larger species, and some flies will just have color and movement to attract fish. Each lake has its own characteristics, and this is an important part of understanding the how, what, when, and where of fly-fishing success on the big fresh waters.

Lake St. Clair

Though Lake St. Clair is not considered one of the Great Lakes—it is usually included as part of the Lake Erie system—I am treating it as a separate entity in this book because of the superb fly fishing it offers. St. Clair can easily stand alone as a

The Michigan side of Lake St. Clair covers much of the Detroit metropolitan area, where there is significant shoreline development. In spite of its urban characteristics, this area is still rated as a top fishery for smallmouth bass and muskellunge.

distinctive body of water based on its size alone. But because it is also recognized as a premier warmwater fishery, it deserves individual mention. *American Angler* magazine has rated Lake St. Clair as "one of the top 100 fly-fishing destinations in the world." In spite of this, relatively few anglers have cast a fly into its waters.

Lake St. Clair is actually a wide spot in the St. Clair River, the outlet of the upper Great Lakes. It has a surface area of 420 square miles and a mean depth of just over 10 feet. The maximum depth of the lake is about 21 feet—except for the shipping channel, which bisects the lake for 18 miles at a depth of 30 feet for the passage of large freighters. St. Clair narrows down into the Detroit River and ultimately flows into Lake Erie.

The lake itself is a study in contrasts. The north and west shorelines are the Detroit metropolitan area, where there is extensive development. The Canadian shorelines on the east and south are much less developed. The St. Clair River Delta is the largest such wetlands area in the Great Lakes. At the delta, too, the Michigan area has been urbanized while the Ontario side is still wilderness, with much land set aside as the Walpole Indian Reservation. The south shore of the lake outside of the reservation has some development, which increases as you head toward Windsor.

The water retention time (the time it takes the total volume of a lake to replace itself) in the Great Lakes is measured in years. In Lake St. Clair, the entire volume of water is replaced every 21 days. This constant flow of cool water from Lake Huron helps to moderate the temperature of St. Clair in the summer, so even in the dog days of August, the lake's fish remain active. Although high winds can cloud St. Clair's water, it clears quickly; the bottom is usually visible nearly everywhere on the lake.

St. Clair supports a wide range of fish species. Of main interest to fly anglers are smallmouth bass, largemouth bass, northern pike, muskie, carp, and a variety of panfish—including yellow perch, rock bass, and crappie. Coldwater species such as

A fly-caught muskie from Michigan's Lake St. Clair, one of the most productive muskie fisheries around. This fish is about 38 inches long and is an average-size fish for the lake.
BRIAN MESZAROS

steelhead, salmon, and brown trout also wander through on occasion and can be an unexpected bonus.

The lake itself is a maze of weed beds, rock piles, gravel bars, sand flats, canals, and channels. It is extremely fertile and supports large populations of sport fish, forage species, and invertebrates like crayfish and burrowing mayfly nymphs. St. Clair is considered by many to be the best lake around for smallmouth bass and muskie. It is arguably the single best warmwater fishery on Earth and looks much like it was designed with fly fishers in mind.

Certain areas in the lake can be fished from shore, especially in the spring. The delta at the north end of the lake has a number of locations where

Riprap along the Michigan shoreline of Lake St. Clair prevents erosion and provides cover for bait, attracting predators. These areas are easy to fly-fish and can be particularly productive in the spring, when most fish move inshore to spawn.

The St. Clair River Delta is an extensive wetlands area that serves as a nursery for many of the lake's species. Much of the area is shallow, offering both wading and sight-fishing opportunities for fly fishers.

Capt. Brian Meszaros shows his approval of a Lake St. Clair smallmouth weighing close to 7 pounds, taken on a blustery day. Since the lake has an average depth of just over 10 feet, bass of this size are reachable with a fly all season long.

shorebound anglers can access extensive grass beds holding an assortment of species. Marinas on the various islands in this same area also support land-based fishing.

However, the best way to fish St. Clair is from a boat. Numerous private and public launch areas surround the lake. Suitable craft can range from a pontoon boat or canoe to a glitzy, high-powered bass boat. If looking to cover any distance, anglers need to pay close attention to weather conditions. As shallow as it is, Lake St. Clair can change from flat calm to a boiling cauldron of waves in minutes.

Fly fishing in Lake St. Clair is a very saltwater-like experience. You can slowly work flats and sight-cast to smallmouth bass, carp, and even northern pike and muskie. Even in deeper areas you are casting to visual rock piles, gravel bars, and weed edges. Many times you will see the fish eat your fly. Muskie appear from nowhere to follow a fly or a smaller hooked fish to the boat, leaving the angler with shaking knees and shattered nerves.

At other times you will find baitfish pushed to the surface as they are chased by larger predators. Groups of both smallmouth and largemouth bass will trap and ambush schools of emerald and spottail shiners. Just as in saltwater, diving birds are the key to locating these feeding blitzes. Here the hunter can also become the hunted. Muskie will sometimes come together to ambush the predatory schools of smallmouth bass, which themselves then push to the surface in their attempt to escape.

Lake St. Clair is one of the most heavily used recreational lakes in North America. The founding families of the American auto industry, including Ford and Dodge, built estates on its shores, and the lake is in a densely populated area of millions. In spite of the pressures from diverse recreational use, Lake St. Clair continually ranks as a top sport fishery. Catch-and-release is practiced extensively for the main species of interest—smallmouth bass and muskellunge. You would be hard-pressed to find—or even to design from scratch—a better lake for fly fishing.

Lake Erie

The shallowest of the true Great Lakes and the smallest in total water volume, Lake Erie stretches more than 200 miles from Toledo, Ohio, to Buffalo, New York. Four states (Michigan, Ohio, New York, Pennsylvania) and the province of Ontario, Canada, share Lake Erie's 810-mile shoreline. The Detroit River contributes the majority of the flow of water into the lake; the river drains the upper Great Lakes and Lake St. Clair. Much of Lake Erie's shoreline and drainage area is urbanized and agricultural.

There is a long history of human habitation along Lake Erie's shores. For thousands of years, Native North American tribes established seasonal settlements to take advantage of the lake's bounty: a wide variety of fish species and mollusks in the shallow waters and abundant waterfowl in the extensive wetlands around the lake.

An evening feeding blitz on Lake Erie. White bass have pushed emerald shiners to the surface, and gulls are joining in the action. Cousins of striped bass, white bass are distributed throughout the Great Lakes.

A steelhead is hooked at a Lake Erie river mouth; steelhead stage in these areas before entering tributaries to spawn. A variety of fly-fishing techniques—including dead-drifting egg and nymph combos, and stripping or swinging streamers—can be used in these situations.

After European settlement, unregulated commercial fishing and industrialization had significant negative impact on Lake Erie. Canada's Welland Canal, which has been around since 1932, opened the door to a parade of invasive fish species. Industrial pollution and farmland runoff turned the lake into a eutrophic soup of oxygen-depleting plants and noxious chemicals. By 1950, once-abundant fish species, such as the blue pike, were extinct.

Back in the 1960s, Erie was called "The Dead Sea" because of extensive pollution and uncontrolled toxic algae blooms. The Cuyahoga River, which flows through the industrial heart of Cleveland, gained international notoriety in 1969 after oil floating on its surface caught fire, an incident credited with securing passage of the Clean Water Act in 1972.

Erie has the shortest water retention time of the five major Great Lakes: its volume is replaced every $2^1/_2$ years. With the reduction in pollutants and farmland runoff, the lake was able to "flush itself out" relatively quickly. Gamefish populations rebounded. By the mid-1980s, Lake Erie had become known as the "Walleye Capital of the World" and was supporting a large charter sportfishing fleet. Lake Erie still supports one of the largest commercial freshwater fisheries on earth, focusing mainly on the harvest of walleye and yellow perch. The smallmouth bass fishery also took on increased prominence, drawing national attention to the quality and quantity of fish it produced.

The most recent development confirming Lake Erie's prominence as a sportfishing mecca is the extensive stocking and management of steelhead trout. Although steelhead have been present since initial stockings in the late 1800s, in the last decade Lake Erie tributaries have become important destinations for anglers in search of these oversize, migratory trout. The steelhead is an exotic species purposely introduced into the lake. Although self-sustaining populations of steelhead exist in Lake Erie, annual stockings maintain the levels needed to support the sport

Top left: Lake Erie is known for producing oversize smallmouth bass. This fish hit a chartreuse and white Deep Minnow—a top pattern around the Great Lakes. *Above:* White bass hit flies readily and are good fighters for their size. They normally travel in schools; where you hook one, you are likely to find more.

Above: Freshwater drum are abundant in Lake Erie and other warmer waters of the Great Lakes. They are strong fighters and will hit a variety of crayfish and baitfish imitations.

offs, flats, and other fish-holding areas. The average depth of this area is 24 feet, and it is the domain of all the warmwater species found in the lake. Smallmouth are found here in all hard-bottom areas; drum and white bass are also common. This is also an area where walleye can be taken regularly on a fly. The western basin of Lake Erie has countless areas of fish-holding structure.

The central basin of the lake runs from the borderline of the western basin east to Erie, Pennsylvania. Fly anglers can focus on nearshore and harbor areas. This section's natural bottom structure, protective breakwalls, and several artificial reefs all attract and hold fish. Avon Point, one of the largest single natural structures in the lake, is a key fishing area. Pennsylvania's Presque Isle Bay is the best fly-fishing area on the south shore, where an angler may encounter any of Lake Erie's fish species. The bay offers sheltered areas from nearly any wind, so it is a great place for float tubes, canoes, and kayaks. Wading anglers will also find many productive areas.

Lake Erie's third and easternmost basin stretches from Presque Isle to Buffalo, New York. Fly-fishing activity is best here on nearshore rock humps and points and also in spots where tributaries enter the lake. Smallmouth are the primary population and the most targeted sport fish, but steelhead may show up both early and late in the

Low-light periods are the best time to cast streamers to migratory trout and salmon. This hefty steelhead hit the author's Arctic Wiggler streamer at the mouth of Ohio's Chagrin River.

season. The area around Dunkirk, New York, is particularly productive. On the Canadian side, rocky areas—from Fort Erie, past Crystal Beach, all the way to Long Point—are prime smallmouth habitat. Long Point Bay also offers excellent fishing for all warmwater species.

Lake Erie is host to an ongoing list of invasive species. The zebra mussel was introduced in the late 1980s through ballast-water discharge from oceangoing freighters. This filter feeder now covers all hard-bottom areas in the lake. The round goby is another established invasive species. Gobies resemble sculpins and compete for habitat with native sculpins and darters. Although both are intruders, their effect on ecosystem has not been entirely negative. Thanks to the zebra mussel, the once-murky waters of Lake Erie are now much clearer, and this increased clarity allows fish to see prey from farther away. The slow-moving, soft-finned goby has become an easy meal for larger predatory fish. The overall long-term effect of these invasives has yet to be determined, but they are established and now play a role in the natural ecosystem.

Lake Michigan

The word "Michigan" is believed to come from the Ojibwa word *mishigami*, meaning "great water." Lake Michigan is the only one of the Great Lakes that is entirely in the United States. The largest freshwater sand dunes in the world are found along the lake's shoreline. Because of its long north-south orientation, Lake Michigan also has small but noticeable lunar tides. The shoreline of the lake measures 1,640 miles, and the lake reaches a depth of 925 feet.

Lake Michigan can be divided roughly in half by a line running from Milwaukee, Wisconsin, to between Grand Haven and Muskegon, Michigan. This line follows a rise in the lake bottom called the Milwaukee Reef, which creates within the lake distinct northern and southern pools, each having a clockwise flow. Prevailing westerly winds across the lake's surface help to moderate temperatures on the Michigan shoreline.

Because pocket-shaped Lake Michigan is situated south of the general west-to-east flow through the Great Lakes system, water circulates slowly through the lake, which has a water retention time of 99 years. Michigan's connection to the rest of the Great Lakes is through the Straits of Mackinac, which lead into Lake Huron. There is also access to and from the Mississippi River system via the Illinois Waterway at Chicago.

Guide Nate Sipple covers water on the Lake Michigan side of the Door County peninsula. Depending on the time of year, both coldwater and warmwater species can be targeted here.

The northern part of the Lake Michigan basin is heavily forested, with a low population density and an economy based on tourism and natural resources. The southern area is heavily populated, with extensive industrial and agricultural development. There are also numerous state parks, state and national forest areas, and several national lakeshore areas along the Lake Michigan shoreline. Among these are the Hiawatha and Huron-Manistee National Forests, Pere Marquette and Escanaba State Forests, and Wilderness and Muskegon State Parks.

The primary native fish species of interest to anglers are lake trout, smallmouth bass, largemouth bass, and northern pike. Steelhead, chinook salmon, coho salmon, brown trout, and carp are introduced species. Pacific salmon were introduced into Lake Michigan in 1967 to control alewives, the herring-like invasive species that reached the Great Lakes through the St. Lawrence Seaway. Lake trout populations had been drastically reduced by commercial fishing and by the entry of the parasitic sea lamprey, another invasive species. Lacking a predator, alewife populations skyrocketed in the late 1950s and early 1960s, and die-offs left millions of rotting fish washing up on the beaches.

Though not native to Lake Michigan, the salmon established themselves, and there are now self-sustaining populations in a number of tributaries. Regular stocking also supports sportfishing opportunities. Steelhead and brown trout, first introduced into the Great Lakes in the 1870s and 1880s, now also have natural populations reproducing in a number of river systems. These too are supplemented by stocking to maintain population levels for sport anglers.

The common carp was brought to North America by European settlers in the 1870s, when populations of native fish began to dwindle due to overfishing, pollution, and habitat loss. The fish was already highly valued in the settlers' native

When walking into areas such as the beaches at Indiana Dunes National Lakeshore, anglers need to carry with them everything they will need: food, water, foul-weather clothing, and extra gear.

Chicago-based angler Jim Linehan connected with this Lake Michigan harbor brown trout in spawning colors. JIM LINEHAN

lands, where carp were raised commercially as food. Adaptable to a variety of habitats and tolerant of pollution, carp spread rapidly throughout the United States. The first plantings of common carp in the Great Lakes were made around 1880. Carp supported a strong commercial fishery for years and recently have gained a growing fly-fishing audience. They have become, in fact, a targeted species for fly anglers, and northern Lake Michigan has become a key fishing location.

The shoreline of the lower half of Lake Michigan consists mainly of sand, silt, and softer materials. Fly-fishing opportunities are mainly in estuaries, where tributary rivers transition before entering the lake. Several examples of these are Muskegon Lake, White Lake, and Manistee Lake. These offer excellent fly fishing for a full range of warmwater species, as well as for steelhead and salmon when these are staging prior to migration.

The upper part of the lake is significantly different from the lower. North of a line from Sturgeon Bay, Wisconsin, across to Frankfort, Michigan, limestone bedrock forms much of the lake bottom and shoreline. Numerous bays and islands create miles of prime habitat for fish and prime fishing opportunities for anglers. The Door Peninsula extends into Lake Michigan at Green Bay, Wisconsin, where—

This Lake Michigan carp was taken along the Chicago-area shoreline by Jim Linehan. Carp have become a popular target across the Great Lakes, as they are often found searching for food in shallows, where they hit flies readily. JIM LINEHAN

despite having the world's highest concentration of pulp and paper mills—Green Bay supports a very productive sport fishery.

Big and Little Bay de Noc, along with Grand Traverse and Little Traverse Bays, provide a variety of angling opportunities—from stalking carp on hard limestone flats, to working rock piles and drop-off areas for smallmouth bass, to targeting salmon busting a cluster of baitfish. This area includes numerous smaller bays, harbors, points, and river-mouth areas, as well as many islands. The largest island, Beaver, has a very colorful history and is becoming an important destination for fly anglers.

Notably, Lake Michigan offers one of the most unusual opportunities to be found anywhere in fly fishing, a phenomenon that generally occurs during the summer. When lake water stratifies due to temperature variations, density differences between warm and cool water cause distinct temperature barriers to form. Thermal upwellings generated by wind cause the cold water to be pushed up the surface. Floating debris tends to accumulate along these "scum lines." Baitfish and insects are trapped in these barriers, and steelhead can be found feeding right at the surface, even though the water may be 300 to 400 feet deep.

Gear anglers, mainly trolling spoons and stickbaits, have fished these thermal lines for years, targeting steelhead. They are easily located by checking surface temperature of the lake (www.coastwatch.msu.edu) from satellite imagery. Adventurous fly anglers can use a larger boat for transport out to these areas, which may be many miles off shore. If conditions allow, they can transfer to a smaller craft or even a float tube to cast for steelhead. Again, this is a very saltwater-like situation, not unlike looking for mahi-mahi under floating debris along the Gulf Stream. Note that you have a narrow window of opportunity, owing to the distances involved and dependency on special weather conditions. However, if everything comes together, the results can be spectacular.

A more dependable opportunity occurs by fishing the temperature "flip," which can occur in one of two directions. Along the Wisconsin shoreline, prevailing west winds push warmer surface waters toward the Michigan shoreline to the east. This, in turn, pushes colder, deeper water back to the west—toward the Wisconsin shoreline. A drop in water temperature of more than 20 degrees F may occur when there are sustained west winds, bringing a bounty of coldwater species to the surface near the shoreline, even in midsummer. If there are sustained east winds, the Michigan shoreline will experience the "flip," and cold water will be pushed toward that shoreline.

This phenomenon is unique to Lake Michigan, owing to its relatively narrow width and the quick drop from shoreline areas to an average depth of nearly 300 feet. By understanding and taking advantage of the temperature change caused by windy conditions, fly anglers can target coldwater species that are usually available only during a short window of opportunity. For the flip to occur, wind speed does not have to be particularly strong as long as it is sustained for a period of three to five days. The longer this condition exists, the longer coldwater species will be available in near-shore areas.

Lake Huron

Lake Huron was the first of the Great Lakes to be encountered by European explorers; much of its basin is still heavily forested and sparsely populated. It is the second-largest of the Great Lakes by surface area (23,000 square miles), with shoreline of more than 3,800 miles, including the perimeters of the thousands of islands scattered through its northern half. Manitoulin Island, the largest in Lake Huron, is also the largest freshwater island on Earth; Georgian Bay and Saginaw Bay are two of the largest bays in the Great Lakes.

Water comes into Lake Huron from Lake Superior by way of the St. Mary's River. With a constant flow of incoming water and a sizeable outlet at the St. Clair River, Lake Huron's water volume of 850 cubic miles turns over relatively quickly; its retention time is 22 years. Huron is similar geologically to Lake Michigan, with its northern section of rocky shoreline and bedrock.

Lake Huron is the home of more than a thousand recorded shipwrecks, the most in the Great Lakes. Several of the most destructive storms to hit the Great Lakes have occurred here. The Storm of 1913 sank 10 ships, grounded another 20, and killed 235 people. The people in the Great Lakes Basin do not forget these losses. Michigan has five lakebottom preserves, and one national park in Ontario (Thunder Bay National Marine Sanctuary and Underwater Preserve) is designated to protect historically important wrecks.

Like all Great Lakes, Lake Huron has undergone significant changes over the last century. The population of deepwater lake trout was nearly exterminated by overfishing and by the invasive sea lamprey, just as in Lake Michigan. Stocking

Alewives are the primary food source for Great Lakes chinook salmon, and a decline in alewife numbers in Lake Huron has caused a shift in the fishery. Lake trout are more opportunistic feeders, able to consume a wider range of forage species. Their numbers are on the increase, while the salmon population is down.

The author conducting research on the St. Marys River. Rocky areas like this attract forage species, which in turn attract a variety of gamefish.

programs have attempted to reestablish lake trout populations, and Pacific salmon were planted to control alewife populations. Now alewife populations have been reduced to the point that salmon populations have begun to decrease as well. Consequently, stocking strategies are being shifted away from Pacific salmon to brown trout, Atlantic salmon, and steelhead. These species are more opportunistic feeders and will feed on another invasive species, the round goby, if other baitfish are not available.

Michigan's "thumb" area of Lake Huron has a number of locations with good early season smallmouth fishing. Using a long switch rod allowed for a higher backcast to maximize casting distance while wading. MIKE SCHULTZ

Warmwater species are abundant in certain areas. Saginaw Bay is the largest drainage system in Michigan, including the largest contiguous freshwater coastal wetlands system in the United States, and Big and Little Charity Islands, part of the Michigan Islands National Wildlife Refuge. The bay supports agriculture, manufacturing, tourism, outdoor recreation, and a diversity of wildlife. It is a productive fishery for walleye, smallmouth bass, and perch.

Georgian Bay, which lies totally within Canadian borders, has long been famous for sportfishing opportunities. It has a surface area nearly as large as that of Lake Ontario and the eastern coast of the bay, known as "the 30,000 islands," is the world's largest freshwater archipelago. The Georgian Bay Biosphere Reserve

The tannic-stained Ocqueoc River enters Lake Huron on a stormy fall day. River-mouth areas around the Great Lakes attract a seasonal variety of gamefish.

stretches from the Severn River north to the French River Delta. Georgian Bay Islands National Park, located near Port Severn, Ontario, is also in the Reserve.

The bay teems with a variety of fish species of interest to fly anglers. Smallmouth bass, northern pike, and largemouth bass are abundant. A developing muskie fishery, which is producing fish that average nearly 50 inches in length, is gaining recognition from a group of adventurous fly fishers. Pacific salmon are also present, and Parry Sound is one of the few places in the Great Lakes where lake trout have been reintroduced and successfully established.

Manitoulin Island separates the main part of Lake Huron from the North Channel. As the world's largest freshwater island, Manitoulin has many miles of shoreline and numerous sizable bays to explore. The island has four major rivers that drain into Lake Huron and attract spawning steelhead and salmon. In addition, the warmwater species found elsewhere around the lake can also be found around Manitoulin and around the many smaller islands throughout the North Channel.

The St. Marys River enters Lake Huron's North Channel at St. Joseph Island after flowing 75 miles from Lake Superior. It's entire length forms the international border between Michigan and the province of Ontario. Lake freighters bypass the St. Marys Rapids by means of the Soo Locks. Bottom draw gates at the head of the rapids regulate the river flow and the level of Lake Superior. Ernest Hemingway experienced and wrote about the rainbow trout (actually steelhead, but to some anglers they are synonymous) fishing here in the 1920s, proclaiming that "the rapids of the Canadian Soo have the best rainbow trout fishing in the world." All the coldwater species in the lakes inhabit the rapids at one time or another during the year. Although there is a population of resident rainbows in the rapids, steelhead are the lake-run fish.

Lake Superior State University in Sault Ste. Marie, Michigan, introduced a program to establish populations of Atlantic salmon in the upper Great Lakes in 1987.

A brown trout with its silvery spring coloring. Browns provide early season action in harbors and other nearshore areas across much of the Great Lakes. They take on more color in fall, as spawning season nears.

Note the tag on the head of this Atlantic salmon being release back into the St. Marys River. If a tagged fish is harvested, the tag should be returned to Lake Superior State University's Aquatic Research Laboratory for data collection.

The fish are raised to yearling size, released into the St. Marys River, and drop into Lake Huron to feed and grow. Atlantics return to the river in the early summer, moving into several power plant outlets and the main St. Marys Rapids. Fly fishers can target these fish both from boat and by wading.

The Bruce Peninsula is a popular sportfishing area and has numerous tributaries that attract spawning salmon and steelhead. The peninsula divides Georgian Bay from the main basin of Lake Huron and, with its two Canadian national parks and inclusion in the Niagara Escarpment World Biosphere Reserve, contains the largest remaining forest and natural habitat area in southern Ontario. Farther south along the Ontario shoreline, the Saugeen and Maitland River mouths provide opportunity for a full range of fish species.

North of Saginaw Bay on the Michigan side of Lake Huron, Tawas Bay attracts interest with a large limestone artificial reef that holds good numbers of smallmouth bass, pike, and walleye. The area where the Au Sable River enters the lake at Oscoda was the first place in the Great Lakes where steelhead were stocked—in 1876. From this spot up to Thunder Bay, there are fishing locations for brown trout, lake trout, and even walleye, along with the ever-present smallmouth bass. The Thunder Bay National Marine Sanctuary and Underwater Preserve, mentioned earlier, is the site of more than 100 historically significant shipwrecks.

From Thunder Bay up to the Straits of Mackinac, anglers can discover a variety of opportunities. Limestone flats around Presque Isle provide some of the best sight-fishing for carp in the Great Lakes. Nearshore anglers can find smallmouth bass, lake trout, brown trout, and salmon, depending on the time of year. The mouth of the Ocqueoc River at Hammond Bay is a top fishing area that attracts all species.

Near the Straits of Mackinac, rocky shoreline areas hold smallmouth bass, and flats are good locations to find cruising carp. Bois Blanc Island has numerous productive areas for fly rodding.

On Upper Peninsula side, St. Martin Bay and the shoreline east to the Les Cheneaux Islands area presents a variety of opportunities: a multitude of bays holding pike and largemouth bass, rocky areas with smallmouth, and hard-bottom flats with excellent carp fishing. These kinds of settings exist all the way to Drummond Island.

The best thing about fly fishing around Lake Huron is the number of state, provincial, and national parks and reserves along the shoreline. These provide shoreline access, launching areas for small boats and kayaks, camping and inexpensive lodging, as well as opportunities to engage in other activities when a fishing break is in order. There are also several guides here who have experience with fly anglers, but most fishers will likely prefer to explore in a "do it yourself" mode. Either way, this is a beautiful, scenic area with countless options for the adventurous angler.

Lake Superior

The largest freshwater lake on earth by surface area, Lake Superior contains 10 percent of the world's fresh water. It could hold the volume of all the other Great Lakes combined, with room for more. Superior drains a forested and sparsely populated area of more than 49,000 square miles, rich in natural resources and scenic beauty. There may be areas along the shoreline that have never been touched by a human footstep. More than 300 rivers and streams empty into the lake; the largest are the Nipigon and the St. Louis.

Lake Superior has a shoreline of more than 2,700 miles. If straightened into a line, it would stretch from Duluth, Minnesota, to the Bahamas. This immense body of water influences weather patterns over a large part of the United States and Canada. Lake-effect snows are generated when moisture picked up by wind blowing over the lake surface becomes snow when it reaches colder land masses. Annual snowfall on Michigan's Keweenaw Peninsula exceeds 200 inches.

In spite of the lake's immense size, man's control is evident even in Lake Superior. The Lac Long and Ogoki Diversions channel water to Superior that would, without interference, naturally be flowing into Hudson Bay. These diversions were implemented to transport logs for the pulp industry and to support the generation of hydroelectric power.

Duluth, Minnesota, at the western end of Lake Superior is one of the busiest ports in the world, despite being more than 2,300 miles from the Atlantic Ocean. More than a thousand Great Lakes– and ocean-going freighters visit annually. At the height of the iron-ore mining industry, Duluth was home to more millionaires per capita than any other city in the world.

Superior is the deepest, clearest, and cleanest of all the Great Lakes. The average depth is 480 feet, with underwater visibility of nearly 30 feet. The average water temperature is 40 degrees F. Water retention time is 191 years, by far the longest of any of the Great Lakes.

The northern shoreline of Lake Superior is rocky and extremely rugged, sitting on the southern part of the Canadian Shield, Precambrian-age rock strata that are

The Lake Superior shoreline features countless scenic vistas with little development. When the leaves are changing colors in the fall, the scenery can be spectacular. JIM LINEHAN

among the oldest on earth. Some rock formations tower more than a thousand feet above the lake. The southern shoreline—from Michigan's Grand Marais to Whitefish Point—is known as "The Graveyard of the Great Lakes" because of all the shipwrecks that have occurred in this area. The most famous of these is that of the Edmund Fitzgerald, which sank during a gale on November 10, 1975.

Despite its size, Superior contains a lower concentration of dissolved nutrients relative to water volume and thus has less capacity to maintain aquatic life. It can support a fishery only about one-tenth the size of that of Lake Michigan. Native species of interest to anglers are

Lake Superior's Chequamegon Bay is famous for the smallmouth bass fishery it supports. Special regulations have created an abundance of trophy-sized smallies. This fish hit a fly called the Tongue Depressor.

lake trout, brook trout, smallmouth bass, northern pike, muskellunge, and walleye. Introduced species such as rainbow trout, brown trout, splake (a brook and lake trout hybrid), and chinook, coho, and pink salmon also contribute to the sportfishing economy.

The overall fishery in Lake Superior has improved significantly over the past few decades. Lake trout populations have increased to the extent of being self-sustaining; stocking is no longer needed. Control of sea lamprey populations has been a key component to this improvement.

Shore and boat anglers work the power plant discharge at Ashland, Wisconsin. The warm water attracts baitfish, and predators follow. These discharges are fishable long after main lake areas have frozen over.

Several large islands and island groups are found in Lake Superior. Isle Royale, in the northwest corner, is part of the state of Michigan, the second largest island in the Great Lakes, and a national park. The park is closed from November to April because of the area's extreme weather conditions. Michipicoten Island, in the northeast corner of the lake, lies in the province of Ontario and is administered as a provincial park. Both of these islands contain lakes, rivers, and creeks that drain into Lake Superior; most angling activity takes place on their lakes.

Off Wisconsin's Bayfield Peninsula, the 22 Apostle Islands and the adjacent shoreline make up the Apostle Islands National Lakeshore. The focus here is sea kayaking, but there are good nearshore angling opportunities for steelhead in spring and for lake trout and salmon in the fall. Smallmouth bass and northern pike can sometimes be found in areas with aquatic vegetation.

Finally, the Slate Islands archipelago in northern Lake Superior, offshore from Terrace Bay, Ontario, is a popular sea kayaking area and source of much of the lake trout brood stock used to repopulate Superior. Northern pike are also found in the shallows of inlets and coves. These islands—now a Provincial Natural Environment Park, with no facilities available—are notable as home to Ontario's largest herd of woodland caribou. The islands were formed from a meteor impact a billion or so years ago and also contain some rare geological formations.

Several areas of Lake Superior are of particular interest to fly anglers. On the south shoreline, northern Wisconsin's Chequamegon Bay lies inside the barrier of Chequamegon Point and Long Island. Much shallower than the surrounding lake, the bay is composed of sand, rock, and other structure that provides perfect habitat. It is 12 miles long and varies from 2 to 6 miles across.

Smallmouth bass are the primary target here, and Chequamegon Bay is one of the best trophy bass fisheries anywhere. The Wisconsin Department of Natural

Capt. Leo Wright connected with this chrome bright steelhead at a Lake Superior creek mouth. Casting a shooting taper and a baitfish pattern produced this fish; this combination works all across the Great Lakes.

Resources has special regulations in place: an early catch-and-release season, followed by a "one fish over 22 inches" rule during the regular season. The peak time here is from mid-May through June, when fish are spread through the shallows to spawn; most are found at water depths of less than 5 feet. The target includes a mix of pre-spawn, spawning, and post-spawn fish, and bass can be taken on a variety of surface and subsurface patterns.

Flies continue to produce through the summer and into fall, when the fish move into deeper water. Offshore rock piles, humps, drop-offs, weed edges, and other structure hold fish; get the fly to them and they can be caught. Shoreline cover still holds some bass, so opportunities continue for the angler in self-propelled craft. In addition, the bay holds good numbers of pike that can show up at anytime, and also walleye that may grab a fly under low-light conditions. Anglers may also encounter steelhead, brown trout, splake, and salmon where creeks enter the bay.

There are numerous ports and harbors along the stretch from Chequamegon Bay east to Sault Ste. Marie, Michigan. Several sizeable rivers enter the lake, along with numerous smaller creeks; there are also bays, points, and islands to explore. The rugged shoreline has numerous state parks and national forest areas. Pictured Rocks National Lakeshore has several fishing access points where anglers may encounter trout, salmon, steelhead, brown trout, northern pike, and smallmouth bass.

To Minnesotans, the "North Shore" of Lake Superior runs from Duluth, Minnesota, past Grand Marais, to the Ontario border. Highway 61 follows this stretch before linking up with Highway 17, the Trans-Canada Highway, in Thunder Bay, Ontario. The scenery here can only be described as spectacular: the highway winds along high rocky bluffs with sheer drops to the lakeshore. A number of river-mouth opportunities as well as port areas are found along this stretch. Steelhead, salmon, lake trout, and northern pike are the species of main interest.

The Nipigon River is the largest of Lake Superior's tributaries. The home of the long-standing world-record brook trout, the Nipigon empties into the lake at the town of Red Rock, Ontario. Nipigon Bay is sheltered from the main part of Lake Superior by Black Bay Peninsula to the west and St. Ignace Island to the south. A good portion of the area is contained in the recently established Lake Superior National Marine Conservation Area.

The bay is home to lake trout, steelhead, several species of salmon, and northern pike. This area is also one of the few strongholds for "coaster" brook trout. Coasters are migratory brookies that cruise the shoreline of the lake but enter tributaries to spawn in the fall. They are one of the true living treasures of the Great Lakes. Nearly decimated by overfishing, special management strategies have brought coasters back from the brink.

With outstanding scenery and crystal-clear water, Nipigon Bay offers the opportunity to sight-cast to cruising lake trout and brook trout on sandy flats or rocky reefs. Numerous creek and river mouths attract fish, and one of the best is the mouth of the Jackpine River. All back-bay areas with aquatic vegetation hold northern pike.

Along Highway 17, the Trans-Canada Highway, to the east, numerous creeks and river mouths present themselves for exploration. Most of these are relatively short in length, often with waterfall barriers limiting any upstream migration, so there is a lot of upstream and downstream movement of fish. Be prepared for a lot of "do it yourself" work to access these places, but the reward is often worth the effort. There is a good system of trails and back roads; however, don't expect a developed ramp to launch a boat in most places.

The drive around Lake Superior's North Shore to Sault Ste. Marie goes through mostly wilderness areas. Rock formations up to 1,000 feet or more rise above the shoreline, and the scenery is breathtaking. The rivers are pure and wild. Countless coves, inlets, points, and bays are virtually untouched, just waiting for exploration by fly anglers. To give an idea of the size of this area, the distance from Duluth to Sault Ste. Marie is nearly 650 miles.

Lake Ontario

The easternmost of the Great Lakes, Lake Ontario is the smallest by both surface area and length of shoreline. It reaches 800 feet at its deepest point. The Niagara River from Lake Erie is the primary source of water for Lake Ontario, which flows into the St. Lawrence River at Kingston, Ontario. Bordered by New York State and the province of Ontario, it is the only Great Lake that does not touch the state of Michigan.

More than a quarter of the population of Canada lives within the Lake Ontario basin, most in the northwest in the Toronto-Hamilton area. The remainder of the shoreline, including that bordering New York, is largely rural. The south shore of the lake is a well-known fruit-growing and wine-making area, with cool breezes from prevailing winds moderating seasonal temperatures. Lake Ontario very rarely freezes over, so the south-shore area is also well-known for its lake-effect snows, when moisture-laden air moves over colder land masses.

Being the most downstream of the other lakes, Ontario has had its share of environmental issues. The infamous Love Canal area received both national and international attention in the late 1970s, when buried toxic waste was discovered leaking into the Niagara River. Canada's Hamilton Harbor is also a major source of industrial pollutants. The lake has also suffered from the initial influx of a number of invasive species.

In spite of these problems, Lake Ontario has a highly developed recreational fishery. Steelhead, brown trout, and Pacific salmon have replaced the native Atlantic salmon that dwindled through the 1800s by overfishing and habitat loss. Recent

Top left: Smallmouth bass are abundant throughout Lake Ontario's shallows. Fly anglers can target them in numerous locations. This fish hit the author's Meatwagon pattern. *Above:* Steelhead are a favorite target of fly anglers across Lake Ontario. They can be caught in harbor and river-mouth areas when staging to run upstream. A baitfish imitation fooled this fish.

Above: Largemouth bass are found in significant number in the shallow bays and ponds that surround Lake Ontario. While generally overlooked by most anglers, this species responds well to fly-fishing techniques.

evidence suggests that efforts to bring back Atlantic salmon are starting to have a positive effect, but long-term outcomes remain unpredictable. Lake trout still populate the lake and are available to sport anglers.

Inshore areas of the lake have good populations of warmwater species: smallmouth bass and northern pike in particular. Ontario also has a number of rivermouth estuaries, similar to those in Lake Michigan, where warmwater species are present year-round and where coldwater species become important as they stage for spawning runs.

The mighty Niagara River flowing out of Lake Erie is the main inlet to Lake Ontario. It offers seasonal fishing for most Great Lakes species and can be fished effectively by shorebound anglers. The Niagara Bar is a shallow area of materials deposited at the mouth of the river over thousands of years. This massive piece of structure is a significant fish-holding area.

As you head east along the lakeshore, fly-fishing opportunities exist at virtually every river and creek entering the lake, either in estuaries or more developed harbors with breakwalls and jetties. Eighteenmile Creek, Oak Orchard Creek, Salmon River, and Sandy Creek are examples of these.

There are also several distinct bays that offer excellent fishing opportunities: Irondequoit Bay, Sodus Bay, Henderson Bay, and Chaumont Bay all provide a seasonal mix of warmwater and coldwater species, with boat, canoe, kayak, and shore opportunities. There are numerous launch areas and state parks with access and facilities.

West of the mouth of the Niagara River, along the Canadian shoreline toward Hamilton, more creek-mouth and estuary areas offer angling opportunities. Despite the effects of industry, even the Hamilton Harbor area can be productive. The same is true for the mouth of the Credit River in the most urbanized part of this area, between Hamilton and Toronto.

The Toronto Islands, just offshore of Canada's largest city, provide opportunity for northern pike, largemouth bass, carp, and a host of panfish. There are plenty of places for a shorebound angler to catch fish, because bike and hiking trails follow much of the shoreline. Even the downtown waterfront offers a number of areas that can be fished with success.

East of Toronto, the mouth of the Ganaraska River is one of the best in the lake and again, a full scope of species is available depending on the season. This may be one of the best areas in the Great Lakes to try for a steelhead in excess of 20 pounds.

Continuing east, Quinte's Isle, also known as the Prince Edward Peninsula, juts south into the lake. The peninsula is surrounded by a series of points and bays, including the Bay of Quinte. This Z-shaped arm of Lake Ontario, with its several smaller arms, is a well-known sportfishing area, featuring several hundred miles of shoreline and a number of provincial parks.

Farther north and east, the Thousand Islands area begins at Kingston, Ontario. Amherst, Wolfe, and Main Duck Islands are still considered part of Lake Ontario. These islands are well known for bass, northern pike, and fall muskie fishing. For the fly angler, this east end of Lake Ontario is unexplored territory with excellent opportunities.

Resources

Compared to the amount of information available for Great Lakes gear and bait anglers, there is virtually no information that focuses on fly fishing. This book is the first comprehensive look at fly fishing across the Great Lakes; I look forward to more information appearing as anglers increase their exploration of this rich area. Local tackle shops and guides, web sites and online forums, magazines, newspaper outdoor columns, books, and other publications can all provide specialized detail and insights that Great Lakes fly fishers can use to their advantage.

I have found that it is helpful to get as much information as possible from local sources, even if they are geared toward conventional angling. With a bit of experience, an angler can usually transpose this data into a workable fly-fishing approach. Sinking lines and flies can easily take the place of light tackle and jigs. Large streamers can be thrown to replace crankbaits. Granted that the substitution may not be parallel in every detail, but the fly angler can often duplicate much of what the conventional angler does.

Sea kayaking has become popular across most of the Great Lakes, particularly on the Canadian side. By searching for kayaking information in an area, an angler can discover lesser-known launch and access locations, reef and shoal areas, camping locations, and sheltered waters, as well as generally picturesque locations. It is surprising that sea kayaking and fly fishing have not already morphed into major crossover activities.

Finally, state, provincial, and municipal web sites are a great resource for fly anglers in the form of general information about such topics as fishing regulations, boating launch areas, and locations and facilities of municipal parks. Again, this information will not be directed to fly anglers, but we can easily put it into a fly-fishing context.

State and Provincial Web Sites

Illinois Department of Natural Resources
dnr.illinois.gov
1-217-782-6302

Indiana Department of Natural Resources
in.gov/dnr
1-877-463-6367

Michigan Department of Natural Resources
michigan.gov/dnr
1-800-292-7800

Minnesota Department of Natural Resources
dnr.state.mn.us
1-888-646-6367
email: Info.dnr@state.mn.us

New York Department of Environmental Conservation
dec.ny.gov

Ohio Department of Natural Resources—Division of Wildlife
dnr.state.oh.us
1-800-945-3543
email: wildlifeinfo@dnr.state.oh.us

Ontario Ministry of Natural Resources
mnr.gov.on.ca
1-800-667-1944
email: mnr.nric.mnr@ontario.ca

Wisconsin Department of Natural Resources
dnr.wi.gov/
1-888-936-7463

Lakeland Boating
http://www.lakelandboating.com/

Lake Michigan Angler
lakemichiganangler.com

Milwaukee County Parks

McKinley Park
county.milwaukee.gov/ImageLibrary/Groups/cntyParks/maps/McKinley1.pdf

Bender Park
county.milwaukee.gov/ImageLibrary/Groups/cntyParks/maps/Bender1.pdf

Marinas.com
marinas.com
(listing of harbors and marinas around U.S. and Great Lakes)

Wisconsin Outdoor
wisconsinoutdoor.com

Great Lakes Angler Magazine
glangler.com

U.P. Hidden Coast Recreation Route
uphiddencoast.com

Buc's Michigan Fishing Report
bucsfishingreport.com
(weekly Michigan fishing reports)

Bays De Noc, Michigan
baysdenoc.com

Pursue the Outdoors
http://www.pursuetheoutdoors.com/boating/nautical-charts/charts.php?id=14908#

A Tight Loop: Fly Fishing the Midwest
ATightLoop.com

Greater Niagara Hotspot Fishing Map
erie.gov/hotspot

Lake Ontario United
lakeontariounited.com
(discussion forum and map of Lake Ontario with ports of call listed)

CoastWatch
coastwatch.msu.edu
*(a cooperative project between the NOAA CoastWatch Great Lakes Regional Node located
at the NOAA Great Lakes Environmental Research Laboratory in Ann Arbor and the Great
Lakes Sea Grant Network. Created & maintained by Michigan Sea Grant and the MSU
Remote Sensing & GIS Research and Outreach Services; supported by MSU College of
Agriculture and Natural Resources and MSU Extension)*

**National Oceanic and Atmospheric Administration (NOAA) Great Lakes
Environmental Research Laboratory**
glerl.noaa.gov

chapter 3

Warmwater Fish

A general definition of warmwater fish is species that prefers a water temperature of about 60 degrees F or warmer. Of course, seasonal changes may well force fish into water temperatures well below this range during the late fall, winter, and early spring. However, water temperatures in the preferred range are necessary for growth, spawning, and even general survival.

Although classified as warmwater fish, there are several species that would be better referred to as coolwater species. Among these are smallmouth bass, northern pike, muskellunge, and walleye.

These fish tolerate a wider range of temperatures than typical warmwater species. Smallmouth bass, for example, start their pre-spawn feeding when water temperatures are in the mid-40s, and they still feed actively when water temperatures reach the 80-degree range.

Muskie and pike also feed actively through the 40-degree range and even into the high 30s. This is particularly true in the fall, as they feed heavily in preparation for winter and spawning activities that begin shortly after ice-out. Pike are readily caught through the ice; they will also eat well during the heat of the summer, though they often seek cooler shaded areas or move offshore to deeper water.

Smallmouth Bass

The smallmouth bass reigns supreme as the most popular and accessible species for Great Lakes fly fishers. They are available from the Thousand Islands at the east end of Lake Ontario to Duluth Harbor at the west end of Lake Superior—and at countless points in between. Though usually categorized as a warmwater species, smallmouth are tolerant of a wide range of water temperatures. They feed in 45-degree F water and continue to eat even when water temperatures push up around 80 degrees.

Smallmouth may actually be the ultimate fly-rod fish. They eat flies readily from top to bottom and, pound for pound, are one of the toughest fighting fish there is. A 3-pound smallie can jump a half dozen times and still have enough left to bend a saltwater 8-weight into the cork. They can be ridiculously easy to catch at times, as well as frustratingly difficult to fool at others.

Smallmouth are not a true bass, but are actually a branch of the sunfish family. Their closest relative, the largemouth bass, is another Great Lakes fish of interest but lacks the distribution of the smallmouth. Smallies are also called bronzebacks due to their dark brown coloration. Their color often varies with the bottom substrate where

Smallmouth Bass

Hot Spots and Peak Times

Lake St. Clair
U.S. waters: mid-May–October
Canadian waters: last Saturday in June–October

Lake Michigan
Door County, WI, waters: May, June
Grand and Little Traverse Bays: mid-May to mid-July
Little Bay de Noc: mid-May–mid-July

Lake Superior
Chequamegon Bay: early May–mid-July

Lake Huron
Port Austin, MI, shoreline: May and June
Georgian Bay: last Saturday in June–September

Lake Erie
South shore estuaries: May
Presque Isle Bay: May and June
Upper Niagara River: mid-May–mid-July

Lake Ontario
Henderson Harbor area: third Saturday in June–July
Lower Niagara River, Niagara Bar–U.S. waters: mid-May–July
Canadian waters: last Saturday in June–July

they are found. Fish on sand or light-colored rock can be nearly golden in color, while those lying on a dark bottom or in shadows may be nearly black. They also have vertical dark bands on their sides that seem to "light up" when active and excited.

Largemouth bass, by contrast, are generally more green in color, with horizontal markings along their sides. Largemouth are generally found in areas with a softer bottom and vegetation. When closed, the jaw of a largemouth bass extends back past the eye of the fish. With smallies, the jaw will be even with the eye.

The average Great Lakes smallmouth will weigh 2 to 3 pounds. The largest ever recorded in the lakes were several fish just under 10 pounds, but anything over 5 pounds is worth talking about. Lake St. Clair, Chequamegon Bay off Lake Superior, and parts of Lake Erie are well-known for their oversize bronzebacks. Any fish in the 3-pound range or better will give a good account of itself on a hook.

Smallmouth bass are usually found on or near hard-bottom areas—the best are rocky, with a mix of rubble and gravel—which give them ready access to their favorite food: crayfish. Depending on time of year and geology, these locations may have depths ranging from a foot or two to more than 30 feet. Smallies will work

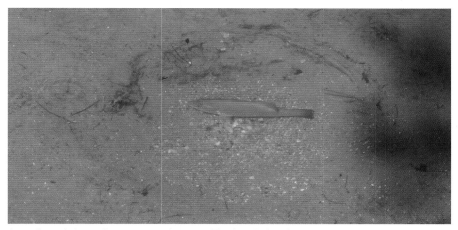

A smallmouth bass sits on a spawning nest. The female has fanned out the bottom to expose clean gravel. After the eggs are laid, the male guards them until they hatch.

sandy areas with mixed weeds as long as there is rock close by. You will not find them in soft-bottom areas.

Here's a prime illustration of this scenario. One day this past spring on Lake St. Clair, we were casting to visible rock piles scattered over a large sandy flat in about six feet of water. A single large rock was visible on the light-colored sand out in the middle of nowhere. We drifted within casting range of the rock and were treated to the sight of a 5-pound-plus smallmouth floating up from the shadow of the rock to engulf a slow-sinking streamer.

Prior to moving into the shallows, smallmouth stage off deeper areas adjacent to spawning locations. This is where they can be productively targeted by fly anglers.

Smallies are primarily sight-feeders, so clear water is a benefit in searching for them. They will sometimes go a long way to chase a fly and often follow right up to your rod before deciding if your offering is worth a taste. They often school with similar-sized fish, especially in the summer and fall. It is also common to have several smallmouth curiously follow a hooked fish, apparently trying to figure out why their friend is acting so strange. A quick cast by another angler will often result in a doubleheader, as one of these trailing bass hits the new fly.

Smallmouth have predictable seasonable movements and are found year after year in the same locations, as long as there has not been a drastic change in water depth. They winter in deep, rocky areas, often adjacent to steep ledges or drop-offs. They may suspend over a rock pile or a hump in the bottom, or along a drop. Feeding in winter is intermittent, so it's not a time to pursue them with a fly rod.

Steve Martinez shows a trophy-size smallmouth from northern Lake Michigan. Here, smallmouth are slow growing, and it takes many years for a bass to reach this size. Studies have shown that in the northern areas of the Great Lakes, an 18- to 20-inch fish is likely more than 15 years old. KEVIN MORLOCK

As spring water temperatures move into the mid-40s, smallmouth move to pre-spawn locations, which are deeper areas just off their spawning grounds. Fifty degrees is the magic number that really jumpstarts their feeding activity in preparation for spawning. Pre-spawning smallies are often found in 10 to 20 feet of water, sometimes deeper. Sinking lines are needed to get flies to these fish, but the reward can be striking it rich with bronzeback treasure, both in size and numbers.

As water temperatures continue to warm, smallies move to shallower areas and become more active. When temperatures stay consistently above 55 degrees, they will move onto their actual spawning areas, usually some sort of hard bottom with a mix of sand and gravel. Feeding will continue until the water reaches 60 degrees. This is absolute prime time for throwing flies, as fish will often be in water at less than 10 feet, in some places as little as two feet, and still eager to eat. Actual spawning depth varies depending on location and water clarity.

Male bass are the ones that fan out the nest. When conditions are right, females move onto the nest, and the eggs are laid and fertilized. The male will continue to guard the nest for the next 10 days or so, until the eggs hatch and the fry move off. The males will attack anything that attempts to invade the nest.

When the round goby first invaded the Great Lakes, it was feared they would have a detrimental effect on smallmouth populations, since they prefer similar habitat. There has been evidence of this occurring in some areas. Underwater video has shown swarms of gobies around smallmouth nests, waiting to eat the eggs. The male fish guarding the nests were driven off at times by a ravenous horde of gobies, who then cleaned out all the eggs on the nest. Fortunately, goby populations have stabilized in most areas, and they have become a food source for bass and other fish.

Most areas have some sort of controls in place to protect smallmouth during the spawn. This may be a closed season or a strict catch-and-release time period. Lake Superior's Chequamegon Bay is a good example: restrictive limits support the maintenance of a world-class smallmouth fishery while giving anglers access to great sportfishing opportunities.

The smallmouth post-spawn period allows first the females and then the males to rest and recuperate. Smallies will move to rocky drop-offs, points, reefs, and offshore rock piles. As summer progresses, feeding stays active, with bronzebacks chasing a mix of crayfish, baitfish, and gobies. Mayfly hatches, particularly *Hexagenia* species, can bring smallies to the surface. Smallmouth may also target smaller fish that are feeding on the mayflies.

Smallmouth may move into the shallows to feed under low light. At times, they may also follow schools of baitfish and suspend over deep water. They may join white bass in herding schools of baitfish to the surface, or lay beneath these schools, waiting for an easy meal as crippled minnows slowly sink down. During bright sun and the heat of the day, summertime smallmouth may move into areas too deep to effectively fish with a fly.

As the days shorten and water temperatures begin to fall, smallies will move tight to rocky points and drop-offs. They will also concentrate on offshore humps and rock piles. Crayfish will start to hibernate; baitfish will become the primary forage as they too migrate back to hard-bottom areas. There will be a pronounced feeding binge as the water temperature falls back into the 50s. Once the water temperature drops below 50 degrees, smallmouth will move to their deepwater wintering areas.

The importance of smallmouth bass to Great Lakes fly fishers cannot be overstated. They are a perfect fly-rod fish, willing to take flies under a wide variety of situations. Smallmouth bass pack an amazing amount of power and strength into their football-shaped bodies. They are widely distributed throughout the lakes, and they are usually ready to eat a fly if you put it in front of them.

Carp

The common carp, a European import to North America, is slowly establishing itself as a premier target of Great Lakes fly fishers. Worshipped and revered in its native Asia, carp were raised throughout Europe during the Middle Ages as a food for clergy and nobility. Few fish have enjoyed such a high place in society.

Carp were brought to North America in 1877 at the ongoing requests of European immigrants and as a viable replacement for native species depleted by over-

Carp have become an import fly-rod target in northern Lake Michigan. Due to its crystal-clear water, extensive rocky flats, and abundance of large carp, Beaver Island has become a popular destination. KEVIN MORLOCK

Carp

Hot Spots and Peak Times

Lake Michigan
Beaver Island: mid-June to mid-August
Door County: mid-June through July
Grand Traverse Bay: June and July

Lake Erie
Upper Niagara River: June
Lake St. Clair: May, June

fishing, pollution, logging, and other practices. The imported fish quickly took hold in their new habitats and, by the turn of the century, were well distributed and readily available.

At about the same time, people started to think of carp as a "substandard" species for several reasons. First, the fish were no longer exclusively a food of the wealthy. Carp became so abundant that they were available to the average person, and the upper class had switched to more costly fish. Second, whereas raising carp had been a precise science in Europe, based on hundreds of years of experience, fish farmers in North America were raising carp in any type of water available, often stagnant, mud-bottomed ponds. In short, carp just didn't taste good.

Although a viable commercial carp fishery still exists today, over time carp began to receive notice as a hook-and-line target. Most likely this can be traced to the British; our good friend Izaak Walton wrote about fishing for carp in the early 1600s. Let's fast-forward to the early 1960s, because it was at about that time that the "modern era" of carp fishing began to take shape. The July 1966 issue of *Field & Stream* magazine included an article titled "Those Copper Colored Bones," written by Mel Ellis, a Milwaukee outdoor writer. The article described Ellis's longtime pursuit of carp with a fly rod along Lake Michigan's Door Peninsula.

This article—and several others by Ellis—inspired angler George Von Schrader, who vacationed in the Lake Michigan area every summer, to follow his lead. In subsequent years, Von Schrader chronicled his carp exploration around the entire Great Lakes and presented his findings in an interesting self-published book, *Carp Are Gamefish*. To my knowledge, this is the first book that deals specifically with fly fishing in the Great Lakes.

Von Schrader's book featured specific locations throughout the Great Lakes where he had found fly-eating carp. He also included information about flies and techniques. This book led fellow Ozark-based fly fisher Dave Whitlock to link up with Von Schrader several times before his death. Whitlock also published several articles on Great Lakes carp, and it has been "game on" ever since. There are now a handful of guides across the Great Lakes who include carp in their repertoire of offerings to clients, and new carping water continues to be discovered.

A European import, carp respond to a variety of bottom-bouncing flies. Barbell eyes and rubber legs are part of many productive patterns such as Kevin Morlock's Tailer Teaser or the Coyote Ugly tied by Dave Pinczkowski. KEVIN MORLOCK

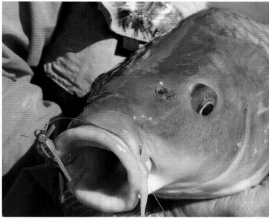

Jeff Liskay hoists a large carp taken in warmwater discharge near Michigan City, Indiana. Fish of this size are powerful fighters and will test an angler's equipment and skill.

There are a number of factors that have brought carp to the attention of Great Lakes fly fishers. First of all, carp are widespread in all of the lakes. Next they grow to a very large size—most in the 10- to 20-pound range, and some even larger. They are strong fighters when hooked, making long sustained runs, and test equipment to the fullest. Conventional anglers have little interest in catching carp, so the areas that hold these fish are uncrowded and underfished. Finally and most important, carp move to shallow flats to feed, where they can be sighted, stalked, and cast to in classic saltwater style.

Carp have one of the most highly developed sensory systems of all freshwater fish. Although their eyesight is quite poor, their other sensory organs are extremely sensitive. Carp employ their soft mouths and barbells to root around soft-bottom areas for prey such as crayfish and insect larvae. This feeding style allows them to feed in all water conditions—clear to extremely muddy. They also have a Weberian apparatus, a physiological feature of some fish that connects to the swimbladder and amplifies vibration received through the lateral line. When caught and released, a carp also excretes a chemical that serves to warn others of potential danger.

Although carp can be caught by blind casting, the favored fly-fishing method is to sight, stalk, and then cast to them. There are many locations around the Great Lakes where this opportunity presents itself. The best part is that many of these are shoreline locations and can be accessed right along roadways. The hard limestone flats of upper Lake Michigan and Lake Huron are prime areas for this. Although carp are present in many other areas in the lakes, chasing them is extremely difficult because of steep shorelines and soft bottoms unsuitable for wading.

Top sight-fishing takes place post-spawn, when hungry carp move onto flats to cruise for food. These fish frequently are opportunistic feeders, looking for any available creepy-crawly morsel. Carp are easy to spot over this light-colored bottom; they should be intercepted so that the cast can be made from an angle in front of them, just as one would cast for bonefish.

The months of June and July are the prime time for stalking carp on Great Lakes flats. As long as deeper waters are cooler than the adjacent shallows, carp will regularly move onto the warmer, shallow flats to feed. Once water temperatures equalize in both shallow and deeper areas, movement to the flats decreases significantly. In the northern parts of Lake Michigan, however, carp can be found working flats well into August.

Beaver Island in Lake Michigan has emerged as a primary destination for serious carp stalking. Capt. Kevin Morlock, of Indigo Guide Service, establishes his base on Beaver Island for most of the summer, chasing carp and smallmouth. The island, which has a colorful history, can be reached only by ferry or plane. It mixes the flavor of "old Michigan" with beautiful scenery, crystal-clear water, and big carp for anglers.

Carp also frequent many of the warmwater discharges located around the lakes, where they can be caught through much of the year. Here again, blind casting may produce fish, but it is also possible to find fish feeding in the shallows where sight-fishing is possible. These discharge areas are localized but offer a time frame that extends well beyond that of regular flats opportunities.

As more anglers seek carp, new fishing areas will be identified. Regardless of where you find them, Great Lakes golden bones provide anglers the opportunity to stalk, cast, and hook a large and powerful fish that will test both their skill and equipment to the limit. The carp has come full circle, once being the choice fish of the wealthy, then demoted to trash-fish status, and now emerging as one of the prime targets for Great Lakes fly fishers.

Northern Pike

The northern pike is another abundant species for fly anglers exploring the waters of the Great Lakes. The southern range of the northern pike ends along the south shore of Lake Erie. They are well distributed throughout the region, generally found in shallow, weedy bays or rocky areas that have mixed-weed growth.

Similar to smallmouth bass, northern pike are usually classed as a warmwater species, even though they are actually more active in cooler temperatures, favoring water below 65 degrees F. During the extreme heat of summer, pike may move into deeper, cooler water or far into the thickest weed cover, where abundant shade keeps temperatures comfortable.

Northerns are well known for their voracious appetite and nonselective feeding habits. Smaller fish are their normal fare, but they also eat frogs, crayfish, and just about anything that swims past them, including ducklings and muskrats. With a mouth lined with razor-sharp teeth and the ability to swallow prey up to one-third its own size, a hungry pike finds few food items to be off-limits.

Northern Pike

Hot Spots and Peak Times

Lake St. Clair
April–May

Lake Huron
Georgian Bay waters: May–June

Lake Ontario
Bay of Quinte: May–June

Lake Erie
Presque Isle Bay: April

Lake Superior
Nipigon Bay: May–June
Batchawana Bay: May–June

Lake Michgan
Big & Little Bay de Noc: April–May

The average size of a northern caught in the Great Lakes is 3 to 5 pounds, but fish weighing more than 20 pounds have been taken. Lake Huron is a focal point for Great Lakes pike anglers, with Georgian Bay one of the prime areas for the larger specimens. Saginaw Bay has an abundant pike population that is generally overlooked in favor of other species. Smaller pike are called "snakes"; anglers often hold them in disdain because they bite off flies targeted for other fish. A bite-tippet is a must when chasing pike.

Northerns are best targeted right at ice-out in the spring. If they are around, they will be found moving to the back ends of bays and to marshy areas with dark bottoms that hold radiant heat. Sheltered marinas that warm up more quickly than surrounding waters also attract fish. Pike will even hit flies before the ice has cleared completely. To target pike under these conditions, anglers need only enough open water to cast and retrieve.

Pike spawn when the water temperature reaches 45 degrees. They do not build nests. Pike are classed as "broadcast spawners"; that is, mating spreads the fertilized eggs over a general area, with no parent protection. After a brief post-spawn recovery period, pike will feed actively in the shallows again for a short time. Anglers can find great action at this point, as the fish are really in a feeding mood and will chase down just about anything put in front of them.

As water temperatures increase, pike seek cooler, more comfortable areas. Summertime fishing for northern can be difficult because the fish have either scattered in deeper water or are in deep cover. Weed beds adjacent to deeper water can produce fish, but not in the concentrations found in the spring; you'll need to do a lot of casting and searching that will require sinking lines.

Northern pike can be found across much of the Great Lakes region. Because of their razor-sharp teeth, a bite-tippet should be used in front of the fly. Note the wire used to keep this fly connected. Opinions vary as to the best wire to use, but the knottable wire now available can be easily tied with a simple clinch knot.

Northern pike are an apex predator in many parts of the Great Lakes. They are generally found in weedy, back-bay areas and are the earliest spawning species. Anglers fish bright, flashy streamers for these fish. BRETT MCCRAE

In the fall, with its cooler temperatures, pike again move back into the shallows. They are in top physical shape at this time, as they have been feeding all summer and continue to pack on weight for the upcoming winter. Look for them around decaying weed beds, rock reefs, and points close to deep water. The key to fall fishing is to cover water. The fish will not be as concentrated as they were in the spring, but the average size in the fall is generally larger. If you are after a trophy Great Lakes pike on a fly, this is the best time to try.

Muskellunge

Few fish excite Great Lakes anglers as much as muskellunge. They are the 800-pound gorilla on the block and take a backseat to no other species. Muskellunge are vicious predators, fearing nothing, and totally unpredictable in their behavior. Even better, they can be caught with flies. The last decade has brought a plethora of equipment and information to aid us. This is the top-of-the-food-chain, apex predator wherever it is found.

This is not to say that catching a muskie on any equipment, let alone a fly rod, is an easy thing to accomplish. I hooked my first one after only several hours of trying. "Not so hard," I thought. Then it took hours that added up to days until I was able to hook and land another sizeable specimen. If you plan to fly-fish for muskie, come mentally prepared for the game.

Muskie are widespread across the entire Great Lakes but are only concentrated in a few locations. Lake St. Clair is a muskellunge factory and one of the best places to try for them with flies. Lake Huron's Georgian Bay, the Upper Niagara River, and

Muskie

Hot Spots and Peak Times

Lake St. Clair
June to November

Lake Huron
Georgian Bay waters: June, September, October
Munuscong Bay: June, September, October

Lake Superior
Duluth Harbor: September, October

Lake Erie
Upper Niagara River: June, September, October

the lower St. Mary's River, connecting Lake Superior to Lake Huron, are other areas worth exploring.

As angling pressure on the species has increased, most areas have put restrictive regulations on the harvest of muskellunge. Most fish caught are in the 8- to 15-pound range. A 40-inch fish is the first benchmark in size, with a 50-incher being the holy grail for serious muskie chasers. Great Lakes waters have produced several fish over 60 pounds, but any muskie over 20 pounds can be considered a lifetime achievement for a fly fisher. With the restrictive limits that are being put in place, the opportunity for trophy muskellunge on a fly should continue to improve.

Muskellunge may live 20 years or more, especially in the northern parts of their range. Researchers have found very large fish that may be up to 30 years old. Muskies reach sexual maturity between three and five years; females grow faster and larger than males. Growth varies according to temperature and the amount and type of available food. In Lake St. Clair, for example, fish grow much faster than in Georgian Bay.

Muskie spawn when water temperatures are between 50 and 60 degrees. They are found in habitats similar to those of pike, and, where the two species overlap, usually spawn in deeper water. Muskie, like pike, are broadcast spawners and do not provide parental protection for their young. At times, pike and muskie may hybridize; the resultant offspring are known as tiger muskie because of their coloration. Tiger muskie are also propagated in hatcheries and stocked in a number of locales.

After spawning, muskie move off to deeper-water weed beds, points, and drop-offs, where they soon begin feeding aggressively to regain weight lost during spawning. This post-spawn feeding period is short-lived. As water temperatures continue to rise, muskie move into their summertime haunts, areas of ample cover and comfortable water temperatures. They are more of a warmwater species than pike and stay active even when the water temperature pushes 80 degrees. Among

The author (left) prepares to release this muskie—a surprise catch—back into the waters of Lake St. Clair. Muskies are opportunistic feeders, and this fish hit a crayfish pattern that was being stripped for smallmouth bass.

Capt. Brian Meszaros with a Lake St. Clair muskie. The spotted coloration is typical of muskie throughout the Great Lakes.

the largest and fastest-growing freshwater fish species, muskie also flourish at latitudes well south of the Great Lakes.

Little is off-limits to a feeding muskie, but their favorite forage is smaller fish, especially yellow perch and white suckers when they are available. Surprisingly, they will target crayfish at times; a number of Lake St. Clair fish have been hooked by anglers working crayfish patterns for smallmouth bass. With an impressive set of super-sharp dentures, muskie—like pike—can handle a wide range of food; again, it is absolutely necessary to use a bite-tippet when targeting them.

In summer, these fish can be very aggressive feeders and somewhat solitary. They often stay in a specific area or range as long as conditions are stable. Loose schools—fittingly called "wolf packs"—may come together to ambush unsuspecting prey. Lake St. Clair fly-fishing guide Capt. Brian Meszaros has seen this behavior a number of times, when full-size smallmouth bass exploded out of the water in terror after being cornered by a group of marauding muskies.

Intense feeding activity occurs again in the fall and continues until temperatures reach about 40 degrees. Actively searching for food, muskies may follow migrating baitfish, at times suspending over deep water. Usually, though, they prefer areas with cover. At this point, very large flies are the norm for anglers, as the fish are now targeting full-grown forage species. The fall period is probably the best time of the year for a trophy fish. Weather changes and fronts that shut down other fish may really get muskies "on a bite," so be prepared for adverse conditions.

The book *Muskie on the Fly* by Robert Tomes is a must-have if you are seriously going to pursue this species. Tomes has fished around the world but finds the muskie of his native Midwest and Great Lakes water as challenging as any species.

Largemouth Bass

They may be called "America's fish," but largemouth bass do not have nearly the distribution throughout the Great Lakes as their smallmouth cousins. They are found through the lower and middle parts of the region but are pretty much non-existent in the upper lakes. Largemouth are most often found among weeds and other cover in harbors, bays, and estuaries. They also hold on breakwalls and jetties that have abundant weeds.

Also called "green fish" or "greenies" by anglers because of their coloration, largemouth bass also have an irregular, dark lateral stripe. The average Great Lakes largemouth weighs 2 to 3 pounds. Some reach 5 pounds; they seem to top-out around 7. They are opportunistic feeders, willing to tackle just about anything they can fit into their oversize mouths. A variety of smaller fish, crayfish, frogs, and even small snakes are fair game.

Largemouth populations have increased significantly over the last decade in some areas, including Lake Erie and Lake St. Clair. Here, as the invasive and filter-feeding zebra mussel became established, they pulled much of the suspended matter out of the water; lake clarity increased dramatically. As a result of increased light penetration, weed growth increased, creating more suitable habitat for largemouth.

Several prime areas to chase Great Lakes largemouth are Lake Erie's Long Point Bay in Ontario and Presque Isle Bay in Pennsylvania. In Lake St. Clair, find woody cover in weeds and you are likely to find largemouth around. They are also abundant in several of the western Michigan estuaries, especially those formed by the Muskegon and White Rivers. If the water is shallow and warm, with weed growth, there is a good chance that green fish will be there too.

Largemouth bass are the largest member of the sunfish family and a true warmwater species. The upper Great Lakes are the northern edge of their natural range. Greenies do not get very active until water temperatures reach about 55 degrees. At this point, these fish begin moving from deepwater winter sanctuaries toward their spawning areas in the shallows. Pre-spawn feeding activity is of shorter duration than that of smallmouth, but of similar intensity.

Largemouth move onto nests at water temperatures of about 60 degrees, and most spawn at 62 to 65 degrees. Their spawning habits are nearly identical to

Overlooked by many anglers, largemouth bass are abundant in many warmer estuaries and bays around the Great Lakes. They are a great target for fly anglers as they will hit a variety of surface and subsurface patterns. Explosive surface strikes have endeared them to fly fishers.

Largemouth Bass

Hot Spots and Peak Times

Lake St. Clair
U.S. waters: mid-May–August
Canadian waters: last Saturday in June–August

Lake Erie
Presque Isle Bay: May–August
Long Point Bay: last Saturday in June–August

Lake Huron
Georgian Bay: last Saturday in June–August

Lake Michigan
Michigan estuaries: May–August

those of smallmouth, except that largemouth generally spawn in shallower water. After the spawning and a brief recuperation period, greenies regroup in areas of cover and abundant food—often flats with abundant weed growth. In some places, largemouth may drive schools of baitfish to the surface. Diving gulls often point the way for anglers; I have seen this happen often on Presque Isle Bay.

Largemouth have a well-developed sensory system and can feed well in turbid conditions. They are also active night-feeders, so in clear lakes, or during periods of continued bright skies, an after-dark adventure can be very productive. A word of advice: become intimate during the daylight with any area you plan to fish after dark. Even familiar places look a lot different after the sun goes down.

In the fall, as weed growth diminishes and water temperatures drop, greenies begin to move along points, ledges, and other areas that give quick access to deeper water. They feed heavily to pack on extra energy reserves for the coming winter. During this period, if you catch one, you are likely to find there are others close by. As temperatures drop through the 50s, largemouth metabolism slows and they drop into their wintering areas.

Largemouth are a great fly-rod fish; smaller ones are generally cooperative and hit surface bugs readily. Anglers often find a variety of panfish in the same areas frequented by greenies, and these can provide additional action. Abundant activity is a great stimulant for beginners, but fly fishing for largemouth can be enjoyable for all. Long casts are not required, the fish are not particularly selective, and the best areas are often close to the shoreline.

Walleye

The largest North American member of the perch family, walleye are one of the most popular Great Lakes fish. They are eagerly chased by thousands of gear

Though not often targeted, walleye can be caught on flies when they move into shallows to feed. Both pre- and post-spawn periods find them accessible the fly anglers. Walleye follow baitfish migrations back to shoreline areas in the fall. They also hit flies well at night.

anglers and support an extensive commercial fishery, most notably in Lake Erie. Walleye are called "pickerel" by many Canadians, but they shouldn't be confused with that diminutive member of the pike family.

Walleye are actively pursued from one end of the Great Lakes to the other. Their value to the region is worth millions of dollars from associated equipment sales and tourism as well as their commercial value as a food fish. Lake Erie is considered the top walleye fishery, but all of the lakes have areas where walleyes are present and support substantial sport fisheries.

Not usually considered a fly-rod fish, walleye are usually caught by accident while anglers are pursuing other species. However they can be targeted and taken successfully under the right conditions. The most important factor is that the walleye be within reach of a fly, and there are several significant situations where this happens.

The first of these is before and after the spawning period. Around the Great Lakes, walleye either ascend a river to spawn or spawn on shallow reef areas. Depending on the locale, there may be a closed season during the spawn, so be sure to check regulations about whether these fish can be targeted. Focusing on pre-spawn and post-spawn periods usually helps avoid any legal or personal ethical problems.

Walleye start to move from their deepwater wintering areas toward their spawning grounds as water temperatures reach 40 degrees F. Spawning takes place in rocky, gravelly areas in 3 to 10 feet of water, and the fish congregate just off of these shallows. Most spawning takes place as the water reaches 45 degrees, but this may vary a degree or two, depending on the locale.

During pre-spawn, a large baitfish pattern like an oversize Deep Minnow or Half and Half can be slowly fished on a sinking line and produce fish. Remember there are no young-of-the-year baitfish present at this time, so flies 6 to 8 inches long are not too big. Also, the biggest fish are likely to be taken after dark, so this is not an easy affair. It involves cold water and cold weather at night—pretty extreme conditions for the prospect of a fish or two. The incentive is a trophy-sized specimen of a species generally not targeted with a fly.

The post-spawn period can also be productive when fish move off the shallows and, after recuperation, begin to feed again. Equipment and techniques used during pre-spawning can be used now as well; low-light times offer the best opportunities. The low-light recommendation carries through most walleye pursuit, especially if you are trying to tag one on a fly.

Walleye

Hot Spots and Peak Times

Lake Erie
Ohio reefs: April
Shoreline areas: April, November

During the rest of the year, through the summer and on into late season, walleye are reachable when they move into shallower water following baitfish. Although some may suspend well off the bottom to feed in deeper water, these fish are nearly impossible to tempt with a fly. Fish that have moved shallow, actively chasing baitfish, are much better targets. They can sometimes be found in water as shallow as 3 to 4 feet.

Again, look for low-light conditions. My experience has been that walleye are much easier to tempt with a fly along shallows where waves are breaking, during periods of rain and drizzle, or after dark. These fish have oversized eyes designed for night feeding and also a well-developed lateral line. A fly that makes noise, pushes water, and has lots of flash—such as the Meatwagon pattern I tie—works best. Eli Berant, of Great Lakes Fly, also adds rattles to the Murdich Minnow and similar patterns in order to make fish-attracting noise.

Expect most of your catch to be in the 2- to 4-pound range, though you can catch larger fish on flies from time to time. Lake Erie provides the best overall walleye fishery, with an abundance of shallow water areas for anglers. Lake St. Clair, and Saginaw Bay in Lake Huron, are also productive; however, you might encounter walleye in many locations when throwing streamers in low light or after dark. Again, walleye are not a primary target for fly fishers, but they do offer novelty for shallow-water fishing.

Freshwater Drum

Much-maligned as a trash fish throughout the Great Lakes area, the drum has a distribution and popularity as both a sport and food fish unmatched in other freshwater parts of its range outside the Great Lakes. Also called sheepshead throughout much of its range, the freshwater drum can be found from the Red River drainage of Manitoba, south through the United States and Mexico, down into Central America. It is present in all the Great Lakes except for Lake Superior. It also supports a viable commercial fishery nearly every place it is found.

The only freshwater member of the drum family on the American continent, this cousin of the saltwater redfish can grow to impressive size and, when hooked, puts up a fight that exceeds that of most freshwater fish. Drum get their name from a special swim bladder capable of producing sound: its purpose is believed to be related to spawning activity.

Capt. Steve Martinez caught this large freshwater drum in Pere Marquette Lake. Drum
move in from Lake Michigan during the late
summer and concentrate here. KEVIN MORLOCK

Drum also have several other special
characteristics. Their lateral line extends
all the way into the tail, providing additional sense receptors for feeding in
muddy water. Freshwater drum also pos-
sess otoliths, circular calcium carbonate
"stones" that are part of the inner ear
and assist in maintaining balance. They
were highly valued by Native Americans
as jewelry and currency. Finally, drum are broadcast spawners. A female drum
releases eggs that float and can drift long distances before they hatch.

Drum are mainly bottom feeders, targeting a variety of insect larvae, crayfish,
and mollusks, including the invasive zebra mussel. Drum also target small baitfish
and may suspend high off the bottom at times to chase them. They also move onto
shallow flats to feed. With their highly developed sensory system, drum can be very
difficult to approach and nearly impossible to catch under these conditions.

Drum hit flies readily, and many are caught by anglers targeting smallmouth
bass. The biggest difference is that while a smallie normally takes to the air when
hooked, drum make a powerful run. The unsuspecting angler can easily end up with
skinned knuckles from a good-size fish. The average Great Lakes drum weighs 3 to
5 pounds and gives a good account of itself on an 8-weight rig. Fish in the double-
digit size range are caught regularly, and a drum of this size should be considered a
trophy for any fly rodder.

Freshwater Drum

Hot Spots and Peak Times

Lake St. Clair
May–August

Lake Erie
Mouth of Detroit River: May–June
Shoreline areas: June–July

Lake Michigan
Green Bay: May–June

Lake Huron
Saginaw Bay: May–June

White Bass

A white bass was the first Great Lakes fish I caught on a fly, starting a journey that continues today. White bass are a true bass, similar to the striped bass of saltwater, and are native to Lakes Erie, Huron, Michigan, and Ontario. Other local names for the white bass are "silver bass" and "sand bass." Most true white bass are in the 1- to 2-pound range; anything larger is likely to be a hybrid from breeding with white perch, a nonnative species.

White bass are most accessible during their spawning period, from mid-May to mid-June. They crowd the lower end of many warmwater rivers and can also be found on rocky points in open lake areas. Of all the Great Lakes, Lake Erie is the one that supports the largest number of white bass; the Detroit River estuary attracts literally thousands of white bass each spring. Despite this abundance of fish, few anglers concentrate on white bass.

For those who target white bass, encountering a school can mean furious action, with a fish taken nearly every cast on any white, flashy baitfish pattern. Birds diving to the surface often identify the location where voracious white bass are driving schools of emerald shiners to the surface; gulls also feast on the shiners. This kind of fishing resembles a true saltwater-style blitz, except that the primary participants are a little smaller.

If no birds are signaling the location of a school, blind casting to shallow rocky areas will quickly reveal whether any white bass are present. If they are, it won't take long for action to start. This is great action for any fly fisher and perfect for beginning anglers: the fish are cooperative even if casts are sloppy. White bass are strong fighters and give a good account of themselves when hooked.

After spring spawning, white bass scatter into deeper water, where they remain for weeks. By mid-July, they are again grouping together and following baitfish schools in open water. Feeding gulls continue to help locate feeding fish. Normally at this time, feeding will be on shallower structure adjacent to deep water. These feeding blitzes may last only a few minutes, with the fish disappearing as quickly as they appeared. At times, though, baitfish stay up for an extended period of time, giving anglers a chance to catch multiple fish.

White Bass

Hot Spots and Peak Times

Lake Erie
Mouth of Detroit River: mid-May–mid-June
Western basin reefs, islands: mid-May–mid-June

Lake Michigan
Mouth of Fox River, Green Bay: mid-May–mid-June

The largest white bass are usually caught at the start of the run. Fish this size are a handful on a fly rod.

White bass also follow baitfish into warmwater discharge and harbor areas. There, these fish always cooperate by hitting a baitfish pattern similar in size and color to their prey. As an added bonus, larger predators such as smallmouth bass and walleye often lie below the white bass schools, picking off an easy meal of crippled baitfish that fall through. In Lake St. Clair, you will also find jumbo yellow perch mixed in with schools of white bass.

Panfish and More

A variety of panfish are also available to Great Lakes fly fishers, including rock bass, bluegill, sunfish, crappie, and yellow perch. Rock bass, also called goggle-eye and redeye, are found in rocky areas of warmer lake regions. One of the smaller species, most weigh less than a pound. They are attracted to breakwall areas with lots of rubble and broken rock and are often found in the same area as smallmouth bass. Rock bass feed on crayfish, various insect larvae, and small baitfish.

Crappie are another species found in bays and around docks and marinas across the southern Great Lakes. This fish hit a Wiggle Bug fished on a sinking-tip line.

Though rarely targeted on a fly, yellow perch hit small minnow patterns well. They are often found along weed edges adjacent to deeper water.

Not considered a sportfish until recently, longnose gar have become a popular target in Lake Ontario's Bay of Quinte. Guide Glen Hales holds a sizeable specimen of this species, which is little changed from prehistoric times. GLEN HALES

Pennsylvania guide Karl Weixlmann shows a male bowfin in full spawning colors from Lake Erie's Presque Isle Bay. A truly unique fly-rod catch, bowfin can be found around marshy areas throughout much of the Great Lakes area. JACK HANRAHAN

Bluegill and sunfish spawn in late May and early June; these larger fish are concentrated in shallow water and easy to locate. Round, circular depressions in the back end of bays and coves signal their presence. Once an angler locates one of these areas, action can be fast and furious on small surface bugs and slow-sinking flies such as Woolly Worms and Girdle Bugs. Smaller-size flies are best because these fish have undersized mouths in relation to the size of their bodies.

Yellow perch are a smaller relative of the walleye, present in all Great Lakes waters and supporting substantial commercial and recreational fisheries. Because they are normally found schooling in deeper waters, they are not a primary fly-rod target. However, they can be caught regularly in Lake St. Clair due to its shallow average depth. Yellow perch are found along weed edges, where they feed on small baitfish and insect larvae.

White perch is an invasive species in the Great Lakes that has become established primarily in Lake Erie. This nonnative competes with yellow perch for food and may be a substantial predator on the eggs of various other native species. A member of the true bass family, white perch can hybridize with white bass. They can be distinguished from white bass because they are smaller, more olive in color, and lack horizontal stripes.

Top left: Bluegill are found in bays throughout the southern Great Lakes. This fish hit a jig-style fly. *Above:* Rock bass are also called redeye or goggle-eye. They are an abundant panfish in many areas and great fun on a fly rod.

Above: White perch are an invasive species related to white bass. They feed on small minnows and invertebrates and are often found along with both white bass and yellow perch.

Crappie are found in various locations around the lakes, but mainly in southern Lake Michigan, Lake St. Clair, and Lake Erie. It is hard to determine how abundant they are because few anglers intentionally target them; crappie are often an incidental catch. Crappie are most often caught in marina areas, around dock posts, and where trees and brush are in the water. They feed on small fish and insect larvae.

Unusual Opportunities

The Great Lakes also offer localized opportunities for several unusual species well off the radar of the fly rodder. In parts of Lake Erie, channel catfish can be caught with regularity on flies, and I assume it is the same in other portions of the lakes. A predator, channel cat will hit baitfish and crayfish patterns. This species can run quite large, often up to 10 pounds or more, and channel catfish give a good account of themselves when hooked.

Channel cats prefer a clean gravel or rocky bottom and are rarely found in weedy areas. Found across the entire Great Lakes area, they tolerate water temperatures in excess of 80 degrees F. They are most often caught during the warmer summer months and are most active at night or during low-light periods.

In Lake Ontario's Bay of Quinte, longnose gar have become the target of a growing group of fly fishers. Gar are stalked in shallow areas and hit both streamer patterns and surface poppers. Acrobatic fighters, gar up to 50 inches long have been taken on flies. Because of their long, bony snout, gar can be difficult to hook, and successful anglers often use a stinger hook system when fly fishing.

Longnose gar, found in backwater areas around the southern Great Lakes, have existed since prehistoric times; the species is little changed in millions of years. Gar have an air bladder that allows them to survive in water with very low oxygen concentrations. Their diet is primarily smaller fish. The best time for fly fishing for longnose gar is during the warmer summer months. Ontario guide Glen Hales specializes in catching gar on flies.

Bowfin are another prehistoric survivor whose species can be traced back 150 million years. Their distribution is similar to that of the longnose gar, and like the gar they also have an air bladder that allows them to survive in waters where other fish can't. The males have an amazing color pattern during spawn. These fish inhabit weedy, back-bay areas around the Great Lakes.

In Lake Erie's Presque Isle Bay, guide Karl Weixlmann has developed a technique to catch bowfin on flies. Although bowfin can be encountered nearly any time during the warmer months, Weixlmann concentrates his bowfin chasing during spawning time in May.

chapter 4

Coldwater Fish

The coldwater species of interest to Great Lakes anglers are trout, salmon, and a close relative, whitefish. These species are most accessible to anglers during spawning runs or when water temperatures are low enough to allow them to move into shallow, nearshore areas to feed. Coldwater fish are generally more migratory in nature, following moving schools of bait and seeking their own preferred water temperatures.

Lake trout, brook trout, and Atlantic salmon are native to the Great Lakes. Lake trout were and still are found in all of the lakes. Brook trout were historically found in Lake Superior and the northern reaches of Lakes Huron and Michigan. Atlantic salmon were found only in Lake Ontario, where efforts to reestablish them as a sport species are ongoing.

Rainbow trout were first brought to the Great Lakes from California in the early 1870s, and migratory populations were well established in a number of areas by the turn of the century. Brown trout were brought to the United States in 1883. First releases of both fish took place in Michigan waters: rainbows in the Au Sable River on the Lake Huron side, and browns in the Pere Marquette River, a Lake Michigan tributary.

Both chinook and coho salmon were brought to the Great Lakes from the Pacific Northwest in the early 1960s. In this instance, exotic species were introduced in an attempt to control another exotic or invasive species, the alewife. Both salmon species have done well, to the extent that naturally reproducing populations are found across the region. Pink salmon, another Pacific native, were introduced by accident and have limited distribution.

Lake Trout

Lake trout were once the most widespread of the native coldwater species found in the Great Lakes. They are still found in all five of the Great Lakes, but their numbers are well below historic levels. Lakers are actually a char and not a true trout. They inhabit cold, oxygenated waters, preferring temperatures of around 50 degrees. In the early part of the twentieth century, lake trout were the most important commercial species in the lakes, but overfishing and the invasion of sea lampreys dealt them a blow that they have yet to recover from.

Lakers are among the largest of freshwater fish—some attain weights of more than 100 pounds. The average size in the Great Lakes is around 10 pounds. Lake

Lake Trout

Hot Spots and Peak Times

Lake Ontario
Niagara River and Niagara Bar: December, January, May

Lake Superior
Nipigon Bay: May–September
Slate Islands: May–September
Isle Royale: May–September

Lake Huron
Tawas Bay: April

trout are slow-growing, reaching sexual maturity at 8 to 10 years and living up to 20 years or more. Their slow maturation has been a factor in the recovery of populations in most areas. Lake Superior and a small area of Lake Huron are the only places where natural, reproducing populations still exist. In the other lakes, they are still maintained by stocking, despite a 45-year program to reestablish self-sustaining populations.

Lake Superior has three distinct populations of lake trout: siscowets, paperbelly, and lean or redfin. Siscowets, the largest of these, are stocked in the lower lakes. Leans and paperbellies, often found in shallower, inshore waters, have many similarities. They are more colorful than siscowets and have a slim body shape. All lakers are typically carnivores, feeding on cisco, whitefish, alewives, and, most recently, round gobies.

Lake trout are most successfully caught during spring and fall. In late fall, they spawn at night over shallow, rocky areas. Be sure to check fishing regulations, as there are closed seasons during lake trout spawning in many areas. However, they may be caught as they move into shallow areas in preparation for spawning; they may also be targeted post-spawn in some places.

In preparation for spawning, lakers come into the Lower Niagara River from Lake Ontario to feed on smelt. They will follow smelt into the river again in the spring, when the smelt are spawning.

Lake trout may also feed on eggs from spawning salmon. The U.S. Fish

Although they are considered a deepwater species, lake trout do come within range of fly anglers at times. Ontario guide Paul Castellano caught this sizeable Lake Ontario specimen when it moved into shallow water to feed on smelt.

and Wildlife Service is presently conducting a study to discover whether lakers are also attempting to spawn in the river.

The best way to target lake trout is with a baitfish pattern fished on some sort of sinking-tip line. When water temperatures consistently stay below 50 degrees, lakers will move into shallow areas to feed on baitfish. When there is insect activity, they may even feed on the surface. Ontario outdoor writer Scott Earl Smith has an excellent primer (http://www.wildernessnorth.com/pdf/fly-rod-lake-trout.pdf) on fly-rod lake trout.

Lakers are identified by their deeply forked tail and light markings over a darker gray or greenish body. Their lower body fins are edged in white. The aptly named redfin variety is more colorful, with reddish orange fins. Splake, a hybrid cross between a female lake trout and male brook trout, rarely are bred in nature; nearly all splake are hatchery-bred.

Brook Trout

Brook trout once roamed the nearshore waters and tributaries of Lake Superior in uncountable numbers. Calling them "coasters" and "rock trout," sportfishing accounts from the late 1800s tell of catching dozens of these fish, up to 5 pounds and larger, in a single day. This fishery attracted anglers from all over the world, and unregulated fishing quickly took its toll. By the mid-1900s, only a remnant of the original population remained. The current world-record-weight brook trout—14.8 pounds—was taken in Ontario's Nipigon River in 1916.

Brookies are also a char rather than a true trout. Like the coal miner's canary, brook trout are vulnerable to the slightest change in their environment and early indicators of potential threats to other species. Overfishing, logging, dams, and pollution, plus competition for food with other stocked trout and salmon, reduced Lake Superior's brook trout to near extinction. In the United States, there are only two documented remnant populations, one in Michigan's Salmon Trout River and the other in the waters around Isle Royale. There are likely small numbers of fish scattered along Lake Superior's South Shore, but not in any concentration.

Coasters are believed to spend their entire life in the lake, apart from spawning. They stage off river mouths in late July and early August, move upstream in late August and September, and spawn for the most part in October. While in lakes, these fish have a silvery coloration, but they develop typical brook trout spawning colors once they ascend spawning streams.

Brook Trout

Hot Spots and Peak Times

Lake Superior
Nipigon Bay, North Shore river mouths,
Isle Royale, MI: June–August

After being nearly decimated by overharvesting, coaster brook trout are making a slow but steady comeback thanks to strict seasons and catch limits. Still showing its silvery lake color, this fish was caught along Lake Superior's North Shore. Coasters may be encountered in a handful of places—in Lake Superior's U.S. shoreline waters and also around Isle Royale.
JIM LINEHAN

A Lake Superior coaster brook trout. The area around Nipigon Bay is the best place to target these large, lake-dwelling brookies.
SCOTT EARL SMITH

The hybrid splake (a cross between a female lake trout and male brook trout) are stocked in a number of locations across the northern lakes. They can tolerate locations less desirable than for either of their parent species. They grow faster than brook trout in the wild and eat a wider range of forage. Splake are often hard to distinguish from brook trout, and it is quite possible that some undocumented coaster catches are actually splake.

Coasters respond well to a variety of streamer patterns fished around shoreline areas and river mouths. Ontario fly-fishing guide and authority Scott Earl Smith prefers colorful, sculpin-like patterns such as the Green-Butt Monkey or Yellow-Butt Monkey. A floating or intermediate head line is generally adequate. Minnesota guide Tim Pearson has had success in Minnesota waters with a pattern he ties—the Black Lake Leech. Both men have spent a lifetime fishing Lake Superior shoreline areas and appreciate how special these lake-dwelling brookies are.

Efforts to get coasters put on the endangered species list have failed because, genetically, they are similar to other brook trout. Behaviorally they are much different, spending nearly all their lives in a rocky, sheltered habitat, often within 50 feet of shore. The province of Ontario has had success in restoration of populations, primarily in the Nipigon Bay area. There is a new research initiative to help protect coaster brook trout. Complete information on the Coaster Brook Trout Research Unit, part of the Greater Lake Superior Foundation, can be found at www.thegreater lakesuperiorfoundation.org.

The book *Superior Fishing* by Robert Barnwell Roosevelt gives a detailed narrative of the Lake Superior coaster fishery of the latter 1800s. Published in 1884, the book chronicles an extended trip to the North Shore of Lake Superior in pursuit of brook trout. The trout fishing in Lake Superior at this time was described as the best in the world.

Atlantic Salmon

The largest freshwater population of Atlantic salmon once lived in Lake Ontario, along with other populations of fish that migrated to the Atlantic Ocean through the St. Lawrence River. Known as the premier sport fish of fresh water, these salmon were once abundant beyond contemporary imagination. In the mid-1800s, farmers collected them with pitchforks during their spawning runs into Lake Ontario tributaries. By the end of the nineteenth century, overfishing—and habitat loss through deforestation, pollution, and dam construction—had eliminated Atlantics from the lake and its tributaries.

Various attempts were made through the 1900s to reestablish Atlantic populations. Until recently, they have been unsuccessful. A long-term goal of Great Lakes fisheries managers is to restore the populations of indigenous species, and both the state of New York and the province of Ontario share the goal of restoring a self-sustaining population of Atlantic salmon to Lake Ontario. Successful natural reproduction has been documented in New York's Salmon River, and Ontario recently launched an ambitious plan called the Lake Ontario Atlantic Salmon Restoration Program (www.bringbackthesalmon.ca).

At this time, given the limited populations, it would be difficult to specifically target Atlantics in the Great Lakes; most of the catches that do occur are incidental. However, with a lot of work and research, coupled with a bit of luck, Atlantic salmon populations in Lake Ontario may, at some future time, again support a predictable fishery.

Right now, the most successful reintroduction of Atlantic into the Great Lakes has been on the St. Marys River at Sault Ste. Marie, Michigan. Here, starting in 1987, the Aquatic Research Laboratory at Lake Superior State University, Edison Sault Electric Power Company, and the Michigan Department of Natural Resources teamed up to stock Atlantic salmon that drop into Lake Huron to feed and then return to the river.

They stocked using a landlocked salmon strain from Grand Lake Stream, Maine. The fish have been returning to the St. Marys Rapids area from late May to early June each year, where they remain until spawning is completed in late October. Although successful reproduction has been limited in the river so far, the returns of stocked fish have been good enough to support a dependable sport fishery during the summer, when other coldwater species are at their lowest numbers. Atlantics in

Atlantic Salmon

Hot Spots and Peak Times

Lake Huron
St. Marys River: June–October

A male Atlantic salmon caught in the St. Marys River Rapids in September. This fish has transitioned into spawning coloration.
WAEL DARDIR

This St. Marys Atlantic salmon shows early summer coloration. It is still bright silver and just showing the kype beginning to form, identifying it as a male. Atlantics generally start to enter the rapids area in mid-June.
JIM LINEHAN

excess of 20 pounds have been caught here, but the average fish is in the 3- to 7-pound range. Anglers can find both boat and shore fly-fishing opportunities.

Fly anglers may encounter a very few Atlantics along the shorelines of Lakes Huron or Ontario. The populations are low to begin with, and the area an angler would have to cover to find them is large. The few that are caught are incidental catches by anglers after steelhead or browns; the salmon most often hit a baitfish pattern.

However, once the fish migrate into the St. Marys, they can be specifically targeted with a variety of techniques and fly patterns. When fish first arrive in late May, they are scattered; local anglers often troll for them New England–style, with sinking lines and classic smelt-imitating patterns such as the Gray Ghost or Magog Smelt. This entails using an 8-weight rig, letting out line, and putting the rod into a rod holder while motoring close along the shoreline. It is a matter of covering as much water as possible until a salmon grabs the fly.

Fish that migrate into the power-plant areas generally hit best on small dead-drifted nymphs. A variety of insects are washed through the turbines and create a smorgasbord for feeding salmon. Generic patterns, such as Hare's Ears, Pheasant Tails, and Prince Nymphs, will produce fish. It may take a bit of experimenting to find the right combination of size and color. A two-nymph rig, fished on a 9- or 9½-foot, 7- or 8-weight rod and floating line, is most popular.

In the rapids, flies can be dead-drifted through pockets and pools, swung through likely holding areas, and stripped when smelt move into the area. Here, 8-weight rods are the norm in order to be able to handle fish in the current. Switch rods are popular for those wanting the option to dead-drift or swing. True two-hand rods up to 14 feet can also be used effectively here. Green Caddis and Black Stones are the most effective patterns to dead-drift. Swung flies range from smelt imitations in the rapids to small, dark, soft hackles in areas where salmon feed on emerging caddis.

Whitefish

Whitefish are one of the most important commercial species across the Great Lakes. They are related to trout and salmon, and prefer cool, deep water, where they often overlap territory with lake trout. They spawn in the fall over shallow shoals and reefs. While not a primary sport fish, whitefish can be caught on flies at certain times during the year.

Good numbers of whitefish move seasonally in both spring and fall into the St. Marys River, where they can be caught in the Rapids area on small nymphs. They can also be taken on small streamers as well as wet flies when they move into harbor areas around the northern parts of the Great Lakes. The most enjoyable way to catch them is when they rise to mayfly hatches during the early summer. The North Shore of Lake Superior is the best area for this activity.

Whitefish hit a variety of small nymphs and dry flies, each at different times. Capt. Brad Petzke shows a sizeable specimen caught in the St. Marys River. BRAD PETZKE

Whitefish are hard fighters when hooked but lack the acrobatics of trout. They have a small, soft mouth, and hooks can pull out easily. Most are in the 1- to 2-pound range, but larger ones have been caught on flies.

Whitefish

Hot Spots and Peak Times

Lake Huron
St. Marys River: June–September

Lake Superior
North Shore river mouths: June

Steelhead and Rainbow Trout

Of the nonnative trout and salmon species found in the Great Lakes, steelhead and rainbow trout have the widest distribution and can be found in significant numbers across the entire region. The original stockings in Michigan's Au Sable River in the early 1870s came from the McCloud River in California. By the turn of the century, these were well distributed throughout the Great Lakes, and localized, self-sustaining populations had become established.

Steelhead and Rainbow Trout

Hot Spots and Peak Times

Lake Erie
Pennsylvania shoreline and river mouths: September and October

Lake Michigan
Menominee Harbor: October, November, April
Ludington Harbor: ice-out–April
Milwaukee Harbor: October, November, April

Lake Huron
St. Marys River: October–December, April–May

Lake Ontario
Lower Niagara River: November, December, March–May

Lake Superior
Minnesota North Shore (Kamloops): March–April

In 1920, a young Ernest Hemingway, working for the *Toronto Star* newspaper, wrote that "the greatest rainbow trout fishing in the world is at the Rapids of the Canadian Soo." This indicated that in less than 50 years since their original introduction, these fish were making a major contribution to Great Lakes sport fishing. Today they are the most pursued of all the coldwater species in the lakes, supporting a significant offshore fishery as well as river-focused opportunities.

Native to the West Coast of North America, all steelhead are rainbow trout, but not all rainbow trout are steelhead. Steelhead have a genetic trigger that causes them at one point in their development to migrate to a larger body of water. There, they feed for several years before returning to tributary streams to spawn. The original McCloud River fish were spring spawners that began entering rivers in late fall. In the last 100 years, a variety of steelhead strains have been stocked in the Great Lakes, and these return to spawn at different times of the year. Consequently, an angler is likely to find steelhead in rivers somewhere across the Great Lakes year-round.

There are also resident rainbow populations in some areas. Both the St. Marys and Niagara Rivers have populations of rainbows that do not migrate. Minnesota stocks a Kamloops rainbow strain that stays nearshore all year, staging near river mouths during the winter and spring, when they are readily accessible to anglers. These nonmigratory fish can be caught on a wide variety of fly patterns, from simple egg and nymphs to elaborate streamers and even Spey patterns. Anglers can also have some success targeting them in harbor areas, where they follow baitfish, as well as around power-plant discharges.

Management strategies for steelhead vary widely across the Great Lakes region. Much of the province of Ontario relies on self-sustaining runs, while in Ohio nearly

A beautifully colored shoreline steelhead. This male is just beginning to take on spawning coloration.

A flashy, brightly colored attractor pattern proved to be more than this shoreline steelhead could resist. Anglers often need to attract fish from long distances, so patterns that are highly visible are often required.

all the fish are stocked because river conditions there are not conducive to significant natural reproduction. Other states rely on a mix of stocking and natural reproduction to maintain steelhead numbers. As steelhead can make multiple spawning runs in their lifetime, closed seasons and strict keep limits also play an important role in managing populations in some areas.

Longevity and growth rates also vary widely across the lakes. In Superior, with its colder water and smaller food supply, steelhead may only reach a total of about 10 pounds, even though they may live for a decade or longer. In Lake Erie, with an abundance of food and warmer water, steelhead can reach 10 pounds in as little as four years but may have a life expectancy of only six or seven years. The average fly-caught Great Lakes steelhead weighs 6 to 8 pounds, although fish in excess of 20 pounds are landed every year. The Great Lakes record is a 31.19-pound fish caught in 2004 from Lake Ontario.

It is interesting to note that the climate of the Great Lakes compresses the natural range of steelhead—from Russia's Kamchatka Peninsula south to Baja, California—into a much smaller region north to south. The northernmost part of the lakes, in Lake Superior's Nipigon Bay, reaches the northern boreal (coniferous) forest. The southernmost point, Sandusky, Ohio, on Lake Erie, is in the temperate zone. Great Lakes steelhead have to survive a wider range of temperature extremes than their West Coast relatives.

One of the special Great Lakes fly-fishing opportunities for Lake Michigan steelhead occurs in the summer. The lake is long and narrow, with many deepwater areas close to shore. Depending on wind speed and direction, there can be a lot of vertical movement of water, bringing layers of water with significantly different temperatures and densities into contact with each other. At times, these layers extend right to the surface, and floating material is trapped here.

Called "scum lines," these areas hold insects and attract baitfish. Steelhead cruise them, often feeding right at the surface—sipping in a variety bugs and crashing schools of bait. Anglers can use satellite imagery to monitor surface temperature and locate temperature breaks. If these occur close enough to shore, gear anglers troll them and experience fantastic action. Under the right wind conditions, adventurous fly anglers have been able to take kayaks, pontoon boats, and even float tubes to the scum lines and cast to surface-feeding steelhead in water hundreds of feet deep.

When caught in the lakes, steelhead will almost always be bright silver and full of fight. They may at times drop back into the lake after ascending a stream to spawn; in that case, they will have a bit of color to them. They can also be found near warmwater discharges, where they will hit eggs and nymphs as well as baitfish patterns.

Steelhead have assumed a place of prominence among fly fishers as one of the most prized freshwater sport fish. Their value to the Great Lakes sport fishery is significant, to say the least. Anglers from all over the world come in pursuit of steelhead and contribute millions of dollars to local economies. The willingness of steelhead to take a variety of fly patterns under a wide range of conditions has endeared them to Great Lakes anglers.

Brown Trout

A European import, brown trout are related to Atlantic salmon. In the Great Lakes Basin, they were first released into Michigan's Pere Marquette River in 1883. The

Wisconsin angler Dave Pinczkowski shows a hefty brown trout from Milwaukee Harbor. Owing to an aggressive stocking program, the west side of Lake Michigan has developed into a premier area for big browns.

This springtime Lake Michigan brown trout hit a goby imitation. When water temperatures keep browns inshore, they will feed heavily on gobies.

Brown Trout

Hot Spots and Peak Times

Lake Michigan
Harbor areas: ice-out–April
Milwaukee Harbor: October–November, March–April
Wisconsin power plants: November–December, March–April

Lake Ontario
Lower Niagara River: October–December
Niagara Bar: March–May
Wilson Harbor, Olcott Harbor: September–October, ice-out–April

Lake Huron
Hammond Bay, Tawas Bay: October–December, ice-out–May

Lake Superior
Chequamegon Bay: October–November, ice-out–April

province of Ontario planted its first browns in 1913. In the lakes themselves, browns did not receive much attention until the late 1960s, when they were planted as part of a strategy to control alewife populations and provide a replacement for native fish populations devastated by sea lampreys and pollution.

In recent years, brown trout stockings have increased in a number of locations because they provide a significant nearshore fishery through much of the year. Both New York and Pennsylvania have reinstituted brown trout stockings in Lake Erie. New York has had a highly successful brown trout program in Lake Ontario for many years. Wisconsin has capitalized on browns with a very aggressive stocking program, particularly in Lake Michigan, where it plants several strains. Michigan has revamped its brown trout program in Lake Huron.

The Seeforellen strain of brown has adapted well to the waters of the Great Lakes. This fish lives longer, grows larger, and is more disease-resistant than other strains. It also tends to be more pelagic, often following schools of baitfish into open lake waters. The current world record, at a shade under 42 pounds, is a tie between two Lake Michigan Seeforellen browns caught in recent years.

Other domestic strains are also stocked, and these tend to stay closer to the areas where they are planted. These browns in particular provide a great opportunity for fly fishers. Many stage off river mouths starting in late summer, drop back into the lake when spawning is complete, and then return to the same river mouths. These are often the first fish available at ice-out, moving into harbor waters that warm more quickly and open up while main lake areas are still covered with ice.

Browns also love to winter in warmwater discharges that attract baitfish and other forage; here, they can move in and out of the current to feed as they desire. Like their stream-bound relatives, lake browns also have a nocturnal streak, often shunning bright sunlight and preferring to feed more actively on cloudy days and even at night. Nighttime forays can be very successful, and some anglers even incorporate luminous materials into their flies to help trigger strikes.

Through most of the year, lake browns are silvery in color, with dark spots. Those of the Seeforellen strain will be almost entirely silver, with fewer spots than domestic browns. As fall approaches, all browns take on more of the color of stream fish. Males especially will darken and develop the large kype typical of most trout and salmon. Spawning may occur on rocky shoal areas as well as in lake tributaries.

While they respond well to baitfish patterns, browns can be taken on a wide range of flies, including crayfish and goby patterns. They will also respond to traditional loch-style techniques used in Great Britain, in which several flies are fished with floating line and long leader from the surface down to several feet. At present, Lake Michigan and Lake Ontario have the biggest populations of brown trout. If their distribution in the Great Lakes continues to expand, browns are likely to become a more targeted species by shore-based anglers.

Coho Salmon

Native to the Pacific Northwest, coho salmon, also called "silvers," were the first Pacific salmon species to be stocked in efforts to combat the exploding populations of invasive alewives that spread across the Great Lakes in the 1950s. They had been planted here earlier with limited success, but natural reproduction was not supporting the population. It was after coho were stocked in Michigan's Platte River in 1966 that the modern era of Great Lakes salmon was born.

In the Great Lakes today, most attention has shifted to chinook salmon for several reasons. First, chinook are a larger fish and more popular with offshore boat anglers and the industry they support. Second, it is easier and less expensive to raise chinook than coho in a hatchery setting; coho require a longer period of care. Coho also seem to get outcompeted by chinook for desirable spawning habitats.

Coho Salmon

Hot Spots and Peak Times

Lake Superior
South Shore river mouths and estuaries: September
South Shore harbors: ice-out–May

Lake Ontario
River-mouth areas: ice-out–May, September

Lake Michigan
South-end harbors: ice-out–May, September
River-mouth areas: September–October

This coho salmon hit a stripped streamer close to a warmwater discharge in Lake Michigan. Coho move inshore in the early fall to enter spawning tributaries.

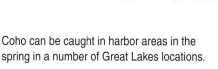

Coho can be caught in harbor areas in the spring in a number of Great Lakes locations.

Nevertheless, coho thrive in Lake Superior, and nearly all of the lake's tributaries support runs of wild, naturally reproducing coho. There are also natural populations in northern Lake Michigan and other small, localized populations across the lakes. For the most part, though, coho rely on annual stocking to maintain their numbers. The average Lake Michigan coho weighs 7 to 10 pounds. In Lake Superior, they average around 5 pounds. The largest coho ever recorded from the Great Lakes was a 33.5-pound fish from Lake Ontario. Coho have only a three-year life span. In the Great Lakes, they spawn from October through December.

From a fly-fishing standpoint, coho are popular because they have a propensity to chase brightly colored flies. They respond to flies long into their spawning cycle. They are also more surface-oriented and opportunistic in their feeding activity. In Lake Superior, coho have been observed feeding on insects blown into the lake on windy days.

Coho action in the lakes is good in spring, when they can be found in harbor areas in reach of anglers on breakwalls and jetties. In the spring and winter, coho are also drawn to warmwater discharges, where they hit baitfish and attractor patterns. In Lake Michigan, they have an observed migration route: fish from the northern part of the lake move south during the winter and spring, and then north again in the summer and early fall, prior to ascending streams to spawn. Like all species of Pacific salmon, cohos die after spawning is completed.

Chinook Salmon

Another Pacific coast native, chinook or king salmon were first stocked in the Great Lakes around the same time as rainbow trout. These first attempts were not successful. The first modern-era stockings took place in several Lake Michigan and Lake

Chinook Salmon

Hot Spots and Peak Times

Lake Michigan
Mouth of Platte River: late August–September
Drowned river mouths: late August–September

Lake Huron
St. Marys River: September

Lake Ontario
Niagara River: September
Niagara Bar: April–May

Lake Superior
Ontario river mouths: August–September

Huron tributaries in 1967, as part of a management strategy to combat the invasive alewife populations. Since then, chinook have become a staple of Great Lakes sportfishing; millions of dollars is spent annually in their pursuit.

Chinook have had significant success establishing naturally reproducing populations across the Great Lakes. In Michigan, 50 percent of returning fish may be naturally reproduced. In New York's Salmon River, millions of wild chinook reproduce in the system that enters Lake Ontario. While this all sounds good, it may lead to problems down the road if there are too many fish for the lakes to support.

The main food for chinook is alewives, and as alewife populations decrease, the ability of a system to support chinook also decreases. This has been the case recently in Lake Huron, where both alewife and chinook numbers are down significantly. Chinook will also feed on smelt, but again, there have to be enough of them in the system.

From a lake fly-fishing standpoint, chinook get mixed reviews. The opportunity to throw flies at them in the lakes is limited because they spend most of their time following bait and feeding in deep offshore waters, out of the reach of fly fishers.

When chinook stage to enter spawning rivers, they usually do so quickly; these fish rapidly reach sexual maturity. This all means that lake anglers generally have a limited time frame to throw flies at chinook. By the time they reach harbor areas in late summer and early fall, chinooks' feeding activity has already started to decrease as the physiological changes for spawning begin to occur.

At night and during predawn hours, staging chinook will hit flies for short periods, whether out of curiosity or just as an instinctive feeding reaction. So there are definite times when they can be caught. Just as with a hatch on a trout stream, timing is everything. Several hours of casting can result in a short period of tackle-busting bedlam if a sizeable chinook grabs your offering and heads back toward the main lake.

Casting a streamer in predawn darkness, Michigan guide Russ Maddin took this chinook in Lake Michigan's Grand Traverse Bay. JON RAY

Challenging to catch on a fly, this Lake Michigan chinook salmon was taken during the early morning hours. Low-light periods are the best time to try for chinook.

There are several other times when Great Lakes chinook will hit flies. One of these is when sustained west winds cause Lake Michigan to "flip," and cold water is pushed up from the bottom and to the Illinois and Wisconsin shoreline. Chinook often move into harbor areas following bait and come into range of nearshore anglers. Alewife imitations cast on sinking-head lines will attract feeding chinook.

Chinook will follow schools of spawning smelt in the spring and may come into range of fly anglers. One of the best areas for this is on the Niagara Bar, where the Niagara River enters Lake Ontario. From mid-April to mid-May, smelt gather on the bar before ascending the river to spawn, and all sorts of fish—chinook among them—gather for the feast. Casting flashy white-and-gray streamers on a sinking head can result in vicious strikes and drag-burning runs.

Most Great Lakes chinook weigh 10 to 20 pounds. Fish over 30 pounds are still caught each year, but as alewife numbers have fallen, so has the average size of the chinook. The long-term future of the chinook fishery appears dependent on alewife stocks. Unlike other species who have found alternate forage, chinook have yet to find a replacement for their preferred prey.

Pink Salmon

The presence of pink salmon in the Great Lakes came about by accident. In 1956, an experimental planting of pinks was being made in Hudson Bay, and the fish were being held at the Port Arthur Hatchery in Thunder Bay, Ontario. While the plane taking the fingerlings to Hudson Bay was being loaded, a hundred or so spilled into Lake Superior. Another several hundred remaining in hatchery troughs were also put into the lake. It was later discovered that an additional 21,000 were flushed into the Current River that empties into Lake Superior.

Over the next several decades, pinks spread across the Great Lakes. At present, they are found in significant numbers only in Lakes Superior and Huron. The

Pink Salmon

Hot Spots and Peak Times

Lake Huron
St. Marys River: mid-August–September

Lake Superior
North Shore river mouths: mid-August–September

stronghold for pinks is in the North Channel area of Lake Huron and the North Shore of Lake Superior. The only place where pinks are targeted by anglers is in the St. Marys Rapids. Large numbers of pinks enter the rapids in late August and spawn in early to mid September. They can be caught on a variety of small streamer, wet fly, and egg patterns. Most will be in the 1- to 2-pound range.

Because runs of pinks coincide with those of chinook salmon, and both seek a similar type of spawning substrate, the two species may hybridize when large concentrations of each is present. The resulting fish, called a "pinook," shows up regularly in the St. Marys and several other tributaries in the area. Pinook show characteristics of both species, and no two look the same.

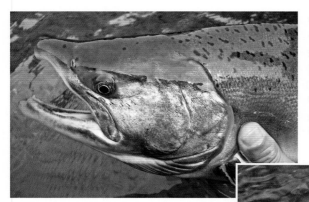

When overlap and competition for spawning areas occurs, species of Pacific salmon can hybridize. Pink and chinook hybrids called "pinook'" are found in the St. Marys River and several other Lake Huron tributaries. JON RAY

A Great Lakes pink salmon. Also called "humpies" because of their body shape during spawning, pinks were introduced accidentally into the Great Lakes. They are abundant in a number of Lake Superior and northern Lake Huron tributaries, as well as in the St. Marys River. JON RAY

chapter 5

Gearing Up

Rods

If I were limited to only one rod for use on the waters of the Great Lakes, I would choose a 9-foot, 8-weight. This rod offers the most versatility for the variety of fish and opportunities that exist here. If an angler is focusing on smaller species such as panfish, a rod as light as a 5- or 6-weight can be used. Going any lighter than this can create problems if there is any amount of wind present. On the other hand, if the goal is targeting muskie and throwing oversized flies, a 10-weight might be the best rod choice.

The 8-weight gives the ability to handle a reasonable amount of wind and throw a fairly large, air-resistant pattern. It may be a bit of overkill on smaller fish, but this weight can provide enough strength to subdue a large specimen if you encounter one. Sometimes you also need to steer fish away from cover after they've been hooked, so I would rather err on the heavier side whenever fishing the big water.

Great Lakes anglers often need to cast for distance to cover water. It pays to practice casting before getting on the water.

On the berm at the St. Marys Rapids. Jeff Liskay carries extra rods and any other gear he might need for a day's fishing.

Switch- and two-hand rods are establishing a niche in Great Lakes fly fishing. The reel becomes a critical piece of equipment in cold weather and when chasing migratory species.

Most Great Lakes fly anglers prefer saltwater-style rods with faster actions, because they are able to push a line for distance, even into wind. In many cases, covering water is the name of the game, and the larger the area in which a fly is visible, the better the chances of its getting eaten. A faster rod also makes setting the hook easier on a longer line. That being said, the lakes also offer sight-fishing opportunities, so a rod also needs to throw accurately when necessary, sometimes at a shorter range. Finding a rod with all these characteristics can be a challenge.

Length of the rod can vary, depending on the specific application. The standard 9-foot length serves well in most situations. When fishing from a canoe, kayak, or small boat, shorter warmwater-specific rods, around 8-foot, are easy to maneuver and control fish in close for landing and release. These can be found in several different line weights from a variety of manufacturers. If most of your fishing will be from these craft, you may want to give a shorter rod a try.

Several species-specific rods have also come on the market. Sage has marketed Largemouth, Smallmouth, and Bluegill models in shorter lengths for a number of years. Echo has worked with Capt. Pat Ehlers of Wisconsin to develop a series of shorter, "boat-length" rods in different line weights.

Working with Scott Fly Rods, Capt. Brian Meszaros designed a rod for muskie fishing on Lake St. Clair; it has an extended rear grip that allows a fly angler to easily do the "figure 8" technique on fish that follow the fly to the boat. This design may become mainstream for chasing apex predators like pike and muskie.

If your angling will be from piers and breakwalls, or in surf, you may want to consider a longer rod. These situations have proven to be a viable application of the switch rods that are popular in river-fishing for steelhead. These normally 10- to 11-

foot rods are light enough to be cast easily single-handed. The grip on these rods is designed for the angler to "switch" and cast with two hands if circumstances require.

An 8-weight switch rod, cast overhead with two hands, can throw a line a long way. Also, the length allows the rod tip to be kept closer to the water while retrieving the fly from an elevated area. In the surf, the longer rod allows easier casting for distance while wading, and it is really not a detriment while stripping the fly. On larger boats, say 16 feet or more, the switch rod is still a usable tool.

The switch rod is also the perfect tool for when you want to use a dead-drift system. I have gone nearly exclusively to an 11-foot, 8-weight switch rod with a heavily front-loaded floating line for this use. This allows a long leader—with indicator, flies, and shot—to be cast and mended efficiently. This rod will also handle fish in excess of 15 pounds, which is a reasonable weight to expect in many Great Lakes waters.

Reels

Depending on what species you are chasing, the reel may or may not be a critical piece of equipment. For chasing warmwater species like smallmouth bass, the reel functions mainly for line storage. Smallies will rarely run any line off the reel, electing instead to head skyward. Pike and even muskie normally thrash and slug it out close to you. If this is all you plan to do, a simple single-action reel may serve well. Keep in mind, though, that even warmwater "trash fish" like freshwater drum and carp can make long, knuckle-busting runs that will strain an inexpensive reel.

If you plan to pursue any coldwater or migratory species, a reel with a strong, adjustable drag system is a necessity. Hooking steelhead, king or coho salmon, brown trout, or even lake trout in shallow water or a stationary location requires a reel that will hold 100-plus yards of backing, with a solid drag to back it up. A sealed drag that is impervious to the elements is also a desirable feature.

These reels continue to function both in blazing heat and below freezing temperatures after being submerged. They are virtually maintenance-free except for the need to clean dirt and grit from the spool frame. The drag surfaces are protected and need no lubrication to function properly. As most coldwater species are available nearshore either very early or late in the season, when freezing temperatures are a possibility, a sealed drag can be an important feature of your reel. Most companies now offer models with a sealed drag system.

Still, there are a number of expensive reels on the market that lack this feature, so a thin layer of water can collect on the drag surface. This is fine in warmer weather but can be disastrous in cold—a reel can go into free-spool even when pulling out line, and major backlash in the line can occur. Bottom line: buy the best reel you can afford and look for a sealed drag.

Lines

There are more fly-line choices on the market these days than ever before. As technology has advanced, lines have become more and more specialized, and this has been a great advantage for fly anglers chasing fish around lakes. Depending on which species you are after and where you are fishing, any number of lines can be applicable.

The simplest line to use is still the weight-forward floater. There are variations of this design to help turn over larger flies and work more efficiently in wind, and one of these would be the best line to start with. Examples are Scientific Anglers' Magnum Tapers and the RIO Smallmouth Taper. The floating line is used to work floating flies and divers on, or just below, the surface. It can also be applied to dead-drift techniques when fishing any type of current areas that enter the lakes. This line will also allow weighted flies to be fished below the surface on a long leader; however, these will be limited to depth of less than 4 feet or so, because all but the heaviest flies will creep toward the surface when retrieved.

Perhaps the most frequently used line for nearshore application is some sort of sinking tip. This can be a short, intermediate (clear) tip for spooky carp on the flats, or a long, high-density tip for throwing off of a pier or breakwall—and variations in between. Looking at the number of sinking lines available can be very confusing. What we try to do is work with several lines to cover as many situations as possible.

The clear-tip lines have a definite place in many Great Lakes applications. They are an excellent tool for stalking fish—carp, smallmouth bass, or any number of species—on flats in clear water, keeping the colored line as far away as possible. This slow-sinking tip will keep a lightly weighted fly holding closer to the bottom and will minimize snags that could be encountered with a heavier fly.

The clear-tip line is also used to keep a fast-moving streamer pattern a foot or two below the surface. This area can be a major feeding zone for many gamefish, and it cannot be covered properly with a floating line. Incorporating a clear-tip line with a wiggle-style foam pattern can become a fly fisher's "crankbait" to fish just below the surface. And results can be exciting visual action and explosive takes.

The clear section on these lines varies from 10 to 30 feet in length. The clear tip is found in combination with a floating line and is also incorporated into an integrated shooting-taper system with an intermediate running line. Nearly all line makers offer these products. For wading, the floating-line/clear-tip combination is best, because the floating line will be easier to pick up without it getting tangled in your feet or in underwater vegetation. You could also avoid this problem by incorporating a shooting basket to gather line into your gear. When you are casting from a structure or boat, the integrated shooting taper allows for longer casts and for holding the fly a bit deeper on the retrieve.

When you want to explore deeper shoreline areas and cover the water column more efficiently from a pier, breakwall, or watercraft, a fast sinking-tip line is the best choice. The grain-rated, integrated shooting tapers have come a long way in their development and offer a lot of versatility. The Teeny lines were the first of this type on the market. Other examples of these are Scientific Anglers' Streamer Express and Wet Tip Express lines, RIO's Outbound series, Cortland's Quick Descent lines, and the Forty Plus lines from Airflo.

With sinking heads usually 25 to 35 feet in length, these lines cast well in wind and have a fixed, known sink rate, so that you can count down to a certain depth before starting the retrieve. Even on a fast strip, these lines hold depth well and keep the fly in the desired zone for a long portion of the retrieve. The sinking line can also be used with a floating fly to carry it below the surface.

You can find these lines with both a floating and intermediate running line. Again, for wading, opt for the floating or you will need a shooting basket to gather line. As noted, the intermediate running line can be used from an elevated platform such as a pier or boat.

If all this is starting to look a bit too complicated and expensive—with multiple reels or spare spools to carry the variety of lines needed—there are ways to simplify the process. The easiest way is to incorporate an interchangeable shooting-taper system. One of the biggest overall advances in recent fly-line technology has been the introduction of welded loops. These have made attachment of leaders and any loop-to-loop connections a simpler, more streamlined process. This type of connection goes in and out of guides easily, with very little disturbance.

Both floating and intermediate shooting lines are available with welded loops, along with shooting tapers of various line weights and densities—from floating to very fast-sinking. One reel can be loaded with a shooting line; carry several different heads (floating, intermediate, fast-sink) for quick, easy adaptation to locations and conditions. Fly anglers have come a long way since the days of having to make our own shooting lines out of monofilament or level fly lines, and from making heads out of lead core or cut-up fly lines.

One of the easiest shooting lines to work with is the Dragon Tail sold by Scientific Anglers. Originally designed for Spey applications, this line also works well for overhead casting, especially in heavier line weights. It has a 15-foot taper to where the head loops on, which helps to roll the shooting taper up to the surface to be recast; this also allows a bit more line to be extended while false-casting. For those unfamiliar with shooting tapers, this is a good one to start with.

Borrowing again from the Spey market, I have started using Scientific Anglers' Custom Express Tips with the Dragon Tail line for overhead casting. These tips are 30-foot lengths of T-10, T-12, T-14, and T-18 looped on both ends. They are thin and dense, sink quickly, and have minimal wind resistance. These have proven to be a great tool for both distance and for reaching deeper than conventional lines off piers, breakwalls, and boats.

Full sinking lines also have a place in the Great Lakes, but mainly for offshore fishing on deeper structure areas and in trolling applications. The focus of this book is nearshore opportunities; full sinking lines are another topic for another time.

A final word on fly lines: technology continues to advance quickly in this area. Several lines with imprinted patterns have come onto the market. The Sharkskin lines from Scientific Anglers have noted advantages over smooth finish lines—they float higher, are easier to pick up and mend, and cast farther. On the downside, they make noise in the guide and require finger protection if stripped continuously. Textured, another patterned line by Scientific Anglers, has the same advantages as Sharkskin, but makes less noise and is less abrasive when stripped. Also, the lines Titan Taper and Saltwater Taper Clear Tip Textured are showing particular promise in the Great Lakes arena.

Airflo has introduced the Ridge Line, with reduced friction that allows casts to be made farther, with less effort. We will likely also see more of these type of lines in the future, and they may well help us to cover water more efficiently and improve our angling success.

Leaders

Depending on the application, leaders for Great Lakes use can be simple or quite complex. Off a sinking tip or sinking head, often all that is needed is a 3- to 5-foot length of 10- to 15-pound tippet. With a regular floating line, a normal tapered leader matched to the fish and fly size may be used. Toothy critters require some sort of bite-tippet incorporated at the end of the leader. If throwing giant flies for late-season muskie, anglers must incorporate an extra-heavy butt section to help turn over these large flies, which can equate to having a small chipmunk on the end of the line.

For floating-line use, a standard $7^1/_2$- to 9-foot packaged leader can be employed. For panfish and smaller species, the tippet should be 6- to 8-pound breaking strength. If you want to start throwing larger, more air-resistant, or weighted flies, go with a heavy-butt leader that tapers to a minimum of 10-pound breaking strength. To lengthen the leader, add additional tippet to the end.

Stalking fish in shallow water often requires a long leader, especially on a calm, sunny day. As lake fishing is like saltwater fishing, saltwater-style leaders can be used. A 9- or 10-foot bonefish leader has a butt-and-taper design developed to turn over flies efficiently. When stalking carp in the shallows, I often add a 2- to 3-foot length of fluorocarbon material to the end to move the line farther away from the fly. As mentioned earlier, the added length also allows an angler to work a fly slightly deeper, to around 4 feet or so.

For places such as power plant discharges, river mouths, and larger connecting waters like the St. Marys or Niagara rivers, I set up a leader for dead-drift/indicator applications a bit differently. Starting with a conventional 9-foot leader tapered to 12-pound, I add 30 inches of 10-pound material and then 24 inches of the same material. The fly is tied on the end, where a dual fly system can also be made, and split shot are attached as needed—above the knot connecting the two added sections.

With the various clear tip and sinking-tip lines available, leaders are much simpler. A single length of 10- to 15-pound material may be all that is needed. A perfection loop or double surgeon's loop can be put into one end, looped to the line, and then the fly tied on. If the line does not have a welded loop on the end, or if the loop becomes damaged, nail-knot a 12-inch length of 20-pound material and then make a loop in the end. The tippet can be looped onto this.

Wire bite-tippets are a necessity when targeting large northern pike and muskie. Recent advances in technology have made it much easier rig up for these toothy predators.

For extra-large flies, start with a length of 30-pound material at the line. In clear water, the length of the tippet may extend out 6 to 8 feet in order to move the fly farther from the line. Fluorocarbon material may be used to reduce visibility and minimize abrasion.

For toothy critters like pike and muskie, a bite-tippet is necessary. Over the years, anglers have tried a number of different materials for the bite-tippet, from standard wire to large-diameter fluorocarbon. Right now, most anglers seriously chasing big guys with teeth are using titanium wire, which is easily knotted to the leader and to the fly. Packaged leader—with wire already tied in—is also available.

For smaller pike, 40- to 50-pound fluorocarbon is suitable and can be fished off a standard bass- or saltwater-style leader. The fluorocarbon material is knotted to the leader tippet with an Albright knot. If you opt for wire, the Albright knot also can be used to attach that to the leader. You may also use a small black barrel swivel that has a breaking strength in excess of the wire. The knottable wire is tied to the barrel swivel with a clinch knot.

If you are in a situation where you want to use large, air-resistant flies for larger pike or muskie, it is best to go to a saltwater big-game-style system. For a floating line, start with a 3-foot length of 40-pound monofilament as a butt section. Loop on about 30 inches of 30-pound material and then add 30 inches of 20- to 15-pound material for the tippet. Then 25- to 35-pound titanium wire can be added to the end. You can also add a small cross-lock snap to the end of the wire to make changing flies simpler.

For sinking lines, a similar system is used, except that the length of the butt section can be shortened to 20 inches or so. Using the knottable titanium wire, you can also premake wire leaders by tying a small, strong barrel swivel on one end and a cross-lock snap on the other. The length of wire is normally 12 to 15 inches. These can be quickly added or removed from the leader as desired.

Other Necessities

In many cases, the Great Lakes fly fisher will be geared up in a fashion similar to that of a saltwater angler: polarized glasses, hat, nippers, pliers, rain gear, sunscreen, first-aid kit, and insect repellant. These are all standard items no matter where you are. Additional items such as a hook hone, flashlight, or headlamp may also be a part of your gear. Sun masks and sun gloves are also becoming a standard part of the equipment.

Many lake area anglers carry a pack of some sort for flies, leaders, and tippet, because fly boxes are often larger than those used for stream fishing. A pack can also accommodate a camera, water, snacks, and other items. For long walks or extended periods on the water, a chest pack/backpack combo may work best.

Waders can be an important item for shorebound anglers. Rubber-bottom shoes with studs are a good all-around choice for sand, rocky shoreline, and jetties, piers, and breakwalls. Korkers sandals with carbide studs have been used by saltwater anglers for years for extra grip on slippery rocky. The latest wading technology for really nasty, slippery rock is Patagonia's Aluminum Bar Wading Shoes and River Crampons. These provide a much larger surface area than studs for gripping traction.

The Great Lakes are large enough to create their own weather systems. Proper foul-weather gear is a necessity to handle rapidly changing conditions.

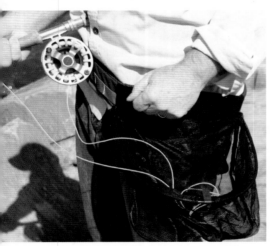

This stripping basket by William Joseph keeps catching rocks and line tangles to a minimum. It slides right into the belt and out of the way when not needed.

In warmer areas, wet-wading may be possible, but this still requires some sort of protective footwear. Though rarely used by freshwater anglers, a stripping basket can be handy when shore fishing and casting for distance; the basket helps to minimize line tangles and snagging on feet, as well as on rocks and debris. Also, if you are wearing some sort of spikes or cleats to improve grip on rock, one nick of sharp metal on a fly line can render an expensive line useless. A variety of different stripping baskets are on the market, but something as simple as a dishpan, a small wastebasket, or even a cardboard box can be used. I have used a small, soft-sided cooler fitted with a bungee cord that served the purpose, and even a 5-gallon bucket can be used when necessary.

Borrowing from our saltwater brethren, a serviceable stripping basket can be easily made from a regular 14x12-inch plastic dishpan. Drill 8 to 10 small holes, evenly spaced, in the bottom. From the bottom, insert a section of weedwhacker monofilament about 3 to 4 inches long into each hole and secure them with hot glue. Add slits on the long sides of the dishpan so you can slip through a wading belt, nylon web belt, or bungee cord that will fit around your waist.

In terms of commercial products, Charlie's Stripping Basket is a great choice due to its light weight and portability. The William Joseph integrated basket/belt is

An artificial grass mat like this on the floor of a boat will help control line and minimize tangles when casting.

also usable, but does not have the opening size some anglers prefer. Orvis offers a functional molded-plastic design, and L.L. Bean also sells a collapsible mesh basket.

In a boat, taller, cylinder-like designs such as the Beachcomber Flyline Tamer and Bucket II can help manage and control line. Capt. Austin Adduci has fashioned several by pop-riviting a section of bendable plastic into a circle around 20 inches in diameter and attaching it to a flat base. Capt. Kevin Morlock uses a rectangular mat of long, artificial grass to control line in his boat. The long fibers hold the fly line as it is stripped onto the mat and keep the coils from tangling.

On the Great Lakes, weather conditions can range from nearly tropical to Arctic-like. Weather is often localized and, in both spring and fall, can change quickly. In the spring especially, shore temperatures may be comfortable while water temperatures are still very cold.

Any wind blowing across the water also can lower the on-water air temperature significantly. I have seen many anglers show up for early-season trips dressed according to the forecast air temperatures, only to encounter a 20- to 30-degrees cooler breeze across the water surface. I always have extra clothing layers with me on adventures along the lakes, regardless of the time of year.

Finally, a cell phone has become a necessary item, especially for a solo angler. When you have a problem—from something as simple as a dead car battery to as serious as a broken leg from an unexpected fall—being able to quickly contact help is invaluable. Smartphones can also serve a variety of other functions, such as checking weather and lake forecasts and finding food and lodging.

Flies

The waters of the Great Lakes hold a wide range of food forms, both native and invasive, for gamefish. Depending on the species and location, everything from alewives to crayfish to mayfly nymphs to spiny water fleas may be on the menu. At times, fly patterns need to be fairly accurate imitations of available foods, but there are also situations where flashy attractor patterns get the job done best.

While this chapter begins with several familiar fly patterns, there are many Great Lakes–area fly tiers who have developed—and are still developing—a host of

This hefty smallmouth hit a Claw Dad. The rubber legs on this fly have movement even when the fly is sitting on the bottom. It is great pattern when fish are in a neutral feeding mood.

patterns for use on the Great Lakes and adjacent inland waters. These patterns range from oversize creations for the largest predators down to small nymphs for panfish and others.

You will find the newer patterns in this chapter interesting and innovative; they are also proven fish catchers. Because of the variety of species available on the lakes at any given time, most of these patterns are applicable in different locations for an assortment of fish species. Most also catch fish in areas way beyond the Great Lakes.

Due to the explosion in fly-pattern creation in recent years, some of these patterns may be similar to those in other areas and by other tiers. There is bound to be duplication of ideas at times, without prior knowledge. I have tried to credit the pattern originator to the best of my information and ability.

Also, please keep in mind that in the listing of useful patterns for a given area, these are not the only flies that will be productive. Patterns from one location will often produce in another place. If the recommended flies are not producing, don't be afraid to experiment. We are still very early in the learning process of fly fishing in the Great Lakes.

Subsurface Patterns

As a variety of fish species may be encountered in a given area, versatility in fly patterns is a key to consistent success. It would be difficult to argue against Clouser's Deep Minnow as the single most universal pattern in the Great Lakes. Depending on size and coloration, it imitates a wide range of baitfish: alewives, emerald shiners, and more. Important for Great Lakes applications are all-white, chartreuse-white, blue-white, gray-white, olive-orange, olive-chartreuse, and perch, sized to range from 3 inches to 6 inches in length.

A box full of baitfish for Great
Lakes applications. Many of
these flies have saltwater
origins, but they have also
proven to be effective on the
"inland oceans."

A box of baitfish and
attractor patterns. Great
Lakes fish will sometimes
key on specific baitfish,
so it pays to have an
assortment of sizes.

Variations of the Deep Minnow with a tail tied-in first add extra length and bulk to the fly. If saddle hackles are used, this is called a Half and Half, because it borrows half of the material from a Lefty's Deceiver. Longer flash material of various types can be used to create the Flashtail version. If bucktail is used for the tail, I call it the D2 Deep Minnow (double deer). Even a rabbit strip can be added for extra effect, creating the RS Deep Minnow. By using coyote or fox tail for the wing, the Coyote Clouser can imitate crayfish as well as gobies.

Lefty's Deceiver is also a solid performer across the Great Lakes. Colors are similar to those of the Deep Minnow, and the Deceiver can be used to create a larger, longer fly—up to 8 inches or so in length. There are variations that incorporate an assortment of materials. Further, many patterns with saltwater applications are usable across the Great Lakes. Eli Berant, of Great Lakes Fly, ties several variations of Deceivers designed specifically for Great Lakes applications.

As forage species increase in size through the seasons, fly sizes should also increase. For example, early in the year, Capt. Austin Adduci uses a small imitation of about two inches long to imitate just-hatched perch fry for southern Lake Michigan smallmouth. On Lake St. Clair, Capt. Brian Meszaros throws perch patterns of 10 to 15 inches during the late season for muskies and oversize smallmouth.

The round goby, an invasive species, has emerged as an important forage species in many areas. This sculpin-like, bottom-dwelling fish has become a favorite food of smallmouth bass, brown trout, lake trout, steelhead, coho, and even carp. Goby imitations are now a must-have for Great Lakes fly fishers. Standard sculpin patterns can be used to imitate gobies, but more specific patterns are being developed.

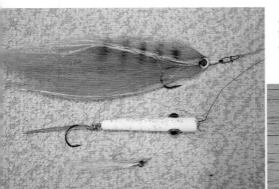

A look at fly sizes for Great Lakes applications. As the size of forage species increases through the season, fly size can do the same.

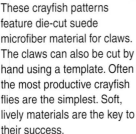

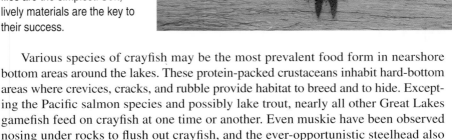

These crayfish patterns feature die-cut suede microfiber material for claws. The claws can also be cut by hand using a template. Often the most productive crayfish flies are the simplest. Soft, lively materials are the key to their success.

Various species of crayfish may be the most prevalent food form in nearshore bottom areas around the lakes. These protein-packed crustaceans inhabit hard-bottom areas where crevices, cracks, and rubble provide habitat to breed and to hide. Excepting the Pacific salmon species and possibly lake trout, nearly all other Great Lakes gamefish feed on crayfish at one time or another. Even muskie have been observed nosing under rocks to flush out crayfish, and the ever-opportunistic steelhead also chase them down.

Crayfish are a staple in the diet of bottom-oriented species. Smallmouth bass in particular have a nearly insatiable fondness for these miniature freshwater lobsters. From the time crayfish emerge in the spring until they hibernate in the fall, smallies feast on them, and so does a host of other species, including carp, freshwater drum, and even jumbo perch. One of the more interesting symbiotic relationships you can see in the Great Lakes is smallmouth shadow-feeding carp. While rooting on the bottom, carp often spook out more than they catch. Smallmouth have learned to follow behind and get an easy meal, cleaning up the leftovers that the carp miss.

One of the holy grails in fly tying is the perfect crayfish pattern. Of the multitude of patterns on the market, those that look most like a crayfish in hand are often poor performers in the water. Many are made with stiff materials that tend to spin on retrieve and tangle the fly into the leader. Patterns made with soft materials that have movement in the water are much more productive. Several productive crayfish imitations have come from the vises of Great Lakes tiers: Mike Schultz's SF Crayfish, Pat Ehler's Crazi Craw, plus my own EZ Craw are examples of these.

Nymph patterns also have a place, especially in river-mouth areas and connecting waters like the St. Marys River. The Superior X-Legs is a nymph pattern that is usually seen only on tributaries and river mouths at the west end of Lake Superior, but I believe it would work in other areas across the lakes. The JQ Caddis I tie has accounted for Atlantics, steelhead, and resident rainbows in the St. Marys. My Great Lakes Stone nymph has also worked there. *Hexagenia* mayflies also emerge in many places across the lakes, so I recommend carrying along Hex nymphs and even adults, because these can be fished at times also.

I would not fish warmwater species in the Great Lakes without having a few of Bill Shearer's Figure 8s or Tongue Depressors in my fly box. The Figure 8 is a versatile fly for toothy critters and big predators like lake trout. Tongue Depressors have a spoon-like action that attracts both largemouth and smallmouth bass as well as walleye and other species.

Dave Pinczkowski, an angler based in Milwaukee, Wisconsin, has several designs that are proven fish-catchers. His Bad Hair Day streamer can be tied in an assortment of colors and sizes to match a variety of forage species. Pinczkowski also contributes here his Simpleech and Coyote Ugly patterns, which attract bottom-oriented species like smallmouth bass and carp.

Capts. Kevin Morlock and Steve Martinez, from Indigo Guide Service, contribute a series of patterns they use to tempt carp at Lake Michigan's Beaver Island archipelago. Though simple in construction, their patterns are specialized for their intended purposes. The Indigo guys also bring an updated twist to longtime Michigan guide John Kluesing's Blueberg streamer, an effective pattern for multiple species in estuary and harbor areas. Before focusing on Beaver Island, Morlock had covered many miles of water chasing carp in northern Lake Michigan and Lake Huron.

Michigan's Eli Berant, of Great Lakes Fly Company (www.greatlakesfly.com), offers a selection of patterns specific to Great Lakes waters. Some are variations of existing patterns like Murdich Minnow and Lefty's Deceiver. Other patterns are new designs of his own—the Bingo, Enforcer, and Bush Pig, to name a few.

Matt Erny offers an interesting selection of warmwater-focused patterns. Erny incorporates hooks from the conventional-fishing side into some of his flies. Nearly all of his patterns have applications for Great Lakes fly fishing. They are interesting and unusual—and they catch fish.

Ohio angler Pat Kelly contributes several mega-size patterns for chasing apex predators. He specializes in catching muskie on flies, and his creations are focused entirely on this species. The flies Kelly ties are not for everyone, as they require skilled casting, but they do attract trophy-sized fish that may not respond to smaller offerings.

There are times when substituting materials in a pattern can make it more usable in certain situations. For example, I have thrown my productive Meatwagon streamer for a number of seasons now. The pattern features a magnum-sized Zonker strip wing. When I went to upsize the fly for pike and muskie, the rabbit strip became heavy and difficult to throw when soaked with water. By replacing the rabbit strip with an Icelandic sheep wool wing, the fly becomes much more manageable in the #/0 sizes.

I also introduced a fly I call a Swaptail Streamer, which is mainly a muskie pattern. It is an articulated, oversize creation tied on a size 4/0 hook. A snap is

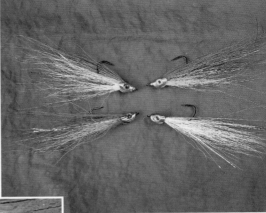

Top left: The author's Swap-tail Streamer pattern. The tail of the fly can be changed out easily to present a different color pattern for larger predators like pike and muskie. *Above:* A selection of Fish-Skull Minnows in productive colors. These flies will catch an assortment of Great Lakes fish species.

Above: Todd's Wiggle Minnow. Originally a saltwater pattern, this fly is productive across the Great Lakes for a variety of species. It can be fished with a floating line but is particularly effective when fished on a sinking-tip line.

incorporated on the hook shank so that the tail section of the fly can be changed or "swapped" as desired. Muskie, in particular, are often responsive to color changes. By having several main head colors and changeable tails, I can experiment with a large number of color combinations to stimulate strikes. In this pattern too, Icelandic sheep wool is incorporated as a primary material to make the fly more manageable when wet.

Tiers featured in this chapter have also contributed several styles of tube and extended-hook patterns. Tube flies are most often used in connecting waters like the Niagara and St. Marys River, although Rick Kustich, Brian Meszaros, and Steve Wascher show versions designed to cast for muskie and pike. My own Arctic Wiggler tube pattern has proven extremely effective and can be cast or swung. Niagara River guide Paul Castellano shares his Niagara Intruder, another pattern that is equally productive as a cast or swung fly.

The streamer patterns that Glen Hales throws for gar are pretty generic. They are large, colorful, and flashy. What makes these flies work is the stinger hook that catches the gar in the softer tissue under its snout. Because a gar's mouth is all bone and teeth, a regular hook rarely stays stuck.

Some well-known Great Lakes Basin tiers—Ian Anderson, Kevin Feenstra, Chris Helm, Ted Kraimer, Rick Kustich, Bart Landwehr, Bob Linsenman, Russ Maddin, Nick Pionessa, Jon Ray, Scott Earl Smith, Jon Uhlenhop, Karl Weixlmann, Matt Zudweg, and others—have contributed both their skill and knowledge in the fly arena. Each of these tiers brings something to the table to help enhance angling success. Some focus on warmwater species, some on coldwater; others cross over—and all species are fair game.

A Niagara River brown trout couldn't resist a Niagara Intruder. This versatile pattern can be cast and stripped, or swung.

Some patterns might best be called fly-rod lures rather than actual flies. One of my favorites is Todd's Wiggle Minnow. Originally a saltwater pattern, this foam cylinder creation comes in several sizes and an assortment of color schemes. It has a quick, tight wiggle and will dive a bit under the surface when used with a floating line. When fished behind intermediate and sinking tips and lines, it will run deeper. In effect, this pattern becomes a fly-rod crankbait.

Ontario fly tier Graham Coombs operates a business called Swim True Flies (www.swimtrue.com). His muskie and pike patterns incorporate synthetic materials to make them more castable, and he adds features such as a diving lip and rattles to add motion and noise. Patterns like these may be pushing the envelope as far as traditional flies are concerned, but they can be thrown on a fly rod with a conventional fly line. In my book, this makes them a legitimate fly pattern.

New tying materials, products, and tying techniques continue to come on the scene and enhance the effectiveness of flies on the Great Lakes. The Fish-Skull manufactured and sold by Flymen Fishing Company shows great promise, as this product adds both weight and color to a pattern. The metal skulls can also be added to a fly after it has been tied, so an angler can quickly modify a pattern as simple as a Woolly Bugger. With their keel-like construction, Fish-Skulls can also be used to make a fly swim with its hook inverted and away from the bottom.

Michigan-based guide and angler Ted Kraimer, of Traverse City, has his Bobble Head Baitfish weighted to make the fly move like an injured baitfish. Motion that is out of the ordinary signals distress, and this movement can elicit strikes from predators that might ignore a standard pattern. Some patterns also have rattles to create extra noise. Whether fishing open-water areas from piers and breakwalls or blind casting from a boat, some extra action and noise can help draw fish from a distance to the fly.

Surface Patterns

Generally, surface patterns have much more limited usage across the Great Lakes.

There are locations—Lake Superior's Chequamegon Bay and Presque Isle on Lake Erie are notable examples—where surface patterns can be consistent producers for both smallmouth and (in the case of Presque Isle) largemouth. Most warmer backwater areas can also produce largemouth and panfish on the surface.

Cork, foam, and deer hair creations can all produce fish. Capt. Roger Lapenter swears by a small Peck's Popper in a color he calls the "Gray Ghost" as the most consistent producer on Chequamegon Bay. Frog imitations are standard in many areas, but don't forget the "bright day, bright fly—dark day, dark fly" adage. On New York's Upper Niagara River, Rick Kustich and Nick Pionessa rely on longer, pencil-style designs to imitate injured baitfish.

When you are looking for a lot of noise to attract fish, the Blockhead Popper, popularized by Minnesota smallmouth guru Tim Holschlag, is a great choice. Michigan's Matt Zudweg has refined the Blockhead design by tapering the back surface area, making it easier to cast, and adding rubber legs. On Lake St. Clair, Capt. Brian Meszaros relies on Bob's Banger, a saltwater popper, to draw smallmouth and the occasional muskie. Minnesota fly angler and tier Paul Hansen turns his foam creations on a lathe, creating lightweight, castable, and durable surface patterns.

When Hex hatches are on, smallmouth, carp, perch, and even walleye and catfish may take a dun or spinner pattern on the surface. One of the biggest thrills I have had fishing the Great Lakes was watching a 16-pound carp come head-out to inhale my Hex dry. On calm summer evenings, whitefish may be found sipping midges at river mouths on Lake Superior's northern shoreline.

Diver-style patterns can be particularly effective for most warmwater gamefish. These can be small minnow imitations up to mega-size versions for toothy predators, but a frog diver is hard to beat in many areas. I have also incorporated Icelandic sheep wool into large diver patterns to make them more casting-friendly.

Fishing divers on sinking-head lines is a great technique when fish are in a more neutral mood. The fly is pulled under on the retrieve and held down by the line. When the retrieve is paused, the fly will hover or float up slightly, with the materials breathing in the water the whole time. This can be deadly at times—too much for predators to resist.

There is no doubt that Great Lakes patterns will continue to evolve. Changes in the forage base may cause species in some locations to concentrate on other food forms. As more fly anglers work the lakes, the learning curve in testing and selecting patterns will be reduced. I can imagine a time when it will be possible to create a more refined selection of flies for certain areas at certain times of the year. The key to determining the overall effectiveness of a fly pattern is assessing how long it's been in use and how consistent it's been in catching fish.

Fly Patterns

Nymphs, Crayfish, Leeches

JQ Caddis

Hook:	#8-12 Daiichi 1120 (or equivalent)
Thread:	Black and chartreuse 70-denier UTC Thread
Body:	Chartreuse stretch tubing over chartreuse thread
Collar:	Black hare's ear blend
Head:	Black bead, sized to hook

Notes: I tied this JQ Caddis, a favorite imitation of the *Rhyacophila* caddis larva that is so common across the Great Lakes Region. It is a great producer in the St. Marys River. Indiana angler Joe Quarandillo created this pattern a decade or so ago, and it has been catching fish ever since.

Great Lakes Simple Stone, Beadhead

Hook:	#8-14 Daiichi 1560 (or equivalent)
Bead (optional):	Black, gold, or copper, sized to hook
Thread:	Black UTC Thread
Tail:	Black goose biots
Abdomen:	Black hare's ear blend
Ribbing:	Black, red, green, blue, or gold UTC Wire (Brassie)
Thorax:	Black hare's ear blend
Wing case:	Turkey, or soft side of a ring-necked pheasant tail

Notes: This is actually a Hare's Ear Nymph to which I added a biot tail; it has caught everything from carp to coho. It will catch fish, whether dead-drifted, swung, or slowly retrieved. I like to vary the color of the body rib just to give a little extra zing to the pattern at times. Good in the St. Marys River and fast-flowing, rocky river mouths.

Stonebugger

Hook:	#4-8 4XL streamer
Weight:	0.020-inch lead wire
Thread:	Black 70-denier UTC Thread
Tail:	Brown marabou
Body:	Coarse fiery brown dubbing
Wing case/back:	Turkey quill
Legs:	Partridge, grouse, or speckled hen body hackle

Notes: This fishy pattern has caught a wide variety of species around the Great Lakes. It is usually tied in this brown version, but black, olive, and tan also produce. I was not able to identify the originator, and I first found it in the Orvis catalog a number of years ago. The body is tied in sections with dubbing first, the leg feather flat on top, and then the wing case pulled over and tied down. This process is repeated until the shank is filled to the eye.

Ted's Swimming Hex

Hook:	#6 TFS 2500
Tail:	Gold variant rabbit strip
Gills:	Pheasant rump feather, lower section
Wing case:	Peacock
Body:	Golden Stone Life Cycle Dubbing
Legs:	Sili Legs, perfectly barred brown
Hackle:	Pheasant rump feather
Eyes:	Bead-chain or lead eyes

Notes: *Hexagenia* mayfly nymphs are a significant food source for carp, and this has been Ted Kraimer's best pattern. Fish it on the bottom to feeding fish, or swim it through laid-up fish. Mix up the sizes of the eyes for various depths. Anything feeding on Hexes will eat this fly, so hang on!

Crawbugger

Hook:	#4-8 Daiichi 1710
Thread:	Brown or olive-brown 70-denier UTC Thread
Tail:	Sculpin olive marabou
Eyes:	Black plastic bead chain
Body:	Coarse olive or brown dubbing, spun in a loop and picked out for legs
Rib:	Copper wire, or color to match body
Hackle:	Partridge, grouse, or waterfowl flank, such as widgeon

Notes: I designed this quick and simple crayfish simulator to attract a wide range of species. Best in clear water, worked slowly.

Sexy Hexy

Hook:	#6-8 Daiichi 1120 (or equivalent)
Thread:	Tan or cream 70-denier UTC Thread
Rear body:	Any light-wire straight eye hook (1 inch) broken off at the bend and attached to the main hook with 10-pound monofilament, tan grizzly marabou tail, coarse yellow dubbing for body, and tan grizzly marabou at eye
Front body:	Coarse dirty yellow dubbing, as in rear body
Hackle:	Tan grizzly hen saddle
Eyes:	Mini-barbell, lead, or machined black nickel

Notes: *Hexagenia* mayflies are found across the entire Great Lakes region. The nymphs in particular become extremely important as a food source when emergence take place, usually mid-June to mid-July. This is my simplified version of Kevin Feenstra's Hex Wiggle Nymph. Cast and strip back slowly. I believe this fly is eaten as a small baitfish too. This pattern can also be tied in an unweighted version, in which case, add a wing case of peacock herl and use black plastic bead chain for the eyes.

Superior X-Legs

Hook:	#8-10 Daiichi 1560 (or equivalent)
Bead (optional):	1/8- to 3/16-inch copper
Thread:	Brown 70-denier UTC Thread
Tail:	Brown or brown grizzly marabou
Abdomen:	Brown stonefly blend ribbed with copper wire
Thorax:	Brown stonefly blend tied heavier and picked out with one strand of brown with orange flecks and Sili Legs

Notes: This pattern is a must-have for the Lake Superior tributaries and river mouths of Minnesota and Wisconsin. It is a key pattern for steelhead and Kamloops rainbows. It can be dead-drifted or slowly twitched and retrieved. It has also been used successfully in other areas around the Great Lakes too. Matt Paulson of the Superior Fly Angler showed me this pattern, but I was not able to find out who originated it.

EZ Craw

Hook:	#4 Daiichi 1710 (or equivalent)
Weight:	Small lead barbell eyes, tied so the hook rides upright
Thread:	140-denier UTC Thread, color to match body and claws
Claws:	Claw-Dad Claws, color to match body
Antenna:	Two strands of rubber hackle
Body:	Crosscut rabbit strip (tan, brown, olive, grizzly orange)

Notes: I have tied this pattern for many years. The precut claws are now available from Eastern Trophies Fly Fishing of Alexandria, VA (571-213-2570), www.easterntrophies.com. This fly is rugged, versatile, and catches fish. It can be stripped, swung, and drifted under an indicator. I would not fish smallmouth anywhere without some of these in my box.

Claw Dad

Hook:	#4-8 Daiichi 1710 or equivalent
Thread:	70-denier UTC Thread, color to match body
Claws:	Claw-Dad Claws, color to match body
Body:	Medium chenille (black, brown, tan, or olive)
Legs:	Round rubber hackle
Eyes:	Medium or small lead barbell

Notes: Nothing fancy or flashy here, just a long-proven, consistent fish catcher from the Kreel Tackle Company. The claws as well as completed flies are now sold by Eastern Trophies Fly Fishing, Alexandria, Virginia (517-213-2570), www.easterntrophies.com. This fly can be stripped, hopped, and fished under an indicator.

Morlock's Tailer Teaser

Hook:	#4 Mustad R74 (or equivalent)
Thread:	Black 140-denier UTC Thread (or equivalent)
Tail:	EP 3D Fibers Everglades with orange Krystal Flash
Body:	0.025-inch lead wire and Rootbeer Estaz
Legs:	Brown and black Juicy Legs
Head:	Orange Estaz
Eyes:	Red or yellow barbell

Notes: This is another top-producing pattern for Kevin Morlock and his guiding crew, which I've tied here. It designed to sink quickly to deep-tailing carp. By adjusting the amount of lead wire on the body and size of the eyes, this fly can be made to sink at a wide range of speeds. It is also a good pattern for smallmouth and freshwater drum.

Warm Water Charlie

Hook:	#6 TMC 200R
Thread:	Yellow 70-denier UTC Thread
Tail:	Tan grizzly marabou with two strands of pumpkin Sili Legs with orange tips
Body:	Yellow and tan Sparkle Yarn and ring-necked pheasant rump hackle
Legs:	Sili Legs (tan with orange sparkles)
Wing:	Tan arctic fox tail
Eyes:	Small, machined black nickel barbell

Notes: Warm Water Charlie designer Jon Uhlenhop is manager of Chicago Fly Fishing Outfitters and has fished the lakeshore area of the Windy City his entire life. He fishes this pattern regularly for the assortment of warmwater species found in the harbors and shoreline areas. He also ties this in an olive variation.

Coyote Ugly

Hook:	#6 Gamakatsu B10S
Thread:	Tan 70-denier UTC Thread
Tail:	Coyote or fox tail and several strands of copper and gold Angel Hair
Body:	Golden olive Petite Estaz
Legs:	Orange and black speckled Sili Legs
Head:	Light brown deer body hair
Eyes:	Small barbell, red with black pupil

Notes: Coyote Ugly designer and Milwaukee-based angler Dave Pinczkowski fishes this pattern religiously for Door County, Wisconsin, carp. It is slow sinking, with great action on the drop, and is often eaten while sinking. Also good for picky smallmouth and jumbo perch.

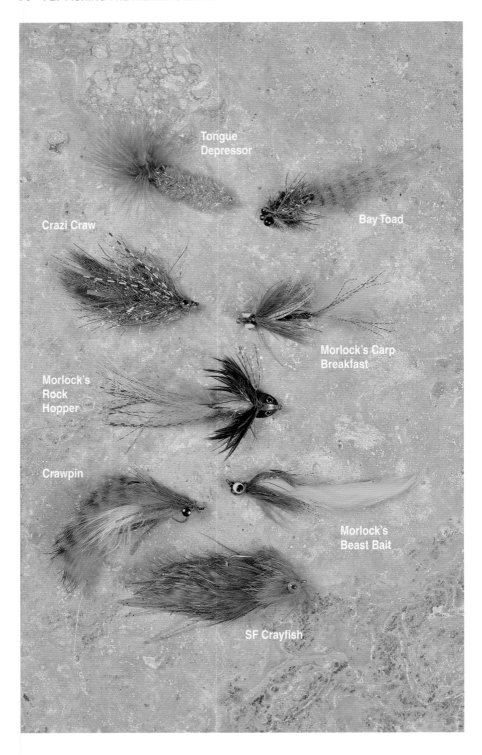

Tongue
Depressor

Crazi Craw

Bay Toad

Morlock's Carp
Breakfast

Morlock's
Rock
Hopper

Crawpin

Morlock's
Beast Bait

SF Crayfish

Tongue Depressor, Olive

Hook:	#4 Dai-Riki 700 B
Weight:	0.030-inch nonlead wire
Thread:	Red or orange 6/0 UNI-Thread
Tail:	Olive marabou
Body:	Olive Cactus Chenille, trimmed flat top and bottom

Notes: This fly designed by Bill Sherer should be fished on a loop knot to maximize its wobbling action. It is a very productive pattern for smallmouth, largemouth, and walleye. Other productive colors are white, black, brown, and perch.

Bay Toad

Hook:	#4 Daiichi 2451 or 2450
Thread:	Olive dun 6/0 UNI-Thread
Tail:	Golden olive Extra Select Craft Fur
Body:	Olive Ice Chenille with pheasant rump feather
Head:	Olive and black EP Fiber
Eyes:	Large black bead chain

Notes: Bay Toad was designed by Traverse City, Michigan, guide Ted Kraimer. Inspired by the Tarpon Toad, this pattern, fished by swimming it, is effective on both smallmouth bass and carp. Tie with both bead-chain and various-size lead barbell eyes in small or extra small to reach the depth you want.

Crazi Craw

Hook:	#2-4 Gamakatsu B10S
Thread:	6/0 UNI-Thread, color to match body
Tail:	Four Micro Pine Squirrel Zonker strips (crawfish orange or olive) with root beer or olive Krinkle Mirror Flash
Body:	Polar Chenille (UV rusty copper or UV olive copper)
Legs:	Centipede Legs (orange or olive)
Eyes:	Psuedo Eyes (medium, red)

Notes: Pat Ehlers is a longtime guide and warmwater specialist who owns the Fly Fishers Fly Shop in Milwaukee, Wisconsin. He has a number of patterns available through Rainy's Flies, tier of this one. The Crazi Craw is a great pattern for off-color water or when you are trying to draw fish from a long distance. It regularly attracts smallmouth, largemouth, and carp as well as other crayfish eaters. Materials for both the orange and olive variations are included.

Morlock's Carp Breakfast

Hook:	#4 TMC 200R
Thread:	Black, brown, olive, or tan 70-denier UTC Thread (or equivalent)
Tail:	Small bunch of marabou with six to eight strands of Krystal Flash
Body:	Three to four peacock herl fibers ribbed with copper wire
Back hackle:	Light yellow mallard flank with several strands of Krystal Flash, same color as tail
Front hackle:	Pheasant body feather
Eyes:	Yellow barbell

Notes: This fly is a favorite of Michigan guide Kevin Morlock. It is tied in four color variations—black, brown, olive, and tan. It will catch carp all across the Great Lakes and beyond.

Morlock's Rock Hopper

Hook:	#4 Mustad R74 (or equivalent)
Thread:	Tan 70-denier UTC Thread
Tail:	Tan Finn Raccoon Zonker strip with orange Centipede Legs and copper/black grizzly Flashabou Accent
Body:	Hot pink Senyo's Laser Dub
Inner collar:	Root beer Palmer Chenille
Outer collar:	Black and brown schlappen with copper/black grizzly Flashabou Accent mixed in
Head:	Small brown Flymen Sculpin Helmet

Notes: I tied this fly based on Kevin Morlock's original. Before sliding on the Sculpin Helmet, pull the collar to each side to simulate sculpin or goby fins. Coat with clear fingernail polish to hold in place. Slide the Sculpin Helmet on from the front. If it is too loose, build up space with thread. Glue in place with Zap-A-Gap. Lake Michigan carp are attracted to pink when cruising in deeper water. Estaz can also be used for the body. This pattern works with an orange body but will attract more smallies than carp in this color.

Crawpin

Hook:	#1 Daiichi 2461
Thread:	Olive 140-denier UTC Thread
Tail:	Cream marabou
Body:	Golden olive Estaz or Cactus Chenille
Wing:	Olive rabbit strip with brown bars
Legs:	Sili Legs (pumpkin with green sparkle)
Eyes:	Medium black nickel

Notes: I designed this fly, tied here by the Pacific Fly Group. This is my favorite color of this crossover pattern. It imitates a crayfish, sculpin, or goby, depending on the color. I also tie this in brown, tan, and black variations. It is another fly with good multispecies appeal. It pushes a lot of water, making plenty of "noise."

Morlock's Beast Bait

Hook:	#2-4 Mustad R90 (or equivalent)
Thread:	Brown 70-denier UTC Thread (or equivalent)
Tail/body:	Yellow-olive rabbit strip
Collar:	Blue Krystal Flash
Hackle:	Brown schlappen
Head:	Brown rug yarn
Eyes:	Large red barbell

Notes: This pattern, which I tied in the yellow color listed, has produced some of Kevin Morlock's largest carp over the years. It is a consistent producer and will also attract smallmouth.

SF Crayfish

Hook:	#1-2 Daiichi 2456 (or equivalent)
Thread:	Brown-olive 140-denier UTC Thread
Tail:	Orange-tipped, pumpkin rubber hackle, gold grizzly Flashabou
Pincers:	Olive variant rabbit strips, one on each side of tail
Body:	Several wraps of orange grizzly crosscut rabbit with olive mallard flank in front
Collar:	Olive variant crosscut rabbit
Eyes:	Medium barbell

Notes: Michigan fly shop owner and guide Mike Schultz tied this fly for a single fly, catch-and-release tournament on Michigan's Huron River. The pattern has been a top performer ever since in rivers and lakes. It is extremely durable and made to be "stripped and ripped"—with a quick, active retrieve to trigger strikes. It will catch any species actively feeding on crayfish and gobies.

Simpleech

Hook:	#2-6 Gamakatsu B10S
Thread:	70-denier UTC Thread, color to match wing
Wing:	Rabbit strip
Eyes:	Medium barbell

Notes: Another favorite of Dave Pinczkowski, this is about as simple as pattern can get. Vary colors for creepy-crawly critters and for baitfish. Push the hook point through the skin side of the rabbit-strip wing and then tie it down over the eyes. You can add Flash for baitfish patterns. This is a proven fish-catcher, and a bunch can be tied quickly in a pinch.

Simpleech

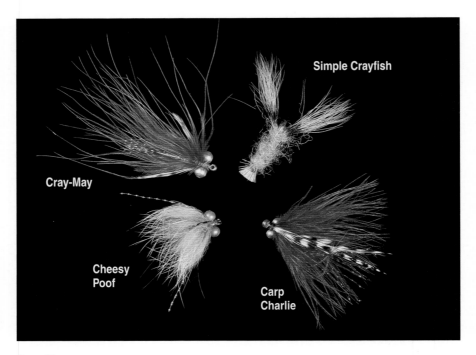

Cray-May

Hook:	#6-8 Daiichi 1560 or equivalent
Thread:	Brown 70-denier UTC Thread
Tail:	Root beer Krystal Flash
Body:	Root beer Krystal Flash
Hackle:	Sculpin olive marabou with a grizzly hackle tip on each side
Eyes:	Gold bead chain (medium)

Notes: Capt. Geoff Kowalczyk guides and fishes the Anchor Bay area on the north end of Lake St. Clair and designed this pattern, which is effective for carp that cruise the shallows in spring and early summer. It represents either an immature crayfish or a swimming mayfly nymph—whichever the fish prefer. Smallmouth and various panfish will also hit this fly.

Simple Crayfish

Hook:	#6-10 Daiichi 1260
Thread:	Fluorescent red 6/0 UNI-Thread
Pincers:	Fox squirrel tail
Body:	Coarse dubbing
Eyes:	Small, black bead chain
Tail:	Butt ends of fox squirrel tail, trimmed short

Notes: A great carp pattern from Nick Pionessa, manager of the Oak Orchard Fly Shop in Williamsville, New York. Pionessa will present this to feeding carp, letting the fly sink slowly into the fish's line of sight. Any movement of the fish forward to where the fly landed often signals a strike, and the line is tightened up until the fish is felt. The pattern also attracts smallmouth and panfish such as rock bass and perch.

Cheesy Poof

Hook:	#8 Gamakatsu C-14S
Thread:	Olive or tan 70-denier UTC Thread
Body:	Red fox body fur, spun in a loop and combed out, one strand of gold Krystal Flash on each side
Eyes:	Gold or black bead chain

Notes: Another proven carp pattern that Pionessa designed and fishes regularly on the Upper Niagara River. It has excellent action on the drop, and the size of the bead-chain eyes determines the sink rate.

Carp Charlie

Hook:	#4-6 Daiichi 1550
Tail:	Copper Krystal Flash
Body:	Copper Krystal Flash
Wing:	Brown marabou with grizzly hackle tips and several strands of copper Krystal Flash
Eyes:	Gold bead chain

Notes: This pattern from Traverse City, Michigan, guide Russ Maddin was designed to target carp on Lake Michigan's Grand Traverse Bay. Smallies also will eat it. (Hint: Tie it larger on a saltwater hook and try it for redfish.)

Nipigon River Leech

Hook:	#2-8 Daiichi 2220
Thread:	Olive 3/0 UNI-Thread
Tail:	Chartreuse marabou with several strands of pearl Krystal Flash
Body:	Dark olive Uni-Mohair with lead wire underneath
Rib:	Medium silver wire
Wing:	Olive chinchilla rabbit strip, twice the length of the hook
Throat:	Red marabou or wool
Collar:	Dark olive ring-necked pheasant rump feather

Notes: First tied by guide and fly shop owner Bill Boote of Thunder Bay, Ontario, this is a must-have for the lower Nipigon River area. It catches brookies, lake trout, steelhead, and salmon.

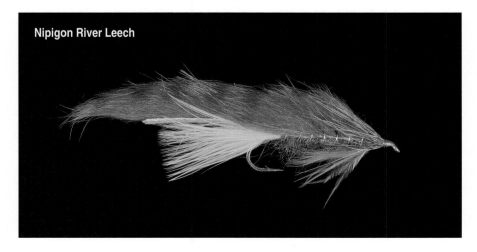

Nipigon River Leech

Standard Baitfish, Sculpin, and Gobies

Deep Minnow

Hook:	#1/0-6 Daiichi 2546, Gamakatsu B10S, Mustad 3366 (or equivalent)
Thread:	Chartreuse 140-denier UTC Thread (or equivalent)
Belly:	Bucktail
Wing:	Bucktail over top of Krystal Flash, Flashabou, Flashabou Mirage, and Krinkle Mirror Flash
Eyes:	Barbell

Notes: This is the best-known baitfish pattern and can be tied in other colors to imitate nearly any forage species. Any baitfish-eating predator can be caught on this fly designed by Bob Clouser. It is most productive when tied sparsely; many commercial patterns have too much bucktail. The chartreuse-white version shown is the most popular around the Great Lakes, but other productive colors are all-white, gray-white, olive-white, olive-chartreuse, olive-orange, and brown-orange.

RS Deep Minnow

Hook:	#1-4 Daiichi 2546, Gamakatsu B10S, Mustad 3366 (or equivalent)
Thread:	Blue 140-denier UTC Thread
Tail:	Rabbit strip
Belly:	Bucktail
Wing:	Bucktail over Flash
Eyes:	Barbell

Notes: RS refers to rabbit strip in my design here. This pattern has been part of my arsenal for several years. It is one pattern that has consistently produced lake walleyes. The rabbit strip adds a little extra movement on a slow retrieve, while giving a more visible profile when fished after dark.

Coyote Clouser

Hook:	#1-4 Daiichi 2546, Gamakatsu B10S, Mustad 3366 (or equivalent)
Thread:	Tan 140-denier UTC Thread
Tail:	Small bunch of shorter hair from coyote or red fox tail
Wing:	Longer hair from coyote or red fox tail over gold and then brown/black grizzly Krystal Flash
Head:	Shorter hair from coyote or red fox tail, tied over top of the wing
Eyes:	Medium or large red barbell

Notes: This pattern can look like a goby, a sculpin, or a crayfish. It is best fished around breakwalls or rocky drop-offs. It is simple to tie and catches fish. Coyote tail gives the fly a grayish tinge, while red fox is more brown.

Flashtail Deep Minnow

Hook:	#1-4 Daiichi 2546, Gamakatsu B10S, Mustad 3366 (or equivalent)
Thread:	Olive 140-denier UTC Thread
Tail:	Krystal Flash, Flashabou, Krinkle Mirror Flash, or similar material, tied approximately twice the length of the wing
Belly:	Bucktail
Wing:	Bucktail
Eyes:	Barbell

Notes: Plenty of flash and extra movement from this Deep Minnow variation. It presents a larger profile and is a good choice in off-color water or when trying to attract fish from a longer distance.

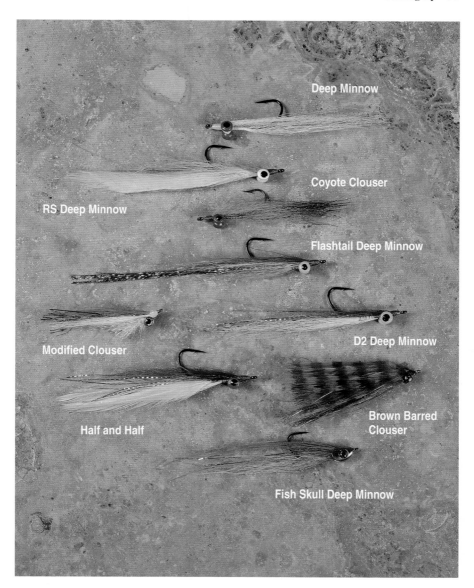

Deep Minnow

Coyote Clouser

RS Deep Minnow

Flashtail Deep Minnow

Modified Clouser

D2 Deep Minnow

Half and Half

Brown Barred Clouser

Fish Skull Deep Minnow

Modified Clouser

Hook:	#1 Daiichi 2546
Thread:	White 140-denier UTC Thread
Wing:	Dark bucktail over white bucktail with Axxel Flash in between
Body:	Pearl Palmer Chenille, trimmed short on the bottom
Eyes:	Blue Sparkle Barbell Eyes from Montana Fly

Notes: Though known best as a deer-hair guru, Chris Helm ties all styles of flies. This pattern of his gives a good silhouette of short, deep-bodied baitfish such as small shad.

D2 Deep Minnow

Hook:	#1-4 Daiichi 2546, Gamakatsu B10S, Mustad 3366 (or equivalent)
Thread:	Olive 140-denier UTC Thread
Tail:	Long, sparse bucktail
Belly:	Bucktail
Wing:	Bucktail over Flash
Eyes:	Barbell

Notes: I designed the D2, which refers to "double deer," as in the bucktail added as a tail. This gives the fly extra length and also provides the opportunity to easily add a third color, if desired. Again the bucktail should be kept sparse on this fly.

Half and Half

Hook:	#3/0-2 Daiichi 2546, Gamakatsu B10S, Mustad 3366 (or equivalent)
Thread:	Olive 140-denier UTC Thread (or equivalent)
Tail:	Two to four saddle hackles tied to oppose each other
Belly:	Bucktail
Wing:	Bucktail over Flash
Eyes:	Medium or large barbell

Notes: This pattern, designed by Lefty Kreh, combines features of both the Deep Minnow and Lefty's Deceiver. The addition of the saddle hackles add length and profile, making this a good pattern to imitate larger baitfish. The same colors as those used for the Deep Minnow are productive.

Brown Barred Clouser

Hook:	#2-6 Daiichi 2546 (or equivalent)
Thread:	Brown 150-denier Lagartun
Body:	Tan Micro Pearl Core Braid
Wing:	Tan/brown Montana Barred marabou with root beer Midge Krystal Flash
Belly:	Pheasant-tail color Angel Hair
Eyes:	Barbell

Notes: This pattern from Ohio's Chris Helm works best in the late spring and early summer. It imitates a young-of-the-year sculpin or goby and other bottom-dwelling critters.

Fish Skull Deep Minnow

Hook:	#1-4 Daiichi 2546, Gamakatsu B10S, Mustad 3366 (or equivalent)
Thread:	White or red 140-denier or 70-denier UTC Thread
Wing:	Light-colored bucktail, flash, and darker bucktail
Head:	Small to large Fish-Skull, depending on hook size

Notes: The Fish-Skull, from Flymen Fishing Company, is a fairly new product that adds weight, color, and flash to streamer patterns. They are quite simple to use, added to the front after the fly is completed. Make sure the heavier side of the skull is to the bottom so the hook rides inverted. Use Zap-A-Gap on the thread before sliding on the skull. I expect we will see Fish-Skulls incorporated into a variety of patterns as time goes on.

Simpleech Baitfish

Hook:	#4-6 Gamakatsu B10S
Thread:	White 70-denier UTC Thread
Wing:	White rabbit strip, with pearl or holo silver Angel Hair
Eyes:	Medium barbell (white)

Notes: An effective, quick-to-tie pattern to imitate smaller, silvery baitfish from Dave Pinczkowski. It is good pattern to work close to the bottom, as it has an upturned hook.

Silver Shiner Clouser

Hook:	#2 Daiichi X472
Thread:	Gray 70-denier UTC Thread
Belly:	White bucktail
Wing:	Gray bucktail over rainbow Krystal Flash
Eyes:	Barbell, red with black pupil

Notes: This color of the Clouser Deep Minnow is a must for New York's Upper Niagara River. This version will outperform other colors by a wide margin. Rick Kustich normally fishes this fly on a sinking-head line.

Jig Clouser, Golden Shiner

Hook:	#1/0 60-degree jig hook
Thread:	White 140-denier UTC Thread (or equivalent)
Belly:	White bucktail
Wing:	Yellow bucktail over gold Flashabou
Eyes:	Medium barbell (gold)

Notes: Pennsylvania guide Capt. Jim Sharpe fishes this pattern in weedy areas around Presque Isle Bay when golden shiners are on the menu.

Fox Tail Minnow

Hook:	#6 TFS 5444 Jig
Thread:	Gray 6/0 UNI-Thread
Tail:	Rainbow pearl Polar Flash, pearl Flashabou, and opal Flashabou Mirage
Belly:	White arctic fox tail
Wing:	Gray arctic fox tail
Eyes:	Small lead barbell (pearl)

Notes: Ted Kraimer's variation of the Clouser Minnow, this works well for smallmouth bass across the Great Lakes. You can change the color of the top wing to olive or chartreuse to imitate various baitfish.

Corsair Spottail Shiner

Hook:	#2 Daiichi 2461
Thread:	Black 70-denier UTC Thread
Body:	Pearl/white Corsair tubing with black thread at tail
Wing:	Peacock Flashabou Accent with peacock herl over top
Throat:	Fluorescent red yarn
Eyes:	3D holographic

Notes: The spottail shiner is a well-distributed forage species across the Great Lakes. In spite of this, there are few patterns that imitate this baitfish. This is Capt. Geoff Kowalcyzk's interpretation.

Boa Minnow

Hook:	#1 Daiichi 2461
Thread:	White or gray 70-denier UTC Thread
Tail:	Gray or white marabou
Body:	Boa yarn, eyelash yarn, or Gala yarn
Wing:	Krinkle Mirror Flash
Head:	Ice Dub

Notes: I normally swing this small baitfish pattern or dead-drift it under an indicator. It has been productive in the Niagara River and around power-plant discharges.

Perch Fry

Hook:	#4 TMC811S (or equivalent)
Thread:	Black 70-denier UTC Thread
Belly:	Tan Craft Fur
Back:	Tan Craft Fur

Notes: A fly pattern hardly gets any simpler than this. Perch fry are targeted by smallmouth, walleye, pike, and other predators in the early summer. Austin Adduci has great results with this pattern in the southern end of Lake Michigan. Add barring to the back with a dark-colored marker.

Tubular Smelt

Hook:	#2-8 Mustad Signature Stinger
Thread:	Fluorescent red 3/0 Danville Thread
Belly/Back:	Pearl/white Metz Deadly Dazzle with pink Deadly Dazzle, mix several strands each of pink Flashabou Mirage, silver Flashabou, blue Krystal Flash, purple Krystal Flash, topped with gray Deadly Dazzle and peacock herl
Body:	Pearl Mylar tube, epoxied, with red marker on back
Eyes:	Painted

Notes: Smelt are a staple forage species across most of the Great Lakes. This pattern by Karl Weixlmann duplicates smelt coloration and is productive wherever smelt are found.

Little Precious

Hook:	#8-10 Mustad 9672
Thread:	Fluorescent red 3/0 Danville Thread
Wing:	Olive arctic fox tail
Belly:	White arctic fox tail
Flash:	Pearl Flashabou
Head:	Brass bead

Notes: This imitation of a crippled minnow designed by Karl Weixlmann will attract a wide range of species. Use it for steelhead, smallmouth, and panfish that are feeding on emerald shiners.

Great Lakes Goby Grub

Hook:	#2 TMC 765SP (or equivalent)
Thread:	Tan 140-denier UTC Thread
Tail:	Brown grizzly rabbit strip
Body:	Olive Estaz with trimmed everglades EP Fiber over top
Head:	Tan sheep wool
Eyes:	Black nickel I-Balz (medium)

Notes: Austin Adduci created this pattern to combat spin fishers who were tossing tube jigs for smallmouth. It has proven to be a productive pattern to target smallmouth and other species feeding on gobies. This is the most common color, but it can be altered depending on locale and time of year.

Bait Bugger

Hook:	#4 Daiichi 1710
Thread:	Olive-brown 70-denier UTC Thread (or equivalent)
Tail:	Olive grizzly marabou
Body:	Golden brown Ice Dub with natural or yellow grizzly hackle palmered over
Flash:	Twenty strands perch Flashabou and grizzly hackle
Head:	Large gold cone

Notes: Tim Pearson is a guide, fly tier, and artist based on Minnesota's North Shore. His Bait Bugger imitates darker, mottled baitfish and will work in many areas around the lakes. It can also represent other baitfish, having a mottled appearance and good movement in the water. Tie in the Flashabou forward at the head and pull it back over the body a few strands at a time with each wrap of grizzly hackle.

Lion Bugger

Hook:	#4-6 Daiichi 1710 (or equivalent)
Thread:	Brown 70-denier UTC Thread (or equivalent)
Tail:	Tan or olive grizzly marabou with orange grizzly marabou and two orange or chartreuse Sili Legs
Body:	Olive or root beer Cactus Chenille or Estaz, palmered with a brown saddle hackle
Legs:	Yellow Centipede Legs
Collar:	Tan or olive grizzly marabou, wrapped
Head:	Black nickel Cross-Eyed Cone

Notes: This is a very productive crayfish imitation designed and tied by Jon Uhlenhop. It can also be used to imitate small gobies. Has great movement from the marabou and legs. Smallmouth sometimes eat this on the drop.

Great Lakes Goby

Hook:	#1-2 Daiichi 2220
Thread:	Brown 70-denier UTC Thread
Tail:	Brown grizzly marabou
Body:	Natural emu with brown saddle hackle palmered through
Collar:	Brown rubber hackle
Head:	Brown sculpin wool
Eyes:	Red plastic bead chain

Notes: This pattern is an offshoot of Kevin Feenstra's Emulator. I have tied this for many years, and it is still a fish producer—both when stripped and on a swing.

Polar Shiner

Hook:	#6 Daiichi 1640 (or equivalent)
Thread:	White 70-denier UTC Thread (or equivalent)
Belly:	White Polar Fiber
Wing:	Olive Polar Fiber
Lateral line:	Peacock Flashabou Accent
Throat:	Fluorescent red wool
Eyes:	3D silver/black

Notes: Capt. Geoff Kowalczyk, who designed and tied this pattern, fishes the north end of Lake St. Clair. This pattern matches young-of-the-year emerald shiners.

Mike's Damino

Hook:	#6 Daiichi 1120
Thread:	140-denier UTC Thread to match fly color
Eyes:	Super pearl 3D Epoxy
Gills:	McFly Foam
Body:	Marabou and SF Flash Blend

Notes: Mike Schmidt of Angler's Choice Flies is developing a reputation for creating fish-catching streamer patterns. This is another imitation of the Great Lakes most-distributed forage species.

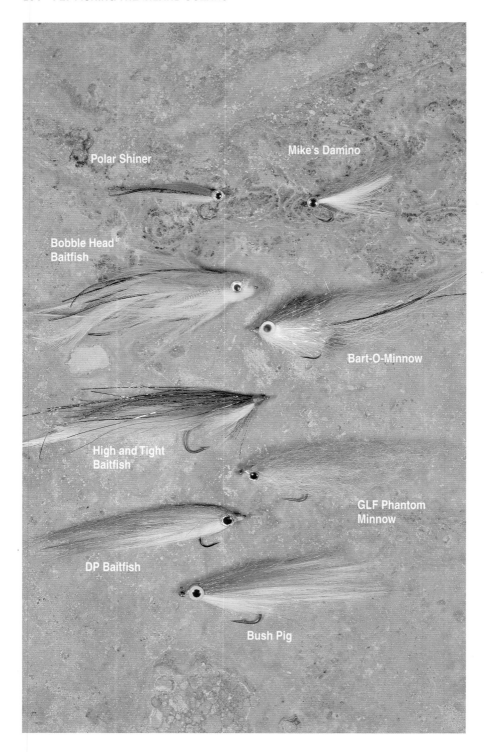

Polar Shiner

Mike's Damino

Bobble Head
Baitfish

Bart-O-Minnow

High and Tight
Baitfish

GLF Phantom
Minnow

DP Baitfish

Bush Pig

Bobble Head Baitfish

Hook:	#1 Mustad S74SZ
Weight:	.30-inch lead wire
Thread:	Gray 6/0 UNI-Thread
Tail:	White rooster saddle (4) and pearl Angel Hair
Body:	White bucktail and white marabou
Collar:	Mallard flank
Wing:	Gray marabou and peacock herl
Head:	White and gray sheep hair
Eyes:	1/4-inch silver holographic

Notes: This fly was designed by Ted Kraimer. The bucktail used in the body is tied in short and prevents the tail feathers from fouling in the hook bend. The lead wire is tied on the upper portion of the bend, which works with the head shape and material to provide a wounded action to the baitfish. Before casting, get the fly wet by massaging water into it; otherwise it will float (which isn't all that bad for surface and near-surface feeding).

Bart-O-Minnow

Hook:	#6 TMC 8089
Thread:	Gray 70-denier UTC Thread (or equivalent)
Tail:	White bucktail with seven strands each of pearl and silver and Flashabou over top
Overwing:	Olive, tan, or gray Icelandic sheep
Lateral line:	Two strands peacock herl on each side
Collar:	White Ice Fur
Throat:	Red rabbit
Head:	White chenille for bulk, EP Sparkle Brush palmered forward over chenille
Eyes:	3D

Notes: This baitfish imitation from Bart Landwehr has a realistic profile from any angle. It can be fished anywhere across the lakes and be effective. Use the color that is closest to the local forage species. For the head, use pearl blue for blue baitfish, pearl magic for olive and gold minnows; color with Prisma marker.

High and Tight Baitfish

Hook:	#1 Mustad S74SZ
Thread:	Gray 6/0 UNI-Thread
Tail:	White rooster saddle (2) and silver Angel Hair
Body:	Pearl Sparkle Braid
Underwing:	Gray bucktail
Wing:	Gray rooster saddle (4)
Overwing:	Speckled silver Flashabou and black Holographic Flashabou
Throat:	White marabou
Gills:	Red Krystal Flash

Notes: Effective on most species that eat baitfish, this classic-looking pattern designed by Ted Kraimer provides motion from its feathers but holds its profile while imitating a number of different baitfish.

GLF Phantom Minnow

Hook:	#1/0, #2 Daiichi 2546 (or equivalent)
Thread:	White 140-denier UTC Thread (or equivalent)
Belly:	SF Flash Blend, reverse-tied
Back:	SF Flash Blend, reverse-tied

Notes: This is a match-the-hatch pattern for a variety of baitfish from Eli Berant. It is best in super-clear water and calm conditions, when predators can be very selective. The material can be colored easily with waterproof markers to add additional detail.

DP Baitfish

Hook:	#1-4 Gamakatsu B10S
Thread:	White 70-denier UTC Thread
Tail:	White Extra Select Craft Fur with opal Flashabou Mirage
Body:	White Extra Select Craft Fur and silver holographic Angel Hair
Eyes:	3D

Notes: This is another Bad Hair Day variant from Dave Pinczkowski. Tie them in all-white and color as desired or needed. For the body, tie in the white Extra Select Craft Fur forward and then pull it back and tie it down. Mix in the silver holographic Angel Hair, and color the top of the fly with a gray or olive marker. An easy-to-tie, durable fish catcher!

Bush Pig

Hook:	#2/0 Daiichi 2546 (or equivalent)
Thread:	White 140-denier UTC Thread (or equivalent)
Belly:	DNA Holo Fusion (white), reverse-tied
Back:	DNA Holo Fusion (sky blue), reverse-tied
Eyes:	Chartreuse 3D

Notes: Eli Berant of Great Lakes Fly has an extensive selection of productive patterns. This is a great multipurpose baitfish imitation. The DNA Holo Fusion is a lifelike material that gives this pattern great flash, movement, and profile.

Chartreuse Thing

Hook:	#2/0 Daiichi or Gamakatsu Octopus
Thread:	Chartreuse 70-denier UTC Thread
Tail:	Chartreuse bucktail with gold Flashabou
Collar:	Chartreuse Estaz
Head:	Large Cross-Eyed Cone (black nickel)

Notes: This is mainly a salmon pattern. It is tied on with a loop knot and fished actively, giving an erratic movement when retrieved. Jon Uhlenhop also ties and fishes a variation called the Pink Thing.

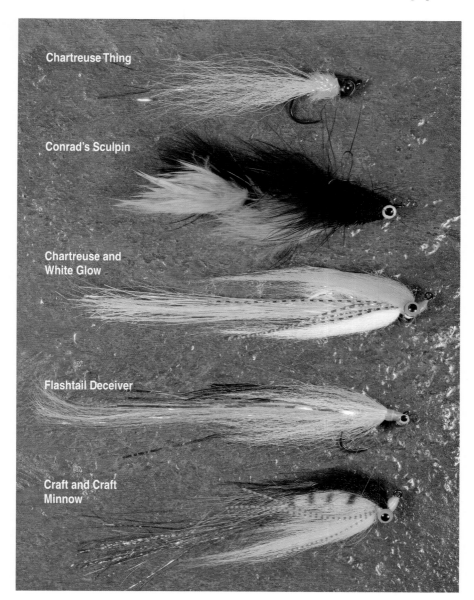

Chartreuse Thing

Conrad's Sculpin

Chartreuse and
White Glow

Flashtail Deceiver

Craft and Craft
Minnow

Conrad's Sculpin

Rear hook:	#6 Mustad 3366
Thread:	Chartreuse 140-denier UTC Thread (or equivalent)
Tail:	Dubbing and schlappen
Wing:	Marabou
Front hook:	#2 Mustad 3366
Thread:	Black 140-denier UTC Thread (or equivalent)
Tail/wing:	Marabou with six to eight strands of flash mixed in
Body/head:	Deer hair
Joining loop:	40-pound hard monofiliament with three or four red glass beads
Eyes:	Large barbell

Notes: This is one of the original "big trout" streamers to come out the Michigan area. It was developed by Indiana tier and angler Jeff Conrad for the Au Sable River. The pattern has performed well on the lakes because it can be tied in a variety of colors to imitate sculpin, gobies, and lampreys. In my experience, you can just break the bend off the rear hook, as anything going after this fly will take it all, rarely short-striking, and be hooked up front. Many variations of this style of fly have followed; they take just about anything that swims in the Great Lakes area.

The tail has a large ball of dubbing in front of bend of the hook. Take two schlappen feathers and cut into V-shaped sections approximately ¾ inch long. Stack three or four of the V sections together and tie them on the side of the hook shank in front of the dubbing ball so that they splay to the outside. Repeat for the opposite side. For the body/head, use clumps of spun and loosely packed deer hair up to the eyes, trimmed flat on the bottom and rounded on top. It should be left wide to give a good sculpin silhouette. Use about six inches of mono for the joining loop, and score the ends of the mono before tying down the loop to help secure it. Coat the thread with Zap-A-Gap after the loop is tied in.

Chartreuse and White Glow

Hook:	#1/0 TFS 5444 60 Jig
Thread:	Bright green Danville Flymaster
Eyes:	Large silver Real-Eyes and 6 mm green plastic eyes
Tail:	Green Glow and pearl Flashabou
Body:	Large UV Polar Chenille (silver) and white schlappen
Legs:	Barred chartreuse and barred pearl Sili Legs
Belly:	White Extra Select Craft Fur
Underwing:	Chartreuse bucktail
Wing:	Chartreuse and bright green Extra Select Craft Fur

Notes: When fishing in low-light or dark, charge the fly with your camera's flash or LED flashlight for best results. This fly from Ted Kraimer works well for salmon and bass.

Flashtail Deceiver, Tutti Fruiti

Hook:	#1 Daiichi or Gamakatsu Octopus
Thread:	Fluorescent pink 140-denier UTC Thread (with green stripe added)
Tail:	Mint green bucktail and mixture of pearl DNA Holo Fusion and pearl Magnum Flashabou
Wing:	Pink bucktail, with eight to ten strands peacock herl over top and mint green bucktail
Belly:	Pink bucktail
Eyes:	Small yellow barbell

Notes: The bucktail in the tail helps minimize tangling the material in the hook when casting. Originally a saltwater pattern, this can be tied in a variety of colors as both an attractor pattern and baitfish imitation. This color combination has proven effective for salmon in Traverse Bay, Michigan. It was designed by Mark Sedotti and tied by Russ Maddin.

Craft and Craft Minnow, Fire Tiger

Hook:	#1/0 TFS 5444 60 Jig
Thread:	Chartreuse 6/0 UNI-Thread
Eyes:	Large gold Real-Eyes and 6 mm green plastic eyes
Tail:	Holographic fire tiger and pearl Flashabou
Body:	Large gold Holographic Chenille and chartreuse schlappen
Legs:	Chartreuse Sili Legs, perfectly barred
Belly:	Chartreuse Extra Select Craft Fur
Underwing:	Fluorescent orange bucktail
Wing:	Fluorescent orange and black Extra Select Craft Fur

Notes: Use a black permanent marker to mark the Craft Fur on this fly by Ted Kraimer.

Emerald Candy

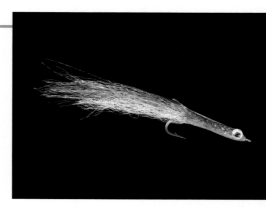

Hook:	#6-10 Mustad 9672
Thread:	Fluorescent red 3/0 Danville Thread
Belly:	White FisHair or similar synthetic
Back:	Mix of silver, blue, pearl, and purple Flashabou or Krystal Flash with olive FisHair or similar synthetic over top and peacock herl topping
Body:	Pearl Mylar tube, epoxied
Eyes:	Painted

Notes: Pennsylvania guide Karl Weixlmann fishes this pattern extensively for early fall steelhead along the Lake Erie shoreline. It should be successful wherever emerald shiners are found.

Redneck Goby

Hook:	#4-8 straight-eye streamer
Thread:	Brown flat waxed nylon thread
Tail:	Gray rabbit fibers
Body:	Dubbed gray rabbit
Wing:	Pine squirrel body fur strip with several strands of rainbow Krystal Flash
Pectoral fins:	Hungarian partridge
Eyes:	Red barbell

Notes: This bottom-hugging pattern of Karl Weixlmann's is another crossover between a goby, sculpin, or crayfish. The squirrel fur strip wing gives a different effect than rabbit.

Moby Goby

Hook:	#4-8 streamer
Thread:	Brown flat waxed nylon thread
Tail:	Gray rabbit fibers
Body:	Dubbed gray and cream rabbit, mixed
Wing:	Pine squirrel body fur strip with root beer Krystal Flash
Overwing:	marabou
Head:	Spun brown wool
Pectoral fins:	Hungarian partridge
Eyes:	Red or yellow barbell

Notes: This is a realistic imitation of a small goby from Karl Weixlmann. Everything from carp to coho can be taken on this fly.

Big Eye Bluegill

Hook:	#1/0-2 Mustad Signature Stinger
Thread:	White flat waxed nylon thread
Tail:	White or cream EP Fiber (or similar material) and pearl Mirage Flashabou, colored with permanent marker
Belly:	Cream or white EP Fiber (or similar material), colored with permanent marker
Back:	Olive EP Fiber (or similar material) and pearl Mirage Flashabou, barred with permanent marker
Eyes:	Gold ½-inch 3D

Notes: Karl Weixlmann's Big Eye Bluegill presents a large profile and can be used to target largemouth bass and toothy critters like pike and muskie where they overlap with bluegill and sunfish.

Goblin

Hook:	#4 Daiichi 2451
Thread:	Camel 6/0 UNI-Thread and tan Flymaster
Tail:	Black barred rabbit strip (gold variant)
Collar:	Natural brown rooster saddle
Fins:	Speckled brown hen saddle
Head:	Cream and olive sculpin wool
Eyes:	Red barbell (extra small or small)

Notes: A cross between a sculpin and a goby—two significant food sources in the Great Lakes—makes this a terrific smallmouth bass pattern from Ted Kraimer. But don't hesitate to fish it to carp.

RL Helmet Bugger

Hook:	#4 Daiichi 1760
Thread:	Olive or brown 70-denier UTC Thread
Tail:	Marabou
Body:	Estaz or Cactus Chenille
Hackle:	Bugger hackle
Legs:	Speckled Crazy Legs
Head:	Small Sculpin Helmet

Notes: The Daiichi 1760 fits perfectly with the Sculpin Helmet, creating a stand-up hook that fishes well along the bottom. I designed this fly, which is most common in olive and brown color combinations. Wind the hackle through the body, with extra wraps of webbier hackle at front of the body.

Zoo Cougar, Olive

Hook:	#1-4 4XL streamer
Thread:	Tan or olive 140-denier UTC Thread
Tail:	Olive and brown marabou
Body:	Pearl Diamond Braid
Wing:	Tan calf tail with olive-yellow mallard flank over top
Head/collar:	Olive deer hair

Notes: This is another pattern originally designed as a trout streamer. Though primarily a sculpin pattern, this color can also work as a crayfish and goby imitation. Spin the olive deer hair and then leave it wide and trim it flat on top and bottom. It has a neutral buoyancy and fishes best on a high-density, sinking-head line. It was created by Kelly Galloup and tied by Jon Uhlenhop.

River Creature, Chartreuse-Olive

Hook: #1/0 Gamakatsu B10S
Thread: Olive 70-denier UTC Thread
Tail: Yellow-chartreuse barred and speckled Crazy Legs
Body: Olive Cactus Chenille or Estaz
Head: Medium gold Fish-Skull

Notes: By varying size and color, a large number of variations of this pattern can be created with this fly from Flymen Fishing Company. The version listed is my favorite, but other productive combinations are all-pearl, orange-brown, orange-olive, and all-chartreuse. For perch and crappie, use a #4 hook with a small Fish-Skull.

Sparkle Grub, Olive

Hook: #4-8 TMC 200R
Thread: White 3/0 Danville Thread
Tail: Olive arctic fox, with strands of pearl Krinkle Mirror Flash mixed in
Body: Olive Cactus Chenille, Estaz, or similar material
Eyes: Barbell

Notes: Other color schemes for this pattern from Karl Weixlmann are white, black, brown, and chartreuse. By changing the size and color, this pattern can simulate a lot of different things.

Jig Baitfish

Hook:	#2-6 Daiichi 4663
Thread:	White 70-denier UTC Thread
Tail:	White marabou with pearl Flashabou or Mirror Flash
Body:	Pearl Cactus Chenille, Estaz, or similar material
Head:	Large silver bead mounted on a straight pin and tied on hook shank

Notes: This is a favorite pattern of Niagara River guide Paul Castellano for fishing under a large indicator. It imitates baitfish that have been injured when passing through the turbines of the power plants on the river. He dead-drifts the fly through slower runs and pockets.

Cross-Dresser

Hook:	#4 Mustad 34007
Thread:	White 6/0 UNI-Thread
Tail:	Three white saddle hackles per side, tied to splay out, silver Krystal Flash in front
Body:	Pearl Estaz
Head:	Red Estaz
Legs:	Pearl with silver flake Sili Legs, to imitate pectoral fins

Notes: Lake Erie guide Jim Sharpe fishes this pattern as an injured baitfish with an erratic retrieve. He also ties variations with pink or chartreuse heads.

Mike's Murdich

Hook:	#1-2 Daiichi 2546
Thread:	White 140-denier UTC Thread
Tail:	White bucktail with silver holographic Flashabou over top and excess material at front
Collar:	White Hi-Viz or Ice Fur with the Flashabou left from the tail pulled over top
Head:	0.030-inch lead wire with Estaz over top (pearl, silver, pink, or chartreuse)
Eyes:	3D

Notes: A simplified version of the Murdich Minnow from Michigan guide Mike Schultz. Weighting the head makes the fly dart erratically on a fast retrieve. Add spot on each side of the collar with a black permanent marker. It is a great general-purpose baitfish imitation for a variety of warmwater and coldwater species.

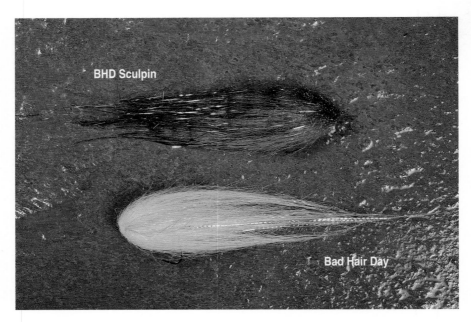

BHD Sculpin

Hook:	#4 Gamakatsu B10S
Thread:	Olive 70-denier UTC Thread (or equivalent)
Tail:	Olive Extra Select Craft Fur and junebug-colored Flashabou
Body:	Olive Extra Select Craft Fur with bronze and chartreuse Angel Hair
Head:	Copper Flashabou and olive Ice Dub

Notes: This color variation of the Bad Hair Day streamer, also from Dave Pinczkowski, is best on tannic or off-color water. Fish it around a rocky bottom with a sinking-head line. For the tail, tie in the Craft Fur forward and then pull it back and tie it down with the Flashabou; put black barring on the top of the body with a permanent marker. Put the copper Flashabou around the body and then a clump of the olive Ice Dub. Darken the top of the Ice Dub with a black permanent marker.

Bad Hair Day

Hook:	#1-4 Gamakatsu B10S
Thread:	White 70-denier UTC Thread (or equivalent)
Tail:	White Extra Select Craft Fur with pearl Krinkle Mirror Flash
Body:	White Extra Select Craft Fur and Angel Hair
Head:	Chartreuse, gray, tan, or pink Extra Select Craft Fur

Notes: This is one of Pinczkowski's favorite patterns. It is simple to tie, extremely durable, and will catch nearly anything that swims. By changing color and hook size, a wide range of food forms can be imitated. It has great action in the water and can be cast and stripped, or swung. For the body, tie the ends of the Craft Fur forward and then pull them back and tie them down with sparse Angel Hair. The head is tied in the same way.

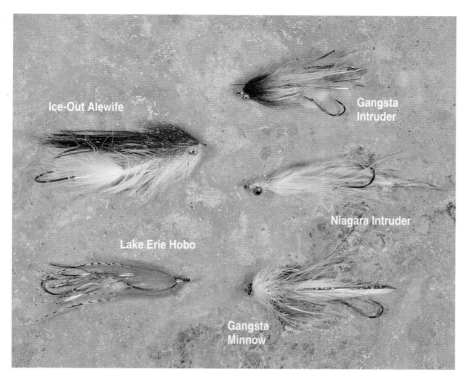

Gangsta Intruder, Emerald Shiner

Shank:	Flymen Fishing Company 20mm Articulated Shank
Thread:	White 6/0 UNI-Thread
Hook loop:	30-pound Fireline with #2 Owner Mosquito Hook
Blade:	#0 Indiana nickel
Body:	Small section of silver minnow belly Laser Dub with pearl UV Polar Chenille in front
Collar:	White schlappen
Wing:	White and chartreuse ostrich herl fibers with silver and green holographic Flashabou over top and peacock as topping
Head:	Olive Australian opossum on top, chartreuse Ice Dub on bottom
Eyes:	Small chartreuse Real-Eyes Plus

Notes: This Intruder-style pattern from Greg Senyo has plenty of flash and movement, with extra vibration from the blade. You can alter the size or colors of the pattern as needed for a variety of applications.

Ice-Out Alewife

Hook:	#1-2 Daiichi 2220 (or equivalent)
Thread:	White 70-denier UTC Thread (or equivalent)
Tail:	White marabou
Body:	Pearl Cactus Chenille palmered with white schlappen
Wing:	Black hanked Lite-Brite with ten to twelve peacock herl strands over top
Head:	Bronze peacock Lite-Brite on top, polar pearl Lite-Brite on bottom
Eyes:	MFC black nickel (medium)

Notes: Indiana river guide Dustan Harley created this pattern for use in the lower part of the St. Joseph River. It is also effective in nearshore situations, where it can be both cast and stripped or swung in current. A good choice when alewives are the target of predators. You can also make it Intruder-style, with a hook loop of .018-inch wire or 30-pound braid.

Niagara Intruder

Shank:	Straight-eye standard hook, broken off at bend after tying
Thread:	White 140-denier UTC Thread
Hook loop:	30-pound braid or .018-inch nylon-coated wire
Body:	White marabou, wrapped as a hackle, with six to eight strands of flash on a side
Wing:	Gray or white rabbit strip
Head:	Pearl Estaz, Cactus Chenille, or similar material
Eyes:	Barbell

Notes: Paul Castellano guides on the Niagara River; he is based on the Ontario side. This pattern is one of his favorites, since it can be either cast or swung, depending on the situation. Castellano usually ties this as a smelt imitation, but it can be tied in many color variations. To ensure the hook loop is secure, tie it down on top of the shank, leaving a bit extra at the front. Then fold the extra length back and tie down again; coat the thread with Zap-A-Gap. Daiichi 2553 (red) or 2557 (black nickel) or Gamakatsu Octopus are the favored hooks to use with these patterns, #2 for steelhead and browns, #1 for lakers.

Lake Erie Hobo

Shank:	Any straight-eye streamer hook
Thread:	White 6/0 UNI-Thread
Hook loop:	30-pound Fireline with #2 Owner Mosquito hook
Target spot:	Fluorescent pink and then chartreuse Ice Dub
Body:	Silver holographic Flat Braid with white Laser Dub in front
Collar:	Gray arctic fox tail with Amherst pheasant fibers
Flash:	Rainbow Flashabou

Notes: This pattern Greg Senyo designed blends natural baitfish colors and a bright "target spot" of color for steelhead to hit. It can be cast or swung in river-mouth and lower-river areas. It also takes lake-run brown trout and lake trout.

Gangsta Minnow, Emerald Shiner

Shank:	Flymen 20 mm Articulated Shank
Thread:	White 70-denier UTC Thread
Blade:	#0 nickel Indiana blade
Hook loop:	30-pound Fireline braid with #2 Owner Mosquito hook
Wing:	White rabbit strip with pearl/silver Polar Flash and chartreuse holographic Flashabou over top
Collar:	White marabou with olive schlappen wound in front
Legs:	Pearl with silver fleck Sili Legs
Head:	White Shaggy Dub
Eyes:	Green plastic bead

Notes: Designed by Greg Senyo mainly for steelhead, this pattern can be cast or swung to imitate an emerald shiner. Senyo fishes this fly at the mouth of Lake Erie tributaries.

Large Baitfish

Figure 8

Hook:	#4/0-2/0 Daiichi 2461
Weedguard:	.030-inch coated wire
Thread:	210-denier UTC Thread to match fly color
Tail:	Bucktail with Krystal Flash over top
Body:	UV Polar Chenille
Wing:	Icelandic sheep with Krystal Flash, holographic Flashabou, and Krinkle Mirror Flash over top
Belly:	Bucktail
Back:	Bucktail with Krystal Flash
Eyes:	3D, epoxied
Head:	Epoxy mixed with glitter

Notes: Bill Sherer of Boulder Junction, Wisconsin, has probably guided more anglers to muskie on a fly than anyone else. This is one of his original toothy-critter patterns, and it is still going strong after a number of years of use. Updates of UV Polar Chenille and holographic Flashabou has freshened up its appearance. Layer colors of sheep and mix types of flash used for the wing. This can be tied in any color combinations imaginable, but Bill normally imitates muskie forage like perch and suckers. This pattern is a must-have for apex predators.

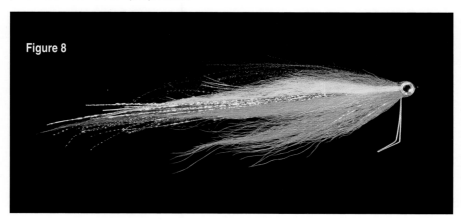

Figure 8

Muskie Meth

Hook:	#8/0 Gamakatsu SL12S
Thread:	White 210-denier UTC Thread
Tail:	Polar Pony Hair with holographic Flashabou on bottom, Big Fly Fiber with Krystal Flash and Flashabou on top
Body:	Reverse-tied bucktail with Flashabou and Krystal Flash blended through it in back, reverse-tied Finn Raccoon in front
Eyes:	Super pearl ½-inch 3D Epoxy Eyes
Head:	Thread finished with superglue and treated with Hard as Hull

Notes: Pat Kelly works at Mad River Outfitters, a longtime fly shop in Columbus, Ohio. He has a passion for chasing muskies and has turned the flies he ties for them into an art form. As the season progresses, forage species get bigger, and larger flies are needed to attract muskies. This is particularly true in big-water situations. Kelly's flies, such as this one, are designed to attract the largest fish. This pattern can be tied to imitate forage species or in bright, contrasting colors. It pays to have both styles when pursuing muskies, as they can be discerning. All-chartreuse, all-white, all-pink, perch, fire tiger, brown-orange, olive-orange, black-chartreuse, black-orange, and black-pink are all key colors.

Muskie Marauder

Rear hook:	#2/0 Gamakatsu B10S
Thread:	210-denier UTC Thread to match fly color
Tail:	Polar Pony Hair with holographic Flashabou
Lateral line:	Grizzly flatwing saddle
Body:	Reverse-tied bucktail
Front hook:	#8/0 Gamakatsu SL12S
Thread:	210-denier UTC Thread to match fly color
Body:	Reverse-tied bucktail with Mirage Flashabou and Krystal Flash blended through
Front lateral line:	Grizzly schlappen
Eyes:	3D Epoxy
Head:	Thread and eyes coated with Big Bond UV Light Cured Epoxy

Notes: Use .024-inch seven-strand Beadalon to join the two parts. Three 6 mm beads are used as spacers on the wire. This is another Pat Kelly fly and the same colors work as with the Muskie Meth pattern.

Natural Born Killer

Rear hook:	#6/0 Gamakatsu S12S
Thread:	210-denier UTC Thread to match fly color
Tail:	Polar Pony Hair with Big Fly Fiber over top, blend in holographic Flashabou, flatwing saddle on each side
Body:	Reverse-tied bucktail with Krystal Flash throughout
Middle hook:	Gamakatsu B10S with bend cut off
Thread:	210-denier UTC Thread to match fly color
Body:	Reverse-tied bucktail with Flashbou Mirage and Flashabou throughout, grizzly flatwing saddle on each side
Front hook:	#8/0 Gamakatsu S12S
Thread:	210-denier UTC Thread to match fly color
Body:	Reverse-tied bucktail with reverse-tied Finn Raccoon in front, Flashabou Mirage throughout bucktail, two flatwing saddles on each side
Head:	Loosely spun deer hair trimmed square
Eyes:	3D Epoxy

Notes: Use .024-inch seven-strand Beadalon to join the sections. Three 6 mm beads are used as spacers on the wire. The same colors work as with the Muskie Meth and Muskie Marauder patterns. Although this pattern from Pat Kelly may seem a bit extreme, keep in mind that it is designed to target the largest predators. It is going to take a mouthful to attract a 50-inch or longer muskie, and this is a fly that can do it. This aspect of our sport, trying to target the largest of freshwater apex predators, is just beginning to be explored.

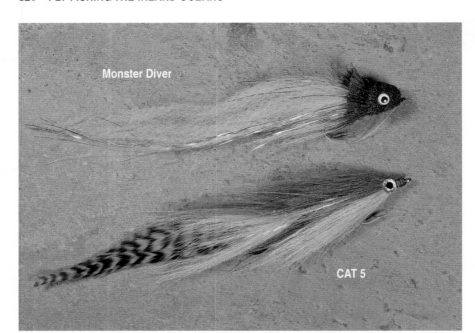

Monster Diver, Olive, Chartreuse

Hook:	#4/0 Daiichi 2460
Thread:	Black 140-denier UTC Thread
Weedguard:	20-pound hard monofilament
Tail:	Chartreuse Frizz Fiber with pearl Mirror Flash
Collar:	Chartreuse bucktail
Head:	Olive deer body, packed tightly and trimmed

Notes: This fly is designed by Scott Currie to attract larger toothy critters. The tail material compresses tightly with minimal water absorption, allowing easier casting of the fly. The size of the head pushes a lot of water and leaves a good bubble trail. This pattern is also productive when fished on a sinking-head line. Other productive colors are olive-orange, black-chartreuse, black-orange, and fire tiger.

CAT 5

Rear hook:	#5/0 Gamakatsu Round Bend Worm Hook
Thread:	210-denier UTC Thread to match fly color
Tail:	Six schlappen feathers
Collar:	Two sections of reverse-tied bucktail with one section regular-tied bucktail in front, Flashabou and Krystal Flash tied in with front section
Front hook:	#5/0 heavy saltwater
Thread:	210-denier UTC Thread to match fly color
Collar:	Two sections of reverse-tied bucktail with one section regular-tied bucktail in front, Flashabou and Krystal Flash tied in with front section
Eyes:	3D
Head:	Epoxy coated

Notes: This is an articulated version of the Great Lakes Deceiver, also designed by Eli Berant. The two sections are joined by .025-inch coated wire with four 6 mm beads as spacers.

Foosa

Hook:	#5/0 Daiichi 2461 (or equivalent)
Thread:	210-denier UTC Thread to match fly color
Tail:	Six saddle hackles with a collar or bucktail and then Finn Raccoon
Body:	Pyrex worm rattle tied down and then glued on the top-middle of the hook shank, pearl Estaz or Cactus Chenille wrapped over top
Front collar:	Two sections of reverse-tied bucktail with mixed Flashabou and Krystal Flash, reverse-tied Finn Raccoon in front
Eye:	3D
Head:	Epoxy coated

Notes: This pattern by Eli Berant has had a lot of time on Lake St. Clair. It has plenty of movement, a big profile, and makes noise. Berant shows key colors on his web site, www.greatlakesfly.com.

Meatwagon Magnum

Hook:	#2/0 Gamakatsu B10S, #3/0-6/0 Gamakatsu Roundbend Worm Hook
Thread:	210-denier UTC Thread to match fly color
Weedguard (optional):	Preformed .030-inch coated wire
Wing:	Icelandic sheep with flash of your choice
Belly:	Reverse-tied bucktail with arctic fox tail in front
Back:	Reverse-tied bucktail with arctic fox tail in front
Head:	Palmer Chenille
Eyes:	3D secured with Liquid Fusion

Notes: This is a larger version of my Meatwagon streamer, substituting Icelandic sheep for the rabbit strip wing. The sheep compresses when wet and picks up very little water weight, making it easier to cast in larger sizes. Plus, it has great movement and is very durable (Thank you, Bill Sherer, for teaching me this). If you are laying colors on the wing, add flash with each layer. If you don't want to make the weedguard yourself, they are available from Bill Sherer, www.wetieit.com. You can also tie this on the Gamakatsu Worm Hook with weedguard. Although pricey, it is a great hook for working flies in cover, and it is available up to a size 5/0. Key colors in this pattern are all-black, black-chartreuse, black-pink, black-orange, fire tiger, olive-orange, and brown-orange.

Great Lakes Deceiver

Hook:	#3/0 Daiichi 2546 (or equivalent)
Thread:	140-denier UTC Thread to match fly color
Tail:	Four to six schlappen feathers
Collar:	Reverse-tied bucktail on top and bottom with Flashabou and Krystal Flash next and then bucktail tied regular on top and bottom
Eyes:	3D

Notes: This take on Lefty's Deceiver from Eli Berant can be fished anywhere around the Great Lakes. It can be tied in natural and attractor colors. Berant's favorite color combinations can be found on his web site, www.greatlakesfly.com.

Foosa

Meatwagon Magnum

Great Lakes
Deceiver

Mega Rattling
Murdich Minnow

Mega Rattling Murdich Minnow

Hook:	#4/0 Daiichi 2461 (or equivalent)
Thread:	210-denier UTC Thread to match fly color
Tail:	Bucktail with flash on top
Collar:	Three to four wraps of Magnum CCT Body Fur
Head:	Pyrex worm rattle on the top of the hook shank with Cactus Chenille wrapped over top
Eyes:	3D

Notes: This oversize version of the Murdich Minnow from Eli Berant has lots of flash and makes plenty of noise. It is a great searching pattern for larger predators. Do not trim the front of the flash for the tail but pull the extra flash over the top of the collar and tie it down.

Muskie Mushy

Hook:	#5/0 Gamakatsu Round Bend Worm
Thread:	Clear monofilament
Body/tail:	Mega Mushy Fibers with pearl Flashabou, treated with Softex
Belly:	Reverse-tied Mushy Fibers and pearl Flashabou
Back:	Reverse-tied Mega Mushy Fibers and pearl Flashabou
Eyes:	3D, glued on

Notes: Based on Dave Skok's saltwater pattern, this version from Eli Berant is designed to attract clear-water muskie from a distance. Berant first fished this pattern on Lake St. Clair, but it can be used anywhere. It relies on flash instead of noise to attract fish.

Bingo

Hook:	#6/0 TMC 800S (or equivalent)
Thread:	Clear monofilament
Body:	Jig rattle secured to top of shank
Belly:	Reverse-tied SF Flash Blend
Back:	Reverse-tied SF Flash Blend
Eyes:	3D

Notes: This a great pattern for large pike and muskie from Eli Berant. It will also attract other large predators. It has flash, movement, and big profile and noise. You can highlight the back with permanent marker.

Angel Hair Baitfish

Hook:	#4/0 TMC 800 SP
Thread:	Clear monofilament
Belly:	White Slinky Fibre
Wing:	Light purple SF Blend with golden olive Angel Hair over and black SF Blend on top
Gills:	Hot pink Fluoro Fibre
Eyes:	3D

Notes: This pattern was designed by Scott Currie.

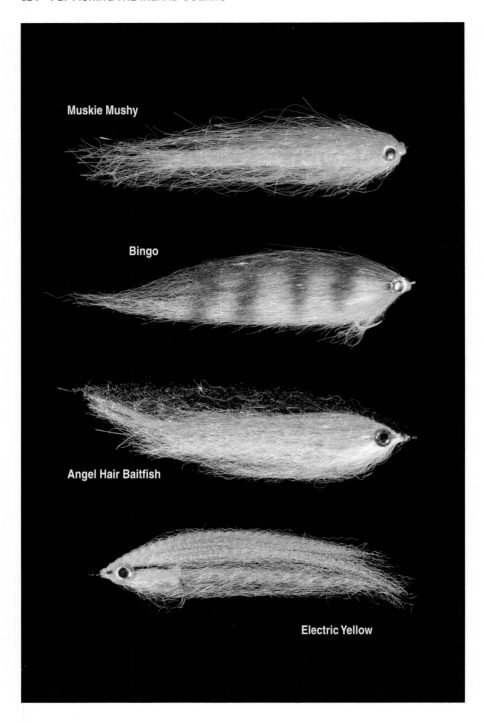

Muskie Mushy

Bingo

Angel Hair Baitfish

Electric Yellow

Electric Yellow

Hook:	#4/0 TMC 800 SP
Thread:	Clear monofilament
Belly:	White Slinky Fibre
Wing:	Shaded chartreuse SF Blend
Gills:	Hot orange Fluoro Fibre
Eyes:	3D

Notes: This pattern was designed by Scott Currie.

Massey Warrior

Hook:	#4/0 Partridge Absolute Barbless Pike Hook
Thread:	White 140-denier UTC Thread
Tail:	White bucktail with white Angel Silk over top
Body:	Pearl UV Polar Chenille with red UV Polar Chenille in front for gills
Wing:	Bleeding black SF blend
Head:	Large black Fish-Skull

Notes: This pattern was designed by Scott Currie.

Attractors

Glow Pig

Hook:	#2/0 Mustad 34007
Thread:	Clear monofilament
Tail:	Reverse-tied creamy white glow-in-the-dark Flashabou
Belly:	Reverse-tied creamy white glow-in-the-dark Flashabou
Back:	Reverse-tied fluorescent green glow-in-the-dark Flashabou
Eyes:	3/8-inch 3D

Notes: Eli Berant designed and fishes this fly for nighttime chinooks. It will also attract brown trout and walleye after dark.

Flash Fly, Blue-Pink

Hook:	#4 Daiichi 2461
Thread:	Fluorescent orange 70-denier UTC Thread
Body:	Chartreuse Palmer Chenille (medium)
Wing:	Two silver doctor blue saddles (long and thin), with silver holographic Flashabou over top
Belly:	Mix of pearl Flashabou and silver holographic Flashabou
Head:	Fluorescent pink UV Ice Dub over top of eyes
Eyes:	Small Real-Eyes

Notes: Jeff Liskay fishes this pattern for Lake Erie steelhead from breakwalls and piers with a fast-sinking Streamer Express line, and at river mouths with the intermediate version. He also ties a variation with a pink body and chartreuse saddles and head; the Flashabou stays the same.

Thunderbolt, Chartreuse

Hook:	#4 Daiichi 2220
Thread:	Chartreuse 6/0 UNI-Thread
Tail:	White marabou
Body:	Light gray UV Ice Dub
Wing:	Opal Magnum Flashabou Mirage with copper DNA Holo Fusion
Legs:	Chartreuse Sili Legs with chartreuse orange-tipped Northland Limber-Legs
Head:	Chartreuse Ice Dub
Eyes:	Small gold bead chain

Notes: Like many of Kevin Feenstra's creations, this is another flashy pattern with lots of movement and an interesting blend of colors. He also ties a version with a yellow tail, gold Holographic Flashabou in the wing, and orange Ice Dub for the head.

Fire Detector

Hook:	#1-4 Daiichi 2461
Thread:	Chartreuse 6/0 UNI-Thread
Tail:	Pearl Krystal Flash with opal Flashabou Mirage
Collar:	Yellow deer hair
Head:	Orange and chartreuse Ice Dub on top and fluorescent pink Ice Dub on bottom
Eyes:	Small gold bead chain, two per side

Notes: Yellow perch are a favored prey of warmwater predators. This Kevin Feenstra pattern is a perch simulator and a favorite of Feenstra during the summer months. Add bars to the tail with brown marker.

Sim's Double Thunder

Hook:	#4 Daiichi 2546 (or equivalent)
Thread:	Chartreuse 140-denier UTC Thread (or equivalent)
Body:	Reverse-tied bucktail in contrasting colors for top and bottom (chartreuse-white, olive-white, olive-orange, chartreuse-orange)
Eye:	Stick on
Head:	Epoxy over bucktail and thread

Notes: Veteran Lake Erie angler Jim Simonelli fishes this pattern in the waters around Erie, Pennsylvania, for smallmouth, walleye, and steelhead. Tie the bucktail forward for the body and then pull it back and tie it down. Match the thread to the top color of bucktail.

Convertible Smelt

Hook:	#2 Daiichi 2161
Thread:	Gray 140-denier UTC Thread
Hook loop:	0.018-inch coated wire
Body:	Steelie blue Ice Dub
Hackle:	Blue marabou wound Spey-style
Wing:	Gray rabbit strip with peacock Flashabou Accent over top
Eyes:	3D stick on, epoxied

Notes: I designed this pattern as a variation of the Niagara Intruder. It gives the option of being fished as a conventional hook design (with a stinger hook added to the wire loop), or of cutting off the bend of the hook and using just the hook on the wire loop. Color combinations are endless, but the design is well-suited to baitfish hues.

Streaker, Black

Hook:	#4 Daiichi 2461
Thread:	Yellow 6/0 UNI-Thread
Tail:	Black bucktail
Body:	Butt ends of tail tied down nearly to the eye of the hook
Wing:	Black bucktail with opal Flashabou Mirage over top
Belly:	Opal Flashabou Mirage
Eyes:	Small bead chain, two on a side

Notes: This pattern gives flash and a hint of color. Other colors Kevin Feenstra ties are orange and chartreuse. Leave short butt ends of bucktail at the eye of hook. Divide bucktail at hook eye with cross wraps used to secure the eyes. Both warmwater and coldwater species will take this fly.

Hammerhead

Hook:	#4 Mustad R74
Weight:	0.035-inch lead-free wire
Thread:	Black 210-denier UTC Thread
Tail:	Fluorescent green and fluorescent yellow glow-in-the-dark Mylar Motion with pumpkin Sili Legs
Rear body:	Any dark yarn
Front body:	Crawfish orange magnum rabbit strip, palmered
Eyes:	Extra-large gold bead chain, two on a side

Notes: Designed by Ian Anderson for Beaver Island (Lake Michigan) carp, this pattern will also take both smallmouth and largemouth bass. The colors given here are the original, but they can be adjusted as desired. The extra-large bead-chain eyes add a bit of rattle and can be trimmed down to reduce weight.

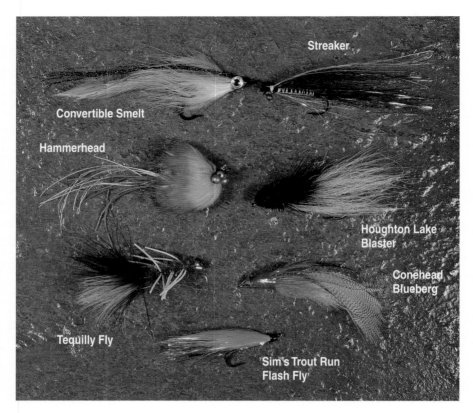

Houghton Lake Blaster, Light and Dark

Hook:	#2 Daiichi 2220
Thread:	Gray 140-denier UTC Thread
Tail:	Red wool
Body:	Black chenille ribbed with flat silver Mylar tinsel
Wing:	White bucktail
Head:	Deer body hair dyed black, spun and trimmed sculpin-style

Notes: This is an updated version of the Houghton Lake Special, an old-time Michigan night-fishing pattern. It adapts well to big-water use, with its contrasting colors that provide good visibility in a variety of water conditions, and a wide head that pushes a lot of water on retrieve. The light version uses natural brown deer body hair, spun and trimmed sculpin-style.

Tequilly Fly

Hook:	#2 Daiichi 1710
Bead:	7/32-inch copper
Thread:	Black 140-denier UTC Thread
Tail:	Yellow and black marabou blood feathers
Body:	Root beer Cactus Chenille
Legs:	Yellow round rubber legs tied in pairs

Notes: This is a great pattern for neutral mood smallmouth and sight-fishing. It sinks slowly, with a lot of movement, and the yellow legs make it easy to spot in the water. I tie and fish this variation of the original pattern: the hook is bigger, and I substitute root beer Cactus Chenille for the body.

Conehead Blueberg, Fire Tiger

Hook:	#4 Daiichi 1720
Thread:	Fluorescent orange 70-denier UTC Thread
Tail:	Orange and yellow marabou with red Krystal Flash
Wing:	Three curved mallard flank feathers and ¼-inch-wide strip of holographic gold sheeting
Hackle:	Orange schlappen with orange Cactus Chenille in front
Cone:	Medium gold

Notes: Kevin Morlock fishes this adaption of John Kluesing's Blueberg streamer in lower river and harbor areas. Color combinations are endless, but this color has proven productive for Lake Michigan salmon and steelhead. The curved feathers give the fly a spoon-like wobble when swung in the current or stripped. Tie the wing feathers on top of the hook shank, smallest on bottom to largest on top.

Sim's Trout Run Flash Fly

Hook:	#6 Daiichi 2441
Thread:	Black 70-denier UTC Thread
Tail:	Kelly green Flashabou
Body:	Fluorescent green glow-in-the-dark Flashabou wound as a body
Wing:	Silver Flashabou
Overwing:	Green arctic fox tail

Notes: Jim Simonelli fishes this pattern at the mouth of Pennsylvania's Lake Erie tributaries for both steelhead and brown trout.

Mike's Meal Ticket

Hook:	#1 Mustad 34007
Thread:	Olive 140-denier UTC Thread
Body 1:	Olive rabbit strip
Body 2:	Pearl EP Sparkle Brush
Body 3:	Gold speckle Sili Legs with a black spot
Connector:	0.018-inch coated wire with 2⅛-inch green glass beads
Head 1:	White lead barbell eyes
Head 2:	White ram's wool

Notes: This articulated streamer from Mike Schmidt is a good alewife imitation and can also work as a spottail shiner. It has plenty of action to simulate a crippled baitfish. You can use red beads for gills.

Blue Belly Dancer

Hook:	#2 TMC 300
Thread:	Black 6/0 UNI-Thread
Tail:	Blue marabou with eight strands of royal blue Krystal Flash
Body:	Blue synthetic dubbing with lead wire underbody
Rib:	Silver wire
Wing:	Chinchilla rabbit strip
Hackle:	Red Chinese neck hackle with natural guinea hackle in front

Notes: The overall length of this fly, a smelt imitation designed by Romeo Rancourt, should be approximately 4½ inches. It is productive on the flats and river mouths of Lake Superior and certainly has application all across the Great Lakes.

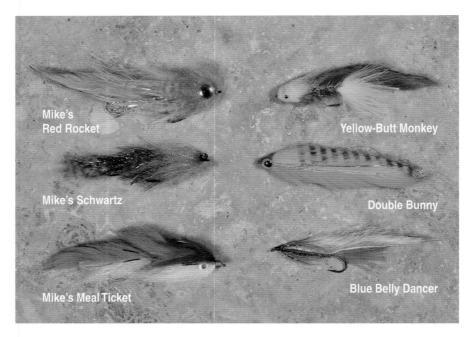

Mike's Schwartz

Hooks:	#2 and #4 Daiichi 2461
Thread:	Dark brown 140-denier UTC Thread
Tail:	Tan grizzly marabou
Body 1:	Polar Chenille
Head 1:	Tan Laser Dub
Head 2:	Golden brown Ice Dub
Collar:	Natural mallard flank
Eyes:	Black plastic beads

Notes: This pattern from Mike Schmidt can double as a sculpin or a goby. It has great movement and flash in the water.

Double Bunny, Fire Tiger

Hook:	#2 Daiichi 2220
Thread:	Olive 140-denier UTC Thread
Belly:	Orange rabbit strip
Back:	Barred olive rabbit strip
Flash:	Several strands of gold Krystal Flash and orange holographic Flashabou on each side
Eyes:	3D stick-on covered with epoxy to form head

Notes: This versatile, rugged pattern by Scott Sanchez can be thrown just about anywhere and will catch just about anything. With all the variations of dyed rabbit strips available, color combinations are endless. Tie some up in your favorite colors and keep them handy. Use a rabbit strip twice the length of hook shank for the belly, run the hook point through the hide side of the rabbit strip, and tie it down in front. Glue the hide side of the back strip to the belly strip hide with some sort of flexible adhesive like Tear Mender or Flexament, and then tie it down in front. Often overlooked as a warmwater pattern, this should be in everyone's fly assortment. This version was tied by Bill Sherer.

Mike's Red Rocket

Hooks:	#1 and #2 Gamakatsu B10S
Thread:	Tan 140-denier UTC Thread
Tail:	Tan rabbit strip with gold holographic Flashabou
Rear body:	Tan Cactus Chenille with yellow schlappen palmered over with tan marabou in front
Front body:	Gold holographic Flashabou and then tan Cactus Chenille with yellow schlappen palmered over
Connector:	0.018-inch coated wire with two 1/8-inch orange glass beads
Head:	Tan marabou, grizzly marabou tips with orange Sili Legs on each side, rusty bronze Laser Dub, and tan Laser Dub in front
Eyes:	Super pearl 3D Epoxy

Notes: Though originally tied as a trout streamer, this pattern from Mike Schmidt is a great golden shiner imitation. It has lots of flash and movement to draw fish from a distance.

Yellow-Butt Monkey

Hook:	#2-4 Daiichi 2220
Thread:	Tan 6/0 UNI-Thread
Tail:	Yellow marabou
Body:	Rootbeer Estaz
Wing:	Rusty brown rabbit strip
Throat:	Red wool yarn
Collar:	Pheasant rump
Head:	Tan ram's wool, trimmed
Eyes:	Small yellow lead barbell

Notes: Scott Earl Smith and Bob Linsenman designed this great pattern for Nipigon-area coaster brook trout. It will also attract coho, brown trout, and various warmwater species.

Glow Flash Tail

Hook:	#4/0 Gamakatsu Octopus
Thread:	Bright green Danville Flymaster
Tail:	Glow Flashabou and chartreuse Flashabou
Hackle:	Chartreuse rooster saddle
Body:	UV silver Polar Chenille
Belly:	White bucktail and chartreuse bucktail
Head:	Pearl, chartreuse Ice Dub
Eyes:	Large red Presentation Eyes

Notes: This pattern from Ted Kraimer is used for fishing salmon in the Great Lakes in low-light conditions. The tail is easily charged by an LED flashlight or camera flash. The action of this body when stripped with pauses provides a jigging action. This is often when the fish crushes it.

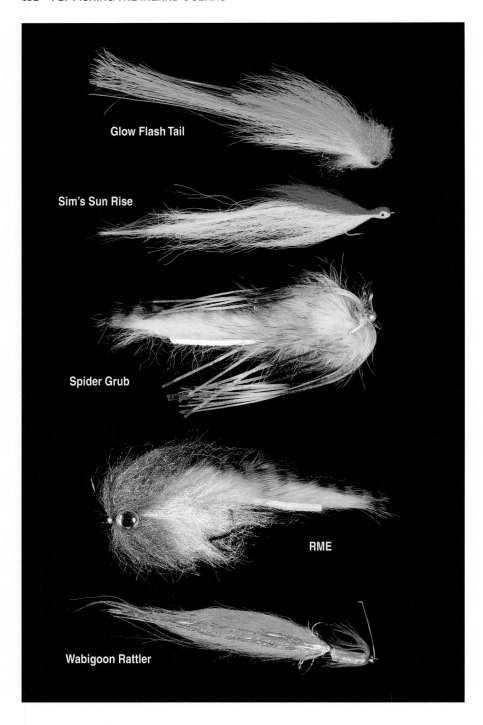

Glow Flash Tail

Sim's Sun Rise

Spider Grub

RME

Wabigoon Rattler

Sim's Sun Rise

Hook:	#1/0 Daiichi 2546
Thread:	Clear monofilament
Tail:	Pearl DNA Holo Chromosome Flash mixed with yellow Fuzzy Fiber, approximately 6 inches long
Back:	Reverse-tied red bucktail
Belly:	Reverse-tied yellow bucktail
Eyes:	1/4-inch yellow stick-on
Head:	Epoxy coated

Notes: Jim Simonelli designed this fly for pike in Lake Erie's Presque Isle Bay. It has attracted pike and largemouth bass in a variety of locations

Spider Grub

Hook:	#2/0 Mustad 90-degree jig hook (with 15 wraps of 0.030-inch lead wire)
Bead:	3/16-inch gold or copper
Thread:	Brown-olive 140-denier UTC Thread
Tail:	Olive-barred rabbit strip
Body:	Olive-barred rabbit spun in a dubbing loop
Collar:	Olive-barred rabbit strip, palmered
Skirt:	One half of a black-chartreuse-olive rubber skirt wrapped around hook, dubbed olive rabbit underneath

Notes: This pattern from Matt Erny is the fly angler's answer to the jig-n-pig. Fish it around pier edges, dock pilings, and similar areas. It will often be eaten on the drop, so watch carefully for any movement.

RME

Hook:	#2/0 Daiichi 2461
Thread:	White 70-denier UTC Thread
Tail:	Olive-barred rabbit strip
Body:	Olive-barred rabbit strip from tail tied over mix of pink and blue Laser Dub
Belly:	Silver minnow Laser Dub
Head:	Sculpin olive Laser Dub
Eyes:	Small lead barbell eyes tied on bottom of hook shank, 5/16-inch super pearl lead eyes

Notes: During spawning, goby often develop a purplish color on their side. The mix of colors in this pattern from Matt Erny imitates this very well.

Wabigoon Rattler, Perch

Hook:	#3/0 Gamakatsu Wire Guard Worm Hook
Thread:	Black 3/0 UNI-Thread
Tail:	Olive and orange Icelandic sheep or FisHair with fire tiger holographic Flashabou
Body:	Large pearl Mylar tubing with glass worm rattle inside, tied to hook shank and epoxy coated
Hackle:	Red schlappen
Eyes:	Bead chain or barbell

Notes: Other hooks such as the Mustad 34007 or Gamakatsu B10S can be used to make this pattern, which was designed by Scott Earl Smith. Mainly a fly for northern pike, it can be tied in a variety of colors.

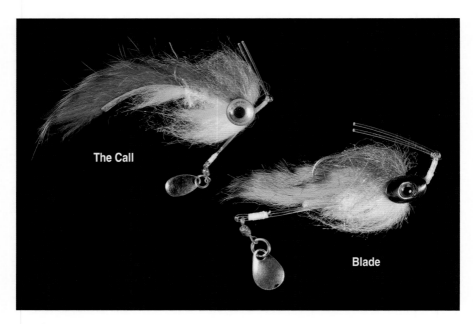

The Call

Hook:	#2/0 Mustad 60-degree jig
Thread:	White 70-denier UTC Thread
Tail:	Olive rabbit strip over chartreuse Laser Dub
Body:	Pearl Cactus Chenille
Belly:	Chartreuse, pearl, and pink Laser Dub
Head:	Olive and pink Laser Dub
Eyes:	⅜-inch Deep Sea Eyes
Weedguard and blade:	60-pound monofilament, micro swivel, #0 Colorado blade

Notes: This innovative pattern from Matt Erny is as much a fly-rod lure as a fly. In off-color water, a little extra noise and flash can help predators locate prey. Pass the 60-pound monofilament through a micro swivel with a #0 Colorado blade and then loop it back. Close the loop with thread by the swivel and attach at the angled part of the hook shank below the eye. Bend back the monofiliament as a weedguard.

Blade

Hook:	#2/0 Mustad 60-degree jig
Thread:	White 70-denier UTC Thread
Tail:	Olive-barred rabbit strip
Body:	Pearl Cactus Chenille with olive-barred rabbit strip over top
Head:	Sculpin olive Laser Dub on top, silver minnow Laser Dub on bottom, and pink Laser Dub for cheeks
Weight:	Medium Fish-Skull (black nickel)
Blade/weedguard:	60-pound monofilament and #0 Colorado blade

Notes: This pattern from Matt Erny is a different variation of the spinner fly. The tail should be kept short to avoid interfering with the spinning blade and to avoid moving the blade so far back that strikes miss the hook. Use 60-pound monofilament with a #0 Colorado blade in the loop, tied in along hook shank to extend behind the tail, ends tied up to eyes and bent back as weedguards.

Coyote Ugly

Hook:	#2/0 Mustad 90-degree jig
Thread:	Brown 70-denier UTC Thread
Tail:	Brown over orange marabou
Body:	Pearl Cactus Chenille colored with a light brown marker
Legs:	Tan-barred, brown and black, gold-flecked rubber skirt material
Collar:	Red fox tail
Head:	Red fox tail underfur stacked and shaped
Eyes:	Large black Deep Sea Eyes with super pearl 3D eyes

Notes: This is Matt Erny's go-to pattern for smallmouth bass in any type of water—river, harbor, or big lake. It is effective all season long, imitating both goby and crayfish.

Bug-Eyed Frog

Hook:	#2/0 Mustad 90-degree jig
Thread:	Olive 70-denier UTC Thread
Tail:	Olive over white marabou
Body:	Pearl Cactus Chenille
Legs:	Olive with blue and green flecks rubber skirt material
Head:	Olive over white sculpin wool trimmed to shape
Eyes:	Large Deep Sea Eyes with super pearl 3D eyes

Notes: There are few subsurface frog patterns, but it is certain that predators feed on frogs when they encounter them swimming below the surface too. This is a sleeper pattern for largemouth bass designed by Matt Erny.

Coyote Ugly

Bug-Eyed Frog

Deep Creeper

Hook:	#3/0 Gamakatsu Wire Guard Worm Hook
Thread:	Black 140-denier UTC Thread
Tail:	Black bucktail
Body:	Orange Palmer Chenille with chartreuse Palmer Chenille in front
Back:	Black magnum rabbit strip
Legs:	Orange and chartreuse round rubber legs, two each color on a side
Eyes:	Large chartreuse lead barbell

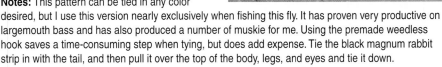

Notes: This pattern can be tied in any color desired, but I use this version nearly exclusively when fishing this fly. It has proven very productive on largemouth bass and has also produced a number of muskie for me. Using the premade weedless hook saves a time-consuming step when tying, but does add expense. Tie the black magnum rabbit strip in with the tail, and then pull it over the top of the body, legs, and eyes and tie it down.

Impulse Bunny T, White

Hook:	#3/0 Daiichi X Point "J" Hook
Weight:	⅜-inch bead
Thread:	White 140-denier UTC Thread
Tail:	White magnum rabbit strip
Body:	White crosscut rabbit
Lower foam:	Red ¼-inch-thick closed-cell
Top foam:	White ¼-inch closed cell
Eyes:	Stick-on

Notes: This weight on this pattern holds the hook point up so the fly can be fished in heavy cover. The placement of the foam strips provide floatation and give the fly a darting "walk the dog" movement when retrieved. Designer Graham Coombs suggests tying it on with a loop knot for maximum movement. This version was tied by Swimtrue Flies. Finished size of the fly should be around six inches. Tie in the bead at the start of the bend of the hook and the tail in front of the bead, hook point, and then push it through the hide side of the rabbit strip. Cut the lower foam ½-inch wide, secure it in front of the bead, and then fold it over and tie it down right behind the eye of the hook. Cut the top foam into a teardrop shape, tie it down at eye forward, and then fold it back and tie it down, glue it to the top of the red foam. Scale pattern decal or glitter can be added.

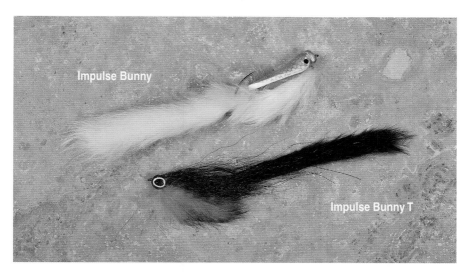

Impulse Bunny, Black-Olive

Hook: #3/0 Daiichi X Point "J" Hook
Weight: ⅜-inch orange-colored brass bead, secured halfway around bend of hook
Thread: Black 140-denier UTC Thread
Tail: Black magnum rabbit strip
Body: Olive crosscut rabbit
Wing: Black bucktail over red Krystal Flash

Notes: The innovative designs by Ontario tier Graham Coombs can be found at www.swimtrue.com. This pattern allows a fly angler to effectively work heavy lily pad beds and other tight cover. The fly can be pulled over and through pads and then allowed to drop into open pockets. Largemouth bass and northern pike are the usual targets with this pattern. As with many patterns, color combinations are limited only by the tier's imagination. Push the hook point through the hide side of the rabbit strip and then tie it down in front of the bead.

Meatwagon

Hook: #1/0 Gamakatsu B10S
Thread: Olive 70-denier UTC Thread
Tail/wing: Olive-barred rabbit strip with olive bucktail underneath
Belly: Cream bucktail with cream or tan marabou in front
Back: Olive bucktail with olive marabou in front and then six to eight strands of olive Krinkle Mirror Flash on each side
Hackle: Red schlappen
Head: Olive Palmer Chenille
Eyes: 3D stick-on

Notes: Experience has shown this to be my most productive color for a host of warmwater species, but a multitude of colors can be created. The fly can also be made weedless by tying in a monofilament loop or using the Gamakatsu Weedless Worm Hook.

Surface Patterns

Baby Bass Popper

Ty's Tantalizer

Tap's Bug

St. Paul Slider

Hula Frog

Blockhead

Zudbubbler

Gray Ghost Popper

Stunned Minnow Popper

Baby Blockhead

Baby Bass Popper

Hook:	#4 Daiichi 2461
Thread:	White 6/0 UNI-Thread for tail and base, 100-denier gel-spun for spinning hair
Tail:	White bucktail with pearl Polar Flash
Body:	Stacked and spun deer hair (white for belly, olive and black for sides and bands)
Eyes:	7 mm plastic doll eyes, white pupil

Notes: This pattern designed by Nick Pionessa makes a lot of noise for its size. It is easy to throw on a lighter weight rod due to the narrow profile it has. Trim the body to shape with a razor blade and coat the front with flexible cement.

Ty's Tantilizer, Frog

Hook:	#2/0 Gamakatsu B10S
Thread:	140-denier UTC Thread for tail and gills, 130-denier gel-spun thread for spinning hair
Tail:	Black-yellow and olive-black Centipede Legs, grizzly saddle hackle (olive-black and yellow-black), peacock Mirror Krystal Flash
Body:	Olive over yellow, over white yearling elk or deer belly hair
Eyes:	4½ mm solid plastic

Notes: The unique head shape of this fly makes it dive, but it still makes a lot of noise, helping to attract fish from a wide area. Color variations are up to the individual. Designed by Chris Helm.

Tap's Bug

Hook:	#2/0 or equivalent Chris Helm Gaelic Supreme Extra Wide Bass
Thread:	130-denier gel-spun thread to match fly color
Tail:	Dyed yearling elk spinning hair
Body:	Dyed yearling elk spinning hair
Head:	140-denier UTC Thread

Notes: This is a favorite pattern of deer-hair guru Chris Helm, designed by H. G. Tapply. The high front is coated with Dave's Flexament, allowing the fly to really make noise when popped. Colors can be varied as desired.

Hula Frog

Hook:	#1/0 Gamakatsu B10S
Thread:	Black 6/0 UNI-Thread
Tail:	Grizzly saddle tips, dyed green
Body:	Shaped and painted EVA foam

Notes: Minnesota guide Paul Hansen designs and fishes a number of shaped-foam patterns. They are very lightweight and will float forever, eliminating the need for the frequent waterproofing required with deer-hair patterns.

St. Paul Slider, Frog

Hook:	#1/0 Gamakatsu B10S
Thread:	Yellow 6/0 UNI-Thread
Tail:	Yellow marabou with gold Krystal Flash
Body:	Shaped and painted EVA foam

Notes: This fly too was designed by Paul Hansen. The slider-style head allows the fly to dive slightly and has a side-to-side darting movement, especially when tied on with a loop knot. By altering color, a baitfish version can be created easily.

Blockhead, Yellow

Hook:	#2/0 Gamakatsu B10S
Thread:	Yellow 3/0 UNI-Thread
Weedguard:	20-pound-test hard monofilament
Tail:	Yellow marabou with gold Flashabou mixed in
Hackle:	Orange schlappen
Body:	Yellow 3/8-inch-thick closed-cell foam
Eyes:	10 mm plastic doll eyes

Notes: Few patterns are as recognized for their Upper Midwest and Great Lakes area roots as the Blockhead designed by Sheldon Bolstad. This version is tied by the Great Lakes Fly Shop. The main feature of this surface fly is that it makes noise—a lot of noise—and will draw fish from a long way. It is a durable, long-lasting fish catcher that is quick and simple to make after the body is prepared. Cut the foam 3/4 inches long, 3/4 inches wide in front and tapered to 1/2 inches wide in back. To make things even easier, preformed heads are now available. Any stinger-style hook can be used, and color combinations are endless.

Zudbubbler, Yellow

Hook:	#1/0 Daiichi 2720 Stinger
Thread:	Yellow 6/0 UNI-Thread
Tail:	Yellow marabou, with chartreuse Centipede Legs on each side
Hackle:	Orange and chartreuse saddle wound over a base of chartreuse Ice Dub
Body:	Yellow closed-cell foam from a flip-flop sandal cut to shape and colored with a marker
Legs:	Yellow and chartreuse Centipede Legs

Notes: This signature pattern from Michigan guide and tier Matt Zudweg is a productive Blockhead variation. With its numerous rubber legs, the slightest move brings this fly to life. It is best fished slowly, allowing the legs to really work. It is a good choice when loud poppers are not producing.

Gray Ghost Popper

Hook:	#6 Mustad 33903
Thread:	Black 6/0 UNI-Thread
Tail:	Grizzly saddle tips
Hackle:	Grizzly saddle
Body:	Foam or cork

Notes: This bare-bones design from Peck's Poppers is another injured baitfish imitation. Capt. Roger Lapenter fishes this on Lake Superior's Chequamegon Bay as young-of-the-year baitfish hatch and become abundant. That's when smallmouth can become selective to the size and color of fly they will hit.

Stunned Minnow Popper

Hook:	#2 Mustad 33903
Thread:	Gray 70-denier UTC Thread
Tail:	Four white saddle hackles, tied splayed, two to a side
Hackle:	Grizzly saddle with two white rubber hackles
Body:	Pre-painted hard foam pencil-popper body, epoxied to hook

Notes: Designer Rick Kustich fishes this on the Upper Niagara River and rocky flats along Lake Erie's north (Canadian) shoreline. When there is little vegetation present, baitfish patterns will effectively draw fish to the surface.

Baby Blockhead, Red and White

Hook:	#6 TMC 8089
Thread:	White 3/0 UNI-Thread
Tail:	Red marabou with pearl Krystal Flash, one grizzly saddle tip on each side
Hackle:	White saddle
Body:	Layered closed-cell foam, ¼-inch white, 2 mm black, ¼-inch red, glued, then cut to shape
Eyes:	7 mm doll eyes, white pupil

Notes: This sized-down version of a Blockhead popper is small enough to hook panfish, but will also make enough noise to attract larger predators. It can also be cast on a lighter rod, such as a 6-weight, when larger line sizes are not required. Colors are unlimited. This was designed by Sheldon Bolstad and tied by Paul Hansen.

Rabbit Strip Diver, Dark Baitfish

Hook:	#1/0-2 Gamakatsu B10S or Wire Guard Worm Hook
Thread:	White 140-denier UTC Thread
Tail:	Chinchilla gray rabbit strip with eight to ten strands of pearl Krinkle Mirror Flash
Collar:	Pearl UV Polar Chenille
Head:	Gray deer belly hair, trimmed to shape

Notes: This is a very versatile pattern template that can be fished on the surface in cover or on a sinking line to work deeper areas. The addition of UV material at the collar is a quick and easy way to add a little extra fish-attracting "bling." Again, color combinations are endless, but the standard color mix—white, black, olive, chartreuse—is critical. Larry Dahlberg designed this pattern.

Rabbit Strip Diver

Todd's Wiggle Minnow

Eyed Gurgler

Frog Diver

Todd's Wiggle Minnow, Black

Hook:	#2 TMC 8089NP
Thread:	Flat waxed Danville Thread
Tail:	Black Polar Fiber and pearl Krystal Flash, 30-pound monofilament tied in a loop to keep tail from fouling the hook
Body:	⅜-inch foam cylinder
Eyes:	Small solid doll eyes

Notes: Todd Boyer originally designed this fly for saltwater use, but it can be used in many freshwater applications. It can be fished on a floating, intermediate, or sinking-head line. Colors are based on the foam cylinders available and your skill with waterproof markers.

Eyed Gurgler

Hook:	#4 Daiichi 1720
Thread:	White 6/0 UNI-Thread
Tail:	White Super Hair with pearl green Ice Wing Fiber
Back:	3 mm white foam, same width as gap of hook
Body:	Pearl green Ice Dub
Head:	Foam folded back and tied down
Eyes:	Solid plastic doll eyes

Notes: This is a great imitation of an injured emerald shiner from Nick Pionessa. It makes a bit of noise and has a great darting movement on a retrieve. Pionessa fishes this pattern on the Upper Niagara River and Lake Erie shallows for smallmouth, largemouth, and white bass. Clip the posts on the eyes to about 3 mm, and glue the posts inside the hole made when the foam is folded back to make the head.

Frog Diver

Hook:	#2/0 Mustad C52S BLN or Gamakatsu Wire Guard Worm Hook
Thread:	Olive 140-denier UTC Thread
Tail:	White arctic fox with pearl Krystal Flash, olive arctic fox with olive Krystal Flash over top
Rear legs:	Two or three grizzly olive saltwater neck hackles
Collar:	White deer belly hair on bottom with chartreuse deer belly hair in front
Head:	Stacked deer belly hair (olive on top, white and yellow on bottom), trimmed to diver shape
Front legs:	One olive rubber Centipede and two yellow round rubber legs per side
Eyes:	7 mm plastic doll eyes, orange or yellow pupil

Notes: I'm not sure who tied the first frog-colored diver, but this pattern is a must for any warmwater fly fishing. I replaced the marabou at the tail with arctic fox, as the fox is a much more durable material and still has great movement. The doll eyes give a bit of extra buoyancy at the head of the fly. The hook used is a bit longer than most deer hair hooks, giving plenty of room to add all the materials.

Sheepy Megadiver, Fire Tiger

Hook:	#3/0 Gamakatsu B10S or Wire Guard Worm Hook
Thread:	Olive 140-denier UTC Thread
Tail:	Orange Icelandic sheep hair, with olive Icelandic sheep hair over top, one chartreuse grizzly saddle on each side, and olive Krinkle Mirror Flash as topping
Collar:	Chartreuse deer belly hair
Head:	Chartreuse deer belly hair trimmed to shape

Notes: The sheep wool has great action in the water, but compresses significantly, having minimal weight and air resistance while casting. The head can be treated with fly floatant or a spray prior to fishing to maintain buoyancy. This fly (which I designed) can also be fished on an intermediate or sinking-tip line, making the fly pull down when stripped but sit stationary, or even float up a bit, between strips.

Tube Flies

Arctic Wiggler Crayfish

Thread:	Brown 70-denier UTC Thread
Tube:	Eumer Ball Tube, 17 mm x 4 mm, copper
Tail:	Light brown or tan arctic fox
Legs:	Three or four brown barred and speckled Crazy Legs per side
Body:	Orange Estaz
Collar:	Brown schlappen with root beer Palmer Chenille in front

Notes: I designed this series of flies. This can also be tied in an olive color variation.

Arctic Wiggler Emerald Shiner

Thread:	Chartreuse 70-denier UTC Thread
Tube:	Eumer Ball Tube, 17 mm x 4 mm, chartreuse
Tail:	White arctic fox with chartreuse arctic fox over, topped by mix of pearl Krinkle Mirror Flash and olive Krystal Flash
Body:	Olive Estaz
Collar:	White schlappen with olive Palmer Chenille in front
Eyes:	Jungle cock or small 3D glued on

Notes: This is one of my favorite pattern platforms for small- to medium-size prey species. I normally fish this style of fly, whether stripping or swinging, with the hook swinging free on a loop to keep snags to a minimum. A Daiichi 2553, Daiichi 2557, or Gamakatsu Octopus, all in #4 are the hooks I use.

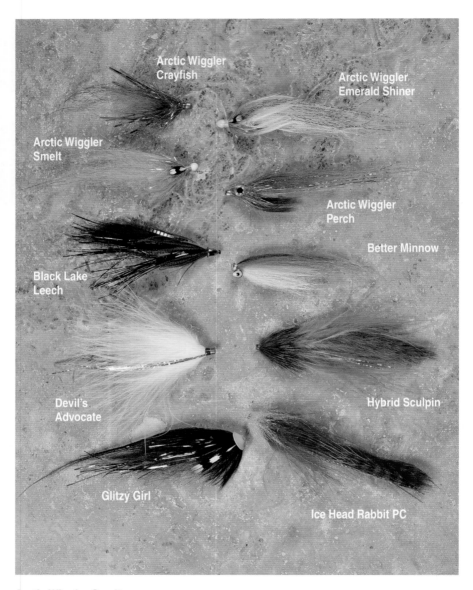

Arctic Wiggler Smelt

Thread:	Gray 70-denier UTC Thread
Tube:	Eumer Ball Tube, 17 mm x 4 mm, white
Tail:	Gray arctic fox with rainbow Krystal Flash over top
Body:	Red Estaz
Collar:	Gray schlappen with pearl gray Palmer Chenille in front
Eyes:	Jungle cock or small 3D glued on

Notes: Tie this so that the overall length of the fly is four to six inches.

Arctic Wiggler Perch

Thread:	Olive 70-denier UTC Thread
Tube:	Eumer Ballhead Tube, 17 mm x 4 mm, gold
Tail:	Golden yellow arctic fox with olive arctic fox over, fire tiger holographic Flashabou mixed in, and bars added with olive or brown marker
Body:	Orange Estaz
Collar:	Olive schlappen with olive Palmer Chenille in front
Eyes:	Medium 3D, gold pupil

Notes: I put several drops of UV Knot Sense at the head to help secure the eyes.

Black Lake Leech

Thread:	Black 6/0 UNI-Thread
Tube:	1-inch small black plastic tube with junction
Body:	Black opal Lateral Scale wrapped around tube
Underwing:	Black Flashabou, about 20 strands
Wing:	Black rabbit strip
Belly:	Black Flashabou, about 20 strands
Collar:	Heron gray mallard flank
Sides:	Black opal Lateral Scale
Head:	Large silver cone

Notes: Minnesota guide Tim Pearson fishes this pattern for North Shore coaster brook trout and other species. He prefers the Daiichi 2451 as a favored hook with tube patterns.

Better Minnow

Thread:	White 6/0 UNI-Thread
Tube:	1-inch plastic, with junction tube
Wing:	Gray Finn Raccoon reverse-tied with natural ostrich over top
Belly:	White arctic fox, spun in a loop with pearl DNA Holo Chromosome flash
Eyes:	Small barbell

Notes: With junction tubing, the leader tippet is run through the fly, tied to the hook, and then pulled back through the fly, and the hook eye is seated in the junction tube. Any straight-eye, short-shank hook is usable. The Daiichi 1650, Owner Live Bait Hook, and TMC 105 are examples of several hooks that can be used with tube flies having junction tubing. Normal hook sizes are #1-4. This fly was designed by Nick Pionessa.

Devil's Advocate

Thread:	Red 6/0 UNI-Thread
Tube:	HMH 2-inch copper with junction tube
Body:	Purple Flat Braid wound over tube
Collar:	White marabou, tip-tied and wrapped with silver holographic Flashabou

Notes: Rick Kustich swings this pattern in the Lower Niagara River, primarily for steelhead. It has a general smelt coloration, but color can be varied depending on water condition. He may also use similar length tubes of brass or aluminum to help control the depth of the fly on the swing.

Hybrid Sculpin, Olive

Thread:	Olive 6/0 UNI-Thread
Tube:	1-inch copper tube with extended junction tube
Wing:	Olive rabbit strip with gold holographic Flashabou
Body:	Olive marabou, tip-tied and wrapped
Collar:	Olive rabbit fur, spun in a loop, wrapped and combed back

Notes: This pattern can be tied in several additional color variations including brown and tan, but olive is Nick Pionessa's favorite color. It can also imitate a goby and a crayfish, depending on location and time of year.

Glitzy Girl

Thread:	Black 6/0 UNI-Thread
Tube:	Small orange plastic with pink junction
Body:	Silver holographic UNI-Flat Braid Tinsel, slide large chartreuse cone in front
Wing:	Purple arctic fox or temple dog with black arctic fox or temple dog over top, with mix of purple, blue, and green Flashabou
Collar:	Purple schlappen with black schlappen in front
Eyes:	Jungle cock
Head:	11 mm Ultralight Monster Cone

Notes: This Scandinavian-style tube pattern is a favorite of Scott Currie's for fishing the St. Marys River and other Lake Superior river mouths.

Ice Head Rabbit PC

Thread:	Purple 70-denier UTC Thread
Tube:	Small Eumer plastic, 1½ inches long
Wing:	Purple rabbit strip with purple Krinkle Mirror Flash
Collar:	Purple marabou wound as hackle
Head:	Chartreuse Ice Dub

Notes: This is a great color combination for steelhead, as it works well in a wide range of water conditions. You can tie this pattern in any color combination desired. I tie the hook in a loop and let it swing free. It can be cast or swung, depending on the situation.

Gar Tube

Thread:	Black 3/0 UNI-Thread
Tube:	One-inch aluminum tube with junction
Wing:	Black magnum rabbit strip, approximately 5 inches long
Belly:	Chartreuse pearl Flashabou
Collar:	Chartreuse rabbit strip wrapped as hackle
Head:	11 mm Ultralight Monster Cone

Notes: Set this up by running a length of leader wire through the tube and then through the eye of a #4 or 2 treble hook. Make a 5-inch-long surgeon's loop in the wire to keep the hook away from the fly, as is often needed for gar.

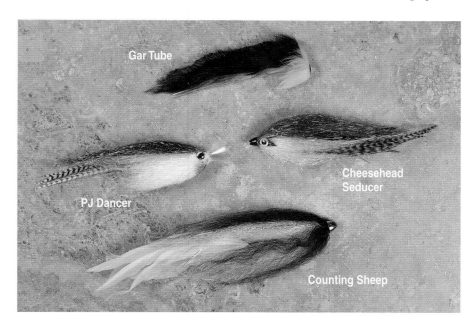

PJ Dancer

Thread:	White 210-denier UTC Thread
Tube:	Large plastic with junction
Tail/body:	Grizzly saddle feathers
Sides:	Pearl green Angel Hair
Belly:	Pearl green Angel Hair
Back:	Blue Ice Angel Hair
Eyes:	3D gold
Head:	Extra large Petitjean Magic Head

Notes: This pattern by Steve Wascher has lots of flash and plenty of movement to draw fish a long way in clear water.

Cheesehead Seducer

Thread:	Chartreuse 210-denier UTC Thread
Tube:	Large plastic with junction
Tail/body:	Grizzly dyed olive, brown, and yellow saddle hackle feathers
Belly:	Pearl gold flash Angel Hair
Sides:	Electric yellow Angel Hair
Top:	Peacock Angel Hair
Eyes:	Brown hackle tip with 3D chartreuse pupil over
Head:	Large brown cone

Notes: Steve Wascher, a northwest New York state guide and fly tier, uses large tube flies like this one for muskie and northern pike. This allows him to adjust hooks styles and sizes as needed as well as easily replace dull or damaged hooks. This pattern does duty as either a perch or smallmouth bass imitation.

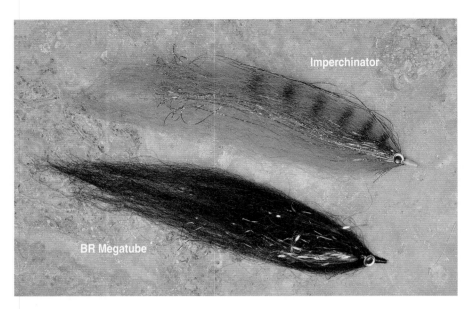

Counting Sheep

Thread:	Black 140-denier UTC Thread
Tube:	Large plastic, 4 to 5 inches long
Tail:	Six white schlappen feathers
Body/wing:	White SF Flash Blend, silver holographic Flashabou, and then black Icelandic sheep hair
Head:	Extra large, silver Cross-Eyed Cone

Notes: This is Rick Kustich's top-producing muskie pattern for the clear waters of the Niagara River. It is tied "in the round," meaning the materials are distributed evenly around the tube. The black-white color combination gives it contrast that is visible from a long distance.

Imperchinator

Thread:	Chartreuse 210-denier UTC Thread
Tube:	HMH 3-inch copper
Back:	Olive yak streamer hair
Belly:	Orange yak streamer hair
Sides:	Fire tiger magnum holographic Flashabou
Throat:	Red Krystal Flash
Eyes:	Extra Large 3D silver

Notes: Yellow perch are a favorite prey species for Lake St. Clair muskie. This pattern from Brian Meszaros gives perch coloration in a big package. Team this pattern with the 7/0 Gamakatsu SC15 hook. Color bars on the back with black or dark brown waterproof marker. The finished length should be 12 to 14 inches.

BR Megatube

Thread:	Black 210-denier UTC Thread
Tube:	HMH 3-inch copper
Back/belly:	Black yak streamer hair
Sides:	Pearl magnum Flashabou and red Flashabou
Eyes:	Extra large 3D silver

Notes: Capt. Brian Meszaros, who designed the BR Megatube, spends many days each year guiding fly anglers to Lake St. Clair muskie. The finished length of this fly should be 12 to 14 inches. Despite the size, it is relatively easy to cast. Meszaros teams a 7/0 Gamakatsu SC15 hook with this pattern for muskies.

Special Patterns

Gar Fly #1

Hooks:	#1 Mustad 9575, #6 treble trailer hook
Thread:	Black 3/0 UNI-Thread
Hook loop:	Kevlar braid
Tail:	White bucktail with black over top
Body:	Silver UNI-Flat Braid Tinsel
Wings:	White bucktail, pearl Krystal Flash, and black bucktail over top
Sides:	Grizzly saddle feathers

Notes: The black-white color contrast is the basis for Glen Hales's gar patterns. This pattern emphasizes that contrast and is one of his favorites.

Gar Fly #2

Gar Fly #1

Gar Fly #2

Hooks:	#2 Mustad 9575, #6 treble trailer
Thread:	Black 3/0 UNI-Thread
Hook loop:	Kevlar braid
Body:	Red UNI-Flat Braid tinsel, with ball of pearl green Ice Dub at front
Wing:	White Angel Silk with black Angel Silk over top
Throat:	Orange Angel Silk

Notes: Hales uses this pattern on days when it takes more flash and color to get the interest of gar. The ball of Ice Dub at the front of the body serves to keep the Angel Silk up and away from the body, where it has more movement and visibility.

Swaptail Streamers, Black Beauty, and Perch

Black Beauty

Hook:	#3/0-5/0 Gamakatsu Worm
Thread:	Black 210-denier UTC Thread
Swivel:	#10 black brass barrel swivel
Wing:	Black Icelandic sheep
Flash:	Peacock Krystal Flash
Back:	Black bucktail
Belly:	Black bucktail
Head:	Black deer belly, spun and trimmed
Eyes:	3D

Swaptail

Hook:	#1/0 Mustad 3366 broken off at bend
Thread:	Black 140-denier UTC Thread
Wing:	Icelandic sheep with Flash and bucktail tied Deceiver-style top and bottom in all-black, all-orange, all-pink, all-red

Perch

Hook:	#2/0-5/0 Daiichi 2461
Thread:	Olive 210-denier UTC
Swivel:	#10 black brass barrel swivel
Body:	Orange Palmer Chenille
Wing:	Olive Icelandic sheep
Flash:	Fire tiger holographic Flashabou
Back:	Olive bucktail
Belly:	Chartreuse bucktail
Head:	Olive deer body, spun and trimmed
Eyes:	3D

Swaptail

Hook:	#1/0 Mustad 3366 broken off at bend
Thread:	Olive 140-denier UTC Thread
Wing:	Olive or orange Icelandic sheep with olive-barred grizzly saddles
Flash:	Fire tiger and gold holographic Flashabou
Back:	Olive bucktail
Belly:	Olive, orange, or chartreuse bucktail

Notes: The concept of this pattern is a main head and hook in one color with tails of several different colors that you can change quickly by attaching and detaching the snap swivel on the hook. This allows you to carry an assortment of colors easily.

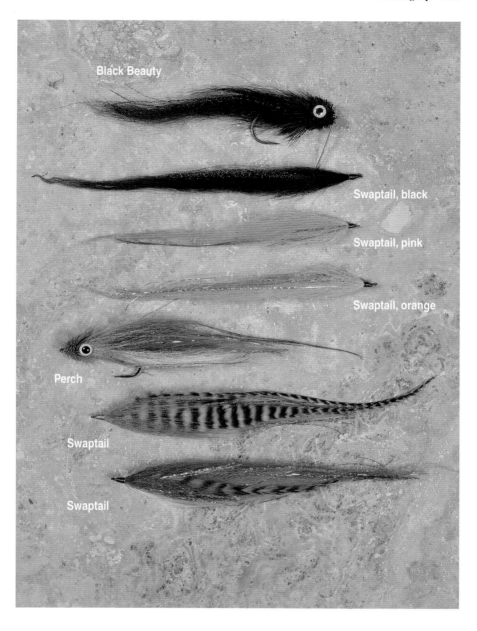

Black Beauty

Swaptail, black

Swaptail, pink

Swaptail, orange

Perch

Swaptail

Swaptail

chapter 6

Fly-Fishing Techniques for the Great Lakes

reat Lakes fish hit flies under a wide range of conditions. The equipment and techniques that are effective here mirror those of saltwater anglers; many of the flies also are adapted from saltwater designs. By incorporating different fly lines, we can effectively present flies to fish in a variety of situations. Anglers are still discovering new areas of the Great Lakes Basin suitable for fly fishing.

One of the most appealing things about Great Lakes fly fishing is the chance to incorporate techniques from both fresh and salt water. We can sight-fish on hard, light-colored flats, enjoying opportunities similar to those in tropical locations. We can blind-cast off rocky points and shoals, or look for feeding blitzes, as anglers also do on the northeast Atlantic Coast. We can drift small nymphs and, at times, drys, in river-mouth currents. We can cast giant flies in quest of apex predators. Whatever kind of fly-fishing action you are looking for, it can likely be found in the Great Lakes.

Much of the thinking about fly-fishing these inland oceans is still in its early stages, with few set rules. And, as we all know, fish don't read the rule books anyway. Don't be afraid to experiment and try different things. As a guide and instructor, probably the biggest mistake that I see people make is the tendency to do the same things over and over: fishing the same place, using the same flies and retrieve. Just because it worked last week—or even yesterday—doesn't mean that it's the best choice for today. Learn to observe and react to what you observe. Different conditions will likely call for a change in what you do. Don't be afraid to experiment and try different things. Be willing to fail and to learn.

Getting Started

Perhaps the most important skill that a fly fisher needs when approaching big water is the ability to cast. You don't need to be a distance champion and throw to the backing; however, as in saltwater fishing, you do need to be able to get the fly out a reasonable distance, and often with some accuracy. The ability to double-haul and shoot line, in the midst of wind coming from various angles, is critical. Lake St. Clair's Capt. Brian Meszaros says the biggest issue he faces with clients is their ability to cast.

When fishing a breakwall, concentrate on any corners or turns, and be sure to cover any other structure, such as logs or rocks, that can provide extra cover for fish.

The rod weight is another factor. When anglers who have only fished trout with a light 4- or 5-weight rig need to work an 8- or 9-weight outfit for a day, they are not conditioned for this and easily tire. Their casting, and their attention to what they are doing, suffer. An angler may cast a 5-weight well on a trout stream, but try an 8-weight sinking shooting taper in a 10 to 20 mph wind and the game changes. In some situations, continuous casting is needed to cover water, and the angler who is able to cover more water will generally catch more fish.

Be prepared to deal with the conditions you are likely to encounter. Athletes practice to improve their stamina and skills. Anglers need to do the same when it comes to throwing heavier lines for extended periods of time, especially when wind and other conditions are going to require more effort.

We anglers can learn from those in other sports as well. For example, many weekend golfers go to the driving range periodically, and even take a lesson once in a while to improve their skills. But few fly fishers practice casting on a regular basis, or take instruction to help them cast better under various conditions. This can create real disadvantage on the water: you can have the fishiest flies ever made, but these are useless if you can't put the flies where fish can see them. Between books, videos, and YouTube, there is no shortage of instructional material for casting. If possible, take a class or two from a skilled instructor. Hands-on coaching can shorten the learning curve significantly.

Another issue in big-water fly fishing is learning how to set the hook properly once a fish hits your fly. The "lift the rod to tighten the line" dry-fly set will not work here. Instead, anglers need to employ the strip strike used in saltwater fishing. This is especially true when using sinking lines. Keeping the rod low and pulling tight with your line hand is a much more effective way to set the hook under the conditions we're talking about here. The dry-fly method of lifting the rod serves to brings the line toward you, creating slack, and does not create enough force to plant a hook in a fish's jaw.

Points and Drop-Offs

The easiest way to fly-fish in the Great Lakes is to simply cast off the shoreline. The question is where to do this. Points that extend off the shoreline and drop quickly to deep water are a prime area. If possible, an angler should first cast parallel to the point and then slowly work out to deeper water. After casts reach the end of the point, the area should be fan-cast.

Depending on the overall depth of the area, an intermediate- or sinking-tip line may be needed. An intermediate line can cover depths down to 6 feet or so, but beyond that, a sinking-tip or sinking-head line gives the best coverage. This is the case especially for a steadily retrieved fly; the longer head maintains depth for a longer time.

Knowing the sink rate of a line allows an angler to cast, count down, and get a general idea of the depth at which a retrieve begins. After a fly fisher has gained some experience with these lines, they can become a very effective tool. They facilitate good depth control and give an angler a good idea of where a fly is.

Although weighted streamer patterns are fished most often in the Great Lakes Basin, patterns with some buoyancy can also be used here. These can be retrieved and then stopped, so a fly hovers nearly motionless in the water—a deadly technique at the right time and place.

Certain floating patterns can also be fished effectively on a sinking-head line. Todd's Wiggle Minnow and the Tullis's Wiggle Bug turn into pseudo crankbait when used in conjunction with a sinking-head line. Both of these flies attract a wide variety of Great Lakes species.

Nearshore drop-offs can also produce fish. Often adjacent to creek mouths and points, these are best early and later in the season, when fish are traveling through to move into the shallows. Work flies parallel to the drop-offs, and, again, incorporate intermediate- and sinking-head lines.

Shallows and Flats

There are many areas around the Great Lakes where an angler can wade into a shallow area and start casting. These locations are generally most productive early in the season and again in late season. Fish come to the shallows for two reasons: to spawn and to feed. Pike, bass, carp, and a variety of panfish move into the shallows as the water warms in the spring. As the season progresses, they drop off to deeper water but may continue to come to shallower water to feed early and late in the day. You may find trout in the shallows in the fall, as baitfish migrate back inshore.

Feeding in shallows occurs both pre-spawn and post-spawn. Fish also hit while they are on spawning beds, but this is more a protective instinct than feeding behavior. Smallmouth beds are easy to spot in the shallows. Throw a sinking fly onto a smallmouth nest, and the fish will likely pick up the fly to move it away rather than to eat it. Yes, in many areas—though not all—it is legal to hook the fish under these circumstances. However, the fish should be released immediately after being landed. Whether you feel it is acceptable to fish to spawners is a personal decision—just be sure it is legal where you are fishing.

Throwing to visible cover also produces fish. Pike aren't normally visible, because they tend to lie over dark bottoms and often right along the edge of emerging vegetation. Working flies in these areas can produce vicious strikes. Largemouth bass generally lie in cover, both weeds and wood, waiting to ambush prey. An angler will want to explore pockets along the edge of weed beds and areas around fallen trees, especially along trunks and under branches. Both surface and sinking flies can produce strikes in cover.

Bluegill and sunfish usually make beds in groups, normally along the edge of vegetation; clusters of saucer-like depressions in the bottom are easily recognized. Fish return to these spots year after year if the bottom substrate and depth hasn't changed. Surface patterns as well as small, slow-sinking flies produce here.

Larger, scattered rocks often hold smallmouth. These fish tend to stay in any shadow next to a rock and even change location as the sun shifts throughout the day in order to stay in the shadows. If they have not been previously disturbed, smallmouth in rock shadows are normally not very selective and eager to hit a well-presented fly. On some days, sinking flies may be more attractive, while on others it is surface flies that prove more productive. If you are not having success, don't be afraid to experiment and try something different.

Bottom depressions also hold fish. If there is an area that you can't see into and that is deeper than its surroundings—cast to it. Some of these areas are small but can still hold a fish or two. Others can be quite large and may hold a number of fish, often several species. These areas provide comfort and security to some sport fish and also attract baitfish, crayfish, and other food.

Larger fish like carp are often easily spotted as they work along flats. It is important to throw flies toward, or in front of, cruising fish. Whether wading or in a boat, an angler needs to maneuver into position so that the cast can be made in front of the fish. This is essentially the same approach used in saltwater fishing.

With respect to targeting carp, try to identify feeding fish—those that you can observe stopping and tipping up to feed. These fish, distracted by their feeding, can be approached more closely and the fly dropped literally on their heads. You will seldom feel the strike from carp in this setting, but you may see the line move or see the fish dart toward the fly. Tighten up the line, and, if you feel weight, give a solid strip strike. Try not to raise the rod tip to strike; this may pull the fly away from the fish.

Cruising carp require a different approach: presenting the fly so that it sinks within view of the fish while the fish is still moving. Cruising fish are not necessarily feeding fish, and you may have to cast to a number of them before you encounter an eater. You can usually observe the strike when a cruiser eats the fly. Choose a sunny day with minimal wind for best visibility on flats.

Brown trout and even lake trout cruise shallows at times, usually at ice-out and again in the fall. At ice-out, flats warm more quickly and attract baitfish. This, in turn, draws in predators. The same thing happens in the fall, as the water cools and schools of bait move inshore again. Under these circumstances, fish patterns that

Freedom Hawk's series of kayaks are designed with the fly angler in mind. This boat is loaded and ready to fish. The rear pontoons are extended, providing stability for the angler to stand and cast.

match the available baitfish. The visual aspect of the strike is the big draw for anglers at these times, along with the opportunity to catch normally open-water species in the shallows.

The presence of birds such as gulls and cormorants is often a signal of baitfish activity. Larger fish may trap schools of bait or push them into the shoreline, and the birds will join in to feed. Seeing gulls and other birds diving to the surface indicates the presence of bait and usually also the presence of larger fish.

Working the edges of shallows can also be very productive. Look for points, pockets, or places where there is a steep drop into deeper water. These are where fish tend to concentrate when they move off the edge of flats. Depending on the formation of the flat you are fishing, you may be able to walk to the edge and cast to deeper water.

When fishing shallows and flats, the depth being fished determines the type of line you need. Floating lines are usable to depths down to 3 feet or so. Much deeper than that and it becomes difficult to fish a fly with any speed and to keep it on the bottom if needed. A longer leader and heavier fly may help to hold bottom, but too much weight increases snags and may spook fish when it hits the surface.

An intermediate- or sinking-tip line may prove useful to let the fly work deeper at the edge of a flat. Also, try to work the fly parallel to edges as much as possible so that you cover more area along the edge lines. Smallmouth bass in particular love to work the edges of flats in search of food. They can at times even be spotted in these areas, offering angler a challenging sight-fishing opportunity. Smallmouth are pretty opportunistic feeders and hit a variety of flies—both baitfish and crayfish patterns.

The Great Lakes also offers early and late season wading opportunities. Shallow activity generally starts with water temperatures in the high 40-degree F range. Most spawning activity will be complete when water temperatures reach the mid-60s. This is still pretty cool but wet-wadable—especially on a warm, sunny day. You'll need waders in any case, and cool, cloudy days may require waders all day. Go prepared for the worst conditions. It's always better to have extra gear and clothing with you and not need it than not to have what you need and be wishing you had brought it.

Watercraft from kayaks and canoes to full-blown flats skiffs can be used to fish Great Lakes Basin flats. Craft can serve simply as transportation to an area or as a fishing platform. The new fishing-specific kayaks such as the Freedom Hawk are a great tool for flats and shallow-water fishing. In addition to transport, they serve as an elevated fishing platform. The ability to stand at surface level significantly improves an angler's ability to observe what's going on in the water; it's also much easier to cast standing rather than while sitting down.

Creek and River Mouths

It is a safe bet that any creek or river flowing into the Great Lakes will attract fish at one time or another during the year. The mouths of these tributaries can range from sizeable areas, such as the mouth of the Detroit River, big enough to handle freighter traffic, to tiny, nearly invisible spring seeps. Even the smallest trickle will draw fish to its flow, and, in most cases, these will be fish looking to spawn. Trout and salmon, in particular, are attracted to smaller flows, many of which are ignored by anglers in favor of more sizeable waters.

Depending on where you are across the lakes, and time of year, these places may also be a source of warmer water in the spring or cooler water in the summer and early fall. (A simple pocket thermometer will tell you this.) The moderated water temperatures can pull both baitfish and predators into these more comfortable areas to hold and feed.

It's also useful to know that stocked fish do not always imprint on the place where they were stocked; some stray to other streams when spawning time comes. That means a stream doesn't necessarily have to have been stocked in order to have a sport fish population. Studies have indicated a significant amount of such "wandering," such that steelhead stocked in one area can show up in streams hundreds of miles away. Both chinook and coho salmon and brown trout show up in Ohio tributaries, although that state does not stock them.

Also, in areas where natural reproduction occurs, localized populations of steelhead and salmon may become established on their own. It pays to become familiar with all the opportunities in the area you plan to fish. If one place is too crowded or conditions are not right, it pays to have a backup plan.

Salmon and trout begin to stage around the mouths of Great Lakes tributaries in advance of spawning. In the northern area of the lakes, this can begin in late summer. Along Lake Superior's North Shore, river mouths may hold trout and salmon all season long. In this case, the flows serve as a feeding corridor.

Since Superior is comparatively sterile with respect to the more enriched habitats of the other lakes, its river mouths are the places where food is most concentrated.

Capt. Kevin Morlock caught this steelhead in Ludington, Michigan, harbor. He was casting a flashy streamer pattern with a two-hand rod when this fish hit.

A chunky smallmouth comes to hand in Door County, Wisconsin. This fish took a leech pattern fished under a float. An indicator can be used to dead-drift flies and also to hop or crawl them along the bottom.

Also, water temperatures here are not a factor that drive fish offshore. Baitfish are attracted to the flow at the river mouths, insects may be washed into the lake at these locations, and there can even be hatches that provide opportunities to fish with drys.

The best time to fish the creek mouths is first thing in the morning. Fish have had all night to recover from any activity the day before. They often move right onto the shallow bar created where the current and main lake meet. You should make your first few casts right onto this area, letting your fly wash off the shallows into deeper water. You may be standing on dry land at this point.

Gradually work your way into the water, and make your casts across and slightly down current. Streamers are usually the first patterns to try. In clear water, say visibilities of 5 feet or better, start with realistic baitfish imitations. In 3- to 5-foot visibility, adding additional flash or color in the fly may help. If visibility is less than 3 feet, attractor patterns with contrasting colors—such as black and chartreuse—are often best.

The fly can be both stripped and swung if there is enough flow for this. An inter-mediate-tip line has proven effective for this work. If there is a sharp drop to deeper water close to the mouth, it may be necessary to switch to a sinking tip. Inter-changeable-tip-line systems can be useful for a variety of nearshore applications around the lakes to minimize the amount of gear you need to carry. (Several of these systems were described in the "Gearing Up" chapter.)

Current may extend into the lake in a relatively straight line, and fish may scatter through the flow. As the sun comes up, they may drop back to deeper water where the flow dissipates and spreads out. Fish as far out as you can. During daylight, a float tube or other craft may be useful to fish areas outside of the flow that are not reachable from shore. As the sun drops, fish will move back to the shore and possibly increase feeding activity.

Be aware that wind can "bend" smaller flows and create areas that concentrate where fish hold. The current will end up in a regular or "reversed R" shape. An eddy occurs on the inside part of the bend, and fish often hold in the position where it is easy to rest and feed if desired. Work these areas thoroughly.

If streamer patterns are not working, it's time to switch techniques. I'll say again, don't be afraid to experiment and try different things. Drifting flies under a float will often take fish when they are reluctant to chase a streamer. Steelhead and smallmouth, in particular, seem to enjoy this type of presentation. This may be a dead-drift presentation or done with a bit of motion; you can incorporate several types of flies.

Some sort of weight is required to sink the fly below the float. Jig-style patterns or mini-jigs are easily used. Deep Minnows—or essentially any fly with barbell-style eyes or a bead head—can be employed. The most important thing is that the float has enough buoyancy to suspend the fly off the bottom. Either thill floats that slide on the leader or peggable ice-fishing floats work well. A float the size of a thumbnail or slightly larger should suspend a fairly heavy fly.

The leader needs to turn over the fly and float efficiently. The leader from the float to the fly should be as much tippet as possible for the fly to sink quickly. Use as light a tippet as you can for the situation you are in. Small, black Woolly Buggers (#8, #10) with bead-chain eyes seem to particularly attract steelhead.

Start with the fly below the float at about half the depth of the water you are fishing. Dead-drift this in the current as far out as you can, trying to cover different lanes in the current. At the end of the drift, hold the line tight and let it rise to the surface, as this motion will trigger hits at times. Increase the distance below the float until the fly begins to drag bottom; this is to entice hits from nonactive fish.

Smallmouth bass are normally fairly aggressive and respond well to both stripped and swung flies. However they can also be found in a neutral mood, willing to eat a fly but not chase it. In this instance, a technique called "the crayfish hop" produces well. Popularized by Minnesota-based smallmouth specialist Tim Holschlag, the smallmouth hop combines a dead-drift with periodic strips of the line that lift the fly and then let it fall.

This is normally done by casting upstream in a river and "hopping" the fly back to you. With a bit of practice, this can be done when dead-drifting downstream or across the current. The best flies for this technique incorporate materials with a lot of movement. Dave Pinczkowski's Simpleech works well for this; it can be tied in any color you want. My EZ Craw pattern is also effective. Deep Minnow–style flies tied with marabou can also be used. This technique also produces well for walleye and freshwater drum.

A final way to rig up with a float is to incorporate an egg-and-nymph pattern, with spit shot for weight. This set-up has produced countless trout and salmon in Great Lakes tributaries; it also works in river-mouth applications. Fishing for Kamloops rainbows on Minnesota's North Shore incorporates this technique, in which small nymphs are dead-drifted under an indicator at the mouth of rivers such as the

Sediment carried by this Upper Peninsula creek has been deposited in Lake Michigan over a long period of time. Gamefish will often hang along a drop-off to deeper water, waiting for food.

French, Lester, and Knife. The Superior X-Legs is a favored pattern here and also works across the Great Lakes.

Switch rods are becoming a more common tool in these locales. Their longer length is an advantage for roll casting and mending line. They also allow an angler standing knee- to waist-deep to make overhead casts easier. Expect to see more of these rods in use in the future.

Larger river mouths allow a wide variety of fishing methods. Many of these also are situated in harbor areas where protective breakwaters offer additional fishing opportunity. In the Great Lakes, there are also a number of rivers with dams located a short distance upstream from the main lake. Several examples of this are the Manistique and Menominee Rivers on Lake Michigan or the Moira and Trent Rivers that flow into Lake Ontario's Bay of Quinte.

The dams block upstream movement and concentrate fish numbers. Some have fish ladders, but even then, migrating fish still must hold below the ladders, waiting their turn to move upstream. Some areas allow fishing right up to the dam face, while others enforce a "safety zone" below the dam for a certain distance. With a mix of both warmwater and coldwater species, some of these places have fish movement from the lake nearly year-round.

Flies can be stripped and dead-drifted in all these places. Some are fishable from both shore and boat, while others are one or the other. Two-handed rods can also be employed, and flies swung for trout and other species. Thinking way outside the box, Wisconsin Spey-casting specialist Dave Pinczkowski incorporates swinging flies for warmwater species such as walleye, freshwater drum, and channel catfish.

Connecting waters such as the St. Marys, Niagara, St. Clair, and Detroit Rivers could be put in a category all their own. Both shore and boat opportunities abound on these waters, allowing a full range of techniques. The mouths of the Detroit and

Niagara Rivers are fertile fishing grounds infrequently explored by fly anglers. It's worth considering that opportunity abounds in these locations for a wide range of fish species.

One of the more innovative techniques I have seen is used on the Lower Niagara River and Niagara Bar by Canadian guide Paul Castellano to swing flies from his boat. First, some background. On the Niagara, the various fish-holding drifts or runs are covered from a drifting boat; anchoring is never done. The drift is slowed by using an electric motor, just as you would back-row a drift boat in a river. In areas of extreme current, the main motor may be used.

Castellano holds his boat stationary in the current while his clients swing flies for steelhead, browns, and lake trout. They use two-hand rods with Skagit lines and sinking tips. After each swing, Castellano lets the current drop the boat back a few feet for the next cast, much like a shorebound angler steps down through a run to cover it. This is another great example of thinking outside the box.

Breakwalls, Jetties, and Piers

Structures on water are built for a variety of purposes—to deflect rough water and create a calm area, prevent erosion, allow boats to tie up, and provide opportunities for recreation. There are hundreds of structures across the Great Lakes, and most are associated with protected harbor areas. Many are located where rivers enter the lakes.

Breakwalls and jetties are rock or steel walls filled with concrete. Piers can be made of wood, steel, or concrete. Along with functioning for their intended purposes, these also serve as fish-attracting structure. Further, they give shore-based anglers access to deeper water that would normally require a boat to fish.

Both migratory and nonmigratory fish species can be caught from these structures. Smallmouth bass are resident in most places around the Great Lakes, except for parts of Lake Superior. Pike and panfish—such as yellow perch and rock bass—are also found in many areas. In the southern parts of the lakes, largemouth bass may also be in the mix.

Smallmouth favor these structure areas because they attract a wide range of food, including shiners, crayfish, and gobies. When there is little other rocky substrate available, smallmouth may hold on these areas continuously. Where there *is* suitable offshore structure available, smallmouth migrate to these areas, especially during summer months if the inshore water gets too warm. However, they still may move back to jetties to follow bait and feed and then drop back deeper again.

Breakwalls and jetties can be fished from the structure itself and also from the water; the choice depends on the amount of activity and how much space is available for casting. For example, the breakwall at Michigan City, Indiana, has an elevated trackway that limits effective fly casting. Other structures are totally open, with unlimited casting room. Fly casting may also be impractical, or even unsafe, when there are a lot of anglers and pedestrians present. Common sense should prevail here.

Most of the time, it is the ends of breakwalls that are most productive. These are much like any point extending into deep water: fish hold here. The wind can also create eddies off the end of the breakwall; here again, bait congregate and attract predators. This can also occur on outside corners, where a breakwall changes direction.

A hand-over-hand retrieve is used to keep a fly swimming at a constant speed. There are times when fish prefer this over a stripped fly.

Be sure to take note of any structure-related features that could attract fish. Weed edges, sunken timbers, and rock scattered away from the breakwall draw in bait and the kinds of predators that rarely hold on any extended straight area. Concentrate your efforts on place that have different characteristics than the main breakwall.

Make your first casts as parallel to the structure as you can and then fan out toward deeper water. You may be able to cover nearly 180 degrees from a location. If the water is clear, you can fish fairly high off the bottom to start, often with an intermediate-tip. Smallmouth in particular—also steelhead—sometimes move a long distance to a fly. Fish deeper as you continue casting, trying to cover to the bottom. Modern sinking lines have a listed sink rate, and you can count the line down to a specific depth before starting your retrieve.

This is another situation where an interchangeable-tip line can be handy. Shooting-taper systems are also useful here, because of their ability to be cast further and cover more water. As many of these places are fairly high off the water, a longer rod may help keep a straighter connection to the fly on the retrieve. The switch rod can be a useful tool here in order to get the tip closer to the water. Some sort of extendable landing net may also be necessary to land larger fish.

Many of these places require a lengthy walk to get to the most productive fishing areas. A pack to carry water, snacks, rain gear, and other supplies can be very handy and will keep you gear organized. Again, a stripping basket will keep your line under control and out of harm's way. During cold, wet weather, waders with studded wading shoes can be worn for protection as well as for better footing.

Another opportunity in structure areas involves migratory species. These also stage off breakwalls and jetties prior to spawning runs, since they pass by these places when they enter harbors on the way to spawning rivers. This gives anglers

Small creeks are the first places to open up during the spring thaw. The warmer flows often attract baitfish and larger predators.

the opportunity to catch these fish from shore while they are still in "big-water" condition. One of the great thrills of Great Lakes fly fishing is hooking a lake-bright steelhead or salmon while shorebound. These fish run and jump, as the angler hopes he has enough backing and his knots are sound.

Sustained offshore winds for several days create the "flip" phenomenon that brings cold water inshore from deeper areas. This occurs mainly on Lake Michigan and, to a lesser extent, Lake Ontario. Bait and predators follow; at times, they will be within casting range from jetties and piers. By monitoring winds and lake-surface temperatures, anglers can predict areas for this activity with reasonable accuracy.

The web site www.coastwatch.msu.edu provides a wide range of useful information for the Great Lakes—surface temperature, wind speed and direction, and more. Anglers can take advantage of this information to help determine the best areas to fish during a particular period. For example, I would not pick an area to fish where there have been strong and sustained onshore winds. It is likely this area has become too murky to fish, and the disturbance has probably dispersed any gamefish in the area. Or it may be the case that warm surface water has been pushed into the area, driving coldwater species to deeper water.

On the other hand, light winds may have had a minimal effect. Time and experience on the water are the best instructors on how a given area reacts under different wind conditions. By combining the information from this web site and others like it, along with personal knowledge, an angler can make a well-informed decision on what may be the best locations to fish when he is heading out.

Breakwall and jetty areas are also fishable from a variety of watercraft, including, but not limited to, kayaks and canoes. These are also necessary for breakwalls that can't be reached from shore. Float tubes can be used in calm areas as long as an angler is mindful of other boat traffic.

When there is ice cover on the main lakes but radiant energy from the sun has warmed the sheltered harbor surface waters, baitfish and predators may move in to the warmer waters. Brown trout, steelhead, and coho feed in these areas and hit streamers fished in the upper few feet of the water column. However, breakwalls and piers may still be ice covered and unsafe or even impossible to walk on, making some sort of craft necessary to reach these fish.

Although tides are not a significant factor in the Great Lakes, wind-generated seiche waves and currents can have a local effect on harbor and breakwall areas with narrow entrances. Sustained winds can push water into an area, and—when it can no longer be held—the water will flow back out. This creates currents at the openings that can have a temporary effect on where fish station themselves and feed.

Most of the Great Lakes harbors also have marinas and docks. These areas are generally off-limits to anglers during the boating season, but they can be productive in the early and late season—pike, largemouth bass, crappie, and bluegill are often found here. Sinking flies are the most consistent producers. Crappie are suckers for small, slow-sinking baitfish patterns. Bluegills will take an assortment of small rubber-legged flies, both below and on the surface.

Warmwater Discharge Areas

Warmwater discharges of all sizes are found across the Great Lakes. These outflows come from water used by power plants and industrial facilities. Water is drawn in from the lake and used to cool power-generating and industrial equipment, processes which raise the water's temperature. This warmer water is then discharged back into the lake.

Since 9/11, there are new restrictions around nuclear plants, so warmwater discharges in these areas are likely to be off-limits. Warm discharges from fossil-fuel plants around the lakes are much easier to access. Many allow boats right up to the discharge outlets; others allow anglers to walk right into the discharge area. Across the lakes, these locations allow anglers to target a wide variety of species throughout the year.

Warmwater discharge areas are often most productive during cold weather, when they attract large schools of baitfish and their associated predators. When the bait is in, the predators are there. If bait isn't there, few larger fish will be present. This is particularly true of migratory trout and salmon. Also, sometimes bait is so abundant in these areas that it can be difficult to get a larger fish to hit.

Some of these locations hold species like carp nearly year-round because of the water temperature. Others draw a seasonal mix of species as the year progresses. During the summer, the water may even become too warm to attract larger fish.

Of all Great Lakes species, brown trout are probably the most targeted of all at warmwater discharges. They tend to stay inshore more than other salmonids, and they are able to tolerate a wider range of temperatures. In addition, browns are more opportunistic feeders, happy to eat gobies, crayfish, and even perch, in addition to smelt, shiners, and alewives. Even without big schools of bait present, a few browns will often hang around.

There are two issues to be aware of when fishing warmwater discharge areas. First, the discharge has to be pumping in order to draw in fish. Depending on consumer need, power plants are not always generating electricity and pumping water. Highest demand is usually during the week, when both business and residential demands need to be met. There are times during weekends—which is when most anglers are able to get out and fish—that a plant may not be generating.

With tailwater fisheries found below large hydroelectric dams on rivers, water levels rise as power generation begins or increases. This becomes a safety issue, and anglers can call to get a generating schedule. My research has shown that power plants around the Great Lakes do not list generating schedules. An angler might be able to contact an individual location and talk to someone who can let them know if the plant is discharging or not. Unfortunately, outside of regular business hours, it is likely no one will answer a call.

Consequently, an angler needs to do a bit of individual research about a particular generating station of interest. Local bait and tackle shops can be a big help here, as most rely on these power plants to help drive business to them. A quick stop to buy a soda and snack can pay big dividends and save time.

As noted, a plant needs to be discharging warm water in order to attract any significant number of bait and predators—especially during the colder times of year. The temperature of the discharged water must be above the lakewater temperature in order to draw in fish. You may not be able to determine whether this is the case until you get on site.

The area closest to the discharge is often a prime location to attract and hold fish. This is particularly true of smaller outlets. Savvy anglers are aware of this and try to claim this area before others. If there is easy access, warmwater discharge areas can get crowded at times, especially on weekends when the word is out that fish are in.

Outlets that pump a large volume of water influence a bigger area. In these cases, specific location becomes less critical, because fish often move along the discharge stream. These larger outlets may also spread warm water over a wider range, even beyond the main outlet stream. There are also locations where the force of the outlet stream and wave action can build up an extensive shallow area in front of the discharge, creating additional fishing opportunities. It should be clear from this brief discussion that all of these locations are unique and individual research is going to be required to fish them effectively.

Discharges are fished similar to rivers. Flies can be stripped, swung, and dead-drifted. Depth and current speed can help to determine the type of line used. For stripping and swinging flies, some sort of sinking-tip is usually employed. Generally, baitfish patterns are the flies of choice: after all, this is why the larger fish are there. Depending on water clarity, bright attractor patterns may also produce. Goby and crayfish patterns should also be tried.

Flies can be stripped across and down the current and fished through pockets and eddies. The integrated shooting-taper lines are best for this. Most of this work is done on an 8-weight outfit with a 250- or 300-grain line. Make sure the reel has at least 150 yards of backing and a drag that will function in subfreezing temperatures. Sealed drag reels are a must for this work in cold weather.

On some of the larger Wisconsin discharges, Dave Pinczkowski uses a two-hand rod to swing flies and cover a large area. He anchors at the edge of the main flow and casts across and slightly down stream, just as one would in a river. The twist to this is that instead of a Spey line, Pinczkowski uses a shooting line and a long, sinking, shooting-taper to get the fly down deep quicker and make longer casts. The boat can be dropped back along the current with the anchor, and depths up to 20 feet or so can be fished effectively.

When fish are not in a chasing mood, don't be afraid to dead-drift flies. Depending on depth and flow, this may be done with or without an indicator. I have done well using this technique with several baitfish patterns, including Zonker-style flies and my Boa Minnow design. A lot of baitfish get drawn in when water is pulled for cooling and are stunned or killed as they travel through the cooling system. These make an easy meal for any nearby predators. Again, the switch rod becomes a handy tool to change between the different techniques.

Some of these discharges are not easily accessible from land and can only be fished by boat; at others, it may be possible to wade and fish. Some can be reached as easily as parking a car right next to the outlet. It may take some advance scouting and several visits to get a handle on how to fish a spot properly. Overall, warmwater discharges present a great opportunity for anglers to catch a wide variety of species, and they help extend the season in many locations.

Estuaries

An estuary is defined "as a partly enclosed coastal body of water with one or more streams flowing into it, with an open connection to the open sea." Great Lakes estuaries are essentially the same, except that a lake takes the place of the open sea. They are a essentially a mixing area for lake water and water from the rivers or streams that feed the estuary.

Estuaries also serve as spawning areas for a variety of food species as well as for larger fish. Some of these places are quite extensive and cover a large area of coastal land. Others have been reduced in size by development. There are few across the lakes that exist totally untouched.

Most estuaries are fairly shallow and lined with vegetation. Other than main channel areas, most are soft-bottomed because of ongoing sedimentation from inflowing waterways. Some are quite small—basically just a small pond and an outflow. Others are quite extensive and break into numerous channels before reaching a lake. Each has its own characteristics, and most are overlooked by anglers in general and by fly fishers in particular.

Great Lakes estuaries are usually best fished from some sort of watercraft because of the soft bottom and vegetation along the shoreline. Some do have open areas suitable for shore fishing, but a boat of some sort will allow a angler to fish a much greater range. Larger estuaries may hold fish all year long, while others serve more as resting or staging areas as fish move from the lake into a river and back.

Pike, smallmouth and largemouth bass, and yellow perch are common in many estuaries. In places like the drowned Michigan river mouths, there seems to be continual travel in and out of the estuary areas. For example, in Michigan's lower

The darker the water, the deeper it is. Working a rocky drop-off on the Door County Peninsula.

Muskegon River, above Muskegon Lake, lake-sized specimens are often caught throughout the various channels leading into the lake.

Coldwater species, in particular salmon, often stage in deeper estuary waters until conditions are right for them to continue upriver; this generally occurs when a rain increases the river flow, triggering a movement upstream. The lower part of the Douglaston Salmon Run, on New York's Salmon River, is a prime example of this staging. Migratory fish stack up in this area, waiting for an increase in flow.

Warmwater fish generally hold in areas off the current, waiting to ambush food. Undercut banks, pockets of vegetation, and overhanging trees and brush are all areas that should be fished. A variety of streamer patterns work here. I'll often throw my Meatwagon pattern in a perch color with consistent success, although any baitfish pattern can work. Look for smallmouth in any rocky or gravelly areas, and be sure to include crayfish patterns in the mix, especially during the summer.

If streamer action stops, switch to topwater patterns, especially in late afternoon. I have seen the streamer bite come to a dead stop and fish become focused on top-water offerings. My favorite fly for this is a frog-colored diver. Fish this in pockets in the vegetation and parallel to weeds and other growth. It is not unusual to see a wake arise from a number of feet away as a sizeable fish moves to attack your fly.

Salmon hold off the main current in the deeper holes. Kings can be tempted to hit a large flashy streamer at times, while coho are much more willing to grab a stripped fly. Black and red combinations are a favorite for Great Lakes coho, but any contrasting color pattern may produce.

Steelhead may also be found in estuaries in late fall and again in the spring. They will hit both swung and dead-drifted flies in holding areas on the edges of the main current. Steelhead can be caught on their way upriver and again as they drop back to the lake. Though rarely targeted, walleye may also be in the springtime mix as they move upriver to spawn. Be sure to check local regulations about open seasons before keeping walleye—or any other species, for that matter.

Open Water

For our purposes here, we will define "open water" simply as an area that is too deep to wade and that must be reached by boat. This can include shoreline points, drop-offs, and weed edges. In addition, gravel bars, rock piles, reefs, and other structure areas unattached to the shoreline are included in this category.

Anything from a simple float tube to a high-dollar tournament-bass or walleye rig can be used to fish these places. Although kayak touring has developed as a significant activity across the Great Lakes, kayak fishing has lagged way behind. The opportunities for kayak fishing are nearly unlimited, and this is a pursuit that should grow substantially as more fishing-friendly craft come onto the market. In addition to the value of a kayak as a fishing platform, paddling a kayak is also good physical activity and a means to quickly scout a wide area.

Canoes have been a staple on much of the northern lakes area for several centuries. Certain styles are well suited to fly fishing. The wider, square-stern models are still seen at times and do provide a stable fishing platform. These also accept smaller motors to help propel them and can certainly function well as a craft for nearshore use.

River drift boats can also be fine under some circumstances. The advantage of these boats is the roomy, stable fishing platform they present, their ability to go into shallow water, and the fact that they are easily rowed. The disadvantage is that the flat bottom will begin to pound or slam in any size waves and, even with a motor, drift boats will not go very fast.

When more area and distance need to be covered, a motorized boat with a hull designed to take waves is a necessity. There are a wide range of V-hull designs—from smaller aluminum models up to high-powered bass boats—that can be made fly-fishing friendly. Flats and bay boats designed for saltwater use are also seen on occasion in the Great Lakes. These styles are designed for fly fishing; they can handle fairly rough conditions but are still able to maneuver silently in the shallows.

Aluminum hulls reduce weight and maintenance issues, but boats made of aluminum tends to be noisy, and sound travels much better in water than air. If you are going to use an aluminum craft for fly fishing, you should apply some sort of sound-deadening material to the inside bottom. This can be as simple as indoor carpeting; there are also materials, such as those used for truck-bed liners, that can be sprayed or brushed on the bottom.

Great Lakes weather can change quickly, so, when in watercraft, be sure to pay attention to conditions and monitor weather channels. It is also important that you carry all required safety equipment. Cell phones and smartphones have minimized the need for marine radios, but these purpose-specific radios can allow you to contact help quickly if it is needed. And no matter how well-prepared you may be, always let someone know where you are going in case of equipment failure. When cold weather and cold water temperatures are involved, any time saved in locating an angler in trouble could prove to be critical.

Open-water fly fishers also borrow other equipment from gear anglers, including depth sounders and GPS. These allow us to find fish-holding areas below the surface. Usually we are not concerned about actually seeing the fish; we want to locate drop-offs and other structure on the bottom that attract fish. GPS allows us to mark and return to these areas easily, as well as providing navigation support should visibility be reduced due to rain, fog, or other conditions.

The least-used line for fly fishing in open water is a floating line; there are only rare occasions where a surface pattern is fished. Subsurface patterns are fished on a sinking line of some sort. Integrated sinking-head shooting lines are preferred by most for this work, because we can control the depth fairly well by monitoring the length of time we allow a line to sink before retrieving.

Fly fishers can easily fish depths from 6 to around 20 feet with this type of line. The deepest I have caught fish in the Great Lakes is around 35 feet, but that was a bit beyond the capabilities and comfort of the standard 8- or 9-weight rig. We could fish an 11- or 12-weight outfit with a high-density, full-sinking line, but I doubt this is something most anglers would be interested in casting all day long.

One question I get asked all the time is, "Why not use a heavily weighted fly and a floating line with an extra-long leader?" There are several problems with this. First, the fly will begin to creep up toward the surface as soon as we start to retrieve. Second, if the fly weighs enough to not do this, it will be too heavy to cast. The sinking-head line allows us to throw lightly weighted and even unweighted flies and let them sink to the desired depth range; these also hold depth much longer on the retrieve. Finally, using a sinking-head with a designated sink rate, we have a pretty good idea of where the fly is through most of the retrieve.

As I have traveled around the Great Lakes and encountered a wider range of fishing situations, I find a shooting-line system that incorporates a variety of heads to be extremely useful. Using one 8-weight rig, I can fish floating, intermediate- and slow-sinking, and fast-sinking heads. This is not a new concept; it has been used by Northeast striped-bass anglers for years. It just hasn't been seen much around the Great Lakes.

Knowing the depth of the area we are fishing is extremely helpful, because then we can know how long to let the fly sink to keep it in the fishy zone near the bottom. This information can be critical for species like smallmouth bass. Also, as we work from a shoreline point, or across a shallow reef or rock pile, we can stop the retrieve and let the fly sink farther before starting again. This provides the opportunity for hits "on the drop."

When we get a strike in an open-water situation, indications can vary—from feeling a little extra weight or resistance on the line (when a fish simply swims to the fly and closes its mouth over it) to arm-wrenching grabs. Setting the hook with a sinking line takes a bit of getting used to. We do not want to lift the rod, as is usually done with a floating line. This just adds slack into the line, and it almost always results in a missed fish.

Instead, we want to do what is called a "strip strike." This is where we give a straight, hard pull-back with the line hand. Retrieve the fly with the rod pointed straight at the fly and the rod tip low. At the strike, we then have a direct pull, right at the fly. Once the fish is hooked, get the line under control as quickly as possible so you can react to the fish's moves.

We can also incorporate a sideways pull of the rod, parallel the water surface, to provide additional force and leverage. Lifting the rod up, perpendicular to the water,

A trench like this is a gathering place for any fish working a flat. Always work these areas, because both baitfish and the predators that feed on them are attracted to the cover these spots provide.

should be avoided as much as possible. This will usually result in a headshake or two and then a slack line—with the fish gone.

Fly fishers are used to having visual information; for example, we see weed edges and a lot of the shallower structure as we cast and retrieve. Using a depth sounder as "eyes" takes a bit of practice, but you will gradually become accustomed to this. The more experience you have using the sinking line in conjunction with the depth sounder, the more confident you will become—especially after catching a few fish. It probably takes most anglers several full days of fishing to get used to the sinking line.

All of this does not mean that we never see fish in open water; there are times when fish come off the bottom to feed. For example, white bass push schools of bait to the surface and trap them there. You'll know this is happening by the activity of birds dropping to the water to also feed on the hapless bait. Try to get within casting distance as quickly as possible and throw into the disturbance. Use the sinking, shooting-taper line for this and retrieve the fly rapidly—as soon as it hits the water.

If the fish are still up, strikes will come quickly. A large school of fish can keep the bait up for several minutes, giving anglers a chance for multiple hookups. Smaller schools may pop up and be gone quickly, only to pop back up 50 yards away. Trying to follow this latter activity can be frustrating, because every time you move, the fish disappear again.

In addition to white bass, smallmouth and largemouth will sometimes exhibit this feeding behavior as well. This is the only situation in which those two seem to school. I have experienced this activity on both Lake St. Clair and Lake Erie's Presque Isle Bay. Surprisingly, under these conditions, the fish would only hit when up on the surface. Blind casting the area was not successful, even though the bass were definitely close by.

Suspended fish, located by a depth sounder, can also be caught in open water. In Lake Erie, walleye and freshwater drum regularly follow and feed on schools of free-swimming baitfish, often in the upper half of the water column. If schools of bait are spotted on the depth sounder, I try to work flies at that depth range. The larger fish tend to hang at the fringes of the schools, picking off stragglers.

I have caught many fish with flies down only 10 to 15 feet, even though the water depth was 30 feet or more. Walleye activity on flies is best under low light or even at night, while drum hit actively under a clear blue sky on a sunny day. Drum are by far the better fighter, often taking off in a fast, knuckle-skinning run as soon as they are hooked. A sizeable specimen will give a good account of itself before coming to the boat.

chapter 7

Fly Fishing
in Lake St. Clair

Several years ago, *American Angler* magazine rated Lake St. Clair as one of the "100 Top Fly Fishing Destinations in the World." You would think this would have caused an influx of fly fishers eager to test its waters. For whatever reason, this has not been the case. Rather, it is still a rare occurrence to see anyone at all throwing a long rod here. Lake St. Clair remains a mystery even to many die-hard Michigan fly fishers, who seem to overlook all the rod-bending, heart-thumping action close at hand in favor of venturing north to hook a trout or two.

Often overlooked as part of the Great Lakes system, the fly-fishing possibilities of this body of water have yet to be realized. If one were going to design a body of water specifically for fly fishing, Lake St. Clair would function as an ideal model. While much of the lakeshore is highly developed, the makeup of the lake, the continuous flow-through, and fertility of the system allow it to maintain a high level of fish production. With an average depth of around 10 feet, it has a myriad of rock piles, gravel bars, weed edges, sandy flats, points, and drop-offs. In addition, it is loaded with smallmouth bass, arguably the ideal fly-rod species. Throw in a host of other fly-eating species to keep things interesting, and you have a combination that is hard to beat.

It is hard not to argue that a boat is the best way to explore Lake St. Clair, but there are some options for shore-based anglers or those having access to only small personal watercraft. Many are in the Metro Beach area, encompassing Point Huron, Sunshine Point, Sand Point, and the mouth of the Clinton River. This area is located near the city of Mt. Clemens and is easily accessed off of I-94.

Metro Beach

The area now called Lake St. Clair Metropark covers 770 acres, including more than a mile of shoreline, several marinas, and eight different boat launches. A map of the area (http:// www.metroparks.com/images/maps/metro_beach_park.pdf) is available online. The park's back basin warms up early in the season, often with water temperatures a number of degrees higher than those in the main lake area. Crappie, perch, and pike are frequently the first fish to show up here, shortly after ice-out. They will be followed by smallmouth and then largemouth through May and into June.

173

Birds work baitfish pushed to the surface by bass. This a common sight around the Metro Beach area during the month of June.

Hex mayflies are an important food source to both gamefish and forage species in many areas. They emerge in significant number in the Metro Beach area.

Small size 4 to 6 Clouser Minnows in chartreuse-white and all-white will attract perch and crappie. These can be slowly stripped or fished two to three feet under indicator, depending on the depth of the water being fished. Hits will be light, so set at the slightest pull, hesitation of the fly, or twitch of the float. Pike will be found around dark-bottom areas and among any emerging weeds. Start with perch-colored streamers four to six inches long. My Meatwagon streamer in a perch coloration—olive on the back, gold with barring on the sides, and orange on the belly—works well here. Chartreuse-white, red-white, red-yellow, and orange are other productive color schemes for pike.

There is also a long stretch of marina areas and canals to explore. Huron Point has a long stone riprap area and a wadable flat near the day-sail area. The main channel (Black Creek) from the back basin to the lake also holds fish moving in and out. This can be covered with a sinking-tip line and a variety of streamer patterns. A chartreuse and white Half and Half is a great choice to start with. The D2 and RS versions of the Deep Minnow in size 1 to 4 are great searching patterns.

This smallmouth bass hit a streamer fly fished on a sinking-head line. These lines are an essential tool to successful fly fishing in Lake St. Clair and across the Great Lakes.

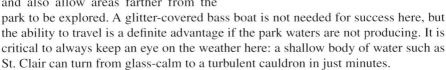

Much of the area can be waded and also easily kayaked. The water is generally clear enough to provide good visibility for wading, but sustained winds from south or east can stir up the bottom. When this happens, tread carefully to avoid any step-downs or soft spots. A kayak is ideal to cover much of this water, providing stealth and quick movement.

Small boats offer great versatility and also allow areas farther from the park to be explored. A glitter-covered bass boat is not needed for success here, but the ability to travel is a definite advantage if the park waters are not producing. It is critical to always keep an eye on the weather here: a shallow body of water such as St. Clair can turn from glass-calm to a turbulent cauldron in just minutes.

The area on the south side of Point Huron remains productive until the weeds get too overgrown; it produces just about anything of interest to wading anglers, including the occasional muskie. On the last Saturday in April, a special catch-and-release bass season begins on the Michigan waters of the lake. This is the time smallmouth move onto this area in big numbers and stay through Memorial Day and or even later into June.

Again, various baitfish patterns are best early in the season. They should be 4 to 5 inches in length and imitate emerald and spottail shiners or yearling perch. As the water warms, crayfish size 4 patterns will be more productive. Goby patterns around 4 to 6 inches long can also work well, especially if the bass are more bottom-focused.

Topwater action can also be had on warm afternoons and evenings. Divers and poppers size 1 in frog, black, or chartreuse cover the color spectrum sufficiently. Carp may be seen working this flat at times too, and these may hit crayfish or Hex nymphs. Smallmouth bass and white bass also start feeding blitzes on the emerald shiners that will school in the area. Keep an eye out for bird activity. When they start diving to the surface, get an emerald shiner imitation to the area where you see them.

As the water warms through late May and June, weed growth becomes more extensive, making wading less productive. A kayak, canoe, or small boat will allow you to work weed edges in three to six feet of water. Pockets and points in the weed beds become key locations to concentrate your efforts. Again a sinking-tip line can often be most productive when fishing sinking patterns. An 8-weight outfit is recommended, because sizeable fish can be encountered at any time and may need to be steered away from weeds.

Boat traffic here also increases around Memorial Day. There will be hordes of emerald shiners and other bait on the weed edges, but they seem to adjust quickly to the increased boat traffic as long as food is available. Fishing with Capt. Brian Meszaros in this area, we have caught sizeable smallmouth and largemouth, along with jumbo perch, literally in the wake of passing boats. Not a wilderness experience, but good to know that these fish can be caught, even with a lot of traffic nearby.

In mid-June, there is an immense emergence of Hex mayflies, so thick at times that streets and sidewalks need to be cleared with snow plows and shovels. This emergence usually takes place after dark, but a calm, cloudy evening may find Hexes appearing and fish eating them while it is still light. This presents a special opportunity to take a variety of fish on the surface, including carp and even walleye. The whole area can develop a fishy smell; the duns and spinners are locally known as "fish flies."

Anchor Bay and Harsen's Island Areas

For a kayak or canoe angler, nearly any small park along the shoreline is a potential launch area. Heading north from Lake St. Clair Metropark and along Anchor Bay, the areas of Anchor Bay Shores, New Baltimore, and Swan Creek Point all have regular boat ramps. Brandenburg Park, in New Baltimore, also has a fishing pier. Here, there is an area of old docks as well as a series of weed beds that can be productive for fly anglers.

If you want to get a bit more adventurous, follow Route 29 around Anchor Bay to Pointe-aux-Chenes and take the car ferry (http://www.michigan.org/property/harsens-island-champion-s-auto-ferry/) out of Algonac across to Harsen's Island. The ferry operates year-round, running several trips an hour across and back from the island. By following Middle Channel Drive, you can get access to Muscamoot Bay. The second yellow gate leads to a dike that goes out into the bay. A walk of a mile or so takes you to a very wadable area of the bay. A kayak can also be launched at various locations to get into the Middle Channel of the St. Clair River or into the bay.

In the spring, pike are the first fish to get active here and can be caught right after ice-out. Look for sheltered areas such as the still-empty marinas and dark-bottom spots that hold radiant heat. Pike can often be spotted laying like logs in the marinas, soaking up the sun's warmth. Throw baitfish patterns with a bite-tippet.

This area, much of which is harder-bottom and wadable, will load with smallmouth when the water temperature consistently holds at 50 degrees and warmer. Most fish will be found at the outer edges of the vast beds of pencil reeds. There are also numerous points, deeper troughs, canals, and corners that all can hold fish. This area is fairly sheltered from the main lake and is normally fishable unless the wind is blowing exceptionally hard.

Smallmouth beds can be spotted easily in the shallows, and most slow-sinking patterns thrown close will get a strike. Capt. Brian Meszaros favors a Tequilly Fly size 2 to 4 or similar pattern for this fishing, because it is visible to both the angler and the fish. As long as fish are released immediately after being landed, there doesn't seem to be a negative impact on spawning success. Jumbo perch are also

A trophy-sized smallmouth taken on a Claw Dad crayfish pattern. A floating line and long leader, extended to 10 feet, worked to attract this fish found cruising the shallows.

often caught in the same areas, while largemouth bass can be found tight to cover, especially to any kind of wood. They are not normally found in the open areas that smallmouth occupy.

On the North Channel, at the end of Anchor Bay Drive off of Route 29, there is a launch ramp that will handle larger boats. This gives access to the east side of Anchor Bay and the islands of the St. Clair Flats Wildlife Area. Carp can be found cruising these flats about the time the smallmouth start to bed. Flies that imitate small crayfish and Hex nymphs get the most attention from carp; the same flies will also attract their share of smallmouth and perch. Capt. Geoff Kowalczyk spends most of his time in the Anchor Bay and St. Clair Flats areas.

Once the smallmouth move from spawning areas, they scatter into deeper areas characterized by isolated weed beds. This is when a larger boat that helps you cover water is an advantage. The fish are less concentrated now, and the wider the area you fish, the better your chances to get into some numbers. Capt. Brian Meszaros covers the whole of Lake St. Clair during the summer and into fall. Often conditions dictate which area he fishes on a given day.

Meszaros favors the 250-grain Coastal Express line from Scientific Anglers to work most of the year. This line allows anglers to easily work flies at the right depth and is easy to cast to cover water. His day-to-day favorite fly is a Half and Half size 2 in chartreuse-white, which imitates the abundant emerald shiners found in the lake. An 8-weight outfit gets the nod for all-around use.

When specifically targeting muskie, he moves up to a 10-weight outfit with an extended fighting butt so the angler can figure-8 the fly when a muskie follows. The

Lake St. Clair Essentials

Primary Species and Peak Times

Smallmouth/largemouth bass: May–
September
Muskellunge: June–October
Northern pike: ice-out through May
Panfish: May, June
Carp: May, June

Useful Fly Patterns

Smallmouth/Largemouth Bass

Deep Minnows, chartreuse-white, olive-white
Half and Halfs, D2 Deep Minnow, RS Deep
Minnows #1-2
Schultz's SF Crayfish #2
EZ Craw #4
Tongue Depressors #2; olive, brown, tan
Tequilly Fly #2-4
GL Goby #1/0
Mega Rattling Murdich Minnow #4/0;
chartreuse-white, fire tiger

Muskellunge

Imperchinator and Black-Red tube flies
Deep Minnow, #1/0-3/0; perch
Figure 8s #3/0; perch and smallmouth-colored
Black Swaptail #3/0-6/0
Muskie Marauder, #8/0
Muskie Meth, #8/0
Natural Born Killer, #8/0
Perch CAT 4, #4/0
Perch CAT 5, #5/0
Mega Rattling Murdich Minnow #4/0; perch,
black-chartreuse, black-white, fire tiger

Northern Pike

Meatwagon #2/0; perch, fire tiger
Double Bunnies; perch, fire tiger, red-white,
yellow-red
Great Lakes Deceivers #2/0
Foosa #5/0; perch, red-white, fire tiger
Mega Rattling Murdich Minnow #4/0; fire tiger

Carp

EZ Craw #4; olive, tan
Sexy Hexy #6
Cray-May

Panfish

Deep Minnow #4-6; all-white, chartreuse-
white
EZ Craw #4

Fly Shops, Guides, Information

Schultz Outfitters

schultzoutfitters.com
734-546-7723

Orvis Royal Oak

www.orvis.com/detroit
248-542-5700

Capt. Brian Meszaros

greatlakesflyfishing.com
734-904-3474

Capt. Geoff Kowalczyk

586-243-3833

Great Lakes Fly

greatlakesfly.com
Eli Berant

Books & Publications

Michigan Atlas and Gazetteer
by DeLorme Publishing
Michigan Blue-Ribbon Fly-Fishing Guide
by Bob Linsenman

Rapidly warming waters in sheltered marinas attract early season pike. This happens well before any boats are at seasonal docks.

longer rear grip also allows a bit more support when fighting a larger fish. A 350- or 400-grain line is used for this fishing. Some sort of a bite-tippet is an absolute necessity.

Meszaros also ties his muskie flies on heavy tubes that allow him to change out hooks easily. This fly will also dive and trigger strikes at those moments when an inexperienced muskie angler freezes and stops stripping because a fish is spotted following. This is a reaction that nearly all anglers have when they encounter their first muskie, and the fish simply turn away when the fly becomes motionless.

Covering water and keeping a fly moving are the keys to successful muskie fishing on St. Clair. Muskies can show up nearly anywhere at nearly any time, usually when least expected. Sometimes it is the shoreline weed edges that are holding fish, but most catches actually occur in weed beds and other structure areas in the main lake.

Smallmouth fishing on St. Clair often lasts into October. and productive muskie fishing can last into December. Although the numbers will likely be fewer, the average size of fish is often significantly larger. Late-season fishing requires a boat to get to fish-holding areas.

I have focused only on the Michigan waters of Lake St. Clair for several reasons. First, a good portion of the Canadian shoreline is governed by the Walpole Island First Nation, and access is restricted. In addition, travel to and from Canadian waters has become more involved as reporting requirements are changing. Due to

The tiger muskie is a hybrid between a northern pike and a muskie. This can occur naturally, as this Lake St. Clair fish shows. BRIAN MESZAROS

the population on the Michigan side, U.S. Customs and Border Patrol monitors the area very closely. At present, it is best to focus angling efforts on Michigan waters.

Lake St. Clair may be one of the best fisheries located by a major urban area. It offers an interesting variety of fly-fishing opportunities. Best of all, it offers even shore-based anglers a chance to sample its bounty.

chapter 8

Fly Fishing
in Lake Erie

The Detroit River drains Lake St. Clair, flowing some 28 miles before connecting to Lake Erie. In addition to being part of the international border between Canada and the United States, it is also one of the busiest waterways in the world. Any freighter traffic bound to or from the upper Great Lakes (Huron, Michigan, Superior) has to travel the river.

The river also divides the Detroit, Michigan, and Windsor, Ontario, metropolitan areas. It has undergone a tremendous amount of restoration in recent decades, running much clearer and cleaner. The Detroit River has been designated as both an American Heritage River and a Canadian Heritage River, and many of its islands are part of the Detroit River International Wildlife Refuge.

A white bass from the lower Detroit River. Countless numbers move in from Lake Erie during the spring and are a great target for fly anglers.

Mouth of the Detroit River

For sheer fish-catching action, few places can match the mouth of the Detroit River in the spring. From early April through June, this area at the northwest corner of Lake Erie attracts a variety of gamefish sure to please any fly angler. Depending on how severe the winter has been, this action can kick off even sooner, but April is generally the time when things really begin.

There are several power plants in the area that discharge warm water back into the lake. As explained earlier, these discharges attract all kinds of bait—which in turn attract larger fish. One of these warmwater-discharging facilities is the Monroe Power Plant at the mouth of the River Raisin in Monroe, Michigan. This area is only accessible by boat, but there are excellent launch facilities at Bolles Harbor and Sterling State Park, a short way off I-75. It is a short run from the launch to Plum Creek Bay, where warm water from the discharge mixes with Lake Erie and where a wide range of fish can be found.

An early April foray to this area with Capt. Brian Meszaros found the water muddied by several days of strong winds. As we were crossing the sand bar at the mouth of the bay and reaching the mixing zone where the water starts to warm up, small pods of emerald shiners exploded out of the water. My second cast toward this activity with a shiner imitation brought a smashing strike and a run into my backing. Several shorter runs later, a 10-pound freshwater drum was brought to hand. Several other fish of similar size came out of this area that day.

Working farther into the main discharge area, we caught a number of small-mouth and then ended the day with a monstrous 14-pound drum that made several knuckle-busting runs before being boated. Over the years, Meszaros has caught largemouth, pike, muskie, carp, walleye, and even big channel catfish out of this area—all on fly. In addition to the main channel, there is an extensive backwater area that is worth exploring.

When the water is clear, flats at the mouth of Plum Creek Bay can show a variety of cruising fish, including drum, carp, and smallmouth bass. To fish the flats, use an 8-weight outfit with floating line to throw a variety of baitfish- and crayfish-like patterns. The patterns described for use on Lake St. Clair will also apply here. Where the water deepens in the main channel, an intermediate- or even sinking-tip line might be needed, depending on how fast the flow is the day you are there.

In addition to serving as a point of access to Lake Erie, Sterling State Park has several fishing lagoons that do not permit motorized boats, making them perfect for canoes and kayaks. Largemouth bass, panfish, and the occasional pike can be encountered in the lagoons. The mouth of Sandy Creek is easily reached and attracts all of the same species. Park information and a map (michigandnr.com/parks andtrails/Details.aspx?type=SPRK&id=497) can be found online.

Another source of warmwater discharge in the area is the Fermi Nuclear Power Plant just north of Monroe; this one, however, is off-limits to anglers and boaters.

Further north in the Trenton Channel, where the Detroit River splits around Grosse Isle, is the Edison Trenton Power Plant. This discharge is fishable by boat only. Anglers launch at the Elizabeth Park Marina off the Grosse Isle Parkway for a short run downstream to the discharge.

Boatside action on the lower Detroit River.

Depending on the time of year, this discharge can attract anything from salmon and steelhead to carp and catfish. March and April provide a real mix of opportunity, as almost any of the species found in Lake Erie or Lake St. Clair might show up. Be prepared to encounter other anglers in places like this though—these areas are fish magnets and hardly secret.

For fly anglers working this discharge, the flow of the river and that of the plant come into play. The strategy here is to anchor your boat at the edge of the discharge and fish across and down the current. Streamer patterns can be swung and stripped on a sinking-tip line. Another technique is to use a floating line and extra-long leader, adding split until the right weight is found to stay close to the bottom. Baitfish patterns and Buggers will usually catch fish. These can be quartered upstream, allowed to sink to the bottom (keeping the line just tight enough to maintain feel), and then allowed to swing up at the bottom of the float.

Another method that's given me great success in these situations incorporates a switch rod, long leader, and indicator. Using a floating line (Scientific Anglers' Textured Nymph Line is the best I have found for this application), single or tandem baitfish patterns are fished below shot and an indicator. My Boa Minnow pattern in size 4 has been very productive for this, but a Deep Minnow size 4 all-white, chartreuse-white, or gray-white is also usable. The switch rod allows an extra long leader (up to 15 feet) and a heavier line to turn over flies, shot, and indicator at short range. This is then fished as a normal nymph rig.

The real gem in this area is Lake Erie Metropark. Located right where the Detroit River widens into Lake Erie, the park is reached by taking Huron River Drive east off I-75. There is a sizeable boat launch area, an additional launch for canoes and kayaks, a full-service marina, and all kinds of onshore activities. A map

Mouth of the Detroit River Essentials

Primary Species and Peak Times

Northern pike: ice-out–May
Smallmouth bass: May, June
Largemouth bass: May, June
White bass: mid-May–mid-June
Freshwater drum: May, June
Panfish: April–June

Useful Fly Patterns

Northern Pike

Meatwagon #2/0; perch, fire tiger
Double Bunnies; perch, fire tiger, red-white,
   yellow-red
Great Lakes Deceivers #2/0
Foosa #5/0; perch, red-white, fire tiger
Mega Rattling Murdich Minnow #4/0; fire tiger

Smallmouth Bass

Deep Minnows; chartreuse-white, olive-white
Half and Half, D2 Deep Minnow, RS Deep
   Minnows #1-2
Schultz's SF Crayfish #2
EZ Craw #4
Tongue Depressors #2; olive, brown, tan
Tequilly Fly #2-4
GL Goby #1/0
Mega Rattling Murdich Minnow #4/0;
   chartreuse-white, fire tiger

Largemouth Bass

Deep Minnows; chartreuse-white, olive-white
Half and Halfs, D2 Deep Minnow, RS Deep
   Minnows #1-2
Tongue Depressors; black, olive, chartreuse
Deer hair divers and poppers #2/0; frog-
   colored

White Bass

Deep Minnow #4; all-white, chartreuse-white
Boa Minnow #4; emerald shiner, silver shiner

Freshwater Drum

Deep Minnows #1-4; chartreuse-white, brown-
   orange, olive-orange
EZ Craw #4; orange, olive, tan
Sparkle Grub; olive, brown

Panfish

Deep Minnows #4-6; all-white, chartreuse-
   white
EZ Craw #4; olive, tan

Fly Shops, Guides, Information

Cabela's

Dundee, MI
734-529-4700

Capt. Brian Meszaros

greatlakesflyfishing.com
734-904-3474

Schultz Outfitters

schultzoutfitters.com
734-546-7723

Books & Publications

Michigan Atlas and Gazetteer
   by DeLorme Publishing

Slow-sinking attractor flies like this Tequilly Fly are often irresistible to shallow-water smallmouth. This fish was taken in a bay off the lower Detroit River.

This large freshwater drum hit the author's crayfish tube pattern.

of the park (http://www.metroparks.com/images/maps/lake_erie_park.pdf) is available online.

As with Lake St. Clair, early fishing starts with pike. These become active as soon as ice-out and move into shallow backwater areas to spawn. Dark-colored bottom areas attract pike because these areas hold the sun's radiant heat. Large, bright streamers with a foot or so of heavy fluorocarbon as a bite-tippet work here for pike. Crappie will also show up where there is a bit of wood or brush for cover; they hit small baitfish flies.

Much of this water can be covered with a canoe or kayak, but a small boat is best because it offers the ability to cover more water and maneuver quickly. I have spent a number of days in this area in just a 14-foot semi-V boat with a 15-hp motor and small electric motor. Weather is always a factor in boat fishing. There are a number of places to duck out of the wind here and still catch fish. However, the worst wind is out of the south, because there is nothing to block it. In addition, the current from the river flows to the south, so waves can stack up, making a boat ride uncomfortable and at times dangerous.

In early May, uncountable numbers of emerald shiners migrate into the Detriot River to spawn. Following behind them are vast schools of white bass who are feeding prior to their own spawning. All this creates a perfect storm of activity, often within sight of the launch ramp at Lake Erie Metropark. On any day from around May 10 to June 15, you might observe numerous pods of gulls working the surface, as shiners are pushed up by feeding white bass. Sometimes this action will be almost within range of the ramp.

The best time to fish using these visual cues is often early in the morning, before there has been a lot of boat traffic. As more boats are launched, the fish get pushed farther out or drop into the deeper channels that cut through the area. They can still be caught, but it takes more time and work to locate them. Work these areas with a 250-grain integrated sinking-head line. This will hold a rapidly stripped fly down 2 to 4 feet, where the fish are usually found. Several casts in an area will let you know if there are white bass around. The most used fly is a Deep Minnow size 2 or 4 in chartreuse-white.

Just south of the launch ramp, you can spot a small island called Sturgeon Bar. Depending on wind direction, it is easily reached by kayak or canoe. The shoreline will cut any wind from the west, but if the wind switches direction, it can quickly get rough. Caution is advised here even though the island is close to shore. Celeron Island is also easily visible, but it is best to head that way with a craft having something more than hand power—again, because of the wind issues.

If you don't see any feeding birds, that does not mean there are no fish. Nearly all of the shallow points along the islands or up the channel toward the power plant will hold fish. Humbug Island is another productive area. Fish the south and west side for white bass and smallmouth. Fish the marsh area inside for pike and largemouth bass.

You will often find other species mixed in with schools of white bass. Smallmouth, largemouth, jumbo perch, and the occasional walleye will be right in there, enjoying the bounty. A quick pull and cut leader may indicate a rouge pike or muskie just ate your fly. Almost anything can show up, especially early in the run.

Most white bass will be in the 12- to 15-inch range. The biggest females often come in first, and some of these reach 18 inches and push 3 pounds—plenty of fun for anyone on a fly rod. Sometimes it seems as if all of the fish in this area are in one giant school, and it's possible to stay in one area for hours. Other days, the fish seem to be in smaller groups, and an angler has to stay on the move.

If you are looking for more variety, the flats by Sugar Island can provide saltwater-style sight-fishing for smallmouth, carp, and drum. Off the flats, the regular mix of species is available. Once you head in this direction, though, pay attention—it is easy to cross inadvertently into Canadian waters. You need an Ontario license if you are in Ontario waters, and there is no reciprocal license agreement. Both the U.S. Border Patrol and Canadian Customs monitor the area closely, keeping an eye out for any suspicious activity.

With all this action going on, you would think that the area is overrun by anglers chasing white bass; the opposite is the case almost all the time. Nearly every boat and person is gear fishing for walleye, working deep channels in the river, or heading into Lake Erie proper. Very little attention is paid to the shallow water areas.

By mid-June, most of the white bass are done spawning and have dropped back to the lake. Vegetation has started to grow up in many of the shallow areas, making them much more difficult to fish. Boat traffic is also more concentrated in the channels of open water. For a month or so, though, this area has been full of activity akin to saltwater blitzes and feeding frenzies. Further, the main player has been a relative of one of the most popular fish for saltwater anglers—the striped bass.

This area is a great example of a nontraditional fly-fishing area that has great fly-fishing action. It is one of many areas close to major population centers around the Great Lakes—easily reached with a bit of effort, and providing a great fly-fishing experience.

Pennsylvania Shoreline

Despite having the least amount of shoreline of any state on the Great Lakes, Pennsylvania makes a significant contribution to the Great Lakes fishery. Its 42 miles provides a full range of warmwater and coldwater opportunities for fly anglers. There are quiet backwater areas to throw popping bugs at largemouth bass, sand flats for chasing cruising smallmouth, rocky beaches where steelhead bust smelt and shiners, and river mouths that attract a wide range of species.

Pennsylvania's waters are smack in the middle of Lake Erie's "Steelhead Alley," which stretches from Buffalo, New York, west to Vermilion, Ohio. The rivers and creeks in this stretch of water are well-known for their fall runs of steelhead. This location on Steelhead Alley also creates productive shoreline and rivermouth opportunities to catch steelhead as they stage to enter tributaries. In addition to steelies, active stocking of brown trout by both Pennsylvania and New York is creating a growing nearshore fishery for brownies.

Warmwater species are also in the mix here too. The same streams that attract steelhead also draw smallmouth bass from the lake. Furthermore, the Presque Isle peninsula, across from the city of Erie, forms a protected bay of some 3,700 acres, which, at some point in the season or another, attracts almost every fish species found in Lake Erie.

Much of Presque Isle Bay is well-suited to the needs of fly anglers: it is shallow enough to be waded or worked with small, portable watercraft such canoes, kayaks, and float tubes. The bay has a variety of fish-holding structure, including weed beds, gravel bars and sandy flats, deeper channels, and fallen trees.

The author releases a shoreline steelhead. At times steelhead will follow bait right to the shore and in range of fly anglers.

The Creeks

Elk Creek is the largest of Pennsylvania's Lake Erie tributaries. It has a sizeable estuary and a rivermouth area that is easily accessed just west of where PA Route 5 crosses the creek. There is a small boat launch here, as well as a trail that leads from a parking lot to the lake. The majority of steelhead entering Elk Creek are fall-run fish. They often begin staging off the mouth in September; some may even be found in late August.

Walnut Creek, a bit farther east toward the city of Erie along Route 5, is also productive right at the mouth. There is a boat launch that gives very quick access to the lake itself. Heading farther east, other productive river mouths that are easily accessed are Cascade Creek on the Erie bay front, Twelve Mile Creek, Sixteenmile Creek, and Twentymile Creek. These all have parking close to the lake. Both Trout Run and Godfrey Run, west of Erie, are designated as special nursery waters. It is unlawful to fish within 50 yards of the mouth of these waters on either side. All of these locations can be reached from PA Route 5.

The pre-dawn period to about an hour after sunrise is the time when lake steelhead are generally shallow and will respond to flies. They will move right into tributary currents during the night, often stay there (unless disturbed), and then move again when daylight forces them into deeper water. During drizzly overcast weather, or if the lake is discolored, fish may stay in the shallows for a much longer period.

There is often a distinct color change or current line identifying the edge of the tributary flow; there is also usually a shallow bar at the mouth of the stream where sediment has built up. Both steelhead and browns will move in and out of the current, often stationing at the first drop-off from the bar, waiting to enter the stream. During high flows, fish will jump the bar and ascend the stream. When flows are low, they will hold in the lake waiting for the right conditions to move.

A river-mouth steelhead that hit a flashy attractor streamer thrown by Jeff Liskay. The current line is visible well out into the lake.

Capt. Jim Sharpe boats a Presque Isle Bay, Pennsylvania, largemouth bass. Although best known for early season smallmouth fishing, the bay provides excellent, season-long largemouth bass fishing.

Silhouetted against the setting sun, Jeff Liskay waits for shoreline action near the mouth of Twentymile Creek.

These fish will respond to an assortment of flies and techniques. The most exciting way to catch them is by stripping a baitfish pattern. They are bright silver, aggressive, and acrobatic. They will actively attack streamers, at times in knee-deep water—resulting in long runs with cartwheeling jumps. Baitfish imitations are usually best, but bright attractors, such as Jeff Liskay's Flash Fly, often get aggressive strikes. The clearer the water, the more realistic the pattern should be. Browns may respond better at times to down-sized patterns like buggy-looking soft-hackle wet flies.

If there is enough flow coming out of the creek, you can also swing flies effectively. This can be done with either a single-hand rod or a switch rod. A floating line with a long leader and weighted fly will normally suffice in this situation. Start right off the shoreline, casting the fly across the current. Let the line swing straight and hang for a few seconds in the flow. Hits often come as the fly picks up speed and rises up as the line straightens out. If brown trout are present, you can also swing soft hackles; steelhead will hit these also.

A final technique is to drift flies under an indicator, as you would in a stream. Keep these high in the water column so they are visible to the fish. Small baitfish patterns can be drifted effectively; so can egg patterns. Sometimes jig-type patterns will work here also. A downsized Deep Minnow, such as a size 6, often works well. All black is a good color, along with baitfish imitations in chartreuse-white and all-white. My Boa Minnow can also be used in this application.

These flies can also be very simple—with just a bit of marabou, bucktail, or artificial hair and a bit of flash on the hook. The clearer the water, the sparser the fly can be. The float and fly or flies are cast into the current and allowed to dead-drift as

Pennsylvania Shoreline Essentials

Primary Species and Peak Times

Steelhead: September, October
Brown trout: August–October
Northern pike: ice-out–April
Smallmouth bass: May, June
Largemouth bass: May–September
Panfish: May, June

Useful Fly Patterns

Steelhead

Emerald Candy, Tubular Smelt, Flash Fly,
    Deep Minnows #2-6; chartreuse-white,
    all-white, and black
Lake Erie Hobo
Gangsta Minnow
Sim's Trout Run Flash Fly
Arctic Wiggler tube; shiner and smelt

Brown Trout

Same as above, often downsized

Northern Pike

Sim's Sun Rise #3/0; perch, fire tiger
Meatwagon Max; fire tiger, chartreuse
Sheepy Megadiver #3/0; red-white, yellow-
    red, chartreuse-orange
Double Bunny
Big Eye Bluegill

Smallmouth Bass

Deep Minnow #2; chartreuse-white,
    chartreuse-yellow, olive-white
Redneck Goby
Moby Goby
Sparkle Grub; olive, brown
Todd's Wiggle Minnow
EZ Craw; olive, tan

Largemouth Bass

Deep Minnow #2; chartreuse-white
Tongue Depressor #2-4
Poppers and divers #1; frog-colored
River Creature #1; chartreuse and brown
Ty's Tantilizer

Panfish

Deep Minnow #6; chartreuse-white, all-white
Sparkle Grub; pearl and chartreuse
Boa Minnow
Little Precious

Fly Shops, Guides, Information

Capt. Steve Brugger
814-833-4040

Elk Creek Sports Store
814-774-8755

Gander Mountain
814-868-0880

Lake Erie Ultimate Angler
shopultimateangler.com
814-833-4040

Presque Isle Boat Livery
814-838-3938

Presque Isle State Park
http://www.dcnr.state.pa.us/stateparks/finda
    park/presqueisle/index.htm
814-833-7424

Capt. Jim Sharpe
sharpefly.com
814-881-8515

Steelhead Alley Outfitters
steelheadalleyoutfitters.com
419-466-9382

Capt. Karl Weixlmann
814-836-8013

Books & Publications

Flyfisher's Guide to Pennsylvania
    by Dave Wolf
Fly Fishing for Great Lakes Steelhead
    by Jerry Kustich and Rick Kustich
*Great Lakes Steelhead, Salmon & Trout:
    Essential Techniques for Fly Fishing the
    Tributaries* by Karl Weixlmann
Pennsylvania Atlas and Gazetteer
    by DeLorme Publishing
*Steelhead Guide: Fly Fishing Techniques and
    Strategies for Lake Erie Steelhead*
    by John Nagy

far as possible and then swung across the current before being picked up and cast again. Be sure to work both sides of the current edge as well as the main flow.

When steelhead first stage in early fall, these areas can get quite crowded with anglers throwing all sorts of gear. As the fish move into the creeks, most anglers will follow them. That means the lake areas get a break from the pressure but still provide good opportunity to catch fish.

When water levels and flows drop, fish may again hold off the creek mouths, waiting for sufficient flow to allow them to move in. This process may be repeated a number of times before the bulk of the fish are able to get into the creeks.

Significant numbers of baitfish in an area can attract and hold both steelhead and browns. True saltwater-style feeding blitzes may occur in these situations, with bait pushed to the surface, gulls diving on them from the air, and steelhead chasing them from below. If these blitzes occur within casting range, getting a fly such as Karl Weixlmann's Emerald Candy or Tubular Smelt into the fray can result in a savage strike—and the fun begins. Usually these occurrences are short-lived, so anglers need to be prepared for when they happen. An integrated shooting-taper-style line requiring a minimum of false casts to achieve distance is a valuable tool for this.

In the spring, steelhead may be encountered at the creek mouths as they drop back to the lake, but these fish often quickly move offshore to recover and feed. However, a new player comes into the game as big Lake Erie smallmouth bass move into position to ascend the creeks and rivers along the south shore of the lake. These fish will spawn in the lower sections of the tributaries, and Pennsylvania has a special trophy-bass season for anglers to target them.

Smallmouth will begin staging at the creek mouths as the water temperature approaches 50 degrees. Once the water stays in the low 50s, smallmouth will enter the tributaries and quickly find suitable spawning habitat. This is usually an area of sand mixed with gravel off the main current flow. They will feed actively until spawning takes place, after which the males guard the nest until the eggs hatch and fry can fend for themselves.

The majority of smallmouth stay in the lower portions of the creeks, rarely traveling more than several miles upriver. Elk Creek in particular draws a large number of lake-run smallies, many of which stay and spawn in the estuary area of the creek. The pre-spawn fish hit a variety of flies, including Deep Minnows, Buggers, and crayfish patterns. These can be stripped or fished under an indicator. A 6- to 8-weight outfit gets the job done. This seasonal activity gives shore-based anglers a short time window to catch lake-size smallmouth in a creek situation.

Steelhead fingerlings are stocked in Pennsylvania creeks in the spring, and most will quickly move downstream and into the lake. They do tend to hang around the mouths of the creeks while getting oriented to the lake environment. Walleye are attracted to this sudden abundance of uneducated prey and provide a brief, nearshore night fishery for fly anglers. A 6- to 8-inch streamer in a white-silver mix, and maybe a hint of pink, can be used to target walleye.

While the creek mouths are generally fished by wading from shore, many types of watercraft can be used to extend an angler's range: float tubes, canoes, kayaks, and motor boats. This allows anglers to explore areas farther offshore when sunlight or other anglers' activity drive fish out of the shallows. Elk and Walnut Creeks and the Northeast Mariana have launch ramps suitable for larger craft. At other locations, smaller craft will have to be carried to the water. Steelhead Alley Outfitters and Karl Weixlmann offer guiding services for river-mouth and estuary areas.

Presque Isle Bay

From a recreation standpoint, this is one of the most heavily used places on Lake Erie. Boaters, swimmers, birdwatchers, and others, along with anglers, make use of this protected harbor. The bay itself is about 5 miles long and 1.8 miles at its widest point. The average depth is 20 feet, but there are extensive areas of shallows. There are a number of no-wake and low-wake areas around the bay, so it is possible for canoes and kayaks to maneuver safely without fear from high-speed boats.

The 7-mile-long peninsula forming the bay makes up Presque Isle State Park. The main part of the city of Erie lies on the shoreline inside the bay. The north side of the peninsula faces Lake Erie. The bay has a historical significance from the War of 1812. It was the location of an American naval base and ship-building operation that helped defeat the British at the Battle of Lake Erie in September 1813. It is a designated National Natural Landmark, with more than 800 species of plants and 300 species of birds calling the peninsula home.

The bay itself is easily fly fished. No matter what the wind direction, there is almost always a sheltered area available. However, even when the bay is too rough to fish, scattered ponds and lagoons on the bay's interior provide ample protection and opportunity. While much of the main bay has hard, sandy bottom suitable for wading, inner areas are soft and muddy, best fished from some sort of watercraft.

Smallmouth bass are the big attraction here, but many other species of fish are available. Largemouth bass, northern pike, muskie, yellow perch, bluegill, crappie, white bass, walleye, along with steelhead and brown trout, can all be found in the bay at one time or another. From ice-out until mid-July is the best time to fish the bay proper. When the ice first clears, northern pike will be found over their favored, warmer, dark-bottom areas. Large, bright streamers will attract pike and should be teamed up with a length of 40- to 50-pound fluorocarbon or wire to prevent bite-offs.

Crappie show up next on the list, usually around areas of flooded brush. They can be caught on small minnow patterns. Smallmouth will begin to move in from the main lake when the water temperatures are in the upper 40s, staging near drop-offs and feeding actively in preparation of spawning. As the water warms into the mid-50-degree range, the bass will move onto shallow flats to begin spawning. Here they will be vulnerable to a variety of fly patterns worked slowly along the bottom; they may even rise to take a popper at times. After spawning, smallmouth will move back into the main lake.

Muskie can show up at nearly any time, often surprising smallmouth anglers with a quick slash at a fly, biting through the light tippet. Bluegill fishing can be exceptional in some of the interior waters reached through canals from the main bay areas. The period around Memorial Day usually finds bay fishing at its peak, with most species close to shore and accessible to fly anglers.

As good as the smallmouth fishing can be at Presque Isle, the largemouth bass fishing may be even better—these are always available to anglers. They are found

Guide Karl Weixlmann fishes a drop-off in Presque Isle Bay. The stripping basket is used to control line when wading deeper.

throughout the bay, especially where there is wood in the water, and along weed edges. Topwater fishing in the summer can be exceptional. The bay water temperatures are moderated by Lake Erie, rarely getting warm enough to put largemouth off their feed in the heat of August.

The Vista 3 Parking Lot is found at the head of the bay, shortly after you enter the state park on Peninsula Drive. Along with excellent shoreline fishing here, there are several shoals marked by buoys a little offshore. A variety of fish can be found here. The area is within a no-wake zone, so powerboats are not a problem. This is a favorite area to work from a canoe or kayak.

Marina Lake is also a popular area. It has a launch ramp for access to the main bay, and the entrance between the east and west piers can be very productive for perch, crappie, and bass. The back end of the Marina Lake area also has productive topwater fishing. The shoreline area from the East Pier toward Misery Bay has several pull-offs and trails down to the water. There are hard-bottom flats along here that attract smallmouth, and shoreline trees and brush attract largemouth.

The Misery Bay area is good for panfish, bass, and northern pike. Another launch ramp here gives quick entry to the bay and Lake Erie. Horseshoe Pond is located right across from the Perry Monument and is known for its panfish. Largemouth are also caught here too. Parts of this area can be reached from the road that leads to the north pier.

The Lagoons are at the west end of Misery Bay. This is a series of interconnected ponds that hold pike, crappie, bluegill, and bass. This area is restricted to manual-powered craft or electric motors. If the bay or lake are too windy for comfortable fishing, this area provides a good backup. Anglers who do not have their own craft can rent canoes and other boats here.

A Presque Isle Bay smallmouth comes to hand. The bay is a great location for kayak anglers. *Right:* Brett McCrae shows a sizeable northern pike from Pennsylvania's Presque Isle Bay. The first gamefish to get active after the ice clears, pike numbers have been on the increase in recent years. BRETT MCCRAE

Thompson Bay is the outermost area of Presque Isle and actually outside of the main bay. Trails off Peninsula Drive lead here, but it has no formal launch area. Canoes, kayaks, or float tubes must be portaged to the water's edge. Wading is tricky here too, as there are pot holes, drop-offs, and soft-bottom areas that can create problems. Extra care needs to be taken, because changes in wind direction and seiche waves cause water levels to change rapidly.

Smallmouth can be targeted in the main lake by boat anglers. Working drop-offs and rock humps in 10 to 20 feet of water can be very productive. There are a series of rock jetties protecting beach areas on the north side of the Presque Isle peninsula; smallmouth and other species can be caught here. There are a number of areas east of the bay entrance that are worth exploring, including the old Sun Oil docks called "the cribs," and Shade's Beach.

Outside the bay, from the North Pier Light to Gull Point, and offshore from Beach 11, it is not unusual to see fish busting bait on the surface. These are often schools of white bass, but I have also seen mixed schools of largemouth and smallmouth bass working emerald and spottail shiners on top. These are true saltwater-style blitzes, with birds giving away the activity as they dive to the surface.

This is one of only a few places where I have seen smallmouth and largemouth work together like this.

There is productive smallmouth fishing along the whole shoreline down to Buffalo, New York. In addition to ramps at Elk and Walnut Creeks, boats can be launched in Erie at Lampe Marina, East Avenue Boat Ramp, and Lawrence Park. Continuing east, Shade's Beach, Charley's Boat Livery, and Northeast Marina all give direct boat access to the lake. The Pennsylvania Fish and Boat Commission has an excellent pamphlet, "Lake Erie Fishing Access Areas" (http://www.fishandboat .com/promo/form/pubs_free.htm), which shows the location of all these places.

Buffalo Harbor Area and Upper Niagara River

Of the major connecting waters found across the Great Lakes, none can match the mighty Niagara River. An integral part of the Great Lakes system, the Niagara flows around 35 miles from the outlet of Lake Erie to Lake Ontario. It also forms the international border between the state of New York and the province of Ontario. At the famous Niagara Falls, the river drops about 170 feet, with a flow of 750,000 gallons per second.

The river came into its present configuration around 5,500 years ago. A huge surge of glacial meltwater reached an older, existing river gorge and cleared out accumulated glacial debris. The 90-degree turn that remained is the present location of the Whirlpool. The largest standing waves in North America are found at the Whirlpool Rapids.

The falls are formed as water plunges over a cliff of dolostone and shale. It is the second largest waterfall in the world next to Africa's Victoria Falls. To put this in a more understandable perspective, all of the water from the four upper lakes (Superior, Michigan, Huron, Erie) flows through the Niagara River and over the falls. Nearly one-fifth of all the freshwater on Earth passes through the river and into Lake Ontario.

The total drop between Lake Erie and Lake Ontario is 325 feet. The Niagara Gorge extends below the falls for several miles, and power-generating stations have been built on both the American and Canadian sides of the river. The Welland Canal on the Canadian side of the river allows boat traffic to pass between Lake Erie and Lake Ontario.

From an angler's standpoint, the Niagara River is divided into two sections, upper and lower. Between both sections, nearly every gamefish found in the Great Lakes is available. Though fly fishers have been coming here for several decades, the full potential of the area is yet to be realized. As in other places, advances in equipment and the application of new techniques are allowing anglers to use flies in situations that have been very limited previously.

Lake Erie Outlet Area and the Upper Niagara River

From the outlet of Lake Erie to the falls, the Niagara is known as a premier warmwater fishery, with smallmouth bass drawing the most attention. It also has muskie, with largemouth bass and a variety of panfish also available. There are also

Buffalo Harbor Area and Upper Niagara River Essentials

Primary Species and Peak Times

Smallmouth bass and largemouth bass: May, June, July

Muskellunge: late June–November

Carp: May, June

Useful Fly Patterns

Smallmouth and Largemouth Bass

Silver Shiner Clouser #2

Tongue Depressor; tan, black, and olive

Simple Crayfish

EZ Craw; olive and tan

Eyed Gurgler

Baby Bass Popper

Stunned Minnow Popper

Muskellunge

Counting Sheep tube

PJ Dancer

Sheepy Megadiver; black, pink, orange

Great Lakes Deceiver; fire tiger, black-chartreuse, olive-chartreuse grizzly

CAT 5; black-red, black-orange, perch

Carp

Cheesy Poof

Simple Crayfish

Cray-May

Fly Shops, Guides, Information

Cattaraugus Creek Outfitters
Vince Tobia
ccoflyfishing.com
716-479-2327

Grindstone Angling
Waterdown, Ontario
grindstoneangling.com
905-689-0880

Oak Orchard Fly Shop
Williamsville, NY
oakorchardflyshop.com
716-626-1323

Books & Publications

Fishing Western New York
by Spider Rybaak

New York Atlas and Gazetteer
by DeLorme Publishing

New York Fly Fishing Guide
by Robert W. Streeter

Sander's Fishing Guide: Western New York Edition by John M. Sander

carp opportunities during the early summer. In early spring and late season, steelhead and stray salmon may also wander into the mix.

The Buffalo Harbor area has limited fly-fishing opportunities from shore, although a small boat or kayak can be used when conditions on Lake Erie cooperate. There is an extensive area of docks, breakwalls, and jetties for exploring. The state of New York has a trophy-bass season on Lake Erie waters. allowing anglers to target smallmouth starting on the first Saturday in May, when smallmouth are already on, or just moving to, shallow water spawning areas within easy reach of fly fishers.

There is an excellent summary of smallmouth fishing in Lake Erie (http://www .dec.ny.gov/outdoor/58757.html) on the New York Department of Environmental Conservation web site. This link also provides an excellent map for anglers, as well as information on additional shoreline areas to explore west of Buffalo.

Rick Kustich hefts a colorful smallmouth from New York's Upper Niagara River. This area is just starting to gain recognition for the quality of its fly fishing.

The best access to the harbor area is at the NFTA Small Boat Harbor Marina. There is some shore fishing here. Erie Basin Marina also has public launch facilities and access to the harbor area. There are several other launch areas as one gets into the river proper, but fly-fishing opportunity is limited.

On the Ontario side, the area from Fort Erie west to Abino Point holds a myriad of hard flats, rock piles, drop-offs, and other structure that attract smallmouth and other species. The smallmouth season in Ontario opens the third Saturday in June, and bass cannot be targeted before then. However, these areas hold good numbers of carp through May and June, and wading is possible in a number of locations.

On the lake side of Fort Erie, Crystal Beach Boat Launch and the Bertie Boating Club both have launches available for public use. There are a number of areas where wading anglers can reach the shoreline to search for carp and other shallow-water cruisers.

As the Upper Niagara River flows north toward the falls, it splits around Grand Island. Wholly within New York waters, the west side of the island provides the best fly-fishing possibilities on the upper river. The West River Parkway runs the length of the island, from the I-190 exit south to Beaver Island State Park. The strip of land west of the parkway is open to the public, and there are several parking areas along here with paths leading to the river. These are open for angler access and to launch canoes or kayaks.

The river in this area is a mix of rocky drops and cuts, gravel flats, and small bays with vegetation and soft bottoms. Distinctive breaks in the current mark the location of underwater rocks and other fish-holding structure. Smallmouth bass are generally found around rocks, while largemouth bass hold around wood and vegetation. Carp are available as they cruise flats looking for food. Muskies can show up

Nick Pionessa lifts a Niagara River carp taken while stalking the shoreline shallows. Wading is much more productive here, as the fish tend to stay tight to shoreline vegetation. This fish hit Pionessa's Cheesy Poof pattern.

Muskie are caught regularly in the Upper Niagara River. Rick Kustich tempted this one to eat his white and black Counting Sheep tube fly. Muskie are fair game in the Upper Niagara from late June through the summer and fall. Look for them along weed edges and drop-offs to deeper water.

at just about anytime as they move in from deeper areas of the river to feed. Well-known fly angler and author Rick Kustich grew up on Grand Island and specifically targets muskie with flies here.

For most anglers, smallmouth are the main target. There is a healthy population of bronzebacks, with some reaching the 5-pound range. The main New York small-mouth season runs from the third Saturday in June to November 30. From December 1 to the third Saturday in June, regulations are in place for catch-and-release with artificial lures—perfect for fly fishers.

The best shore fishing is in the spring and early summer. There are good numbers of fish in close, and river vegetation has not grown up heavily yet. An 8-weight outfit with a floating line works fine during most of this period. Deep Minnows and other streamers are generally productive. A favored pattern is Rick Kustich's Silver Shiner Deep Minnow. Surface patterns like the Eyed Gurgler and Stunned Minnow Popper work well early and late in the day, and also when skies are overcast.

Carp fishing is best on sunny days with little or no wind, when fish are easier to spot as they move across the shallows. Like carp anywhere, these are challenging targets; getting one to eat a fly is an accomplishment. Crayfish and buggy-looking nymph patterns are used when targeting carp. Nick Pionessa, from the Oak Orchard Fly Shop in Williamsville, New York, chases carp here regularly and does best on a small pattern he calls the Cheesy Poof.

Boat fishing is productive spring through fall. There are launch areas for motor-ized boats at Six Mile Creek Marina and at Beaver Island State Park Marina. Sink-ing-tip lines are usually more productive when boat-fishing, allowing deeper areas to be covered more efficiently. Integrated sinking, shooting-taper lines, such as Sci-entific Anglers' Streamer Express, work extremely well. If specifically targeting muskie, bump up both the line and fly size. A 10-weight set-up will handle both larger flies and larger fish. The new knottable titanium wire works well as a bite-tip-pet and doesn't seem to bother any smallmouth interested in an oversized meal.

Fish both sides of any visible breaks in the current. Fish can hold both in front of and behind the obstructions that are altering the river flow. Shoreline cover can also be targeted, especially when adjacent to deeper water. Boat anglers need to be aware that the international boundary runs down the center of the river; you must have an Ontario fishing license if you pass the center on the Canadian side.

From Beaver Island State Park launch to the takeout at the Eagle Overlook is a distance of about 8 miles. There are several other launch/access areas in between. It is possible to launch at the state park and do a float down to one of the launch areas. You can plan a float anywhere from several hours to a full day, depending on how much distance you want to cover. Car-spotting needs to be done on your own, or you could call a taxi to pick you up and take you back to your car at the launch area.

The Canadian side of the upper river has a number of access/launch points and also provides shore-fishing opportunities. Nicholls Marina has a ramp and limited shore fishing. Millers Creek Marina offers full facilities. Frenchman's Creek, Black Creek Ramp, and Navy Island Ramp are suitable for canoes, kayaks, and car-top boats. These are all located along the Niagara Parkway as part of the Niagara Recre-ation Trail (www.niagaraparks.com). Keep in mind that smallmouth fishing on the Ontario side of the lake and Upper Niagara is open from the fourth Saturday in June to November 30. There is no catch-and-release season.

An interesting anomaly takes place here: steelhead actually migrate down-stream, starting in the fall and continuing through the winter. This is not for spawn-ing but to feed on the abundance of shiners and smelt that move into this area. Anglers can wade into several areas along the Niagara Parkway and swing flies on a two-hand rod.

Cleveland Area Shoreline

I am based close to Cleveland, Ohio, and have been fishing flies in Lake Erie for over 30 years. I have caught many fish right along the Cleveland lakefront—among them steelhead, smallmouth bass, largemouth bass, white bass, freshwater drum, walleye, and yellow perch. What really opened this whole area up to me was the assortment of modern sinking-fly lines now available that allow angler to fish effec-tively to depths of 20 feet and beyond.

The Cleveland Lakefront State Park (http://www.dnr.state.oh.us/Portals/2/park maps/clevelandparkmap.pdf) includes three separate areas—Edgewater Park, E. 55th

Cleveland Area Shoreline Essentials

Primary Species and Peak Times

Steelhead; mid-September–October
Freshwater drum; June, July
Largemouth bass; April–May
White bass: June, July

Useful Fly Patterns

Steelhead

Deep Minnow #1-2; chartreuse-white, blue-
  white, pink-chartreuse
Flash Fly
Tubular Smelt
Ice-Out Alewife
Arctic Wiggler tube; chartreuse-white, olive

Freshwater Drum

Deep Minnow #2; chartreuse-white, olive-
  orange, brown-orange
EZ Craw; orange and olive

Largemouth Bass

Half and Half #1; chartreuse-white
Meatwagon #1; perch and fire tiger
Tongue Depressor #2; black and olive

White Bass

Deep Minnow #2-4; all-white, chartreuse-
  white

Fly Shops, Guides, Information

Backpacker's Shop

backpackersshop.com
440-934-5345

Chagrin River Outfitters

chagrinriveroutfitters.com
440-247-7110

Erie Outfitters

erieoutfitters.com
440-949-8934

Orvis Cleveland

www.orvis.com/cleveland
216-591-1681

Books & Publications

Ohio Atlas and Gazetteer
  by DeLorme Publishing

Marina/Gordon Park, and Wildwood. All three places have boat launch ramps and protected harbor areas with some shoreline access. They can be easily fished from a small boat or kayak. The months of mid-April to mid-June are best; there will be an assortment of both pre- and post-spawn species available. Opportunity comes around again in the fall, as steelhead and walleye follow schools of baitfish inshore.

The Cleveland Harbor itself also has a number of private marinas. The break-wall areas of these are often productive, and you can generally venture inside of these areas in a small boat until the docks begin to fill with customers. Largemouth bass in particular have made a strong comeback into the area. Rock bass are also found in good numbers, along with some crappie.

On sunny, calm days early in the season, as water temperatures are warming, action here can be quite surprising. Fly anglers may encounter an interesting grab bag of species, including both smallmouth and largemouth bass, rock bass, crappie, perch, and drum. The odd northern pike may also appear, as well as steelhead.

A largemouth bass from the breakwall at the mouth of Rocky River. Increased water clarity due to zebra mussels has increased aquatic vegetation in many places, leading to an increase in largemouth numbers.

Freshwater drum are abundant along the Cleveland shoreline. Larger specimens like this are great fighters, often taking off on knuckle-busting runs.

Although various patterns will produce fish, it is hard to beat a size 2 or 4 chartreuse-white Deep Minnow as a starting pattern. There are a lot of sheltered corners that warm quickly, attracting baitfish and then predators. Check the calm side of breakwall areas if they are receiving direct sunlight, since warmer water will be trapped there.

I try both floating and sinking lines on these days. There are times when a slow-sinking fly fished on a floating line with a long leader (10 to 12 feet) can be very effective. With the warmest water on the surface, fish will stay high in the water column and often tight to any structure holding warmth. I might cast a simple white bead-head Woolly Bugger in size 4-8, allow it to sink for a bit, then slowly crawl it back. I watch the line carefully for any movement and tighten up at any twitch or pull.

A sinking-head line is best to hold the fly down in the water column when a more active retrieve is employed. And, as water temperature increases, a more active retrieve may be needed. A rapid strip is really not moving a fly that fast, compared to the speed at which conventional anglers are moving lures with their geared-up reels. Try to keep track of how long you let a fly sink before starting your retrieve. If you get strikes, continue to work that depth for a while.

Other areas I have fished are around the mouth of Rocky River and Avon Point. These places are best fished by boat. They offer good early summer action for white bass, freshwater drum, and the occasional walleye. White bass signal their location when they are busting bait on the surface—generally emerald shiners. Sometimes the schools will stay on the surface for a while, allowing multiple catches, but generally they pop up and disappear and then come back up a couple hundred feet away. This makes tracking them with a boat a bit challenging, but adds to the fun.

Freshwater drum go on a feeding spree around the middle of June after spawning. Although they are considered bottom-feeders, they do come well off the bottom to chase baitfish. I have caught many by stripping baitfish patterns in the upper half of the water column, even though the water was 25 to 30 feet deep. Walleye will often exhibit similar behavior, although they seem more inclined to hit flies at night and during low-light periods. A integrated sinking-head line is useful nearly all of the time.

chapter 9

Fly Fishing
in Lake Huron

L ake Huron offers a diverse assortment of both species and angling venues. Its northern reaches are a rocky maze that includes Georgian Bay and its 30,000 islands. This area abounds in rocky reefs, gravel bars, sunken islands, and scattered weed beds. Georgian Bay alone would require multiple lifetimes to explore all of its fishy places. As you head south, the shoreline transitions to more and more sand; harbors, breakwalls, and river mouths become the primary structure.

The northern part of Lake Huron has relatively little development. This is especially true on the Canadian side. There are more signs of change as you head south, but still much less than on Michigan shores. Instead, much of the southern Canadian side of the lake is surrounded by farmland and wooded lots. The pace of life is much slower, with picturesque harbor towns and beaches.

Michigan's Sunrise Shoreline

The eastern coast of the state of Michigan is also called the "Sunrise Shoreline." Like the west side of the state, there are numerous locations that provide a full-range of fly-fishing experiences for adventurous anglers. For the most part, the Lake Huron side of the state receives less publicity and therefore less fishing pressure than the west side of the state.

The Thumb Area

The shape of Michigan's Lower Peninsula resembles a mitt. Just hold your left hand out in front of you and you get the idea. Your thumb would represent the area between Saginaw Bay and Lake Huron. Looking at the outside of the thumb area on a map, Port Sanilac is the first significant harbor area as you head north up Michigan Route 25. There is a sizeable boat-launching facility here, and easy access to the north breakwall. That area, which offers the best fishing opportunity, is also beginning to receive some attention from kayak anglers.

Farther north, toward the tip of the thumb, Harbor Beach is a prime location for a base of operation and boasts "the world's greatest man-made freshwater harbor." There are boat-launch areas as well as access to an extensive breakwall system. Trescott Street Pier is more than 1,000 feet long and lighted for night fishing. Harbor

A blustery fall day on Lake Huron's Tawas Bay makes for tough fly fishing. Too much wind makes casting and boat control extremely difficult and even dangerous to wading anglers.

Beach is also beginning to get some attention from kayak anglers, who can enjoy a reasonable amount of protection from wind inside the sizeable harbor area.

There are several county parks with boat launches close by that give access to shoreline areas. Camping and other amenities are also available. Wagener County Park is five miles south of Harbor Beach off Route 25. Stafford County Park is located at Port Hope, seven miles north of Harbor Beach.

The tip of the thumb area—from Harbor Beach to Flat Rock Point west of Port Austin—provides a wonderful smallmouth bass fishery from late April through much of June. There are wadable rocky flats easily accessed from the numerous parks, launch ramps, and marinas throughout the area. One of the favored areas is Eagle Bay at Grindstone City.

Streamer patterns thrown on intermediate and floating lines will get plenty of attention. Early in the season, baitfish patterns will be most productive. When the water temperature is still in the lower 50s, stray lake trout can also show up. As the water temperature warms, goby and then crayfish patterns will become more productive. During low-light periods, and on cloudy, drizzly days, walleye can also show up. Anglers may also encounter carp, especially in June.

Eli Berant, of Great Lakes Fly (www.greatlakesfly.com), fishes much of this area regularly and is a great source for information and fly patterns. The fly-fishing potential here has hardly been tapped. There is an extensive area of shoreline waiting to be explored. This out-of-the-way part of the Lower Peninsula receives little attention compared to other parts of the state.

The offshore fishery has been in a state of transition, owing to the fact that chinook salmon numbers have decreased dramatically in recent years. This is blamed on the crash of the alewife forage base. On the one hand, it can be said that the salmon have done the job they were originally stocked to accomplish—eliminating the alewives. The downside is that the offshore recreational fishery and the businesses dependent on it are in danger of being lost.

However, there are hopeful signs. At the same time the chinook population is going down, lake trout numbers are on the upswing. There is even evidence that natural reproduction of lake trout has increased dramatically. And although they are not stocked in Lake Huron by either Michigan or the province of Ontario, coho salmon numbers have been stable. Stocking strategies have changed recently for both steelhead and brown trout, and both of these species appear to be doing well.

Chinook salmon have a narrow range of preferred forage and do poorly when they have to switch to other prey. Most other species are much more adaptable. For example, lake trout, steelhead, brown trout, and coho are much more accepting of other food sources, so the influx of invasive gobies has created a significant prey base that these fish are able to exploit. Warmwater species such as smallmouth bass and walleye have also adjusted well to feeding on gobies and now target them as a primary food source.

Baitfish move into the harbor areas along the shoreline in both spring and fall. This can be a mix of emerald shiners, spottail shiners, and gizzard shad. The shad frequently seem to be the preferred target of the larger predators, which could be salmon, steelhead, browns, lake trout, smallmouth, or northern pike, depending on water temperature.

An onshore wind will help bring bait and larger fish closer to harbor areas. When on foot, anglers should look for surface-feeding birds and boils from feeding fish. If fishing from a boat, it often pays to slowly motor around an area, identify pods of bait on a fish-finder, and then cast to the bait pods. In the fall, fish can be found throughout the water column, so a heavy sinking-head line (300- to 450-grain) may be needed to reach deep feeders.

The Ocqueoc River estuary downstream from the boat ramp. Any fish entering or leaving the Ocqueoc system has to pass through this area. The boat is beached on a sandbar right at the mouth of the river.

Michigan Shoreline Essentials

Primary Species and Peak Times

Smallmouth bass: May, June, July
Northern pike: ice-out–May, January,
    February (warmwater discharge)
Carp: May, June, July
Steelhead: ice-out–May, September, October
Brown trout: ice-out–May, September, October
Lake trout: April, May, October

Useful Fly Patterns

Smallmouth Bass

Deep Minnows #1-4; chartreuse-white,
    gray-white, all-white
Half and Half #1/0-2; chartreuse-white,
    gray-white, all-white
Crawpin #2; brown and olive
SF Crayfish
Conrad's Sculpin #2; olive and brown
Mike's Murdich; chartreuse-white, silver-white,
    pink-white
EZ Craw; olive and tan

Northern Pike

Meatwagon Max #3/0; fire tiger and perch
Sheepy Megadiver #3/0; fire tiger and perch
Great Lakes Deceiver; red-white, black-
    chartreuse
Foosa; perch
Mega Rattling Murdich Minnow; chartreuse-
    white and fire tiger
Double Bunny #3/0 red-white, chartreuse-
    orange

Carp

Stonebugger
Crawbugger
EZ Craw; olive and tan
Sexy Hexy
Cray-May

Steelhead

Deep Minnow #1-4; chartreuse-white and
    gray-white
Mike's Murdich; pink-white, chartreuse-white,
    silver-white
Flash Fly
Arctic Wiggler tube; smelt and alewife color

Brown Trout

Deep Minnow #1-4; gray-white, olive-white
Flash Fly
Arctic Wiggler tube; smelt and olive
Great Lakes Goby Grub
Olive Zoo Cougar #2

Lake Trout

Great Lakes Deceiver; chartreuse-white,
    olive-white
Half and Half #1; all-white
Meatwagon #1; all-white
Niagara Intruder; all-white, pink-white
Mike's Murdich; silver-white
Bush Pig; olive-white, gray-white

Fly Shops, Guides, Information

Dave Barkman
Schmidt Outfitters
231-676-0822 (Saginaw Bay)

Eli Berant
Great Lakes Fly
greatlakesfly.com

Frank's Great Outdoors
franksgreatoutdoors.com
989-637-9841

Little Forks Outfitters
littleforks.com
989-832-4100

Kelly Neuman
Streamside Custom Rod & Guide Service
michiganstreamside.com
989-848-5983

Capt. Leo Wright
Leo Wright Guide Service
leowrightguideservice.com
616-302-0558

Books & Publications

Flyfisher's Guide to Michigan by Jim Bedford
Michigan Atlas and Gazetteer
    by DeLorme Publishing
Michigan Blue-Ribbon Fly-Fishing Guide
    by Bob Linsenman

An 8-weight rod would be the minimum for this work for several reasons. First, it is often necessary to make a longer cast to reach fish and cover water. Anything less than an 8-weight is too light to handle any type of wind and still allow control over the line. Second, the heavier rod becomes necessary to fight the larger fish you are likely to encounter. The reel needs a dependable drag, with a minimum of 100 yards backing, 150 to 200 yards being more desirable.

In the spring, most fish will feed in the warmer surface waters. Here, an intermediate line is often most productive. Longer clear-tip heads are becoming very popular, because they can keep a fly in the upper several feet and minimize visibility from the line itself. Fluorocarbon tippet of 10- to 15-pound test is used for the attachment for the fly. If specifically targeting pike, use a bite-tippet.

Saginaw Bay and North

Saginaw Bay itself is a challenging place for fly fishers. Once you get inside the thumb, the shoreline becomes less likely to attract and hold fish. Most of the bay is soft-bottom, and much of the action is offshore at the various islands scattered around the east side of the bay. There are some hard-bottom areas in the bay, but they are not easily reached from the shoreline.

One area of the bay of interest, though, is just outside of Bay City. The Karn Weadock Power Plant at the mouth of the Saginaw River attracts an interesting mix of fish species during colder weather. Of particular interest are the pike and walleye that roam the edges of the discharge area in search of forage during the coldest months.

Guide Dave Barkman, of Schmidt Outfitters, guides anglers through this area during the winter, when he has encountered some very sizeable pike that have eaten large, flashy streamers. This kind of fishing can be very demanding; to begin with, it requires a lengthy walk in and back from the fishing area. As with any cold-weather adventure, preparation is important for safety. Be sure to carry along an extra change of clothes and gloves in case you happen to get wet while wading and fishing.

Tawas City and Tawas Bay is the next of interest for fly fishers and is easily reached off of I-75, the major north-south route through the state. This is one of the best natural harbors on the Lake Huron side of the state. The bay has populations of smallmouth bass, northern pike, and walleye. In the spring and fall, steelhead, brown trout, lake trout, and whitefish move into the shoreline.

An artificial reef was constructed on the north side of the bay to enhance lake trout and walleye spawning, and it has helped to attract a variety of gamefish.

A silvery springtime brown trout. This fish was taken on a small baitfish pattern cast from the shoreline. AUSTIN ADDUCI

A view from the mouth of the Ocqueoc River across Hammond Bay, a fishy area of Lake Huron. Hammond Bay offers trout and salmon in the spring and fall. During the summer, smallmouth, northern pike, and walleye are available.

The reef is easily spotted in the bay's clear waters and can be quickly reached from the East Tawas State Dock by boat, canoe, or kayak.

Tawas Point State Park gives access to a long stretch of shoreline and extensive shallows that drop quickly to deeper water. Canoes and kayaks can be easily launched here to allow casting from the edge of the shallows. It is also possible to wade much of the area and fish to deeper water. You can find smallmouth bass here in the early summer; look for steelhead, brown trout, and lake trout in the spring and fall.

The town of Oscoda sits at the mouth of the Au Sable River. The upper Au Sable is considered one of the best trout streams in the Great Lakes area. The lower river, below Foote Dam to Lake Huron, is host to a variety of warmwater species, including smallmouth, pike, and walleye. Seasonal migratory fish include salmon and steelhead. Brown trout and lake trout also frequent the river-mouth and harbor area.

As with most of Michigan's Lake Huron shoreline, brown trout and steelhead numbers have rebounded here in recent years, along with the noticeable increase in lake trout numbers. Again, this is associated with a change in stocking strategies owing to the drop in the chinook salmon population. This is good news for fly anglers, as steelhead, browns, and lakers are much more willing to take a fly than fussy chinooks.

A state-run launch ramp in Oscoda gives access to the lower Au Sable and Lake Huron. The south pier at the mouth of the river is available for shorebound anglers, who can encounter trout and walleye here. Fishing will be best in the spring and fall, during low-light conditions, and in dreary weather.

The Thunder Bay River enters Lake Huron at the city of Alpena. There is a launch ramp and breakwall complex adjacent to Bayview Park. For nearshore anglers, this is a spring/fall fishery for mainly lake trout, browns, and some steelhead.

North of Alpena, Presque Isle State Harbor has a launch ramp that allows anglers to work the area around Presque Isle Point. There are also several roads out on the peninsula that allow easy access to the shoreline; these also take visitors to the old and the new lighthouses. Anglers can walk the shoreline or launch canoes or kayaks. In early summer, smallmouth bass and carp frequent the shoreline.

The mouth of the Ocqueoc River is located in Hammond Bay. This river also draws the full range of seasonal species we've been finding in other locations: steelhead, brown trout, lake trout, and some salmon. In the warmer months, look for smallmouth bass, pike, walleye, and perch.

There is a launch ramp right off Route 23 that gives smaller craft access to the lower river area and the river mouth at Lake Huron. Another launch at Ray Road allows larger boats to work Hammond Bay.

Northern pike and some smallmouth bass inhabit the lower river. A smelt run in April attracts larger predators to the river mouth. In the late summer, salmon begin to show up, and through October and November, brown trout, steelhead, and lake trout will all make an appearance.

The Cheboygan River enters Lake Huron at the city of the same name. The river is part of an inland water system that allows travel from Burt Lake to Mullet Lake to Lake Huron. A small dam and power plant a short way up from the lake serves as a barrier for any migratory fish coming in from Lake Huron. There is shore access on each side of the river here, and it is fishable nearly year-round.

Early season brings steelhead that can be caught by dead-drifting and swinging flies. Pike and walleye are also available. As the water warms, a mix of smallmouth and largemouth bass show up. Summer brings bass, pike, walleye, and panfish, and, later, salmon. Steelhead usually appear in October, followed by browns, and then lake trout.

Turner Park, at the mouth of the river on the north side, provides access to the breakwall and Cheboygan County Marina. Duncan Bay, just to the east of the river mouth, is a popular fishing area. Cheboygan State Park is located on the east side of Duncan Bay. Little Billy Elliot Creek enters the bay in the state park and is popular for shore fishing. Look for steelhead, browns, and lake trout in the spring and fall. During the summer, bass, pike, and even some carp can be found in the area. A launch ramp in the park is suitable for smaller boats, canoes, and kayaks.

The North Channel and Georgian Bay

The St. Marys River feeds into the North Channel of Lake Huron, a narrow tongue of water between the Ontario mainland and a series of islands that include Manitoulin, Cockburn, Drummond, and St. Joseph. The North Channel feeds into Georgian Bay—and into the main body of Lake Huron—through the False Detour Channel and Mississagi Strait.

Several rivers feed the North Channel, among them, the Blind River. This stream can be reached right in the town also named Blind River, off Highway 17. The town's Marine Park has a launch ramp, and a series of trails provide access to

Kayaks allow anglers to explore hard-to-reach water throughout the Great Lakes. Use of kayaks designed specifically for fishing is on the rise in Georgian Bay.

shoreline areas. Along with hosting a variety of warmwater species, Blind River also serve as a conduit for a significant run of pink salmon in early September.

The town of Spanish sits at the head of the Spanish River Delta. The Spanish River was used as a transportation corridor for centuries, first by native peoples and later by fur traders and explorers. Until the 1950s, it was used to move logs to Georgian Bay, where tugs then towed them to sawmills. The river is now a waterway provincial park. The Lower Spanish River Forest holds the world's oldest stands of red and white pine.

The delta area has been designated an Ontario Provincially Significant Wetland. It holds a wide array of warmwater fish species, including smallmouth bass, northern pike, walleye, muskie, largemouth bass, and panfish. A muskellunge reintroduction program has been ongoing, and there are indications that muskie are again reproducing naturally in the river. The delta is also a walleye sanctuary and is closed to all fishing from October 1 to mid-May.

A multitude of weed edges, rocky ledges, and other structure here can be worked with a mix of floating and sinking flies. An 8-weight outfit with floating, sinking-tip, and sinking-head lines provides the versatility to fish a variety of depths with a range of fly sizes. A bite-tippet of some sort is recommended because of the number of pike likely to be encountered—and also because of the chance that the fish that eats the fly might be a muskie. A 12-inch length of 60-pound fluorocarbon can serve as a bite-tippet. The newer, knottable titanium materials on the market are slowly becoming the material of choice for these.

The Municipal Marina Complex in Spanish gives quick access to the delta area and to Whaleback Channel in Lake Huron proper. Whaleback Channel itself is a myriad of islands, reefs, and rocky shorelines, interspersed with weeds. It offers outstanding fishing for smallmouth bass and northern pike. It is also one of the better areas to target walleye on a fly. Muskie are also regularly encountered.

Each spring, the area gets a massive run of smelt that enter the Spanish River to spawn. This starts in late April and continues through May. When the smelt are thick, saltwater-style feeding blitzes occur, with gulls and cormorants diving on bait pushed to the surface by underwater predators. All gamefish of the area take advantage of the smelt bounty, so multiple-species catches during an outing are common during this period.

Scott Currie, an expatriate Scotsman, has opened a fly shop in Massey, Ontario, a short distance from the mouth of the Spanish River. Currie is very knowledgeable about all the fly-fishing opportunities in the region and offers guiding services for the area. At present, he is the only fly-fishing specialist in the entire Georgian Bay area.

Manitoulin Island is the world's largest island in a freshwater lake. It covers an area of 1,068 square miles and has 108 freshwater lakes of its own. Manitoulin is reached by taking Ontario Route 6 south from Highway 17. You can also take a ferry to the island from the town of Tobermory on the Bruce Peninsula to the south. There are four major rivers on the island: the Kagamong, Mindemoya, Manitou, and Blue Jay Creek. All receive spawning runs of steelhead and salmon.

Of the island's four rivers, the Manitou River and Blue Jay Creek are the best for fly fishing, with strong runs of both coho and chinook, as well as fall and spring steelhead. Both empty into Lake Huron's Michael's Bay, which can be reached off Government Road west out of the village of Tehkumma. A secondary road, just west of the bridge over the Manitou River, goes south to the mouth. There is also a small provincial park that covers much of the Blue Jay Creek area.

This oversize smallmouth hit a pike fly in the lower Spanish River. When in an aggressive mood, smallmouth often attack patterns that are meant for larger predators. SCOTT CURRIE

North Channel and Georgian Bay Essentials

Primary Species and Peak Times

Smallmouth bass and largemouth bass: fourth Saturday in June–August
Northern pike: ice-out–June, September
Muskellunge: third Saturday in June–October
Pacific salmon: ice-out–May, mid-August–mid-September
Steelhead: ice-out–May, October
Brown trout: ice-out–May, September, October
NOTE: Be sure to check fishing regulations carefully, as open seasons vary depending on which Fishery Management Zone you are in. The waters described above touch three different zones. If you have any questions, contact the Ontario Ministry of Natural Resources.

Useful Fly Patterns

Smallmouth and Largemouth Bass

Deep Minnow #1-2; chartreuse-white, olive-white
Half and Half #1; chartreuse-white, olive-white,
Impulse Bunny, sinking and topwater, 3 inch and 6 inch, black, white, olive, frog poppers and divers #1

Pike

Massey Warrior
Angel Hair Baitfish
Electric Yellow
Monster Diver
Figure 8 #3/0; perch, fire tiger
Sheepy Megadiver; olive, red-white
Double Bunny #3/0; chartreuse-orange, red-white

Muskellunge

Muskie Meth
Muskie Marauder
Natural Born Killer
CAT 5; perch, black-orange, black-chartreuse
Swaptail Streamer

Steelhead

Phantom #2; olive-white, chartreuse-white
Bush Pig; olive-white, gray-white, olive-gold
Flash Fly
Tubular Smelt

Brown Trout

Same as above for steelhead

Pink Salmon

Deep Minnow #4-6; chartreuse-white, pink-white
yarn flies #8; pink, chartreuse, or orange

Fly Shops, Guides, Information

Fly Mart
flymart.ca
888-811-1163

Grindstone Angling
grindstoneangling.com
905-689-0880

Graham Bristow/Georgian Bay Muskie Charters
anglerspro.ca
416-937-4911

Hartley Bay Marina
hartleybaymarina.com
705-857-2038

Swim True Flies
swimtrue.com

Books & Publications

Kayaking Georgian Bay by Jonathon Reynolds and Heather Smith
Ontario Blue-Ribbon Fly Fishing Guide by Scott E. Smith

Guide Graham Bristow and a 50-pound-class Georgian Bay muskie. Serious fly anglers should concentrate their efforts here if their goal is hooking a fish like this. GRAHAM BRISTOW

Large northern pike are found in good numbers in Lake Huron's Georgian Bay. They will often follow a fly, viciously attacking it just as it is being lifted from the water—as this fish did.

As in much of Ontario's waters, fishing regulations can be quite complicated and change frequently. There are special fish-sanctuary regulations in place here at certain times of the year, so be sure to check where you can legally fish. Waters adjacent to the river mouths are open, but at present, the river and mouth on both Manitou River and Blue Jay Creek are closed from March 1 to the Friday before the second Saturday in May. They are also closed September 25 to October 31.

From the North Channel, an angler can travel east through an area called the Bay of Islands, and past the towns of Little Current and Killarney. You will then enter the waters of Georgian Bay. With an area nearly the size of Lake Ontario, the amount of water for exploration is mind-boggling. This is another region totally off the radar screen of fly anglers—except for a few locals.

From north end to south end, Georgian Bay contains over 30,000 islands, with a nice, round 1,200 miles of total shoreline. According to area guide Graham Bristow, it probably contains 30,000 reefs, shoals, inlets, weed beds, and rock piles. Except for the extreme south end of the bay, there is structure everywhere—and very little fishing pressure in all but a few areas.

The Moon River Delta area of Georgian Bay contains thousands of islands of all sizes. These create countless fish-holding places where anglers may cast productively. Much of the Georgian Bay shoreline is a maze of rocky islands. Most are among the oldest exposed rock formations on earth. GRAHAM BRISTOW

For the most part, nearshore anglers focus their efforts on warmwater species, both largemouth and smallmouth bass, pike, and muskie. Gar are also beginning to attract a following here, much as they have in Lake Ontario's Bay of Quinte. There is seasonal opportunity for salmon and trout, but much of this is focused more in the south end of the bay and on the Bruce Peninsula.

I can suggest a few spots as starting points for fly anglers, but with the sheer size of the area here—and much of it being near-wilderness—Georgian Bay is pretty much an untapped area for fly fishing. One thing the bay has become is a major destination for sea kayaking. The Paddling Centre in Parry Sound, Ontario, can provide a wealth of information regarding access points and routes along the Georgian Bay shoreline. The "links" section off of their web site takes you to a full range of maps, plus weather and marine forecasts for the Great Lakes. The book *Kayaking Georgian Bay* by Jonathon Reynolds and Heather Smith provides very detailed information about shoreline areas that anglers too will find extremely useful.

French River, Killarney, and Massasauga Provincial Parks all border on the bay shoreline, along with Bruce Peninsula, Georgian Bay Islands National Park, and a host of other public areas. These will provide all kinds of shoreline access. Of these, French River Provincial Park may be the most interesting, as it is reachable only by water and offers a real wilderness experience. The web site www.visitfrenchriver .com gives a good overview.

Hartley Bay Marina in Alban, Ontario, offers a boat and canoe launching service and canoe rentals, and can provide all information needed to access the park. You can also find lodging and supplies here. The French River was the main water-travel route from east to west from the 1600s until the 1820s, so there are well-established canoe routes throughout the area.

The entire delta area is a maze of islands with weeded bays for pike, and shoals and reefs for bass and walleye. Muskie are normally found on the edge of deeper water but can show up anywhere. This area is slowly emerging onto the muskie scene as an area capable of producing a world-record-size fish. Fish in the 60-pound range have been caught here, and Georgian Bay has the ingredients needed to produce larger fish: light fishing pressure in a large area with an unlimited food supply. Graham Bristow, of Georgian Bay Muskie Charters, guides muskie anglers during the open season and has experience working with fly anglers.

There are many lodges and camps across the entire area, but from a fly-fishing standpoint, most of this is do-it-yourself. Georgian Bay Fish Camp, also in the French River Delta, has had exposure to fly anglers through Graham Coombs, of Swim True Flies. Coombs has fished out of the camp a number of times, using his unique swimming patterns with excellent results.

There are certainly other areas that can be explored by fly anglers. Graham Bristow focuses a lot of his fishing in the Moon River Basin, although he will fish as far south as the bay Honey Harbor. He prefers the Moon River area because of its diversity of structure and cover, as well as for the abundance of fish. Much of this area is part of Massasauga Provincial Park, with no road access, so a boat, canoe, or kayak is required to get around.

The extreme south of Georgian Bay is mainly trout and salmon water, with minimal structure. There are some smallmouth wherever any sort of hard bottom can be found, and carp cruise the shallows in the early summer prior to spawning. Three of Ontario's premier steelhead rivers, the Beaver, the Bighead, and the Nottawasaga, drain into Georgian Bay on the east side of the Bruce Peninsula. This makes the area from Wasaga Beach to Owen Sound prime ground for coldwater exploration.

The Nottawasaga River may have the largest steelhead run of any of Ontario's rivers, with a run-time that can extend for a very long period. This is a very diverse population of wild fish that often begins to stage in Nottawasaga Bay at Wasaga Beach in early September. Some fish may not complete spawning until late May.

Wasaga Beach Provincial Park has both shore-fishing access and boat and canoe launch areas. Steelhead, chinook and coho salmon, brown trout, splake, and even whitefish can be caught in the lower river and adjacent lake area. Sturgeon Point Marina has access to the river mouth at the lake. Keep in mind that this is the world's longest freshwater beach and a major summer vacation area, so it's best to schedule fishing before Memorial Day or after Labor Day.

The Beaver River meets Lake Huron at the town of Thornbury. There is a dam a short distance from the lake, with a fish ladder to allow the passage of migratory trout and salmon. This area has excellent access right at the river mouth, including a municipal marina complex for launching all kinds of watercraft. The usual mix of migratory fish will be found here, and there is a decent population of resident smallmouth. There is extended fishing in the lower river to December 31.

The Bighead River enters Georgian Bay at the village of Meaford. This is another of the pleasant harbor towns found along the Bruce Peninsula. The harbor has several launch facilities and a small breakwall complex. Seasonal migratory trout and salmon are the main focus here also, but you can catch resident smallmouth during the summer.

The area from Wasaga Beach to Wairton, on Colpy's Bay, provides excellent opportunities for a variety of shore fishing. The town of Owen Sound has an extensive area of shoreline for trout and salmon. Beyond Wairton, the opportunity for these fish decreases, along with the numbers and size of tributaries.

The area around Craigleigh provides some of the best shore- and small watercraft-fishing. Centrally located between the major spawning rivers, this area attracts good numbers of salmon and trout in the spring, late summer, and fall, holding them close to shore in reach of anglers. Craigleigh Provincial Park gives access to the shoreline and places to launch smaller watercraft from the flat bedrock areas that extend into the water. Again, you will find smallmouth bass here, but so far they receive little attention from anglers.

If we cut west across the bottom of the Bruce Peninsula to Lake Huron proper, we arrive at the town of Southampton at the mouth of the Saugeen River. Denny's Dam, located 4 kilometers upstream from Lake Huron, is a collecting point for any migratory fish waiting to ascend the fish ladder there as they head upstream. There are numerous places to access this part of the river.

Most of the interest here is for salmon and steelhead in the fall and spring, but there are also opportunities in the summer for anglers to chase both smallmouth bass and northern pike. In summer, the Saugeen will look like an entirely different river than in spring and fall, with very little fishing pressure.

The mouth of this sizeable river has two breakwalls that extend into the lake, as well as an easily reached large beach. There is also a boat launch area right near the mouth, with quick access to the lake. Steelhead and salmon often begin to stage here in mid to late August. Other available species include brown trout, lake trout, and whitefish.

I have managed to touch on just a tiny fraction of the vast waters available to anglers in this region. As with most places around the Great Lakes, local information will come from gear and bait anglers and it will be necessary to translate this into fly-fishing language. This book hopes to encourage fly fishers to venture into these new areas with fly rod in hand—and to hook fish.

Regulations and catch limits are fairly restrictive on Georgian Bay and surrounding waters, so there is certainly an awareness of the value of the resources. There are closed seasons, protected nursery waters, and slot-size limits. These can vary widely depending on the area. In addition, many lodges and guides are now practicing catch-and-release. This is particularly true of the expanding muskie fishery in Georgian Bay.

St. Marys River

As the outlet of Lake Superior and connector to Lake Huron, the St. Marys River winds almost 75 miles, its entire length forming the international boundary between the state of Michigan and province of Ontario. Of particular interest to fly anglers is a short stretch of river, including "the Rapids," where most of the 23-foot fall in elevation between the lakes takes place.

The St. Marys River Rapids from the International Bridge. The Canadian berm, visible on the left side of the photo, is the main area for shore and wade fishing.

As mentioned earlier in this book, the St. Marys has a long fishing history, first as a commercial fishery for native North Americans and later as a sport fishery. It was mentioned as early as 1884 by Robert Barnwell Roosevelt in the book *Superior Fishing*. When Ernest Hemingway fished the area in 1920, rainbow trout had become well established, despite being planted barely 50 years earlier.

Two cities named Sault Ste. Marie are located at the Rapids, one in Ontario, one in Michigan.

Both are important centers for lake transportation, each having a set of locks allowing boat traffic up and down the river. These locks played an essential role in the development of the Great Lakes region, allowing the transport of iron ore from the mining ranges at the west end of Lake Superior to the steel mills of the southern Great Lakes. The Soo Locks still pass an average of 10,000 recreational and commercial boats a year, despite being closed for three months of the year (January through March).

Several hydroelectric plants supply power for the locks and provide electricity to large areas of northern Michigan and Ontario. The Edison Sault Power Plant on the American side is the longest hydroelectric plant in the world, 1,340 feet in length. The Edison Sault Power Canal was constructed to channel water into the Edison plant from the river. The Army Corps of Engineers operates a second generating station to power the Soo Locks, which are the busiest ship locks in the world in terms of tonnage passing through.

On the Canadian side, the Francis H. Clergue Generating Station supplies power for locks and industry. A concrete berm was constructed on the north side of the Rapids to maintain water levels for fish spawning. Sault Ste. Marie, one of the largest cities in northern Ontario, is a center for steel and paper making as well as a

St. Marys River Essentials

Primary Species and Peak Times

Steelhead: October, November, April, May, but can be encountered nearly anytime

Atlantic salmon: June–October

Chinook salmon: mid-September–mid-October

Coho salmon: October

Pink salmon: early September

Rainbow trout: May–July

Whitefish: May, June

Warmwater species; May, June, July, August, September, October

Useful Fly Patterns

Trout and Salmon

Smelt-colored streamers #1-4
Tubular Smelt
Modified Clouser
Bart-O-Minnow
Flashtail Deceiver
Daminno
Ice-Out Alewife
Sexy Hexy #6-10
JQ Caddis
Great Lakes Simple Stone #8-12
Pheasant Tail, Hare's Ear, Prince Nymphs, #4-12 heavy wire hooks
Egg flies to match spawning salmon eggs and attractor colors #8-10
Arctic Wiggler
Devil's Advocate
Better Minnow
Glitzy Girl
Other tube patterns to match smelt and other baitfish

Warmwater Species

Clouser Minnows #1-4; gray-white, chartreuse-white
Meatwagon
Double Bunny #1/0-4; natural grizzly gray and white, olive
Great Lakes Deceivers; fire tiger, chartreuse-white, baby rainbow, black-chartreuse
Crawpin #2-4; brown and black
SF Crawfish
Crazi Craw
EZ Craw
Moby Goby
Great Lakes Goby Grub #2

Fly Shops, Guides, Information

Capt. Brad Petzke

Rivers North Fly Fishing Guide Service
riversnorth.net
906-458-8125

Capt. Travis White

St. Mary's Guide Company
whitesguidedfishing.com
906-748-1353

John Giuliani

Northern Fishing Adventures
705-942-5473
Canadian waters and the Rapids

Soo North Fly Shop

Sault Ste. Marie, ON
soonorthflyshop.shawwebspace.ca
705-575-7738

River Conditions

www.lssu.edu/arl/conditions.php

Books & Publications

Michigan Atlas and Gazetteer
by DeLorme Publishing
Michigan Blue-Ribbon Fly-Fishing Guide
by Bob Linsenman
Ontario Blue-Ribbon Fly Fishing Guide
by Scott E. Smith

Capt. Brad Petzke shows an Atlantic salmon taken on a nymph at the Edison Sault Power Plant on the St. Marys River. Atlantics are present in the river from late May into October. BRAD PETZKE

A beautiful Atlantic salmon from the St. Marys Rapids. This fish hit a Spey pattern swung on a two-hand rod. JIM LINEHAN

jumping-off point for all sorts of outdoor activities. The entire area, both American and Canadian sides, is often collectively referred to as "the Soo."

The St. Marys was among the beneficiaries of the stockings of Pacific salmon throughout the Great Lakes in the 1960s to control invasive alewife populations. Both chinook and coho salmon were stocked extensively and now reproduce naturally in the Rapids. Pink salmon were introduced in Lake Superior by mistake, and today the largest spawning concentration in the Great Lakes is found here. A chinook-pink hybrid called a pinook has been documented in the St. Marys and several other nearby tributaries. It is thought that the extreme concentrations of fish that overlap to spawn in the berm area of the Rapids allowed this to occur.

The occasional brown trout can also be found around the power plants and the Rapids. Northern pike inhabit weedy areas off the main flow, and even smallmouth may wander upstream from the warmer lower part of the river. There is something for anglers nearly year-round. Chinooks often begin entering the Rapids in late August, and spring steelhead usually peak in late May. In between, there is always something available for anglers.

In 1987, Lake Superior State University (LSSU), the Edison Sault Electric Company, and the Michigan Department of Natural Resources began a program to introduce Atlantic salmon into the upper Great Lakes. This program, headed by Roger Greil of LSSU, has had success establishing a fishable population of Atlantics that drop into Lake Huron to feed and then return to the river near where they were stocked.

The Atlantics being stocked are a landlocked strain from West Grand Lake, Maine. The eggs hatched for stocking are taken from fish returning to the LSSU Aquatic Research Laboratory on the St. Marys River. The fish are held for a year-and-a-half after hatching before being stocked. This gives students the opportunity to collect and hatch eggs and then work with yearling salmon. The main purpose of

Jeff Liskay checking out the St. Marys River inside the berm. The main rapids are beyond the cement wall.

the program is to train students, with the added benefit of creating a unique fishery for the public.

Natural reproduction of Atlantics has been limited up to this point, so the population is maintained by annual plantings averaging 40,000 yearlings. Fish will return starting as two-year-olds, weighing around 2.5 pounds. Fish in the 20-pound range have been caught and, best of all, Atlantics fill the summer timeframe, when numbers of migratory fish are at their lowest.

Atlantic salmon begin to show up in the Sault Ste. Marie area in early June, after most of the steelhead have vacated. Most salmon initially move to the Edison Power Plant, since this is where they were initially stocked. There is an underwater camera at the Aquatic Research Laboratory that can be viewed live by going to www.lssu.edu/arl/fishcam/php.

A specialized style of boat-fishing has developed here, in which anglers attach to the power plant outflow wall with specially designed hooks. Flies are cast directly into the turbine outflow tunnels where the fish typically hold. When an Atlantic is hooked, the boat may be unhooked from the wall to allow the angler to fight the fish. The same technique can be used for the other migratory species that travel the river, as well as for the resident rainbows and whitefish.

The other power plants are a bit different in that boats cannot be tied up to them. At these locations, a boat can be pulled up as close to the discharge as possible and then allowed to drift back with the flow. Flies can dead-drifted, cast and stripped, and even trolled to produce Atlantics. There is some limited shore access to the Canadian power plant. One important thing to keep in mind—if you plan to fish the Canadian plant, even from a boat, an Ontario license is required.

Fly selection depends on food available in the river at a given time. In early June, with large numbers of smelt in the river, streamers are very productive. These can be cast and stripped, swung, and even drifted under an indicator. It is important to be in the general size range and coloration of the smelt.

Any number of smelt-imitating patterns can be used to tempt St. Mary's Atlantics. A gray-white size 2 Deep Minnow is a good starting point. Smelt in the river can vary in size from three to six inches in length. On some days, the size of the fly can be more important than the actual pattern. It pays to experiment with the size.

Wisconsin angler Dave Pinczkowski has had good success in the Rapids swinging his Bad Hair Day pattern. If I get back to the St. Marys during smelt time, I will definitely throw my Arctic Wiggler and also give Paul Castellano's Niagara Intruder a try too.

In mid-June, significant numbers of *Hexagenia* mayflies begin to hatch in slower areas of the river. Many of these flies drift down to the Soo, becoming fair game for feeding salmon. The nymphs are not present in this area, so an adult pattern can be fished subsurface, imitating a drowned mayfly. An indicator rig with a long leader can be employed, or a bottom bounce rig used. Salmon may also take adult Hex patterns on the surface.

Atlantics also feed on a variety of smaller nymphs that come down the flow. Various generic patterns, such as Prince Nymphs or Hare's Ears in various color shades, should be dead-drifted. Both standard and bead-head versions of these patterns can be used. They should be tied on a heavy wire hook that will be strong enough to hold a fighting salmon.

For nymph fishing from a boat, a 9- or $9^{1}/_{2}$-foot, 7- or 8-weight rod with a floating weight forward or shooting line is used. The reel should have a smooth drag and hold 100 yards minimum of backing, in case a sizable Atlantic is hooked. Long leaders with fluorocarbon tippet are favored. 2X is a starting point, but this may need to be downsized on a bright, sunny day. The water in the St. Marys is vodka-clear, and salmon can get very selective when hitting flies.

Streamers are usually fished behind a sinking-tip line. Integrated sinking, shooting-taper lines are the most popular. The same rod used in nymphing will work for fishing streamers. A short butt section (1 foot or so) of 20-pound monofilament is tied to the tip and a 5-foot length of 10- to 14-pound tippet added, and then the fly tied on. A sparse Clouser Minnow or rabbit strip pattern in smelt colors can be stripped, or any number of baitfish imitators may be used.

Trolling flies behind a full-sinking line—in the style of fishing for landlocked salmon that has been used in New England for decades—can also be employed successfully. This method allows for a large area to be covered quickly, targeting active fish. Finding the right speed is often the key to success with this method. Traditional patterns such as the Gray Ghost, as well other streamer patterns, can be used in this application.

Shore-based fishing is from the Canadian shoreline only. There is a parking area adjacent to the power plant that is only a couple of minutes from Canadian Customs and can be reached from Canal Street. A trail reached by crossing the White Island Reserve is used to get to the Rapids. This takes 15 minutes or so by foot along a well-worn trail. This area is administered by the Batchawana First Nation.

The compensating gates at the top of the St. Marys Rapids influence the water level in Lake Superior.

The Rapids are actually divided into two parts by the concrete berm that parallels the river flow. The berm is designed to maintain suitable spawning habitat on its inside, while flows can fluctuate significantly in the main river at times. Water-compensating gates at the head of the Rapids actually help control water levels in Lake Superior; gates can be closed and opened as needed.

The majority of fish coming into the Rapids to spawn will stay inside the berm. This is particularly true of the Pacific salmon species. Steelhead can be found on either side of the berm. On the Rapids side, they will hold on the edges of the fastest flows where there is suitable bottom substrate. Resident rainbows will inhabit similar areas. Atlantics tend to hold and spawn in the fastest flows and thus present a special challenge.

The main river is pocket-water fishing at its extreme. The exceptional water clarity makes depth hard to judge, but the deeper the water, the darker green in color it is. Rocks can vary from golf-ball size to as big as a house. Most of the rocks are very hard, with a smooth surface.

Fishing the main river beyond the shoreline requires extra care and preparation. Studded shoes are absolutely necessary, along with a stout wading staff. Water temperature in the Rapids is often in the 50-degree F range and lower, and any spill in cold weather can quickly result in hypothermia. An inflatable vest can be a lifesaver, and carrying an extra set of dry clothes with you is not a bad idea.

In the lower part of the Rapids, there are a number of recognizable deeper cuts and pools where fish will stage before moving to the upper flows. Depending on water flows, some of these spots can be reached without too much difficulty. At times it may be possible to work most of the way across the Rapids prospecting the suspected holding areas.

Pacific salmon are normally targeted with a variety of egg and nymph patterns. Just-arrived chinook and coho may also chase streamers. Pinks are taken on small nymphs and yarn flies. These fish all ascend the Rapids starting in late August. As the salmon get into full spawning mode and start dropping eggs, rainbows and steelhead will often move in to feast on this nutritious bounty. At this time, it is often necessary to "match the hatch" with egg patterns for consistent success.

Atlantics can be found in the Rapids from mid-June through October. They tend to hold in the deeper, fastest flows, and these places need to be fished carefully. Again, a variety of techniques can be used. Caddis are abundant, especially the *Rhyacophila* or green rock worm. A green caddis pattern in sizes 8 to 12 can be dead-drifted under an indicator or fished bottom-bounce style. Atlantics will also hit swung flies in the Rapids. Baitfish patterns, attractors, and even traditional drys such as Bombers all produce fish. The use of two-hand rods continues to grow for swinging flies.

Steelhead can be found in the Rapids any month of the year, but the peak time frame is April and May. With no salmon eggs present at this time, nymphs are the most productive flies. Green caddis and black stones, again in sizes 8 to 12, are most popular, but other patterns can produce too. Attractor eggs will still produce fish, as steelhead just can't seem to resist them. An egg/nymph combo bottom-bounced is probably the most effective method for St. Marys steelhead. Be sure to use high-quality, heavy-wire hooks on flies. Current speed in the Rapids helps both steelhead and Atlantics easily detach from lighter wire designs.

Swung streamers also attract their share of steelies, especially in the late spring, as fish begin to drop back to Lake Huron after spawning. Both baitfish and attractor-style patterns will work. Sinking-tip lines are used to swing into holding areas. Skagit-style lines are favored with two-hand rods.

The favored outfit for fishing the Rapids has been a $9^1/2$- to 10-foot, 7- or 8-weight rod. Again, a quality reel with a floating line and ample backing is needed. There is a growing group of anglers employing two-hand rods and Spey casting. An interchangeable tip line is useful to swing flies at various depths from top to bottom. A 13-foot, 7- or 8-weight two-hand rod works well for Spey casting and techniques. An 11-foot, 8-weight switch rod may be the ultimate tool to fish the Rapids, allowing the angler to easily change from dead-drifting to swinging flies and back again.

Below the Rapids area, where the river splits around Sugar Island, warmwater species become more abundant. Munuscong Lake is known for its smallmouth bass and muskie fishing. Downstream from here, the St. Marys widens into Lake Huron proper at Drummond Island. On the Canadian side, the river flows into Georgian Bay, which is an entity all its own to be explored. There are numerous areas along this stretch of water that provide access for canoes and kayaks as well as for power boats. This is a major tourist area, so food, camping, and lodging are also readily available.

The St. Marys River provides a unique experience for Great Lakes fly anglers. Giant freighters pass by while anglers are pursuing a variety of seasonal species. The average angler can fish for both Atlantic salmon and several species of Pacific salmon, sometimes all in the same day. Some of the best water can be reached from shore. But be cautioned, the Rapids are a challenging area and every fish landed there is well-earned.

The Soo is also a popular tourist area, so food and lodging choices are found in abundance. Nonanglers can find a variety of outdoor activities to keep them occupied. Boat tours of the Locks and river run several times a day, providing a glimpse of the work done in harnessing the power of the river and maintaining the Great Lakes as an avenue of commerce.

chapter 10

Fly Fishing
in Lake Michigan

ake Michigan is the second largest of the Great Lakes by volume and the third largest by surface area, boasting a square mileage nearly the size of the state of West Virginia. It is the only Great Lake totally within the United States, its shoreline helping to define the boundaries of Illinois, Indiana, Michigan, and Wisconsin.

With both the cities of Chicago and Milwaukee located on its shores, nearly 12 million people call the Lake Michigan region home. In spite of this, the lake is a significant recreational and tourist destination. In addition, it supports perhaps the most diverse and most developed sportfishery in the Great Lakes.

Door County, Wisconsin

A book could very well be written on the angling opportunities of the Door County peninsula alone. With nearly 300 miles of shoreline, Door has more waterfront than any other county in the continental United States. With Green Bay to the west and Lake Michigan to the east, Door County offers anglers nearly every fish species found in the Great Lakes. The smallmouth bass fishery ranks among the best anywhere, and nearshore fishing for both steelhead and brown trout can be outstanding.

Door County can also stake its claim as the "birthplace of modern Great Lakes fly fishing." In 1990 an enterprising angler named George Von Schrader self-published a book titled *Carp Are Gamefish*. In this book, Von Schrader tells the story of spending summers in Door County during his youth. In 1966 and 1967, he had read articles in *Field & Stream* magazine by Milwaukee nature writer Mel Ellis, who described fly fishing for carp in Door County on both the Green Bay and Lake Michigan sides.

Von Schrader followed Ellis's lead and began chasing carp religiously on his home waters. His passion continued for more than 30 years, during which he chronicled carping locations across the entire Great Lakes. To my knowledge, this is the first book to take a comprehensive look at fly fishing in the lakes themselves. Though its focus is strictly on carp, it covers the essentials: where, when, and how. Von Schrader also introduced a number of fly-fishing notables, including fly-fishing legend Dave Whitlock to Great Lakes carp.

Crystal-clear water is typical of Door County. Jim Oates casts into a deeper pocket on a flat. Pre-spawn smallmouth will often stage in areas like this before moving up to the shallows.

In the past decade, Door County has emerged as a premier destination for small-mouth bass anglers, at least in part because of the presence in Lake Michigan of two invasive species: zebra mussels and round gobies. As filter feeders, zebra mussels pull particulate matter out of the water and increase its clarity, making it easier for smallmouth to see their prey. The round goby fish offers a more direct benefit; it has come to provide an additional and significant source of protein for hungry small-mouth. However, gobies can be a threat as well, because they will attack small-mouth nests and eat their eggs if the opportunity presents itself.

From a fly-fishing standpoint, increased water clarity and an easily imitated food source work in our favor. Smallmouth (and also brown trout) feed voraciously on gobies and in clearer water, may spot a goby—or, for our purposes, a goby imita-tor—from some distance. The opportunities are similar around the Great Lakes where gobies are found.

On the Green Bay side, the best fly-fishing opportunities in Door County start in the area around Little Sturgeon Bay and continue out to Gills Rock on the tip and across to Washington Island. Countless rock piles, reefs, ledges, troughs, and other structure provide areas to feed and nest. All of the harbor areas offer sheltered bays for wading anglers and launch areas for small craft. Both Peninsula and Newport State Parks have numerous locations where shorebound anglers can cast a fly.

Sawyer Harbor in Sturgeon Bay is one of the best-known locations for small-mouth, but an adventurous angler will find fish around almost any rocky area in the bay. The Sturgeon Bay Ship Canal offers accessible opportunities for smallmouth and migratory species. On the Lake Michigan side of the ship canal, fish congregate around a series of rock piles at the end of the breakwall near the Coast Guard sta-tion. When bait is holding in the area, it will attract a wide range of predators.

To the north, a wading angler can connect with bronzebacks in Egg Harbor, Fish Creek, Sister Bay, and Ellison Bay, and float tubes, canoes, and kayaks can be launched from many spots. Peninsula State Park is a popular area, with miles of shoreline to explore and easy access to Von Schrader's fabled Strawberry Islands.

The Lake Michigan side of Door County has more sand and shallower bays. Baileys Harbor, Moonlight Bay, North Bay, and Rowleys Bay are all good fly-fishing areas where another type of structure comes into play—stands of reeds and bullrush that can hold good numbers of smallies. Working the edges of the reed beds, and even pockets back in the reeds, can produce exciting strikes from bass and the occasional northern pike.

Rowleys Bay—especially near the mouth of the Mink River—is known for its smallmouth and early season pike fishery. An interesting technique here is to dead-drift simple leech patterns under an indicator for smallmouth. Because the Mink River has a noticeable flow, this method works well—although fish here will also respond to a stripped fly. This area also attracts plenty of migratory fish in the spring and fall: salmon, browns, and steelhead, along with pike and smallmouth.

Fly anglers here can find many locations for wading and for launching small craft. Water clarity is generally excellent, so it's easy to locate rock piles, cuts, and troughs and to identify and avoid unproductive water. Kayaks and canoes allow anglers to cover water quickly, and the new stand-up kayaks provide visibility unmatched by wading. Fishing paddleboards have just come on to the scene. In addition, saltwater designs with features such as poling platforms and other elevated structure to increase visibility are being seen more frequently.

Smallmouth fishing usually starts on the first Saturday in May, with the opening of the regular gamefish season. At this time, look for smallmouth along the edges of the shallows that lead to deeper water. These pre-spawn fish are usually active feeders after a long, cold winter. As the water warms, they move to shallow areas, where

Dave Pinczkowski caught this carp on a Door County flat. This is possibly the first area to be associated with Great Lakes fly fishing, based on articles in fishing magazines from the 1960s and books referring back to that time.

This bass took a diver worked slowly along the edge of the reeds.

Door County Essentials

Primary Species and Peak Times

Trout and salmon: ice-out–April, September,
October
Smallmouth: mid-May–mid-July
Carp: June, July
Note: Be sure to check regulations for the
specific area of the peninsula where you
are fishing, as rules may vary between the
Green Bay side and the Lake Michigan
side.

Useful Fly Patterns

Trout and Salmon

Deep Minnow #1-2: chartreuse-white, gray-
white
Half and Half #1/0-2; chartreuse-white, gray-
white
Bad Hair Day #1; white, gray, and chartreuse
Bart-O-Minnow #1; white
Great Lakes Deceiver; chartreuse-white, gray-
white

Smallmouth Bass

Deep Minnow #1-4; chartreuse-white, gray-
white, brown-orange
Bad Hair Day #1-4; white, gray, olive, brown
Bart-O-Minnow #2; white, brown, olive
Claw Dad #2; olive, black
Simpleech #4; black, olive, brown, white
Crazi Craw #2; olive and brown

Carp

Coyote Ugly #4
Simpleech #4; black, olive
EZ Craw #4; olive, tan

Fly Shops, Guides, Information

Tight Lines Fly Fishing
De Pere, WI
tightlinesflyshop.com
920-336-4106

The Fly Fishers
Milwaukee, WI
theflyfishers.com
414-259-8100

Dave Pinczkowski
414-412-1838

Nate Sipple
704-304-7581

Books & Publications

Carp Are Gamefish by George Von Schrader
Fly Fishers Guide to Wisconsin and Iowa
by John Motoviloff
Wisconsin Atlas and Gazetteer
by DeLorme Publishing

they continue feeding actively until spawning. This period often produces the largest fish of the year. Most Door County bronzebacks will be 16 to 18 inches long, but there are good numbers of fish longer than 20 inches.

Smallmouth can be easily targeted and caught when they go onto spawning beds, where the males stay to guard the eggs and protect just-hatched fry. However, it is not a good idea to focus on these guardian males, because pulling them off the beds puts the eggs in danger of being eaten by gobies, crayfish, and even by marauding carp. Plus, there's no need to target them. Not all bass spawn at the same time; their patterns even vary to some extent from bay to bay. Anglers can usually find enough fish to avoid spawning beds, or keep that target to a minimum. Also, the beds are only one of many predictable locations for smallmouth. Blind

A stand-up fishing kayak is a great tool to work the flats of Door County.

casting to the shadowed side of larger rocks and off edges of the flats will also produce fish.

Smallmouth also can be found following the movement of alewives into the
shallows in June, an opportunity for exciting fishing because the smallmouth here
will aggressively attack baitfish patterns. September and October can be productive
for large smallmouth bass as well, as these fish are feeding heavily for the coming
winter and may make a push back to the edges of the shallows in search of prey.

As for carp, the best time to stalk this species on the Door County flats is mid-
June and July. Bass are still around, but many have moved off to deeper areas. Carp
are easily spotted on the lighter-colored bottoms, and a variety of "creepy-crawly"
patterns can be cast to them. Flies that imitate crayfish and those that mimic larger
bugs, such as Hex nymphs, will entice strikes.

Nate Sipple, a guide from Tight Lines Fly Fishing Company in De Pere, Wisconsin, is a frequent visitor to Door County waters. He prefers the sheltered flats around
Baileys Harbor, where he often stations himself on rock with a higher vantage point
to wait for carp to swim into casting range. In water deeper than 2 feet, he prefers to
drop a crayfish pattern with heavier barbell eyes in front of feeding carp. In shallower
water, he switches to a lightly weighted fly.

An interesting opportunistic feeding pattern can sometimes occur, in which
smallmouth bass follow behind feeding carp and feast on the critters dislodged from
the bottom and missed by the carp. This may be a single or a small group of bass.
This is another of those saltwater-like fishing opportunities that can be found in the
Great Lakes Basin: smaller fish flowing behind a larger fish that is feeding in shallow, crystal-clear water. Carp will also feed of the edges of flats and in troughs,
where, like smallmouth bass, they will hit small baitfish imitations.

Carp hooked in Door County will average about 10 pounds; monsters exceeding 30 pounds are caught there. I myself have seen carp on these flats that I'm sure were in the 50-pound range. Although they lack the speed of bonefish, carp will make strong runs. Anyway, the sheer size of the fish makes up for the lack of sizzling runs.

Steelhead and brown trout are fairly easy to target in Door County; all of the streams and rivers, either on the bay or lakeside, attract them. In both spring and fall, fish will be holding at the mouths of these tributaries, either staging to move upriver or just returning from spawning back to the lake. In the fall, salmon may also be in the mix in these locations.

When flows are up, the streams often have a distinct tannin color, so there is a distinct line at the point of entry into the clear waters of the lake. Concentrate on this color-change area; it will hold the baitfish that attract larger fish. There may also be a temperature change at this borderline, and larger fish will hold on the more comfortable side.

If you observe that fish are rolling, try an intermediate-tip line, so that an actively retrieved fly stays a foot or two under the surface. If you don't see any activity, use a sinking-tip line to probe deeper water. And, if baitfish are visible, try to "match the hatch" with a streamer similar in size and color to the bait.

The Deep Minnows, Half and Halfs, and Murdich Minnow are all usable patterns. Guide Bart Landwehr, from Tight Lines Fly Fishing Company, ties a local favorite named the Bart-O-Minnow. If blind casting, use a larger pattern—anywhere from 5 to 8 inches in length—and experiment with color.

You should always be prepared to deal with some wind here. One great feature of the area is that if one side of the peninsula is windy, the other is usually calm. Plus, there are plenty of sheltered bays and coves, so you can usually find somewhere productive to move if the winds become too troublesome where you are.

An 8-weight outfit is the minimum for Door County fly fishing. Because this area offers the potential to hook carp or brown trout in the 30-pound class, a 9-weight—even a 10-weight—may be desirable at times. Don't go undergunned, and make sure you have at least 200 yards of backing on your reel.

Fly anglers have the opportunity to fish Door County from ice-out to ice-up: usually early April to mid-November. This is arguably one of the top areas in the Great Lakes for season-long fly fishing and trophy catches.

All factors considered—accessibility, amenities such as abundant lodging and eateries, and spectacular scenery—Door County is a great fly-fishing destination. Wisconsin Route 57 out of Green Bay is the main artery to the area. Despite Door Country's popularity as a tourist destination, a visiting fly angler will find plenty of uncrowded water, no matter the time of year.

Drowned River Mouths

As you travel up the east shoreline of Lake Michigan, a noticeable feature is a series of smaller lakes located at a number of port cities along the shoreline. These are referred to as "drowned river mouths" because of the way in which they were created. As the earth's crust slowly rebounded from the massive weight of glaciers that covered the area some 10,000 years ago, rivers entering the lake become flooded.

Pockets along deep weed edges are prime fishing areas. Capt. Kevin Feenstra works just such a fishy spot in the Muskegon Estuary.

A large smallmouth caught in harbor waters. Many Lake Michigan harbors have populations of smallmouth bass that are largely ignored by anglers. This fish hit a Conehead Blueberg. KEVIN MORLOCK

Water levels increased and back-up into the rivers created these lakes and associated wetland areas.

These estuary-like areas offer transition habitats between lake and river. Some have sand bars that separate them from the main lake; others have developed harbor areas with extensive breakwall and jetty areas. They are important wetland areas that support a wide range of birds, wildlife, and fish.

Drowned river mouths are important staging areas for various migratory species that enter their rivers to spawn, and the mouths also are home to a variety of warmwater species. While some of these areas have received a bit of fly-fishing attention, for the most part they are overlooked by even gear anglers much of the time. We're going to take a look at the fly-fishing possibilities.

The Muskegon River breaks into series of braids and channels flowing through the Muskegon State Game Area before flowing into Muskegon Lake. Beginning at the lake and going upstream several miles, you'll find this area resembles the Florida Everglades more than a well-known trout and steelhead river. Tea-colored water flows along banks lined with head-high vegetation. Shallow areas off the main current hold patches of lily pads.

Sunset on the harbor in Frankfort, Michigan. Dozens of locations like this around Lake Michigan and the rest of the Great Lakes are largely overlooked by fly anglers.

In spring, steelhead are prime targets in harbor areas, which have open water before the main lake. Try patterns matching local baitfish. KEVIN MORLOCK

Well-known Muskegon River guide Capt. Kevin Feenstra has been exploring this area for a number of years, and he says he is still working to determine the full fly-fishing potential of the area. Feenstra has encountered a surprising assortment of fish: smallmouth and largemouth bass, pike, king salmon, brown trout, and steelhead. Most of his time here has been in the late summer.

I took several trips with Feenstra on this water, throwing a variety of streamer patterns and surface bugs. Action was consistent, catches a mix of smallmouth and largemouth bass. Most fish were lying tight to the bank along logs, or in pockets along the bank. Rabbit strip streamers and frog divers produced fish for us.

Several dirt launch ramps are located on the south sides of the river, at the ends of Sheridan and Mill Iron Roads. These put you right into the middle of the game area. There are also ramps where the river ends at the head of Muskegon Lake. The river is floatable from the upper ramps to take-out at the lake. This area is easily reached from U.S. Route 31.

Fly fishers can also use any of the ramps on the lake to get to a small power plant located where Muskegon River enters Muskegon Lake. To my knowledge, no one has fly-fished this discharge, but I would guess it attracts all the species that live in the lake and enter the river.

Feenstra also fishes the estuary of the White River at the town of Whitehall. This is essentially a smaller version of the Muskegon area. Anglers can launch from a small dirt ramp on the south side of the river, where Business Route 31 crosses over the stream. This is a great opportunity to move up-current and fish one side and then float downriver and fish the other side of the river or one of the braids.

In both the Muskegon and the White River mouth areas, two different 8- or 9-weight rigs should be carried: a floating line and a sinking-head line. Depending on the character of the water and the time of day, streamer patterns might be the recommended fly. I have had good success with my Meatwagon pattern in perch and fire tiger colors, while Feenstra has thrown his Fire Detector and Thunderbolt designs. It is likely that almost any bright, flashy pattern will draw strikes.

Matt Erny, of Day 5 Flies, has several designs, such as the NEO, that incorporate blades into their designs. These help attract fish when these waters cloud up after a heavy rain. His Spider Grub is a great pattern for both largemouth and smallmouth bass, and not just here—anywhere they are found. Surface patterns can be effective early and late in the day. Frog-colored poppers and divers have both produced fish for me, and because I've fished here mostly in late summer, the species I've encountered most often have been bass and pike. However, there are many migratory species that move through, so both the Muskegon and White River mouths should provide a variety of fly-fishing opportunities throughout the year.

In addition to the seasonal movement of walleye, steelhead, lake-run brown trout, and salmon in these waters, there seem to be localized movements of both smallmouth and largemouth bass. Both move regularly into and out of the transitional area

Sunrise silhouettes Capt. Kevin Morlock as he casts overhead with a two-hand rod. Two-hand rods can be cast this way for increased distance, making them a valuable asset when trying to cover as much water as possible. KEVIN MORLOCK

Drowned River Mouths Essentials

Primary Species and Peak Times

Chinook salmon: mid-August–September
Coho salmon: September, October
Steelhead and brown trout: ice-out–May,
  October, November
Smallmouth and largemouth bass: May–
  September
Northern pike: May–September

Useful Fly Patterns

Salmon
Bush Pigs
Great Lakes Deceivers; glow-in-the-dark
  colors
Conehead Blueberg #1-2

Steelhead and Brown Trout
Bush Pig
Phantom Minnow
Ice-Out Alewife
Half and Half #1-2; chartreuse-white, gray-
  white

Largemouth and Smallmouth Bass
Meatwagon #1; perch and fire tiger
Thunderbolt
Fire Detector
Spider Grub; smoke and watermelon
Conrad's Sculpin #2; black
Tongue Depressor #2; brown and tan
Zudbubbler popper
Deer hair poppers and divers #1/0; frog colors

Northern Pike
Meatwagon Max; fire tiger, perch
Great Lakes Deceiver; red-white, chartreuse-
  white
Double Bunny #3/0-1/0; red-white, olive-
  orange

Fly Shops, Guides, Information

Great Lakes Fly Fishing Co.
Rockford, MI
troutmoor.net
616-866-6060

Schmidt Outfitters
Wellston, MI
schmidtoutfitters.com
231-848-4191

The Hex Fly Shop
Grand Rapids, MI
thehexshop.com
616-977-3655

The Northern Angler
Traverse City, MI
thenorthernangler.com
231-933-4370

Feenstra Guide Service
feenstraguideservice.com
231-652-3528

Indigo Guide Service
indigoguideservice.com
231-848-4320

Streamside Custom Rod & Guide Service
michiganstreamside.com
989-848-5983

Books & Publications

Flyfisher's Guide to Michigan by Jim Bedford
Michigan Atlas and Gazetteer
  by DeLorme Publishing

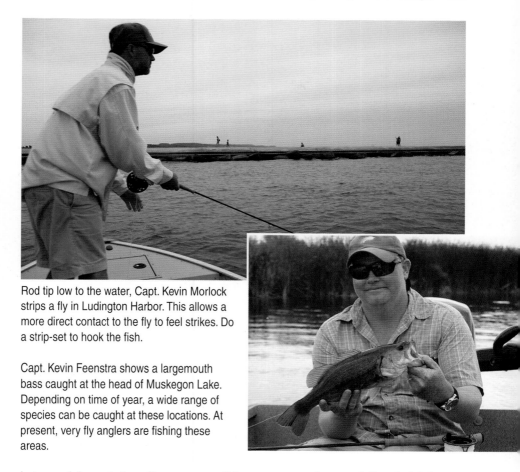

Rod tip low to the water, Capt. Kevin Morlock strips a fly in Ludington Harbor. This allows a more direct contact to the fly to feel strikes. Do a strip-set to hook the fish.

Capt. Kevin Feenstra shows a largemouth bass caught at the head of Muskegon Lake. Depending on time of year, a wide range of species can be caught at these locations. At present, very fly anglers are fishing these areas.

between lake and river. I'm not sure of the reason—perhaps to follow baitfish or to find more comfortable water temperatures. In any case, there is definite movement going on, and it's worth it for fly anglers to take note.

Farther north along U.S. Route 31, the next significant river entering Lake Michigan is the Pere Marquette, which has a significant place in American fly-fishing history: it was one of the first places where brown trout were introduced into North America. The trout fishing on this river is still very good, but it is overshadowed these days by naturally reproducing populations of steelhead and chinook salmon.

The Pere Marquette River enters the lake at the town of Ludington, one of the best-known sportfishing ports on Michigan's west coast. A well-developed harbor area, with a breakwall that is easily reached by foot, offers one important fishing venue. There is also the sizeable Pere Marquette Lake, best fished from some sort of watercraft. Numerous boat ramps provide access to the lake and harbor.

Capt. Kevin Morlock, of Indigo Guide Service, who fishes this area regularly, suggests the best time to fish the main harbor area is early in the spring, before the ice has gone out on the main lake. The harbor ice melts off faster, the water warms up, and this warmer water attracts bait for larger predatory fish.

Ice-out along a Lake Michigan harbor breakwall. Finding pockets of warmer water holding baitfish is the key to finding predators like steelhead and brown trout at this time of year. KEVIN MORLOCK

At these times, steelhead, brown trout, coho salmon, and even some lake trout will be in feeding here on a mix of alewives and shiners in warmer surface waters. A clear-tip line works well here, along with a floating line and long leader. Try to spot baitfish and match the size you see. Generally, a fly in the 3- to 5-inch length is productive.

You may also see larger predators cruising just under the surface in the warmer water, having just entered the

An ice-out harbor brown taken on a baitfish tube pattern. Along with steelhead, brown trout are prime targets in harbors, as they move in to feed on baitfish in the warmer water. KEVIN MORLOCK

harbor from the main lake. Try to cast in front of these fish and bring the fly past them. Use an 8- or 9-weight outfit so you can cast for distance and so you can handle the sizeable fish you are likely to encounter. Also make sure to have at least 100 yards of backing on the reel, especially if you are shorebound.

Depending on conditions, the breakwalls may be walkable; if they are heavily ice covered, anglers may need to use watercraft. A number of launch ramps are located around the lake. When fishing here in early spring, use extreme caution whether on-shore or in a boat: the water is still extremely cold, and getting wet can quickly result in hypothermia.

As the main lake continues to lose ice, pike will become active in its back shallows. Some of these can be quite large, and many may actually be migratory fish that move in from the main lake to spawn. As elsewhere, for early season pike, focus on soft, dark bottom areas that hold radiant heat longer.

As the season progresses, a mix of warmwater fish will appear, including smallmouth bass, largemouth bass, freshwater drum, and panfish. Depending on the day, they will respond to any one of an assortment of surface and subsurface patterns. The bright, flashy designs recommended for the mouths of the Muskegon and White Rivers will also draw attention here. Morlock also fishes a conehead version of a local pattern called the Blueberg with consistent success. The area where the Pere Marquette River flows into the lake, and the shoreline to the immediate south and west, can be particularly productive.

In midsummer, smallmouth bass also show up regularly along the rocky areas of the breakwall, where they chase crayfish and gobies. A sinking-head line is the best tool here to keep a fly deep in the water column and visible to bottom-dwelling smallmouth. Freshwater drum and even the occasional channel catfish can also be caught from the breakwall area in the summer; they will hit the same patterns that attract smallmouth. An added bonus in summer is enjoying an evening's fishing and then watching the sun set into Lake Michigan. As the sun gets lower, fish will become more active and start to feed, and this activity can sometimes extend past sunset.

A good portion of the shoreline in this area has been commercially developed. This is also the home of the S.S. Badger, the largest car ferry on Lake Michigan, which makes daily runs from Ludington, Michigan, to Manitowoc, Wisconsin. For safety reasons, boaters need to stay clear when the Badger is leaving and returning to dock, because this large craft has minimal maneuverability. However, the activity does not prevent fishing in Pere Marquette Lake from being quite productive near where the ferry docks.

The Platte River enters Lake Michigan. A variety of migratory species can be caught here; chinook salmon are the first to arrive in late summer.

The author casting for chinook salmon at the mouth of the Platte River with a switch rod. This type of rod allows for a higher backcast when wading, making it much easier to achieve distance.

In mid-August, chinook salmon start to move into the harbor and Pere Marquette Lake as they begin their spawning migration into the Pere Marquette River. This activity will last for a month or so. Once the word spreads that the salmon are in, boat activity from trollers increases significantly in both the inner and outer harbor areas and in Pere Marquette Lake. Most chinook fishing action takes place in low-light periods or at night.

I have spent several sessions throwing flies at chinook with Capt. Kevin Morlock around Ludington Harbor and in Pere Marquette Lake. In the clear waters off the breakwall, several fish followed flies right to the boat but did not grab. Maybe doing a figure-8 move, as in muskie fishing, would have triggered a strike, but I didn't think that fast at the time. We need more anglers putting in time with flies to unlock this mystery.

Boat traffic also appears to affect these fish; often they will not even strike lures until well after dark, when traffic has decreased. Getting chinook to hit a fly under these conditions is challenging to say the least, but, nevertheless, they can be caught. Patterns incorporating luminescent materials are showing promise and producing fish; for example, glow-in-the-dark Flashabou, Everglow Flash, and Tinsel. These can be activated with a camera flash to make them glow for a period of time.

Eli Berant, of Great Lakes Fly, offers glow-in-the-dark colors of several of the patterns he sells. The Great Lakes Deceiver, Half and Half, and Glo Pig are examples that have been successful attracting salmon after dark.

As the chinook move into the river and head upstream to the spawning areas, steelhead and brown trout often follow behind. Coho salmon will also make their appearance after the chinook. None of these will be in the same numbers as the chinook, but they are much more apt to hit a fly. Lake trout may also show up in late October, if there is enough bait moving inshore to draw them close.

Although there are many other places worth exploring, our final stop heading north along U.S. Route 31 will be the mouth of the Platte River and Platte Bay, where the Great Lakes salmon program was started in the late 1960s. The first coho were raised at the Platte River State Fish Hatchery and stocked in 1966. Chinook salmon followed a year later. Both species were planted in hopes of controlling the population of invasive alewives that had exploded out of control in Lake Michigan and other parts of the Great Lakes. A weir on the Platte River is still in operation in order to collected eggs from salmon for stocking purposes.

The mouth of the Platte River and adjacent waters has been a popular fishing area since the first salmon stockings. The area is now part of the Sleeping Bear Dunes National Lakeshore, which includes more than 50,000 acres of land and 35 miles of picturesque Lake Michigan shoreline. Anglers reach the river mouth by following Lake Michigan Road off MI Route 22. There is a boat ramp here, and an easy trail to the lake.

Most angling activity takes place here in late August, September, and October, when chinook salmon are staging in preparation for their spawn. Early in the morning, and again in the evening, anglers line up along the current outflow of the Platte River into Platte Bay. Most will be gear slingers, but there is often a fly rodder or two mixed in.

Kelly Neuman, of Streamside Custom Rod & Guide Service, frequents this area at this time of year, fishing the river mouth and adjacent bay waters in the evenings and after dark. He has consistent success in catching chinook and coho by casting large glow-in-the-dark patterns with sinking-head lines.

To get to Platt Bay, a small boat can be launched at the river ramp off MI Route 22; it is a short run of about a quarter mile downstream to the bay. There is a sand bar at the river mouth and, depending on water levels, at times it may be necessary

The Platte River, a Lake Michigan tributary, was the first stream in the Great Lakes to be stocked with Pacific salmon. A mix of chinook and coho wait for the weir to be opened to allow for passage upriver.

to get out of the boat and pull it out over the bar. It's a fact at all fishing areas of the Great Lakes that conditions can change very quickly, so anglers—especially those in small craft—should train themselves to constantly monitor wind shifts or other signals of changing weather.

Chinook are normally the earliest species to show up here, followed by coho and some steelhead. In the spring, this area fishes well for browns, steelhead, lake trout, and the odd remaining coho. Action can start as soon as open water shows at the river mouth. Fish will hang around the area until mid-May or so, when they will move offshore to feed and find more comfortable water temperatures. Fly-fishing opportunities can last well into October, with lake trout the latest species to appear. Brown trout may also be encountered at just about any time.

This is also a place for wonderful scenery, with fabulous sunsets and Sleeping Bear dunes vistas. In 2011, viewers of ABC's *Good Morning America* voted this area "The Most Beautiful Place in America." There are also plenty of activities to keep nonanglers busy: hiking, biking, canoeing, and general sightseeing. And the shoreline towns have quaint harbor areas for shopping and dining.

Grand Traverse and Little Traverse Bays

Just a few years ago, Traverse City, Michigan, was selected as one of the top fly-fishing towns in the United States by *Fly Rod and Reel* magazine. Sitting on Lake Michigan's Grand Traverse Bay, the city offers a multitude of opportunities for local and visiting gear anglers, but until very recently, nearshore fly fishing has been pretty much ignored.

Grand Traverse Bay covers some 320 square miles and has more than a hundred miles of shoreline. It features extensive hard, white sand flats; rocky points and drop-offs; river mouths; weed beds; and just about any kind of fish-attracting structure imaginable. Anglers can target both warmwater and coldwater species here. What has kept the bay out of the fly-fishing limelight has been its proximity to some of the top fly-fishing rivers and streams in the Great Lakes area.

Thanks to the efforts of several local anglers and guides, the fly-fishing bounty of the bay is becoming better-known and explored, but its full potential has yet to be discovered. In terms of seasonal fishing opportunities, nearshore prospects extend from ice-out in the spring to ice-up in the winter. Whenever there is open water on the bay during that period, there will be something to fish for.

River-mouth areas and places where seeps or springs enter the bay are the first to lose ice in the spring. These will be a few degrees warmer than surrounding lake water and will attract brown trout, lake trout, steelhead, coho salmon, and the odd northern pike. Techniques and fly patterns for these fish are the same as those discussed previously; recall that they are usually hungry and ready to grab any reasonable fly pattern, such as a Deep Minnow, Half and Half, and even a Woolly Bugger. Often the key to success is simply being at a location when the fish are there.

The Boardman River, which enters the bay in downtown Traverse City, is the largest tributary entering the West Bay. There is easy access to the river mouth right off Route 31; there is also a boat launch a short distance from the lake. Because of the Boardman's urban surroundings, it is heavily fished. Because migratory fish are

The author on Lake Michigan's Grand Traverse Bay. Fishing kayaks are useful for exploring the nearshore waters of the Great Lakes. JON RAY

always on the move, a day—sometime even an hour—can mean the difference between angling success and disappointment. As with all fishing in river mouths, tackling the Boardman is best done first thing in the morning or on cloudy, dreary days, when gamefish are most likely to hold longer in the shallows.

The East Bay is fed by several small tributaries; Mitchell Creek, Acme Creek, and Yuba Creek all attract fish. They can be reached from the Dock Road Launch and Acme Township Park off Route 31. Anglers can walk the bay shoreline as long as they stay in the water. Note that there is a lot of recreational activity here in the summer. There is generally less before Memorial Day and after Labor Day, although warm, clear weather may attract crowds in the off-season.

The Elk River at the town of Elk Rapids is also a top Grand Traverse Bay location. There is a dam here just a short way from the lake, and its steady outflow feeds the marina basin area. The flow from the dam attracts a wide range of fish, and you can never be sure which ones will be present on any given day. This area is good for shore fishing, and a launch ramp gives quick access to the marina basin and channel leading to the bay.

Based on water volume, the Elk River is the largest tributary entering Grand Traverse Bay. In addition to the main dam outflow, there is also a secondary river outlet that attracts some fish. Access to the main bay area is by way of beach areas on either side of the channel that leads to the lake. Many places can be fished on foot, but a float tube, canoe, kayak, or small boat offers more versatility. This holds true for most areas of the bay that are open to watercraft.

Along Route 22 on the West Bay, anglers can use a launch ramp at Elmwood Township Park, close to where the outlet of Cedar Lake enters the bay. Farther north, the harbors at Suttons Bay and Northport both have launch ramps and are worth exploring.

Grand Traverse and Little Traverse Bays Essentials

Primary Species and Peak Times

Chinook salmon: mid-August–September
Coho salmon: September, October
Steelhead: ice-out–May, October, November
Smallmouth bass: May, June, July
Carp: mid-May–mid-July

Useful Fly Patterns

Salmon

Flashtail Deceiver #1; chartreuse-pink,
   chartreuse-orange
Glo Pigs
Great Lakes Deceivers; glow-in-the-dark
   colors
Chartreuse and White Glow

Steelhead

Phantom Minnow
High and Tight Baitfish
Bobble Head Baitfish
Half and Half #1-2; chartreuse-white
Ice-Out Alewife

Smallmouth Bass

Deep Minnow #1-4; chartreuse-white
Fox Tail Minnow
Coyote Clouser
Goblin
EZ Craw
RL Sculpin/Bugger

Carp

Bay Toad
Ted's Swimming Hex
Brown Barred Clouser

Fly Shops, Guides, Information

The Northern Angler
thenorthernangler.com
231-933-4730

Capt. Jon Ray
Hawkins Outfitters
hawkinsflyfishing.com
231-228-7135

Capt. Jon Kestner
jonsguideservice.com
877-636-5063

Ted Kraimer
current-works.com
231-883-8156

Capt. Leo Wright
leowrightguideservice.com
616-302-0558

Books & Publications

Flyfisher's Guide to Michigan by Jim Bedford
Michigan Atlas and Gazetteer
   by DeLorme Publishing
Michigan Blue-Ribbon Fly-Fishing Guide
   by Bob Linsenman

Start by throwing alewife and smelt patterns. Early in the spring, the warmest water is close to the surface, where both bait and predators will be cruising, so use an intermediate line or even a floating line with a long leader. If a standard baitfish fly is not getting results, try a bright attractor. If that doesn't work, go to something dark—maybe even a simple black Woolly Bugger. Be sure to cover the color spectrum before giving up and moving on.

Once the water temperature reaches the high 40s, pre-spawn smallmouth will move to the drop-offs adjacent to spawning areas. A sinking-tip line and an assortment of baitfish and goby imitator patterns can be thrown. An 8-weight outfit is the norm to handle the larger flies often used at this time. The best way to reach the

Capt. Jon Ray shows a carp from Lake
Michigan's Grand Traverse Bay. The bays
shallows are easy to wade, and the light-
colored bottom aids in spotting fish. JON RAY

This chinook hit a Flashtail Deceiver, a bright,
flashy pattern with lots of movement, in a river
mouth. Great Lakes chinook are a challenge to
catch on flies before they enter spawning
rivers, but they are great fighters when hooked.
JON RAY

drop-offs is usually by watercraft, but there are a few areas where shorebound and wading anglers can score.

Beyond the pre-spawn period, Elk Rapids may be the best season-long small-mouth area in the bay, with shore access as well as several rocky points adjacent to deep water that can be reached by wading. Don't overlook the various river and creek mouths or the marina and harbor areas; basically anywhere there are rocks, you will find bass.

In both East and West Bay areas, you will find a very visible drop-off, from hard, white sand to deeper blue water. Any rock, cinderblock anchor, or other such structure along the drop attract smallies. It also pays to check out cuts, sharp turns, or corners on the drop-off itself.

If an earlier angler has not already gotten to them on the day you are fishing, bass here are often quite easy to tempt to a fly. Cast close to the promising drop-off spots, let the fly sink, and then begin your retrieve. Bass will often hold in the shadows but scoot out to grab an easy meal. Clouser-style flies work well for this. All-white, char-treuse-white, and the Coyote Clouser are the main colors you will want to try.

Once the bass move up onto spawning beds, they are easily spotted and caught. On the hard, white sand of the bay, beds may show up as darker spots on the bottom, often in only a foot or two of water. Michigan's special catch-and-immediate-release season allows bass to be targeted during this spawning period. As long as fish are not removed from the area where they are caught, they will move right back to the bed after release. Fishing for smallmouth at this time is a matter of personal choice.

Most of the shoreline along both the West and East Bays is accessible from roadside rest areas, township parks, and beaches. Michigan law permits anglers to walk the shoreline as long as they stay below the high-water line and have entered the water at a public location.

Either a floating- or intermediate-tip line can be used. With the floating line, a leader of 10 to 12 feet will hold the fly on the bottom a bit better. A good technique is to get a standard bass leader of 9 feet, tapered to a 10- or 12-pound tippet. Add about 2 feet of 10-pound fluorocarbon tippet and you have a very serviceable leader.

On calm evenings, you may also get bass to come up for a surface bug. Once you locate bedding areas, cast right over top. Let the fly sit for a minute or more and then give the slightest twitch. Let the fly sit and then give it a slight twitch again. Takes are often very deliberate, with the fish rising slowly under the fly, pausing, and then gently sucking it in. Vary the fly size here: panfish-size bugs generally work the best. Young-of-the-year baitfish have just started to hatch, and smallmouth can get really keyed on miniature flies during this period.

Carp have actually become the biggest draw for fly anglers on Traverse Bay flats. From mid-May to early July, they are the prime target. Some of these fish are true monsters—in the 30-pound range. A big carp on a hard, white flat sticks out like a sore thumb; it can be seen from a hundred or more yards away.

It's usually best to cast to singles or small pods of fish, because larger schools are often on the move and not so interested in eating. There are also a lot more eyes in large schools, so a greater chance that a movement or line flash will give the angler away. A sunny day gives the best visibility for catching carp—also the best opportunity for carp to see the line and flee.

Most of these flats are two- to three-feet deep, in some places a bit deeper. An intermediate-tip line is often favored by anglers here to help hold the fly down and make the line less visible. Again, a 10-pound fluorocarbon tippet is the norm to present a variety of creepy-crawly offerings that resemble crayfish and Hex nymphs.

It's best to cast to tailing fish if you can, but cruisers sometimes will take a fly. Hits are usually seen rather than felt, so you need to watch a fish and how it is reacting. Often you won't be able to see the fly, but if you see the fish dart forward and flare it gills, or make a quick turn of its head, there is a good chance it grabbed the fly. Tighten up, and, if you feel weight, strip-strike and get ready. Once a big carp realizes it is hooked, the fun begins.

Carp begin to move off the flats in early July, as deeper water begins to warm and they can find a comfortable temperature to feed in. Carp-fishing at Mission Point often lasts a bit longer; it is in the open and takes longer to warm up. There is plenty of hard bottom with scattered rock and stone, which makes Mission Point another key location for smallmouth as well as for carp.

The heat of summer is the slowest period for fly fishing Grand Traverse Bay. Most fish have moved off to deeper water, where they are hard to reach. However, the Elk Rapids area, with its extensive rocky flats and influx of water from the dam, will continue to hold decent numbers of smallmouth. Work the edge of the drop-offs leading to deep water, where bass work along the edge of the shallows in search of food. The marina there will also have a few largemouth and pike hanging around the abundant weed beds.

In late August and early September, chinook salmon will move in toward the river mouths in anticipation of spawning. Coaxing a Great Lakes chinook to eat a fly can be a challenge, but the earliest fish moving to spawn can be quite aggressive and

Launching at Petoskey, Michigan, harbor. Most towns along the lakes have well-maintained boat ramps.

will hit flies. Experience has shown they respond best during a short, predawn time frame, or for short periods of time after the sun sets.

Local guide and angler Russ Maddin chases chinook with flies every fall at bay river mouths. He prefers to go after them during low-water periods when the salmon are congregating at these locations, waiting for the next push of high water to ascend the spawning streams. Maddin fishes flies with both flash and color, and he finds that the "hot pattern" may not be the same from year to year. However, the Flashtail Deceiver has been a consistent producer for him.

As the chinook numbers decrease, coho and steelhead numbers increase. Cohos are naturally later spawners than chinook, and steelhead are following the chinook in to feast on eggs. They usually begin to enter rivers in early October. In addition to baitfish patterns, Egg Sucking Leeches and other bright/dark contrast flies will often work for them.

There are a few lake-run browns that enter bay streams, but they are unpredictable. Some will run in September, others not until December, without any real pattern. Lake trout will move inshore to feed when the water temperature drops below 50 degrees. After two to three weeks, they will then move to offshore reef areas to spawn. Generally, nearshore areas of the bay start to ice up in December, shutting down fly fishing.

Capt. Jon Ray, of Hawkins Outfitters, offer fly-fishing guide services on Grand Traverse Bay. Ted Kraimer, of Current Works, LLC, leads walk and wade trips on the bay. The web site of Capt. Jon Kestner, of Jon's Guide Service, features write-ups about smallmouth and carp fly fishing on Grand Traverse Bay that anglers will find interesting and informative. Kestner also gives some good general information about bay-access areas for wading and launching boats.

Although much smaller, Little Traverse Bay, a bit farther north, offers a fishing season that reflects the pattern of Grand Traverse Bay. The Bear River enters the bay right in the town of Petoskey. Shore-fishing opportunities are much more limited here. Little Traverse does a public launch area, and it is best fished by boat. Capt. Leo Wright offers guided trips for this area.

The Big and Little Traverse Bay areas are among the top vacation destinations and recreational areas of Michigan, whether both anglers and nonanglers can find a wide range of activities to keep them busy. Stream and river fly fishing has been the mainstay in this area, but more anglers are beginning to take notice of the big-water fly-fishing opportunities. The scenery and water are beautiful here. For anyone looking to combine a family vacation with fishing, this area would be hard to beat.

North End

The north end of Lake Michigan is an angler's paradise. A fly-fishing presence here has been minimal at best, but it is now growing thanks to the efforts of a few pioneering guides such as Capt. Kevin Morlock, Capt. Brad Petzke, and Capt. Leo Wright. More fly anglers are interested in experiencing the bounty that it offers. The areas presented in this book are by no means the only places to explore with a fly rod. These are simply the places already known to hold promise for fly fishers.

Beaver Island, the largest island in Lake Michigan, has a colorful history: it was once a Mormon settlement ruled by an eccentric leader who declared himself king. From a fishing perspective, in the 1880s, Beaver Island was the largest supplier in the United States of freshwater fish for consumption as food. Today, it is a popular tourist and vacation destination, with a growing reputation in the fly-fishing community.

The island covers about 56 square miles and lies about 32 miles from the mainland city of Charlevoix, Michigan. It can be reached only by air or water. Several local airlines fly to the island, and a scheduled ferry service runs from Charlevoix, Michigan, from April through December. Beaver Island has about 600 year-round residents.

A rich Gaelic heritage can be found on Beaver Island; many of the original commercial fishermen came from Ireland, in particular, from County Donegal. A number of the island's permanent residents are of Irish descent, and Beaver is often referred to as America's Emerald Isle.

Beaver Island emerged onto the fly-fishing scene several years ago after Michigan guide Capt. Kevin Morlock, of Indigo Guide Service, set up shop there during the summer months. Morlock had been scouting the area for a number of years and came to realize that it offered some of the best flats-fishing opportunities in the Great Lakes. A number of smaller islands are part of the Beaver archipelago, and between them, they provide extensive areas of shallow, crystal-clear flats.

Carp are the main quarry here, and the area around Beaver Island abounds with them—some reaching epic proportions. Though carp are easy to spot on the shallow flats, getting them to strike a fly is an altogether different matter. Successful angling here requires accurate presentations after a careful, stealthy approach—and moody carp may still refuse a fly.

Wilderness State Park, at the top of Michigan's Lower Peninsula, offers anglers miles of shoreline access along Lake Michigan.

Fly patterns are usually creepy-crawly creations with varying amounts of weight, depending on depth, current, and wind conditions. Great descriptions and recipes of the carp flies that Morlock and the Indigo crew use at Beaver Island can be found on their web site. In addition, the site also has links to several helpful articles with detailed information about how to fish the area.

Hooking a carp is only part of the excitement for a fly angler. Many of these fish will be 20 pounds or more in size, and while they may not bring the fast runs and jumps of a steelhead to the contest, a big carp will make long, dogged runs and test tackle to its max. A minimum 8-weight rod is necessary, along with a matching reel loaded with 200 yards of backing.

With respect to other species, smallmouth bass are making a steady comeback around Beaver Island after controls were enacted to reduce cormorant populations in the area. Bass fishing was legendary here for decades until a population increase of the fish-eating birds resulted in a significant decline in the number of smallmouth. The slow-growing, localized smallmouth populations were vulnerable to a quick decline, but they have now increased to the point where they can be a target. However, it should be noted that smallmouth cannot be specifically targeted until the season officially opens on July 1.

Smallmouth are often found in the same areas as carp and will often hit the same flies. Likewise, standard bass patterns may also attract carp. Many of the Beaver archipelago "smallies" will actually be quite large, because these are the ones that have been big enough to avoid cormorant predation.

This area used to have substantial northern pike and perch fisheries that likewise fell victim to the cormorants. These species are also slowly recovering. Anglers fishing deeper drop-off areas may also encounter transient salmon and trout as they make their way around the lake following baitfish.

North End Essentials

Primary Species and Peak Times

Steelhead and brown trout: ice-out–May
Salmon: mid-August–mid-October
Northern pike: ice-out–May
Smallmouth bass: mid-May–July
Carp: mid-May–July

Useful Fly Patterns

Trout

Deep Minnow #1-4; chartreuse-white, gray-
   white
Phantom Minnow
Ice-Out Alewife

Salmon

Great Lakes Deceiver; glow colors
Flashtail Deceiver
Glo Pig
Chartreuse and White Glow

Northern Pike

Great Lakes Deceiver; red-white, chartreuse-
   orange
Figure 8 #3/0; perch and fire tiger
Meatwagon Max; perch and fire tiger

Smallmouth Bass

Deep Minnow #1-4; chartreuse-white
Coyote Clouser #1-4
Crawpin #1; olive and brown
Todd's Wiggle Minnow #1; black, fire tiger

Carp

Simpleech
Coyote Ugly
Sexy Hexy
Ted's Swimming Hex

Fly Shops, Guides, Information

Capt. Kevin Morlock

indigoguideservice.com
231-898-4320

Capt. Brad Petzke

riversnorth.net
906-458-8125

Capt. Leo Wright

leowrightguideservice.com
616-302-0558

Books & Publications

Flyfisher's Guide to Michigan by Jim Bedford
Michigan Atlas and Gazetteer
   by DeLorme Publishing

Though the reputation of the region is growing, on any given day, fewer than a handful of anglers are working the miles of shallow shoreline areas around the Beaver Island archipelago. This area has so much to offer, including a fly-fishing experience rivaling Caribbean saltwater scenarios. Sight casting to large fish in shallow water—just as in the tropics—is the name of the game at Beaver Island.

For the do-it-yourselfer, both Beaver Island Marina and the Bill Wagner Memorial Campground have launch ramps where you can drop in your own boat if you trailer it over on the ferry. If you do have plans to take a boat to the island, be sure to make reservations at least 6 months in advance. Car space sells out quickly for the peak summer season. The Beaver Island Boat Company can be reached at 1-888-446-4095 or through their web site, www.bibco.com.

Much of the island is state-owned, and many places along the shoreline road can be reached by driving or biking. A kayak or other small craft can be quickly and easily launched in many areas. The best fishing for carp on the main island is in June; by July, many of the fish have moved to outlying areas that can be reached only by boat.

Little Bay de Noc and Big Bay de Noc both open into Lake Michigan opposite Wisconsin's Green Bay. In a sense, they are extensions of Green Bay. Escanaba, one of the larger cities on Michigan's Upper Peninsula, is here; it is a focal point for a full range of outdoor activity. Fly fishing in the area has been minimal, and this is another locale where more fly anglers are needed to get out there and start exploring. Capt. Brad Petzke, of Rivers North Fly Fishing Guide Service, has been exploring these waters for a number of years and offers guided fly-fishing trips.

The area is well known to the gear-fishing community as a hot spot for walleye fishing and trolling for salmon and trout. A growing smallmouth bass population is also beginning to attract widespread attention. Northern pike are available in good numbers, and largemouth bass may also be encountered in some places. Flats-fishing for carp in this area was mentioned several decades ago in the book *Carp Are Gamefish* by George Von Schrader, but only a handful of anglers are presently chasing them.

The ridge that created the islands at the tip of Wisconsin's Door County continues across to Michigan. There are additional islands on the Michigan side, and then the ridge emerges as the Garden Peninsula that separates Little and Big Bay de Noc from the main part of Lake Michigan. The peninsula has more than 200 miles of shoreline comprised of rocky bluffs, sand beaches, and shallow, weedy bays.

The Michigan shoreline area from Menominee north to Escanaba features several river mouths with both shoreline and small-boat access. Both the Cedar River and the Bark River technically flow into Green Bay, but because they are well into Michigan, I have included them here. Both have steelhead in the spring, and salmon and browns in the fall, along with the possible appearance of lake trout and splake. Smallmouth bass and pike are available during the summer months.

A large school of carp moves along a shallow edge. These fish are in a pocket of warmer water that has been pushed up along the shore by the winds. LEO WRIGHT

This carp was caught near Waugoshance Point in Wilderness State Park. This area has both wading and boat access for anglers.

Sight fishing for big smallmouth bass is possible throughout much of the Great Lakes area. The northern end of Lake Michigan has miles of rocky shallows that provide an exciting fly-fishing opportunity.

The Ford River just south of Escanaba provides a similar mix of seasonal warmwater and coldwater species. As an added twist, the Ford seems to get a run of smallmouth bass from Green Bay in its lower reaches in the summer. Fishing a variety of crayfish and baitfish patterns here can produce smallies in excess of 4 pounds. In late August and early September, salmon show up and provide the opportunity for fishing an interesting species mix.

In terms of access, Ludington Park in Escanaba has a boat launch and fishing pier: the North Shore Boat Launch on the Escanaba River is one of the biggest in the state. In addition, there is a wooden walkway that goes through the wetlands along the river, connecting a series of fishing piers. This walkway gives access to most of the lower river area all the way to its mouth in Little Bay de Noc. The usual seasonal mix of species is available here.

North of Escanaba, just upstream of where Route 2 crosses the river, there is convenient public access below the dam controlled by the Upper Peninsula Power Company. This is the first barrier that fish hit as they travel upriver, and it will concentrate any of the migratory species. During the summer, expect to find a mix of warmwater species, with smallmouth bass the most abundant. Fall and spring attract a mix of salmon and trout.

The towns of Gladstone, Kipling, and Rapid River all have bayside launch areas. Smallmouth bass and northern pike are the main fly-rod targets here; migratory fish can be found at river-mouth and harbor areas as they stage to enter spawning streams. The lower Whitefish River, from Route 2 to the bay, is excellent for northern pike and also for white bass during their spring spawning run. The lower stretch is all private shoreline, so you would need to get to this area from the Rapid River boat launch or from one of the several private campgrounds.

Beaching a carp hooked on the lee side of a point on a windy day. KEVIN MORLOCK

On the east side of the bay, the only public launch ramp is at Hunter's Point in the Little Bay de Noc Recreation Area. The small town of Stonington is farther south along County Road 513. There is personal watercraft access to the shore in the area. At the end of County Road 513 is the Point Peninsula Lighthouse, a site administered by the U.S. Forest Service, with access to an extensive area of shoreline, along with a place to carry in kayaks and canoes.

Capt. Brad Petzke shows a fish hooked off Lake Michigan's Garden Peninsula. BRAD PETZKE

Big Bay de Noc also has a number of boat-launch and access areas spread along its shoreline. The Ogontz Bay launch is an area with productive water for northern pike, smallmouth, and perch. There are also several shallow areas where carp sometimes cruise.

There is additional access across the bay at the towns of Nahma and Garden. There is also access at the mouth of the Little Fishdam River. Garden Bay is a great area to explore by kayak; it also provides a more sheltered setting if it is too rough to venture out to the main bay. Smallmouth bass and northern pike are the mainstay here, along with a variety of panfish—including rock bass and yellow perch.

This area is part of the Garden Peninsula that extends to the southwest from the mainland. The tip of the peninsula is considered one of the top carp-fishing areas in the Great Lakes. During late June, July, and August, schools of carp cruise the shallows around the tip of the peninsula and the Summer Islands. This was one of George Von Schrader's favorite areas for consistent flats action. There are plenty of smallmouth around, along with pike.

Beaver Island is located in northern Lake Michigan. Its colorful history and isolated location make it an interesting fishing location. KEVIN MORLOCK

Fayette State Park is the main jumping-off point to reach the tip of the Garden Peninsula by boat. This historic park features the preserved remains of the iron-smelting facility that existed here in the late nineteenth century. The park has a launch ramp and a small, sheltered marina, along with camping facilities and recreational options.

Route 183 traverses the west side of the Garden Peninsula, offering many places along the bay where an angler can park, take a quick walk to the water, and wade in and explore. Just make sure you are not crossing private property to reach the water. County Road 483 goes to the tip of the peninsula, ending at Fairport. Several small, private launches here can provide access to the Summer Islands just offshore.

The town of Manistique is just east of the Garden Peninsula. With a small, picturesque harbor, pier and breakwall access, and a boat launch, this spot at the mouth of the Manistique River is considered one of the most productive harbor and river-mouth areas on the north shore of Lake Michigan. Smallmouth bass, pike, salmon, and trout are available seasonally. A short way upriver is a favorite area for anglers: a dam that serves to concentrate migratory fish.

There are many fishy waters along Route 2 from Manistique to St. Ignace: Dutch Johns Point, Seul Choix Point, Scott Point, Naubinway, Epoufette Bay, and Pointe Aux Chenes areas all offer possibilities for smallmouth, northern pike, and carp. River-mouth areas attract a variety of species in fall and spring. Public and private launch areas, and campgrounds, beach, and park areas all provide access.

Across the Straits of Mackinac in Michigan's Lower Peninsula, Wilderness State Park, just west of Mackinaw City, has more than 26 miles of shoreline on Lake Michigan, much of it easily wadable. The area has seen some fly fishing over the last decade or so, with anglers concentrating on the area from the end of the park road out to Waugoshance Point.

This five-mile stretch is a myriad of shallow flats, coves, rock bars, and several cuts between islands that give easy access to the north or south side of the point. The Sturgeon Bay area has particular appeal to anglers because it offers protection from nearly any hard wind. From mid-May to mid-July, smallmouth bass can be found here when they move into the shallows to spawn. Carp are found in the shallows during the early summer. Northern pike are also caught regularly, especially early in the season.

Fishing this area requires a bit of planning, and anglers should be in decent physical condition. Although the terrain is flat, much of the walking will be on loose sand, in and out of water. Be sure to take an adequate supply of drinking water with you; once you leave the parking area, you are on your own, without any options for obtaining more. Mosquitoes and black flies can also be a problem during much of June, so be prepared with a head net or bug dope.

Both kayaks and canoes can be used here to quickly cover shoreline areas. The new, stand-up-style fishing kayaks are particularly good for this area because they allow the angler to see further when standing. It is even possible to paddle up one side of the point, cross at one of the channels between the islands, and then paddle back the other. Kayaks can be carried to the shoreline from a parking area on the north side, just before the end of Waugoshance Point Road, which goes to the point.

To reach the south side of the point, go a bit farther to the turnaround and then follow the south trail to the water. This is a walk of several hundred yards. This may seem like a lot of work, but it can be well worth the effort for an adventurous angler: a reward of white sand, crystal-clear water, and scenery more reminiscent of the Bahamas than northern Michigan. The fishing can seem like an extra bonus.

If you decide to fish this area, in addition to taking plenty of water, carry a GPS to mark the parking area and keep track of the distance back to your car. This gives extra security, and can help you time your return to avoid having to walk back in the dark or rush to reach the parking area. Treat this outing as a true wilderness experience. To get a taste of what's ahead if you fish here, take a look at the map of the area (http://www.michigandnr.com/publications/pdfs/RecreationCamping/wilderness_map.pdf) that is available online.

There is a boat launch on Big Stone Bay for larger motorized craft. From here it is easy to make the run west to Waugoshance Point itself. A short way off the point is the old lighthouse, which was built in 1851 and abandoned in 1912. The light from the lighthouse was used for bombing practice in World War II. An angler might expect this offshore shoal to be full of smallmouth bass, perch, and other species, but the legions of cormorants living here have consumed anything of edible size.

If you have a larger craft, make sure you have a chart of the area to avoid grounding. The bottom is visible when there is sun to highlight the water color at different depths, but in low-light or overcast conditions, it is extremely difficult to see the bottom. Caution and a good chart will help avoid a potentially dangerous and costly situation.

The south side of Waugoshance Point was noted as a "guaranteed" carp spot by Great Lakes carp fishing pioneer George Von Schrader. Large flat slabs of white limestone cover the bottom, extending from the shallows out to deeper water. Large carp are easily visible over the white bottom, while marauding smallmouth hide in cuts and crevices waiting to ambush unsuspecting prey.

This is also an area that can see significant hatches of *Hexagenia* and Brown Drake mayflies from mid-June to mid-July. Both carp and smallmouth may rise to feed on these on calm, overcast evenings.

One of my most interesting Great Lakes flats-fishing experiences took place here with Capt. Leo Wright. We were slowly working our way back toward the launch area when a disturbance in a slick of calm water caught our attention. Moving in quietly for a closer view, we saw a small group of carp on the surface, sucking in the nymph shucks left by emerging Hexes. While Capt. Leo moved us into position to cast, I tied on a surface Hex pattern.

When I made my first two casts to the closest fish, it changed directions just as I cast each time, moving away from the fly. On the third cast, the fly landed about two feet in front of the cruising fish. A large carp head came totally out of the water as it inhaled the fly. Ten minutes later, after several strong runs, a 16-pound Lake Michigan carp was secured by the Boga-Grip. The other fish were spooked by the disturbance, but I had taken my first-ever surface-feeding Great Lakes carp.

Capt. Leo has also found that smallmouth will come up out of deeper water all summer long to cruise the edges of the shallows, looking for food. When wind and light conditions are right (low wind, high sun), it is possible to spot and cast to these fish with a good chance of success. A favorite pattern for this is one we call the Coyote Clouser. This Deep Minnow variant is tied with coyote tail fur, so the brownish-tan color scheme simulates a small goby, crayfish, sculpin, or possibly even a Hex nymph.

Wilderness State Park has camping facilities and cabins for rent. There is a swimming beach and a small store for necessities. Mackinaw City is close by, with abundant lodging, shopping, food, and plenty of activity for the entire family. Capt. Leo Wright guides anglers to a variety of fly-fishing opportunities in northern Michigan.

Wisconsin Shoreline

Despite a good portion of the area being industrialized and populated, the Wisconsin shoreline of Lake Michigan provides an amazing assortment of fly-fishing opportunities. These can vary from true urban settings, such as Milwaukee Harbor, to hard-to-reach areas on the Door County peninsula. In addition, a series of power plants along the coast—several of which can be accessed quite easily—attract a variety of gamefish throughout the year.

It is hard to focus on just one or two locations, because this area has so much to offer. The larger cities and towns, including Milwaukee, Racine, and Sheboygan, have harbor areas with fishing platforms as well as piers and breakwalls that serve as fish-attracting structure. Before moving onto any one of these, make sure that it is available for public access and that it is open to anglers. Some have limited access and others may belong to a private marina or other business.

Most harbor areas are located where a tributary enters the lake, and these will have seasonal runs of fish from Lake Michigan returning to spawn. Generally, these will be brown trout, and chinook and coho salmon in the fall, and steelhead in the spring. There may also be a chance for lake trout early and late in the season. These

This brown hit a goby pattern swung on a sinking-tip line in the discharge current from a Wisconsin power plant.

seasonal fish will often stage in the deeper harbor areas adjacent to the river mouth before ascending tributaries. At ice-out, brown trout will also congregate in these areas to feed before heading out into the lake. Warmwater species like northern pike and smallmouth bass are often available in the summer.

These areas are best covered by throwing streamer patterns on some sort of a sinking-tip or sinking, shooting-taper system. Fly patterns vary with sea-

Great Lakes brown trout have found gobies to be a great food source and readily strike flies that imitate them.

sons and species. Chinooks should be targeted with baitfish patterns like the Great Lakes Deceiver or larger versions of the Bad Hair Day in alewife colors. A Deep Minnow size 1/0 in all-white or gray-white is also a good choice.

Browns, cohos, and steelhead will respond to a variety of patterns, including baitfish, gobies, and crayfish. Try Bad Hair Days in alewife colors, along with the Ice-Out Alewife and Deep Minnows. The Crawpin and Bad Hair Days in darker colors imitate crayfish and gobies. I have also had good success here with my Arctic Wiggler tube pattern in both lighter and darker colors.

It often takes an erratic, jerky retrieve, simulating a crippled baitfish, to trigger strikes from chinook and steelhead. Browns and coho seem to respond well to a standard strip retrieve.

Wisconsin Shoreline Essentials

Primary Species and Peak Times

Steelhead and brown trout: ice-out–May, October, November, also when flip occurs

Chinook salmon: mid-August, September, when flip occurs

Coho salmon: ice-out–May, September, October, when flip occurs

Northern pike: ice-out–May, September, October

Smallmouth bass: May, June

Useful Fly Patterns

Steelhead and Brown Trout
Deep Minnows #1-4; all-white, gray-white
Ice-Out Alewife
Bad Hair Days; light and dark colors
Arctic Wiggler; light and dark colors

Chinook Salmon
Great Lakes Deceiver in white, chartreuse-white
Half and Half #1/0, #1; white, chartreuse-white
Ice-Out Alewife

Coho Salmon
Ice-Out Alewife
Bad Hair Day; light and dark colors
Arctic Wiggler; light and dark colors
Bart-O-Minnow

Northern Pike
Great Lakes Deceiver
Figure 8 #3/0
Meatwagon Max; red-white, perch, fire tiger

Smallmouth Bass
Deep Minnow #1-4; chartreuse-white
Coyote Clouser
Bart-O-Minnow
Crawpin; olive and brown
Crazi Craw

Fly Shops, Guides, Information

The Fly Fishers
West Allis, WI
theflyfishers.com
414-259-8100

Tight Lines Fly Fishing
De Pere, WI
tightlinesflyshop.com
920-336-4106

Trout & Grouse
Northbrook, IL
troutandgrouse.com
847-480-0111

Dave Pinczkowski
dpheron@aol.com
414-412-1838

Capt. Brad Petzke
riversnorth.net
906-458-8125

Books & Publications

Fly Fisher's Guide to Wisconsin and Iowa by John Motoviloff

Wisconsin Atlas and Gazetteer by DeLorme Publishing

On the warmwater side, for northern pike, try the same flies you would use for chinook. Smallmouth often eat flies similar to those used for browns and steelhead. None of this is written in stone, so don't be afraid to experiment.

Also, remember to keep the "flip" phenomenon in mind when selecting a place to fish. As described earlier, sustained west winds will bring cold water to the shoreline on this side of the lake. Trout and salmon will often follow this coldwater movement and come within reach even during midsummer. This phenomenon can be very localized and is totally dependent on the wind direction, duration, and velocity.

The Lake Michigan Angler web site (www.lakemichiganangler.com) provides very useful information on nearly every harbor area around the lake, including action reports, weather reports, and lake conditions. Although its focus is on gear and bait fishing, it is a great tool to research areas for fly-fishing potential.

North of the Illinois border, the harbor areas of both Kenosha, at the mouth of the Pike River, and Racine, at the mouth of the Root River, offer great opportunities, with piers and breakwalls that make it possible to fish both open lake and inner harbor areas. A small boat or kayak is also very useable in either location.

Despite being a large metropolitan area, the city of Milwaukee offers an interesting assortment of angling prospects. With an area of 2,400 acres, Milwaukee Harbor itself is arguably one of the top urban fisheries around anywhere. It is best known for its trophy-sized brown trout. Throw salmon and steelhead into the mix—along with a growing resident smallmouth bass population, northern pike, and perch—and you have plenty to keep fly anglers busy.

The harbor, at the mouth of the Milwaukee River, receives numerous warmwater discharges. It remains open except during the coldest weather. With prevailing westerly winds, the "flip" phenomenon pushes colder water from the depths of Lake Michigan back toward the Wisconsin shoreline. This can hold steelhead, browns, and salmon closer to shore, and sometimes these fish can be found in the harbor itself, even during the hottest months of summer.

As a large harbor with only several small outlets to the lake, Milwaukee Harbor can experience very noticeable seiche currents, depending on wind strength and direction—sometimes strong enough to cause fish to take up feeding stations as they would during tidal flows. It pays to be aware of seiche currents any time you fish nearshore areas across the Great Lakes, because they can have a significant influence locally.

Brown trout are the primary target of Milwaukee harbor anglers, and they are available in good numbers for about nine months out of the year. From mid-June to mid-September, most will be out in the lake itself, although some may be pulled back into harbor entrances by when flip occurs. There is fishing access by means of numerous piers and walkways around the harbor. In addition, there are several launch ramps for small boats and kayaks: McKinley Marina is the largest of these. Lakeshore State Park has shore-fishing access, and shoreline areas can also be reached from Veterans Park.

North of Milwaukee, the quaint town of Port Washington provides shoreline and pier access, as well as a sheltered harbor for small boats, kayaks, and even float tubes. The nearby Wisconsin Energy Corporation power plant helps to moderate water temperatures in both early and late season. Warmwater discharges attract baitfish, which in turn attract predators. All Lake Michigan trout and salmon species are found here, along with smallmouth bass and northern pike.

The north breakwater provides the best opportunities for fly rodders, but both sides can be productive, depending on wind conditions and the time of year. From a fly-fishing standpoint, it is always easiest to fish the side with the least wind whenever possible. The inside areas hold more fish during the colder months, because baitfish are drawn to the warmer water. During warmer weather, work the lakeside areas of breakwalls, where the water is cooler.

This Milwaukee Harbor steelhead couldn't resist a stripped Arctic Wiggler tube fly. Though it is a true urban setting, the harbor provides a great opportunity to catch a variety of species, including steelhead, brown trout, salmon, and an assortment of warmwater species.

The city of Sheboygan is the next area of interest for big-water fly anglers. Here the Sheboygan River—arguably the best of the Wisconsin tributaries for migratory fish—enters Lake Michigan. Again, a breakwall and sheltered harbor area provide the opportunity to throw flies to the same mix of fish found elsewhere along Wisconsin's eastern shore. A boat launch at Deland Park allows small-boat anglers quick and easy access to the river.

The power plant just south of town is worth exploring; you can get there by walking the beach from Lakeview Park. Potential fishing spots include several easily reached warmwater discharge points, large flats that extend out from the discharge areas, and the shoreline south of the power plant.

A Menominee River brown. The river below the first dam attracts nearly every species of fish found in the Great Lakes. BRAD PETZKE

The next towns of interest, a little further north, are Manitowoc and Two Rivers. The shallows off the harbor marina in Manitowoc are wadable and can be productive for trout and salmon. A long breakwater that extends into Lake Michigan provides shorebound anglers the opportunity to walk and cast. Smallmouth can be found here in the summer. The USS Cobia, a World War II submarine built in Manitowoc, is on display in the harbor and open for tours.

The East and West Twin Rivers enter Lake Michigan at Two Rivers Harbor. Salmon, steelhead, brown trout, and lake trout can all be caught seasonally from both the north and south piers. Shoreline areas adjacent to the harbor can be waded, or fished by float tube. A significant number of large smallmouth bass also inhabit this harbor. Although ignored here as elsewhere by anglers targeting the "glamour" species of salmon and trout, it bears reminding that smallmouth are a good, available target during the summer months, when most coldwater species are offshore in deeper water.

The town of Kewaunee straddles the banks of the Kewaunee River. This Lake Michigan tributary receives heavy stockings of steelhead, brown trout, and chinook salmon. This is one of the better locations to target shoreline steelhead with a fly, because deep water comes in close to the breakwalls. The area inside the breakwalls can be waded from several locations; it can also be fished from kayaks and float tubes. One of the few Lake Michigan tributaries without any dams or obstructions, the Kewaunee serves as a brood-stock river for steelhead.

Algoma, at the mouth of the Ahnapee River, is the next stop up the coast and a top sportfishing port with a large charter-fishing fleet. There is a public launch ramp inside the harbor, and good access to the lower river. The gateway to the lake side of the Door County peninsula, Algoma features deep water that comes in close to shore and helps hold fish year-round.

Algoma offers good fishing opportunities for brown trout and steelhead in the fall and spring. The area's trophy-size northern pike—which can be found in the harbor area from ice-out into May,

This fall coho hit a leech pattern stripped by the author at a power plant discharge. Coho will aggressively hit attractor-style streamer patterns and are a great target for fly anglers.

and from late September until ice-up—receive little angler attention. The pike respond best to larger, flashy baitfish patterns and attractors. During the warmer months they likely move into deeper offshore waters.

From here we jump across the Door County peninsula to Green Bay, separated from Lake Michigan by Door County and Michigan's Garden Peninsula. Green Bay is 120 miles long and from 10 to 20 miles wide. The Fox River enters Lake Michigan at the city of Green Bay, and the area offers fly-fishing opportunities for an interesting assortment of warmwater species: smallmouth and largemouth bass, northern pike, muskellunge, freshwater drum, walleye, and panfish.

Anglers probably need some type of watercraft to be most effective here. There are a number of launch areas for small boats, but shore access is limited. This again brings us back to urban fishing, with piers, docks, riprap, and even old shopping carts providing cover. While not the most picturesque area, the quality of fishing is quite good, with smallmouth the primary target.

Continuing up the coast, the towns of Pensaukee and Oconto have picturesque harbor areas. Both are productive in the fall and spring for trout and salmon. They also have populations of smallmouth bass, northern pike, and walleye to fill the time between. Both have launch ramps that give instant access to the harbor areas, breakwalls, and bay.

The Peshtigo River enters Green Bay at the Green Bay Shores State Wildlife Area. A boat ramp at the mouth of the river gives access to Green Bay. Here are salmon and trout during seasonal migrations in the spring and fall; smallmouth bass and northern pike are year-round residents.

The Menominee River forms the border between Wisconsin and Michigan's Upper Peninsula. The twin cities of Marinette, Wisconsin, and Menominee, Michigan, are at the mouth of the river. The harbor itself is mostly deeper water, with limited shore access, best fished from a boat. The north pier gives the best access to anglers looking to fish the mouth of the river. The Hattie Street Dam, which prevents fish coming in from Green Bay from moving upriver, offers fly anglers the opportunity for great success below the dam when water levels are cooperative.

The Menominee holds a nice seasonal mix of fish species. In the fall, an angler may encounter salmon, steelhead, brown trout, lake trout, and splake. Guide Capt. Brad Petzke has landed as many as seven different species in one day of fishing flies here. Spring species include steelhead, along with possibilities for browns, lakers, and splake. The warmer months bring smallmouth bass, walleye, northern pike, muskellunge, and a variety of panfish.

There are several of public boat launch locations on both the Wisconsin and Michigan sides of the river. The River Park Boat Launch in Menominee gives access to the river itself, while the Marina Boat Launch is located on the lakeshore. The city of Marinette has launches at Red Arrow Park, Stephenson Island, Boom Landing Park, and Sixth Street. These locations also provide access to both the river and the Green Bay shoreline. This is another high-quality fishery in an accessible urban area whose opportunities have been hardly explored by fly anglers.

Chicago Metro Area

The Chicago metropolitan area has the largest population of any location on the U.S. border of the Great Lakes. In spite of its size and its identity as a major metropolitan area, Chicago offers fly-fishing opportunities that are both varied and abundant. From the north, these opportunities start just below the Wisconsin state line at Illinois Beach State Park, and continue south, and then east, past Gary, Indiana.

Jon Uhlenhop, the manager of Chicago Fly Fishing Outfitters, grew up in Waukegan, Illinois, and has fished the shoreline here with flies all his life. He is a wealth of information on the area for locations, species, timing, and fly patterns. The folks at Trout and Grouse in Northbrook, Illinois, can also help with the northern Chicago area and southern Wisconsin shoreline.

Uhlehop notes that winds out of the westerly area produce the best fishing for two reasons: First, the "flip" phenomenon brings cooler waters inshore during the summer. Second, wind from this direction also means the shoreline is providing protection from the wind, which will be generally at the angler's back when casting.

A combination of resident warmwater species and migratory coldwater species means anglers have a long time frame for fishing. Browns, coho, and steelhead action can kick off as early as March and continue through April; the same species will show up again in October. Both steelhead and browns will stay in the picture into December.

Smallmouth are active from April through June, as are carp in some areas. Perch and drum appear in May and remain through the summer. Warmwater discharges may move the timetable forward in localized areas. A sustained increase in water temperature in a given area can cause activity to start earlier in the year.

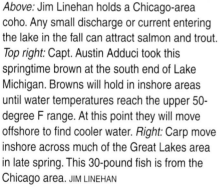

Above: Jim Linehan holds a Chicago-area coho. Any small discharge or current entering the lake in the fall can attract salmon and trout. *Top right:* Capt. Austin Adduci took this springtime brown at the south end of Lake Michigan. Browns will hold in inshore areas until water temperatures reach the upper 50-degree F range. At this point they will move offshore to find cooler water. *Right:* Carp move inshore across much of the Great Lakes area in late spring. This 30-pound fish is from the Chicago area. JIM LINEHAN

The surprising thing about Chicago is that it offers fly-fishing opportunities for nearly 10 months of the year, something few places can sustain.

Baitfish patterns are definitely in play here. Several color schemes are important to imitate alewives, smelt, perch, and gobies. Crayfish and leech imitations are important in the warmer summer months. An 8- or 9-weight outfit is best to prevail in winds, cover water, and handle larger fish; both carp and brown trout can exceed 20 pounds. Different lines are needed depending on the situation: floating, intermediate, and sinking-head lines will all have their place.

As noted, fishable areas start south of the Wisconsin line at Illinois Beach State Park, where spring steelhead cruise the mouth of the Dead River after a heavy rain. The same area also draws fall browns. This is a shallow area where an intermediate line gives the best fly presentation.

Chicago Metro Area Essentials

Primary Species and Peak Times

Steelhead and brown trout: ice-out–May,
   October, November
Coho salmon: ice-out–May, October
Chinook salmon: September
Smallmouth bass: mid-April–June
Carp: May, June

Useful Fly Patterns

Steelhead and Brown Trout

Deep Minnow and Half and Half #1-4; gray-
   white, olive-white
Bad Hair Day #2; baitfish and olive
Ice-Out Alewife
Great Lakes Goby Grub
Lion Bugger
Zoo Cougar #2; olive

Coho Salmon

Chartreuse Thing
Bad Hair Day #2; baitfish and olive
Ice-Out Alewife
Great Lakes Goby Grub

Chinook Salmon

Bad Hair Day #2; baitfish
Ice-Out Alewife
Chartreuse and White Glow
Flashtail Deceiver
Half and Half #1; glow-white

Smallmouth Bass

Great Lakes Goby Grub
Perch Fry
Bad Hair Day #2; baitfish and olive
Zoo Cougar #2; olive
Lion Bugger
Deep Minnow #1-4; chartreuse-white, olive-
   white

Carp

Anderson's Hammerhead
Simpleech
Coyote Ugly
Warm Water Charlie

Fly Shops, Guides, Information

Chicago Fly Fishing Outfitters

chifly.com
312-944-3474

Orvis Chicago

www.orvis.com/chicago
312-440-0662

Trout and Grouse

troutandgrouse.com
847-480-0111

Capt. Austin Adduci

grabyourflycharters.com
630-866-1964

The South Rocks area of Waukegan Harbor offers both coho and smallmouth in the spring. Coho will hit mostly alewife/smelt patterns and bright (pink and chartreuse) attractors. Smallmouth prefer perch and goby imitations. In the fall, browns can be tempted with alewife/smelt and goby patterns.

Tower Road at Winnetka, Illinois, has a shut-down warmwater discharge that is still frequented by carp from April through June. Throw floating or intermediate lines for cruising fish, depending on their depth. Small crayfish flies and other creepy-crawly patterns will tempt carp up to 30 pounds.

At the village of Wilmette, the Gilson Park Pier and the North Harbor Break Wall allow opportunities for coho in April and carp in May. Throw the usual patterns for these. An added bonus here is large yellow perch, which move inshore in

A group of carp hold in the flow from a clear-water discharge. Though very spooky under these conditions, they might hit a dead-drifted crayfish or Hex nymph pattern. JIM LINEHAN

May and are reachable most of the summer on small Deep Minnows. Line choice varies, depending on the depth being fished.

In Montrose Harbor, the Horseshoe Pier area attracts large freshwater drum, starting in May and continuing through the summer. Cast black-and-olive bunny leeches (try Dave Pinczkowski's Simpleech) and small baitfish patterns for these tough fighters. Coho are available March through April, and again in November. Browns will be around in March and April, and again from October into December.

The Montrose Inner Harbor will have coho and browns at about the same time as the Horseshoe Pier. Perch will also be in the harbor through most of the summer. In both pier and inner harbor, intermediate and sinking-head lines can be used. You'll observe that there is a general theme here with respect to species, time of year, and fly patterns. There will be a lot of consistency for the entire Chicago area. Any exceptions will be noted.

Belmont Harbor is the next area of shoreline interest, although the rocks between there and Montrose Harbor hold smallmouth and cruising carp that are feasting on crayfish and gobies in the early summer. There are breakwalls on both sides of the entrance to the harbor, and because of this narrow opening, Belmont is subject to localized seiche currents. This is a top area for seasonal migratory fish, and a good place to night-fish for browns.

One thing to keep in mind here, and in a number of these areas, is the difficulty of landing fish. Getting down to the fish's level is challenging if not downright impossible at times. Although it is a nuisance to carry, a long-handled net can be a great help and will remove the possibility that you might have to hoist a good fish up on just the leader tippet.

Borrowing from saltwater fly anglers, Capt. Austin Adduci uses a stripping tube to control line on the deck of his boat.

At Dog Beach in Belmont Harbor, it is possible to wade and fish for a seasonal mix of fish, working from the beach south to the next point of land. Although casting can be a challenge, the back end of the harbor holds a good mix of panfish.

Diversey Harbor is the next stop south and is a fairly "fly-fishing friendly" area. The harbor entrance is quite narrow and there are breakwalls on both the north and south sides. Again you will see the complete seasonal mix of fish in this area. The south breakwall seems to fish better, perhaps because prevailing winds are from the southwest.

Inside the harbor, the north end has a good concentration of warmwater species, while the east wall is loaded with rock bass. The west side is difficult to fish because it is a boat-mooring area and anglers are required to stay 100 feet away from the craft. In October through mid-November, dying weed beds inside the harbor attract good numbers of pike—some of substantial size. Pike can also be caught at the harbor entrance in that late fall period.

An interesting phenomenon occurs in the Rowing Lagoon south of the Fullerton Bridge. After heavy rains, run-off from Lincoln Park flows through a storm drain outlet by the Ulysses S. Grant Memorial and into the lagoon. This actually creates a current that attracts carp, who feed on the assortment of material washing in. Dead-drifting the current here will often be successful; the water is too murky for sight fishing.

The Chicago Harbor and Navy Pier area can generate action from smallmouth, but Burnham Harbor and the Planetarium Peninsula just to the south are probably a better bet. There is a lot of rocky riprap along the shoreline here to attract and hold smallmouth. The south side and southeast corner of Northerly Island can be particularly productive.

There are also several tubes or tunnels between the lake and the harbor where seiche currents will occur and attract fish. Even migratory salmon and trout can be attracted to this flow if it lasts long enough.

A pier at the 57th Street Harbor is easily fished, and the outer harbor at Jackson Park is also a very fishy area. Both are good places for early season browns; activity

Despite being a huge urban area, Chicago offers an assortment of fly-fishing opportunities for adventurous anglers. This angler fishes Diversey Harbor for smallmouth bass. JIM LINEHAN

seems to start here a week or so earlier than the areas north of the city. Spring coho action can also be good. Any rocky structure will attract smallmouth, and carp will frequent the area through May and June.

So far this discussion focused on Chicago's shore-fishing opportunities. Watercraft adds a whole new dimension. All of these harbors have launch ramps

This shoreline brown was taken stripping a streamer at night. Finding schools of bait are the key to locating fish like this. JIM LINEHAN

that can handle nearly any size and type of craft, which adds significantly to the size of the area that an angler can cover.

Much of the Indiana shoreline is industrialized and although lacking in scenery is a place to consider fly fishing. Capt. Austin Adduci, of Grab Your Fly Charters, fishes the south end of the lake for a variety of species including steelhead, brown trout, coho salmon, smallmouth, and carp. He has a flats-style boat that allows him to pole saltwater-style on shallow flats in order to sight-fish. Capt. Austin also fishes several warmwater discharge areas late in the season and extra-early in the spring.

Boat access to the Indiana shoreline is from the Portage Public Marina. Dunes State Park and Indiana Dunes National Lakeshore are also located here. It is possible to reach the NIPSCO power plant discharge after a long hike on a series of National Lakeshore trails.

On the Scum Line

Let's do one final stop on Lake Michigan. There are times during the heat of the summer when wind and current force cold water from the depths up to the surface and distinct vertical lines of different water temperature and density are created. Called thermal bars, these places are easily identified by satellites that measure surface temperature of the lake.

Also known as "scum lines," the different water densities trap and concentrate a variety of materials—including both lake- and land-bred insects. Baitfish also congregate in these areas. Scum lines mainly attract surface-feeding steelhead, which can be caught on baitfish patterns and even dry flies. Enterprising anglers have dropped float tubes from larger boats on calm days to work the thermal bars.

Capt. Jon Ray of Hawkins Outfitters (231-631-5701,www.hawkinsflyfishing.com) can be contacted to set up trips for this kind of fishing, if conditions allow. Few things in the Great Lakes can match a silver-bright steelhead hooked at the surface. A potential day can be selected and, if Lake Michigan conditions are not right, stream trout fishing is the back-up.

Depending on weather patterns, this opportunity can occur anytime from late June through August. A variety of baitfish imitation flies can be used, including Deep Minnows, Murdich-style streamer, or Bad Hair Days. They should be in standard baitfish colors such as all-white, chartreuse-white, or gray-white, and approximately 4 to 6 inches long.

Any steelhead found on the scum line will be on-the-feed and super-aggressive. Finding the fish is the key, and if you can get a fly in front of one, this kind of fishing can provide a once-in-a-lifetime experience. Use of kayaks and even paddle boards are the next stage in the evolution of working scum lines from a larger boat.

chapter 11

Fly Fishing
in Lake Ontario

Fly fishing in Lake Ontario encompasses all of what we have discussed previously—with a little bit extra thrown in. With a substantial forage base, the lake consistently produces some of the largest migratory fish caught across the Great Lakes each year. The nearshore fishery is outstanding around the entire lake, and this includes Canada's largest city, Toronto—another quality urban fishery.

The Lower Niagara River may be the single most productive stretch of water in the Lakes for variety, numbers, and individual size of species. It can be effectively fly fished from shore and by boat. All Great Lakes sport fish are present here, and the Niagara can be fished nearly year-round.

In Lake Ontario, we also encounter a new species, the longnose gar, which is proving to be an exciting fly-rod fish and is attracting the interest of anglers in other areas. The story of the gar is a prime example of a local angler, Glen Hales, taking advantage of an abundant local species and pioneering an exciting sport fishery.

The Bay of Quinte and Kingston, Ontario, Area

Located at the extreme eastern end of Lake Ontario, the Bay of Quinte is a long, Z-shaped waterway made up of a number of arms and inlets and fed by several rivers. It winds and twists for about 75 miles from the city of Trenton to where it meets the lake at Adolphustown Reach. Although the bay is a stronghold of gear anglers, fly fishing is slowly making its presence known.

For decades, the Bay of Quinte suffered from an influx of poorly treated sewage and nutrient-rich agricultural run-off. Algae blooms stopped sunlight, and there was little weed growth. Like some other parts of the Great Lakes, Quinte's waters were a noxious soup that supported little more than rough fish.

In the late 1970s, sewage treatment facilities were upgraded, controls were put in place to regulate agricultural run-off, and water quality improved. Gamefish began to return, and Quinte became recognized as a premier walleye fishery.

Then the bay underwent another transformation when the filter-feeding zebra mussel became established. Weed growth became more widespread, water clarity increased, and now a wide range of species are fair game for fly anglers.

The bay emerged onto the fly-fishing scene several years ago after being featured in *Canadian Fly Fisher* magazine. Stalking longnose gar on shallow flats was the

This angler is working an open pocket in a weed bed. Gar or largemouth bass are the target.
GLEN HALES

main focus in these articles, giving fly anglers around the Great Lakes a new species to pursue. At the same time, smallmouth bass, largemouth bass, pike, freshwater drum, pike, walleye, muskie, yellow perch, and carp have all become fair game.

Glen Hales, a guide out of Belleville, Ontario, was the first to popularize fly-fishing for gar, and this specialty now has a developed a devoted following. Fly fishing in the bay continues to improve as the recovery in water quality has been maintained. Bass fishing in particular, for both largemouth and smallmouth, has become outstanding. In addition, the rivers entering the bay also get seasonal runs of both salmon and steelhead, giving fly fishers a lengthy time frame to work with.

The city of Bellville, located on the northern shore of the Bay of Quinte at the mouth of the Moira River, serves as a great base for fly fishing the area. In fact, there are fly-fishing opportunities right there. Weed edges hold largemouth bass and pike, while shallow, weedy flats are the haunts of gar.

Both the Gorge Street and Herchimer Boat Ramps give quick access to surrounding waters. Smaller craft—float tubes, kayaks, and canoes—can also be carried in at a variety of locations. A series of public shoreline trails also provide wading access.

The Moira River in Belleville also provides a wide range of opportunities, from the mouth upstream to the first ice-control dam. Resident bass, pike, and carp are here, but the seasonal assortment of migratory fish from Lake Ontario also deserves mention.

In early spring, the river receives a substantial spawning run of walleye, with a few steelhead mixed in. This is followed in early June by freshwater drum, many of which can be in excess of 10 pounds. Drum are powerful fighters and more than willing to smash a baitfish pattern swung on a two-hand rod. In September, naturally reproducing chinook salmon return to the river. These are followed by a procession of coldwater species, including brown trout, steelhead, whitefish, and lake trout.

Another key area worth checking is at the town of Trenton, where the Trent River enters the bay. The Trent is larger than Belleville's Moira River, and the tailwater below the first dam also attracts a similar seasonal mix of species. The resident smallmouth in this area also tend to be a bit larger than those in the Moira.

Fly-fishing areas can be found around the entire bay; most communities have public ramps for larger boats as well as bayside park areas convenient for launching a canoe or float tube, or for wading. The web site www.fishingbayofquinte.com has a link to a map of marinas, public ramp locations around the bay, and other facilities.

Eastern areas of the bay tend to be better for smallmouth, because here the soft, weedy bottom gives way to more gravel and rock. The Picton Bay area is particularly productive where a series of rocky cliffs extend right to the shoreline. There are launch ramps in Picton Harbour and McFarland Park. There are also a number of resorts and motels in this area that cater to sportsmen. Merland Park Resort (www.merlandpark.com) rents boats, canoes, and kayaks.

Another good area for smallmouth is the Telegraph Narrows area of the bay near the town of Deseronto. There is a public ramp in town, and again bayside parks and green spaces that provide additional access to anglers.

Because the eastern areas of the bay are generally more rocky, the flats here also have a harder bottom substrate, usually a mix of sand, gravel, and rock. These areas attract carp as well as smallmouth. The carp will move onto these flats in early June for pre-spawn feeding, making another variation of flats-fishing available.

The Napanee River enters the Bay of Quinte at the town of Napanee, offering seasonal variations: substantial walleye run in the spring, and the largest run of chinook salmon in the bay is found here in September. Access is from boat launch areas and parks, with Riverside Park in Napanee a popular area. Part of the river is designated as a fish sanctuary during walleye spawning in April and May, so be sure to check the latest regulations.

Guide Glen Hales caught this sizeable gar while wading the edge of a weed bed. GLEN HALES

Bay of Quinte and Kingston, Ontario, Area Essentials

Primary Species and Peak Times

Steelhead and brown trout: ice-out–May,
   September–November
Salmon: mid-August–mid-October
Northern pike: May, June
Muskellunge: September, October
Smallmouth and largemouth bass: July
Gar: June, July, August
Freshwater drum: May, June
Carp: May, June

Useful Fly Patterns

Trout and Salmon

Deep Minnow and Half and Half #1/0-4;
   all-white, chartreuse-white, gray-white
Ice-Out Alewife
Flashtail Deceiver

Northern Pike

Double Bunny #1/0; red-white, black-white,
   chartreuse-orange
Meatwagon Max #3/0; perch, fire tiger
Figure 8 #3/0; perch, fire tiger

Muskellunge

Swaptail Streamer
Great Lakes Deceiver; perch, black-
   chartreuse
CAT 5; black-orange, black-chartreuse, perch
Muskie Meth
Muskie Marauder
Natural Born Killer

Smallmouth, Largemouth Bass

Deep Minnow and Half and Half #1-4;
   chartreuse-white
Tongue Depressor; olive, black, and brown
Rattling Murdich Minnow #2/0; chartreuse-
   white, olive-white, midnight
Frog poppers and divers #1/0
Zudbubbler

Gar

Gar Flies #1-3

Freshwater Drum

Deep Minnow #1-4; brown-orange, olive-
   orange, chartreuse-white
Crawpin #2; olive and brown
Brown Barred Clouser

Carp

Coyote Ugly
Simpleech
EZ Craw #2-4; tan, olive
Stonebugger
Crawbugger

Fly Shops, Guides, Information

Glen Hales

glenhales@hotmail.com
613-396-6797

Fishing Bay of Quinte

fishingbayofquinte.com

Amherst Island

amherstisland.on.ca

Books & Publications

Ontario Blue-Ribbon Fly Fishing Guide
   by Scott E. Smith

On the outer edges of the bay and in Lake Ontario proper, Waupoos Island and the Ducks (a series of islands that include Main Duck Island, the False Ducks, and the Duckling islands) are becoming well known for their smallmouth bass fisheries. These places are definitely off the beaten path, and reaching them requires a bit of work as well as a seaworthy boat. However, trophy smallmouth, pike, and even muskie can be the reward.

It was gar fishing that originally brought the Bay of Quinte onto the fly fishers' radar screen. These are most common in the shallow, weedy areas prevalent in the western areas of the bay. An 8- or 9-weight outfit with a floating line is used for them. Most will be in the 24- to 36-inch range, but specimens longer than 50 inches have been caught.

Gar have rows of razor-sharp teeth in their long snouts and something beyond a regular monofilament leader is needed. Glen Hales and others attach a three- to four-foot length of Kevlar braided line as a leader, although some anglers will use a short mono leader and a length of wire.

For targeting gar, attach a flashy baitfish pattern to the leader and add a stinger hook to trail behind the streamer. The stinger is usually a small treble hook on six- to eight-inch length of wire that is tied off the hook on the streamer. The new knottable wire leader on the market makes rigging the stinger quick and simple.

Several of Glen Hales's favorite patterns for gar are in this book. You will notice that they do not have specific names to them; rather, they are different color schemes, because gar may show color preference. All-white, black-white, and mixed colors such as black-orange and chartreuse-orange are popular with anglers and productive with fish. Flies should be four to six inches long, with plenty of flash. Patterns like the Figure 8 can be used, because the Icelandic Sheep wing material will tangle in the gar's teeth. Unfortunately, a single gar can destroy the fly.

Gar are easily spotted, often lying close to the surface in gaps in the weed beds. They are also quite approachable, allowing anglers to get close, accurate casts just in front of them. Gar are not normally too fussy, but vary the retrieve until you find the one that interests them on that day.

As a gar's mouth is all bone and teeth, the hook needs to be set with force when one of them grabs a streamer. Even so, you'll probably find that only about a third of your strikes actually result in a hookup. Usually it is the treble hook that catches a bit of tissue and makes a solid connection between angler and fish. When hooked, gar often tail-walk across the surface—more than once. Use caution when unhooking them, because their teeth can cut quickly and effortlessly: use pliers or hemostats.

The Bay Quinte is easily reached from Highway 401, and this entire region has a long-standing history of providing services to anglers. There is plenty of information available from its numerous bait and tackle shops. Some shops can offer specific help to fly anglers, but it is often best to ask for general fishing information and convert it as needed to fly-fishing applications.

Throughout the bay, an 8- or 9-weight outfit will serve multiple functions for all species. Floating and sinking-tip lines, or even sinking-head lines, will have applications. Fly patterns may range from crayfish for smallmouth, to frog divers for pike and smallmouth, to giant baitfish streamers for late-season pike and muskie. Time of year and species pursued should be your guides.

Hot fly-rod action in the Bay of Quinte. Gar are fierce fighters and provide a lot surface acrobatics when hooked on a fly. GLEN HALES

Prince Edward County and the shoreline area surrounding the Bay of Quinte are rich in a variety of art and cultural activities. There are also many provincial parks with picturesque beaches, and orchard, vineyards, and farms offer interesting side trips. Bed and breakfasts and small resorts provide a wide range of accommodations.

Amherst Island, at the mouth of the Bay of Quinte, can be a wonderful "off-the-beaten-path" experience. The island is best known for being a quiet, artistic location with quaint farms and flocks of sheep, but a short ferry ride from the mainland at the village of Millhaven can take anglers a few miles across the North Channel to the village of Stella. Small boats, canoes, and kayaks can be brought over on the ferry and launched at Stella's boat ramps, giving access to waters that have rarely, if ever, seen a fly angler. A map of the island at http://www.amherstisland.on .ca/maps/index.htm shows boat ramps in Stella and on the southwest side of the island in Amherst Bay.

Action can start early in the spring, when a few warm days will trigger smelt to move into shallows to spawn. Lake trout follow, along with browns and steelhead, to take advantage of this feast. Walleye show up a bit later, but they can be difficult to target with flies unless they are concentrated. It's possible to find walleye here again in the fall, when they feed on shad to put on their winter weight in preparation for the spring spawn.

In summer, smallmouth and panfish can be caught from rocky shallows and anchorages, mostly on the southwest side of the island, in the vicinity of several other small islands (Nut, Grape, and the Brother Islands).

Despite its charm and relative isolation, Amherst Island is not without controversy. In 2012, residents were facing the possibility that a large wind-turbine farm might be established there. They feared that the facility would destroy the atmosphere of the area, giving the island an "industrial" look; that tourism would disappear; and that land and home values would decrease significantly. The outcome was not yet known when this book was completed.

Kingston, Ontario, at the head of the St. Lawrence River and bordering the Thousand Islands, is another developing area for fly fishers. Here, the Cataraqui River—part of the Rideau Canal system—enters Lake Ontario. The mouth of the Cataraqui forms much of the inner harbor area of Kingston.

Smallmouth bass are more prevalent in the harbor closer to Lake Ontario, while largemouth and pike are more common farther up the mouth of the river. A variety of panfish, including rock bass and yellow perch, are also scattered throughout the harbor.

Brown trout have been regularly stocked in the Kingston area for several decades. Nicholson Point and Parrot's Bay are the most popular sites for chasing browns, beginning right after ice-out in the spring and continuing until warming temperatures move them to cooler, deeper water. Browns move inshore again in the fall.

Public boat ramps in Collins Bay and the village of Millhaven give quick access to this area. The Lemoine Point and Parrot's Bay conservation areas both offer access to shoreline areas as well as the opportunity to launch portable watercraft.

Use caution when venturing out in any type of watercraft: the Bay of Quinte can get rough very quickly. The same is true of any of the nearshore Lake Ontario locations. Fortunately, there are plenty of options for anglers to develop a "Plan B" and find a sheltered spot to fish.

Also, fishing regulations can be quite complicated, so study them well for this area—or whichever area you may be fishing. Here, fishing is open all year for most coldwater species, with the exception of lake trout. Warmwater species have varied closure times and open periods. Fish sanctuary closures in the Moira River, Belleville Harbor, and Napanee and Trent Rivers protect spawning walleye from April 1 to the Friday before the first Saturday in May. No fishing is permitted in these areas during that time.

Lower Niagara River and Niagara Bar Area

From below Niagara Falls north to Lake Ontario, the Lower Niagara River flows approximately 14 miles. The Niagara Bar in Lake Ontario proper may also be considered part of this fishery. Best known for its seasonal runs of migratory trout and salmon that move up the river from Lake Ontario, this area also boasts numerous warmwater species. The Lower Niagara offers anglers a truly year-round opportunity, and few places can match its diversity.

Shore Fishing

The sheer size of the Niagara River and the volume of water that flows through it can be very intimidating to anglers; so can trying to access the water in some locations. There are several primary locations for productive fishing from shore on both the American and Canadian sides, but reaching these areas can be both strenuous

The Lower Niagara River can be fished from shore in several places. These anglers are near the Lewiston, New York, boat ramp.

and treacherous. Some trails to the river have switchbacks and steps in series, and there is a drop of more than 300 vertical feet from the top of the gorge. When wet— or snow- or ice-covered, these trails can be extremely dangerous.

While anglers will have greatest success in locations where deeper water comes close to the shore, these spots also are likely to have steep banks that have to be dealt with, and it may be difficult to make long casts. For fly anglers here, the most popular technique is to tight-line drift flies on the bottom. An extra-long leader, with weight to get the flies down, is roll cast on a weight-forward floating line and drifted with a bit of tension on the line. The weight should touch bottom once in a while, as the rod follows the drift. When the end of the drift is reached, let the flies swing up along the edge of the rocks until they are picked up and cast again.

Steelhead are the most sought-after species by fly fishers in the Lower Niagara; their season here runs from October into June. Although January and February are top months for steelhead, shore fishing can be impossible during those months because of the ice and snow buildup on shore. Fortunately, late March, April, and into May are also great steelhead times, with a mix of fish still coming in—spawners, as well as post-spawn fish dropping back to Lake Ontario. Most steelhead caught here will be in the 6- to 10-pound range, but fly fishers do catch some that weigh close to 20 pounds.

Anglers will encounter lake trout beginning in early October, when the lakers are entering the river to spawn. However, lake trout should not be specifically targeted at this time because the season on them is closed for at least a couple of more months—from October 1 to January 1 in New York, and from October 1 to November 30 in Ontario. Lake trout will be around again in the spring, following spawning

This laker hit a swung fly on a cold, drizzly day. The Lower Niagara River is a great place to target lake trout on a fly.

smelt into the river in April. You can expect an average weight of 10 pounds for lakers caught here, but some can hit 20 pounds or more.

Brown trout are likely to be a bit smaller than the lakers; most will be in the 5- to 10-pound range. Fall is the time when browns come in from Lake Ontario to spawn, and they often stay in the river until spring when the water warms up and forces them back to the lake.

Chinook are more successfully fished from boats than shore, as it is nearly impossible to land a hooked one. Lake Ontario kings can push 30 pounds or more at times, so shore fishing usually results in a lot of broken gear with no fish to the bank.

From shore, tippet any lighter than 10-pound breaking strength is a waste of time: too many fish will be lost. Flies should be on heavy wire hooks. Egg patterns are productive, along with baitfish patterns. Try GloBugs, Sucker Spawn, and simple yarn flies, varying the color according to water clarity: the clearer the water, the more muted the colors. Go brighter if the water is stained. Hooks are normally size 8.

Baitfish flies can be kept simple here. A white standard Woolly Bugger is very useable, along with Zonker styles. Smelt,

Smelt are a primary food source in the Niagara River. This tube pattern is a close imitation of the real thing.

emerald shiners, and spot-tail shiners are in abundance, so white or gray with a bit of pink, chartreuse, or olive mixed in are main color schemes. Nymphs are not very useful, as they are not an abundant food source here.

Most hits will be light, and indicators might be the line stopping or maybe feeling a bit of a tick. Tighten up and, if you feel a pull-back, hang on. In some areas there is room to follow a hooked fish, in others you need to hold your ground. Regardless, it is difficult to wrestle any large fish out of the current and bring it to shore. Steelhead in particular love to shoot into the main flow and head downriver at full speed; 100 yards of backing can disappear quickly here, and many encounters

Lower Niagara River and Niagara Bar Area Essentials

Primary Species and Peak Times

Steelhead: October–May
Brown trout: October–December (river), March, April (Niagara Bar)
Lake trout: December–May
Chinook salmon: September (river), March, April (Niagara Bar)
Smallmouth bass: May–August (catch-and-release until third week of June)

Useful Fly Patterns

Steelhead and Brown Trout

Niagara Intruder
Arctic Wiggler tube
Devil's Advocate tube
Better Minnow tube
Hybrid Sculpin tube
Boa Minnow
Ice Head Rabbit tube
Egg patterns

Lake Trout

Niagara Intruder
Half and Half #1/0; all-white, gray-white
Ice-Out Alewife
Ice Head Rabbit tube

Chinook Salmon

Niagara Intruder
Arctic Wiggler tube
Flashtail Deceiver
Ice-Out Alewife
Chartreuse and White Glow
Egg patterns

Smallmouth Bass

Deep Minnow and Half and Half #1/0-2; all-white, chartreuse-white
Meatwagon #1; all-white, perch
Crawpin; olive and brown
Boa Minnow
SF Crawfish
Mike's Murdich; all colors

Fly Shops, Guides, Information

Capt. Paul Castellano

Niagara Falls, Ontario
castadventures.ca
888-512-8127

Cattaraugus Creek Outfitters

Vince Tobia
ccoflyfishing.com
716-479-2327

Grindstone Angling

Waterdown, Ontario
grindstoneangling.com
905-689-0880

Oak Orchard Fly Shop

Williamsville, NY
oakorchardflyshop.com
716-626-1323

Books & Publications

Fishing Western New York by Spider Rybaak
New York Atlas and Gazetteer by DeLorme Publishing
New York Fly Fishing Guide by Robert W. Streeter
Ontario Blue-Ribbon Fly Fishing Guide by Scott E. Smith
Sander's Fishing Guide: Western New York Edition by John M. Sander

Korkers and other styles of studded wading sandals improve grip on the slimiest rocks. They can be helpful when walking shoreline areas during snowy, freezing weather.

are short-lived. If you land one steelhead out of three or four hooked, you've achieved a good average here.

Another method that can be very productive is dead-drifting a streamer or an egg/streamer combo under an indicator. On some days, this will outfish the tightline rig significantly. I think it works best when there is some clarity to the water, so the fish can see farther. You will need to use enough weight to sink the flies quickly and hold them down, and the indicator needs to be buoyant enough to suspend the weight used. Use a leader with a heavy butt section to turn over the

The Devil's Hole and Whirlpool State Parks have trails down into the Niagara gorge that provide access to shore anglers. Use caution if you venture to fish these areas, as footing can be quite treacherous in cold weather.

rig and then add a long tippet section to help sink the flies and hold them down. A 7- to 8-foot bass leader tapered to 12 pounds, with 4 feet or so of extra 10- or 12-pound tippet gets the job done most days. Tie the egg onto the tippet and then add 15 to 20 inches of tippet from the egg, and tie on the streamer. Attach shot to the leader 15 to 20 inches above the egg; usually four or five BB shot get the job done.

For years, a 10-foot, 8-weight rod was the popular choice for this kind of fishing. Lately, switch rods have become more popular. An 11- to 12-foot, 8-weight switch is a very efficient tool for the constant roll casts and mending needed to fish shoreline areas. The extra length also helps to control fish from the shore. The reel needs to hold at least 100 yards of backing and have a drag able to withstand a lot of abuse and function in freezing temperatures. A front-loaded weight-forward line will help turn over the dead-drift rigs at short range. The new Textured Nymph Taper from Scientific Anglers has proven particularly useful here.

Shoreline anglers work flies along areas with deep cuts and pockets close to the shoreline. Strikes often happen almost at the angler's feet, and then the challenge is to keep the hooked fish out of the main current. RICK KUSTICH

A growing group of anglers, led by Rick Kustich and Nick Pionessa, are swinging flies from the shoreline. Compact Skagit-style lines are teamed up with 15-foot tips of T-14 to swing baitfish patterns through holding area. Rods are normally 12- to 13-foot, 8-weight two-handers. Although hits are fewer on the swung fly, you will likely find that you land a higher percentage of fish because hook size is significantly larger and tippet strength greater than in dead-drifting. Tube and Intruder-style flies in baitfish colors are popular, since hooks can be easily changed for size or if dulled by rocks.

The Niagara whirpool area is the closest place to Niagara Fall for shore fishing. From the American side, you get to the whirlpool by way of Whirlpool State Park off the Robert Moses Parkway. On the Canadian side, anglers can reach the river from the Niagara Glen area off the Niagara Parkway. I can't remind you strongly enough that extreme care must be taken when descending any of the trails down to the river. Rubber lug soles on boots with studs probably give the best traction under most conditions. Felt is a detriment when there is snow and ice on the ground.

From the stairs at Whirlpool Park to the stairs at Devil's Hole is approximately one mile. On the American side, this is a slow-moving side pocket off the main river, with a number of shallower areas and rock piles to move around on and fish. Reached from Devil's Hole State Park or by following the trail from the whirlpool area, this is one of the most popular spots on the river for both steelhead and salmon. A shore-based fly angler actually has a chance to land a chinook here.

To get to Devil's Hole from the other side, Canadian anglers have to walk a side road that cuts off the parkway just north of the Niagara Glen and then follow several steep trails down to the Devil's Hole Rapids. This is a very challenging area, with little room to maneuver for casting, fighting, or landing fish. The remainder of the

Canadian side of the river has few good access areas for fly fishing until you reach the Queenston area.

Downstream several more miles is the very popular New York's Artpark State Park, with more than a mile of river shoreline and a network of trails that lead to the river at productive locations. This is the easiest area of the river to get to, with less vertical distance between land and water's edge. Because it lies downstream of the power plants on the river, this area is subject to frequent fluctuations in water level and strong surges of current. It can be frustrating to hook—and finally be close to landing—a good fish, only to have a surge of current carry it off on a tippet-busting trip to oblivion. Such is shore fishing on the Niagara. Every fish landed is well earned.

In the summer, smallmouth bass are abundant in these same areas, along with a mix of other warmwater species including walleye and even muskie. Surprisingly, fishing pressure is often very light as most anglers focus on the more prestigious targets of salmon and trout. The same techniques recommended for steelhead and salmon can be used to go after warmwater species. These will also be more responsive to stripped fly on a sinking-tip line. The Lower Niagara in summer is also a great time and place for anglers to get an extended opportunity to use switch rods. Use baitfish, crayfish, and goby patterns.

A description of shore access areas (www.dec.ny.gov/outdoor/67913.html and www.niagaraparks.com/nature-trails/niagara-river-recreation-trail.html) on the lower river can be found online. You can also contact Oak Orchard Fly Shop (www.oak orchardflyshop.com, 716-626-1323) in Williamsville, New York, for walk-in guides and river information. Again, keep in mind that shore fishing can be a strenuous, and at times hazardous, adventure. This especially true in the late fall and winter, when weather conditions are at their worst.

A chrome-bright steelhead from the shore. Due to the strong main current and limited walking to follow fish, they are a challenge to land in the Niagara River.

This Niagara River brown trout hit an Intruder-style pattern. Stocking programs have increased populations significantly in the past decade and trophy-sized fish are caught regularly.

Boat Fishing

A boat provides the best way to move around and consistently catch fish on the Lower Niagara. Unfortunately, kayaks and canoes suitable for the Upper Niagara do not have a place here. The size of the area covered, current speed, and other hazards requires the use of a power boat. Below Artpark, where the river widens and the current slows, a 14-foot V-bottom boat with a 25-hp motor is adequate. Upstream of Artpark, where the river narrows in the gorge and the discharge from the power plants come into play, a 16-foot boat with a 50-hp motor is the safe minimum.

There are boat launches on the American side of the river at the villages of Lewiston and Youngstown. The launch at Fort Niagara State Park provides access to the lower river, the Niagara Bar, and the adjacent waters of Lake Ontario. On the Canadian side, a launch at the town of Queenston is centrally located to fish either the gorge or the lower area of the river. Keep in mind that this area and the upper river have the same requirements about whether a New York or Ontario fishing license (or both) is required. Fishing seasons are a bit different on the Lower Niagara, so be sure to check the calendar before you get on the water.

Nearly all boat anglers and guides will be using gear or bait. However, flies can be extremely effective and you can use set-ups similar to the ones you use from shore. Some guides will allow clients to try flies; others will refuse because they either don't understand how to rig properly or they have no confidence in their effectiveness.

One guide who actually encourages the use of flies is Paul Castellano, from Niagara Falls, Ontario. Castellano—well into his second decade as a full-time, year-round guide—grew up fishing the Niagara and the adjacent waters of Lake Ontario. An experienced fly angler himself, he has spent a lot of time adapting the use of flies to the boat-fishing techniques used in the river.

Boat anglers cover specific areas of the river referred to as "drifts." As the board drifts with the current, an electric motor is used to slow the boat. This creates conditions similar to fishing from shore: the flies are cast, allowed to sink toward the bottom, and then drift with the current before being picked up and cast again.

Techniques that work here include tight-line drifting and indicator dead-drifting. In addition, flies can be swung effectively from the boat, just as on shore, using the same equipment. The line is cast slightly downstream with a mend or to sink the fly, and then the line is tightened up and the rod tip follows to the bottom of the swing. When the fly is straight below and "on the dangle," the motor is slowed. The boat drops back in the current, setting up the next cast and swing—not unlike stepping down while wading. Castellano's favorite fly for this kind of fishing is his Niagara Intruder pattern.

Castellano will sometimes also cast and strip streamers in a traditional drift-boat style, working shoreline areas. He does this more often in warmer weather—in spring and fall—when fish are more apt to chase. It is his favored method for smallmouth and muskie, but it can also produce all of the coldwater species.

The Niagara Bar, where the river empties into Lake Ontario, was created over the centuries, as river sediment dropped out of the current and accumulated on the bottom. Depths of water around the bar range from 80 feet to 8 feet. With the current from the river passing over it, the bar attracts hordes of baitfish—and their predators.

Depending on the time of year, anything from lake trout to chinook salmon to smallmouth bass can be found cruising the bar in search of food. April and May are considered the best months to fish the bar for variety, although it will produce fish any month of the year. Smallmouth bass are at their peak in June, July, and August. Salmon are abundant in August and September. Steelhead may be encountered from October to June. Lake trout are best in the winter months, and brown trout may show up at almost any time.

The Niagara Bar can be fly-fished effectively when the wind on Lake Ontario is manageable. If the wind exceeds 15 mph, casting becomes a challenge, and the river may be a better option. To cover the most water, an integrated sinking shooting taper gets the job done. Lines from 250 grain to 350 grain can be used. The location of fish varies. Sometimes they will hold on deeper edges, but you may also find them right on top in the shallowest areas. Keep an eye out for where gulls are feeding, because they follow baitfish pushed to the surface by larger predators.

One December morning when Lake Ontario was dead-calm and a light drizzle was falling, Castellano and I found lake trout busting smelt on the surface at the shallowest part of the bar. We caught fish both by stripping streamers and also by using the same swung-fly technique that Castellano uses in the main river. You can also use streamers on the Lake Ontario shoreline on each side of the bar. Like much Great Lakes fishing, this is a very visual, saltwater-like experience, with an assortment of fish available to smash a stripped streamer at any given moment.

From the outlet of Lake Erie to Lake Ontario, the Niagara River is one of the most interesting fly-fishing areas in the Great Lakes; it is also an area of extremes. There are calm backwaters that calls for stealth techniques, and there are some of the biggest whitewater areas found anywhere. The river offers year-round fishing challenges for a wide range of gamefish, and the top areas can be accessed quite easily.

New York Shoreline Areas and Lake Ontario's East End

As with other areas in the Great Lakes Basin—particularly in Wisconsin and Michigan—there is a long history of fly fishing in Lake Ontario's New York tributaries, but little in Lake Ontario proper. East of the Niagara River, the towns of Wilson, Olcott, Point Breeze, and others have well-developed, fishable harbor areas: plenty of fishing activity, just not a lot of fly fishing.

Again, the lack of fly fishing in these harbors is not for lack of opportunity: salmon, steelhead, and brown trout are available seasonally. Smallmouth bass can be found in rocky areas in the harbors as well as in the lake itself, and largemouth bass, pike, and panfish in back areas of the harbors.

In addition to town harbors, state and county parks along the shoreline are also good access areas, some with ramps for launching watercraft. Just west of Rochester, a series of small bays off the main lake—including Braddock Bay, Cranberry Pond, Long Pond, Buck Pond, and Round Pond—provide sheltered fishing for largemouth bass, pike, and panfish.

Braddock Bay, which opens into the lake, receives seasonal migrations of trout and salmon heading for the Salmon and Buttonwood Creeks. On the east side, launch ramps at the Braddock Bay Fish and Wildlife Management Area and Braddock Bay

Patrick Ross caught this steelhead at the head of the Salmon River Estuary. Winter conditions here can make fishing extremely challenging. Water temperatures are normally in the mid to low 30s and air temperatures can be considerably lower. The area also receives significant lake-effect snows. WAEL DARDIR

An eastern Lake Ontario smallmouth. Fly fishing is rarely seen in this area, even though the opportunities are virtually limitless.

Park can be reached from the Lake Ontario Parkway. Buck Pond, Cranberry Pond, and Long Pond are in this area and have channels to the lake that are open intermittently, depending on the wave and current action that deposits or removes shifting sand and gravel from the entrances.

For fly fishers favoring watercraft, Rochester's Irondequoit Bay—with bass, pike, and panfish in the bay itself, and seasonal runs of trout and salmon— is easily fished from a kayak or small boat. Bay Park West has shoreline access and a launch ramp, while Irondequoit Bay Marine Park, located at the outlet to Lake Ontario, offers access to the bay, the lake, and a breakwall area. The web site www.irondequoitbay.com gives great information for this area.

Sodus Bay, located midway between the cities of Rochester and Syracuse, is a popular sportfishing and vacation area, offering both sheltered bay waters and access to Lake Ontario. Sodus covers about 3,000 acres; most of the bay is less than 20 feet deep. Bass, pike, walleye, and panfish are year-round residents, and steelhead, browns, lake trout, and salmon are taken seasonally at the piers located at the bay inlet.

Following the lead of Canadian anglers across Lake Ontario at the Bay of Quinte, fly fishers are slowly beginning to target longnose gar, using techniques and flies similar to those used in Ontario. When water temperatures hits 65 degrees F— usually in early June—Sodus also gets a sizeable run of freshwater drum. Look for these hard fighters around the islands in the bay and where shallow edges are close to deeper water. Bowfin are also common in the back coves here, giving anglers the opportunity to target a particularly unusual species on a fly.

Sodus Bay has many launch areas; local tackle shops are good sources of up-to-date fishing information. If you ask about fly fishing in the bay, you'll likely get a

The Lake Ontario shoreline just outside of New York's Henderson Harbor. Rocky drop-offs, islands, and shoals provide an abundance of fish-holding structure.

blank stare, but any general fishing information can get you started in the right direction.

Further east, Selkirk Shores State Park—between the mouths of the Salmon River and Grindstone Creek, off Route 3—is a location where you can easily fish both the estuaries and the areas where they enter Lake Ontario. Although best known for their salmon and steelhead runs, both of these areas also have opportunities for fly fishing for warmwater species, and if you go anytime from May through August, you won't find the crowds associated with migratory fish runs.

The parking area at the southwest corner of Selkirk park is the access point for the mouth of Grindstone Creek; it is only a short walk from there to the lake and river mouth. At the creek mouth, flies can be swung, cast, and stripped, or dead-drifted under a float. The peak activity here will be in late August and September, when chinook salmon are staging and moving into the creek. If your goal is to fish the estuary from the water, a canoe or kayak will require a short portage.

Steelhead, brown trout, coho, and the odd lake trout can be caught at the mouth after the chinook have finished their run and again in the early spring. The estuary fishes best in late spring and summer. Throw streamer patterns and fish topwater in the estuary for bass and pike.

Access to the lower Salmon River from Selkirk park is off Pine Grove Road, where a boat launch allows quick access to Lake Ontario. Again, most activity here focuses on salmon and trout in the lake. Except when salmon and steelhead are migrating, the estuary of the Salmon River receives very little attention from anglers. The river itself starts at the lower end of the Douglaston Salmon Run, several miles from its mouth, past the highway crossing.

New York Shoreline Areas and Lake Ontario's East End Essentials

Primary Species and Peak Times

Steelhead and brown trout: ice-out–May, October, November

Chinook and coho salmon: mid-August–mid-October

Northern pike: May and June

Smallmouth and largemouth bass: mid-May–July; no early catch-and-release season in Jefferson County waters; season opens third Saturday in June

Useful Fly Patterns

Steelhead and Brown Trout

Deep Minnow and Half and Half #1-4; all-white, gray-white

Mike's Murdich; all colors

Ice-Out Alewife

Niagara Intruder

Hybrid Sculpin tube

Devil's Advocate tube

Arctic Wiggler tube

Better Minnow tube

Chinook and Coho Salmon

Niagara Intruder

Flashtail Deceiver

Ice-Out Alewife

White and Chartreuse Glow

Glo Pig

Arctic Wiggler tube

Northern Pike

Double Bunny #1/0; red-white and chartreuse-orange

Great Lakes Deceiver; red-white, chartreuse-white

Meatwagon and Meatwagon Max; perch and fire tiger

Figure 8 #3/0; perch and fire tiger

Smallmouth Bass

Deep Minnow and Half and Half #1/0-4; chartreuse-white

Mike's Murdich; all colors

Crawpin #2; olive and brown

SF Crawfish

Crazi Craw

Largemouth Bass

Tongue Depressor #2; black, olive, brown

Frog divers and poppers

Hula Frog

Meatwagon #1/0; perch and fire tiger

Zudbubbler popper

Fly Shops, Guides, Information

Carl Coleman's Fly Shop
Rochester, NY
colemansflyshop.com
585-352-4775

Books & Publications

Fishing Western New York
   by Spider Rybaak
Flyfishers Guide to New York
   by Eric Newman
New York Atlas and Gazetteer
   by DeLorme Publishing
New York Fly Fishing Guide
   by Robert W. Streeter

A seiche current has lake water flowing back into Lake Ontario's Henderson Harbor rather than flowing as expected from the harbor into the lake. A sustained seiche can influence where fish will hold, just as currents affect fish-holding patterns in a river.

The estuary cannot be fished from shore; it must be fished by boat, canoe, or kayak. Work streamer patterns for trout and salmon during low-light periods. An intermediate sinking-head line is often best in conditions where water is not very deep. This keeps the fly up and visible in the water column, holding it a few feet under the surface. In this setting, a fast-sinking head could actually sink the fly to a level where it would not be able to be seen by the fish.

The estuary has excellent fishing for pike as soon as the season opens in early May. Throw large, flashy streamers and add a bite-tippet to your leader. Be sure to work areas of dark bottom and emerging weeds. Pike will often sit motionless, waiting for prey to swim past, and then react with a lightning-quick ambush.

Smallmouth bass enter the estuary to spawn, offering good action throughout May and into June. Keep in mind that all bass must be released immediately until the regular season opens on the third Saturday in June. Anglers may also find largemouth bass in the estuary. A 9-weight outfit would be the choice to fish this area across the seasons—to handle the large salmon that can be encountered and to throw larger, air-resistant flies for bass and pike.

North and South Sandy Ponds are just past the Salmon River, separated from the main lake by a sand barrier–beach formation that is the largest barrier-beach ecosystem on Lake Ontario. This is also the only freshwater dune site of significant size in the northeastern United States.

Covering a surface area of 3,000 acres, about four miles long and two miles wide, both ponds offer excellent fishing for bass and pike, along with a variety of panfish. The North Pond is the larger of the two and connects to the South Pond by

Targeting Henderson Harbor smallmouth, this angler works a fly along a shoreline drop-off. Smallies are an important sport species in this area of Lake Ontario.

a narrow waterway. Little Sandy Creek, which flows into the North Pond, receives runs of salmon in the fall and steelhead in the spring.

There is a small-boat launch off County Route 15 in Sandy Island Beach State Park, which divides the two ponds. While motorboats cannot be launched at this location, a number of private ramps and marinas on North Sandy Pond will handle larger boats. These include Sandy Pond Resorts, Sandy Pond Marinas, and North Sandy Pond Marina, among others.

The east end of Lake Ontario—a well-known sportfishing area also called Lake Ontario's "Golden Crescent"—has several large bays and a number of islands where fish can be caught on flies. Chaumont Bay, Black River Bay, and Henderson Bay all hold smallmouth bass, pike, walleye, and panfish. Weedy back-bay areas also hold largemouth bass.

Henderson Bay reaches a depth of about 30 feet and is full of fish-holding habitat, including weed beds, rocky drop-offs, flats, islands, and shoals. Look for largemouth and panfish along the weed beds near the launch area at the west side of Henderson Harbor. This spot, off County Road 178 (Military Road), provides access to the back part of the bay.

At the cut between the mainland and Hoveys Island, seiche currents often create flow both into and out of Snowshoe Bay. It is possible to fish from shore here, and also to launch and fish from small craft such as kayaks and float tubes. Look for largemouth bass and pike in the weed beds, and target smallmouth along rocky areas.

Westcott Beach State Park, on Henderson Bay south of Sackets Harbor, has a small, protected harbor with a boat launch. Two rock jetties hold smallmouth bass and panfish.

Black River Bay is one of the most productive areas on Lake Ontario. It is most widely recognized as a top walleye fishery, but it also has some reputation for its smallmouth bass. Largemouth bass are also here in significant numbers, along with some pike. While bluegill are also very abundant, they receive little attention from most anglers.

At the mouth of the Black River and scattered across the eastern end of Black River Bay are the wetlands of New York State's Dexter Marsh Wildlife Management Area. There is fishing access to the bay from shore. Boat access is available on the north side at Perch Creek off County Road 59, and on the south side of the bay at Muskellunge Creek off Route 180 and Lloyds Landing off Military Road.

You will want to fish weed edges for largemouth bass, pike, and panfish; look for smallmouth bass along deeper edges and in areas with rocks and sand. Smallmouth habitat becomes better as you head west into the bay.

At the dam a short way upriver in Dexter, there is a fish ladder for migratory salmon and steelhead. These often hold below the dam before moving upriver. There are a series of rapids, pools, and shelves from the dam to the bay, and this area could be considered one of the more interesting in the Great Lakes area for its assortment of fish. The Black River receives significant plantings of chinook, steelhead, and Atlantic salmon, and also sees spawning runs of walleye, smallmouth, and assorted panfish. Movement of fish from Lake Ontario into the bay and then into the river occurs nearly year-round.

There is shore access to the Black River in the village of Dexter, as well as from the boat launch at the Route 180 bridge. A map of the Black River Bay area (www .blackriverny.com/BlackRiverNYMap.pdf) showing launch and access areas can be found online.

Chaumont Bay, the final stop in this look at Lake Ontario's New York shoreline, is the largest of the three bays that make up the Golden Crescent; it is also well known as a premier walleye and smallmouth fishery. Three Mile Bay and Guffin Bay can be considered part of this area, which has relatively less development than other places along the lake.

The Chaumont River, which enters the bay at the village of Chaumont, is a warmwater fishery with seasonal activity from trout and salmon. Smallmouth, pike, largemouth, and panfish are the main targets for fly fishers, and anglers should focus on the area from the shallows on the east side of the bay head to the Duck Bay area. There are several launch ramps in the village.

The best fly-fishing prospects for Guffin Bay are at the head, where Guffin Creek enters, and at the tip of Point Salubrious, where there is a shallow, rocky area. Again, the focus is warmwater species, but brown trout can be found in the fall and spring along the drop-off at the mouth of Guffin Creek. Guffin Bay Resort (www.guffin bayresortandmarina.com), which offers boat and motor rentals and a launch ramp, is a source of current fishing information.

Access to Three Mile Bay is available in the village of the same name, with launches within the village itself, and east of the village off Route 12, at the end of Bourcy Road. Fly anglers will want to work the east shoreline of the bay, where a combination of weed edges and rocky areas attract and hold fish.

Long Point Bay State Park is located across Chaumont Bay from the village of Chaumont. There is a launch ramp here as well as boat rentals. Work the shoreline area back to the west toward the area called the Isthmus. This is a narrow strip of land that separates Chaumont Bay from Lake Ontario.

An added bonus in the Chaumont Bay area is the yellow perch fishery. Don't expect to catch them in great numbers, but they often take a Deep Minnow pattern being fished for bass. It is possible to find perch here longer than 16 inches in length and weighing more than two pounds. A handy booklet of nautical charts for the Chaumont and Black River Bay areas is available online (http://ocsdata.ncd.noaa .gov/BookletChart/14811_BookletChart_HomeEd.pdf).

Note that Lake Ontario bass fishing regulations change once you hit Jefferson County, which includes the Henderson, Black River, and Chaumont Bay areas. Here, the season opens on the third Saturday in June, and anglers may not intentionally target bass before that date. There is no early catch-and-release bass season, as in other parts of the state.

Little recorded fly-fishing activity takes place in Lake Ontario east of the Niagara River. Nevertheless, the opportunities are there, and equipment is now available to allows angler to more easily explore estuaries and nearshore locations. There are countless bait and tackle shops that can provide up-to-date information on local gear fishing. The challenge is to take this information and apply it to fly fishing.

Greater Toronto Area

On the Ontario side of the Great Lakes, Canada's largest city, Toronto, offers fly-fishing opportunities in the midst of an immense metropolitan area. Rivers that flow off the Niagara Escarpment into the Greater Toronto Area (GTA) bring a rush of cold water and attract runs of migratory fish. Toronto Harbour includes a series of islands, a large man-made peninsula, and several parks that serve as access locations for both shore-based and boat anglers. Wilson's Toronto fly shop can provide information about local fishing.

The Toronto Islands host an assortment of warmwater species, including pike, largemouth and smallmouth bass, carp, freshwater drum, and panfish. To reach the islands, anglers will need to take a ferry from the mainland. The canals around Hanlan's Point are good for early season pike and later for bass and panfish. Rocky areas in the lagoons around Ward's Island attract smallmouth bass. Boat rentals are also available on the islands, making exploration of the area much easier.

Just east of the Toronto harbor islands is the Leslie Street Spit, a man-made peninsula constructed with dredgings from the Outer Harbour and excess fill material from city construction. It extends more than 3 miles into the lake, and with its numerous coves, bays, and points and lakeside riprap, holds the usual Great Lakes Basin mix of warmwater species.

Tommy Thompson Park, on Leslie Street Spit, is a popular fishing area, well-known for early season pike fishing that starts right after ice-out in sheltered, dark-bottom areas. The park is open on weekends and most holidays. You can walk and bicycle in the park, but cars are not permitted when the park is open. There is a shuttle service, however.

Pike are found around the Toronto Harbor Islands as well as in the Leslie Spit area. Look for them around shallow, weedy areas. BRETT MCCRAE

Just east of the Leslie Street Spit, Ashbridge's Bay Park offers excellent boat-launch facilities as well as good seasonal shore fishing. The marina lagoon has excellent early season fishing for pike and also for panfish. Keep in mind that pike fishing shuts down in the entire Toronto area from April 1 to the first Saturday in May to allow the pike to spawn. There are usually enough pike around for several weeks after the season reopens to keep things interesting.

It's possible to catch some bass and carp here in the summer, but things pick up again toward fall, when the lake water begins to cool and brown trout move inshore. Actually, the trout move in because the baitfish move in; when the food source is close to shore, the browns will be with it. This shoreward movement occurs as long as there is open water, with October being the peak time. Steelhead and even lake trout can also be caught here, especially later in the fall.

The shoreline drops quickly into Lake Ontario at Bluffers Park, at the base of Scarborough Bluffs. There is some early season opportunity here for pike and pan-fish, but the area really comes alive when several days of strong offshore summer winds cause a "flip" to occur, bringing cold water—and with it, trout and salmon—close to shore.

As elsewhere, normal cooling water temperatures through late August and into September more predictably bring browns and salmon close to shore. At that time, salmon will be searching out spawning streams. Browns may sometimes move into streams to spawn, but they often stay in the lake with steelhead and lakers. A small boat can be useful here to cover more area.

On the west side of the GTA, where Humber Bay Park sits at the mouth of the Humber River, marshy areas on the lower river hold early season pike. Anglers may also encounter steelhead, first as they head upriver and later as they drop back to the lake. Brown trout are also a common catch in the early season.

Greater Toronto Area Essentials

Primary Species and Peak Times

Brown trout and steelhead: ice-out–May, October, or when flip occurs

Salmon: mid-August–September, or when flip occurs

Northern pike: May

Smallmouth and largemouth bass: July

Carp: May, June

Useful Fly Patterns

Brown Trout and Steelhead

Deep Minnow and Half and Half #1-4; gray-white and olive-white

Flash Fly

Tubular Smelt

Niagara Intruder

Arctic Wiggler tube

Salmon

Deep Minnow and Half and Half #1/0-4; white with glow, gray-white, olive-white

Flashtail Deceiver

Great Lakes Deceiver; glow colors

Northern Pike

Figure 8 #3/0; perch

Meatwagon Max; perch, fire tiger

Great Lakes Deceiver; red-white, black-chartreuse

Smallmouth Bass

Deep Minnow and Half and Half #1-4; chartreuse-white, olive-white

Crawpin #2; brown and olive

SF Crayfish

Crazi Craw

Great Lakes Goby Grub

Coyote Clouser

Largemouth Bass

Half and Half #1; chartreuse-white, olive-white

Tongue Depressor #2; black and olive

Meatwagon #1/0; perch and fire tiger

Popper and diver #1; frog-colored

Carp

Coyote Ugly

Simpleech; black and brown

Anderson's Hammerhead

Fly Shops, Guides, Information

Grindstone Angling

grindstoneangling.com

905-689-0880

Wilson's

canadasflyfishingoutfitter.com

416-869-3474

Books & Publications

Ontario Blue-Ribbon Fly Fishing Guide by Scott E. Smith

Trout action slows in May, but at that time the area becomes a prime spot for trophy carp. The river also receives a run of white bass in late May. Summer fishing is a mix of largemouth, smallmouth, pike, freshwater drum, and panfish. This area can also experience a "flip."

A sizeable run of chinook salmon will stage at the mouth of the Humber in late summer before moving upriver to spawn, and browns and steelhead move in until ice-up. Anglers can gain access to the mouth from either shore, but the east side generally provides the most consistent fishing.

The GTA provides an assortment of opportunity for the shore-based fly fisher. The web site www.torontofishing.net gives excellent descriptions of the various locations available for fishing around the city. One more point: in most of the

This smallmouth bass hit a fly being thrown for pike. In rocky areas with vegetation, pike and smallmouth populations will overlap. KEVIN MORLOCK

Largemouth bass around the Toronto Islands can be caught with a variety of fly patterns, but fishing topwater flies along weed edges is the most fun. Since pike may also be encountered, the addition of a short bite-tippet is recommended. KEVIN FEENSTRA

Toronto-area locations, a long-handled net would be a very useful piece of equipment to help land fish from rocky shorelines and elevated areas.

While the shoreline from Mississauga to Burlington can still be considered part of the GTA, much of this area is better fished from small watercraft in order to cover more water. Spring, late summer, and fall are the main times for migratory coldwater species, and both Bronte Creek (between Burlington and Oakville) and the Credit River (Mississauga) attract runs of these fish.

Anglers can easily get to and fish from several piers and breakwalls at the mouth of the Credit River. The Credit hosts a significant run of steelhead in the spring, and the area fishes well from March into late May. The standard mix of warmwater species is available during the summer.

There are rocky shoreline areas and numerous pier footings along with other structures along this stretch. Smallmouth bass are found here along with an occasional muskie. During the heat of the summer, the Shell Refinery Pier in the city of Oakville is a hot spot for smallmouth. In the city of Burlington, a hotel pier at Spencer Smith Park provides one shore-fishing location, but the area is better fished from watercraft. Grindstone Angling, in Waterdown, Ontario, provides guiding services.

chapter 12

Fly Fishing
in Lake Superior

As one of the world's largest freshwater lakes, Lake Superior seems an intimidating body of water for any fly angler to tackle. On the other hand, the sheer depth of most of Superior immediately eliminates most of the lake from angling consideration, so the more comfortable focus will be on bays, harbors, and river mouths. In addition, we are fortunate to have the work of experienced anglers who provide a solid foundation for exploring the largest of the inland oceans.

Fishing Lake Superior by Shawn Perich and the *Ontario Blue-Ribbon Fly Fishing Guide* by Scott E. Smith helped to narrow down the search areas for this book; both give valuable "what, when, and where" fishing information. Although Perich's book is mainly gear-based, there is plenty of fly-based information to work with. Scott E. Smith, based in Thunder Bay, is one of the most recognized of Ontario's fly fishers, and Nipigon Bay and the north shoreline of the lake are his home waters.

The areas I have focused on—some of the most scenic areas of the Great Lakes—already have a fly-fishing legacy. You can get to some of these places easily, while others require extensive planning. There are unique fly-fishing opportunities for both common and uncommon species.

Chequamegon Bay

Chequamegon Bay on Lake Superior, the coldest and deepest of the Great Lakes, is a true anomaly: the bay is best known as a warmwater fishery, with most action taking place in less than 10 feet of water. There is even good action in areas shallower than 5 feet. Smallmouth bass are the primary target of fly anglers, but other species, especially northern pike, are also available at various times of the year.

In addition to its warmwater reputation, the bay does support a substantial coldwater fishery in spring and fall: chinook and coho salmon, steelhead, brown trout, and lake trout. Although rarely targeted by fly fishers, these species can become incidental catches during their peak seasons. Multiple species may overlap—feeding in the same areas on the same forage.

Located near the west end of Lake Superior, Chequamegon Bay is about 12 miles long and from 2 to 6 miles wide, covering about 84,000 acres. It is considered the site of the first European settlement in what is now the state of Wisconsin

Discharge from the power plant at Ashland, Wisconsin, attracts a variety of Chequamegon Bay fish.

because in 1658, several fur traders built a dwelling somewhere along the west shore. Native Americans had been traveling to the area for thousands of years to take advantage of abundant fish and wildlife.

The watershed draining into Chequamegon Bay covers nearly one million acres. It is the largest undeveloped wetland complex remaining in the Great Lakes area, an important nesting area for migrating waterfowl, and a nursery for many fish species. The Northern Great Lakes Visitor Center (nglvc.org), just west of Ashland, highlights the heritage and history of the Lake Superior region.

The smallmouth bass fishing on the bay moved toward world-class status when special regulations were instituted several decades ago. A few local anglers, including fly-fishing guide Capt. Roger Lapenter, realized the value of the smallmouth fishing in the bay. Through intensive lobbying, they helped convince the Wisconsin Department of Natural Resources to enact a one-fish, 22-inch minimum-size limit during the open season. Because of the short growing season, it takes Lake Superior smallies a long time to mature, so a 20-inch Chequamegon bass is likely 18 to 20 years old. As a result of protective regulations, the average smallmouth caught in the bay will be about 18 inches and 3-plus pounds.

Fly fishing begins as soon as ice clears the bay in the spring, usually in the first or second week of May. Bass will have moved from their wintering areas to the edge of the shallows in the east end of the bay. Areas such as Kakagon Slough and the Sand Cut slough attract huge numbers of pre-spawn fish. Salmon and trout may also be found in the same areas on a post-winter feeding spree.

Much of the bottom in this area is a mix of sand and gravel with scattered larger rocks—perfect spawning habitat for smallmouth bass. Bulrushes, wild rice, and other aquatic vegetation also attract and hold bass. Find vegetation and the proper bottom, and you have a smallmouth hot spot.

There are also areas with logs and old timber on the bottom. These are leftovers from logging days and provide additional cover for smallmouth and forage species. This wood attracts and holds smallmouth—along with walleye and even pike—all season long.

As radiant energy from the sun increases water temperatures, smallmouth feed aggressively on several forage species: smelt, suckers, and emerald and spottail shiners. A variety of baitfish patterns—including Clouser Minnows and Zonker-styles—on a floating line will be very productive. If there is wind, an 8-weight rod is best to handle these hard fighters and to work flies. A simple leader tapered to 10 pounds will get the job done.

When the water moves toward 60 degrees F, fish will bed and start to spawn, usually in 2 to 3 feet of water. Most spawning activity takes place in June. Bedded bass are easy targets, but in order to maximize spawning success, these fish are best left alone. There is an ample supply of both pre- and post-spawn fish available, so fishing the spawning beds should not be necessary.

Topwater fishing will be at its best at this time, offering exciting action when the wind is down. A variety of poppers and sliders—small Blockheads, Boogle Bugs, Eyed Gurglers—and many generic styles will work. The fish may show preference for a particular style, size, or color on any given day. Some fish aggressively smash a fly on the surface; others may slowly rise, inspect the fly, reject it, or sip it in as gently as any brown trout taking a mayfly.

After spawning, bass will begin to scatter toward the edges of the shallows, with some moving into deeper areas of the bay. Smallmouth may also congregate in the deeper troughs and pockets scattered throughout the shallows to feed on just-hatched shiner and smelt fry. Fishing under this situation can be quite technical in that the size and color of the fly is critical. This is a "match the hatch" situation, and bass will often refuse flies of the wrong size or color.

A good example of a successful fly choice is the Gray Ghost popper fished by guide Capt. Roger Lapenter. This fly, which resembles a bluegill popper, will draw the largest smallmouth to the surface when they are not responding to larger patterns. The Gray Ghost's size, shape, and color closely resemble the abundant, just-hatched fry in the bay.

Anglers can determine where to cast by looking for fish swirling and pushing bait to the surface. These bass are likely stationed next to a log or some other structure and then rush out to ambush any forage that comes close. Accurate casts are important, and casting parallel to visible logs, or into the "X" where logs cross, can attract hidden fish. Because bay waters are normally very clear, the strike is often visible when a fish darts out to attack your fly.

The phenomenon of seiche waves, already noted in other areas of the Great Lakes, also occurs in Chequamegon Bay. Seiche waves, you may recall, are created by sustained winds from one direction pushing water to the downwind side of a body of water. This most frequently occurs in areas with a general east-west orientation, in which the prevailing, and often the strongest, winds are from the west. When the wind dies down, or the weight of the water becomes too much for the wind to hold it, the water flows back in the opposite direction. It may even "slosh"

Chequamegon Bay Essentials

Primary Species and Peak Times

Smallmouth bass: May–July
Northern pike: May, June
Steelhead and brown trout: ice-out–May;
    September, October
Salmon: September

Useful Fly Patterns

Smallmouth Bass

Peck's Gray Ghost Popper
Stunned Minnow Popper
Eyed Gurgler
Baby Blockhead
Zudbubbler
Deep Minnow and Half and Half #1/0-4;
    chartreuse-white, gray-white
Tongue Depressor; olive and brown
Crawpin #2; olive and brown
Rabbit Strip Diver #2; olive, brown, white

Northern Pike

Double Bunny #3/0-1/0; red-white,
    chartreuse-orange
Meatwagon Max; perch and fire tiger
Figure 8 #3/0; perch and fire tiger
Great Lakes Deceiver; red-white, chartreuse-
    black, fire tiger

Trout and Salmon

Deep Minnow and Half and Half #1/0-2; all-
    white, chartreuse-white, gray-white
Ice-Out Alewife
Flashtail Deceiver

Fly Shops, Guides, Information

Anglers All
Ashland, WI
anglersallwisconsin.com
715-682-5754

Bow-Fly
Ashland, WI
bowfly.net
715-682-3277

The Superior Fly Angler
Superior, WI
superiorflyangler.com
715-395-9520

Capt. Roger Lapenter
Anglers All
anglersallwisconsin.com
715-682-5754

Capt. Jake Lapenter
Anglers All
anglersallwisconsin.com
715-682-5754

Capt. Ouitdee Carson
Arrowhead Fly Angler
arrowheadflyangler.com
218-590-1712

Books & Publications

Flyfisher's Guide to Wisconsin and Iowa
    by John Motoviloff
Wisconsin Atlas and Gazetteer
    by DeLorme Publishing

Capt. Roger Lapenter nets a smallmouth bass. Strict regulations maintain the high-quality smallmouth fishing in Chequamegon Bay.

back and forth a number of times until the energy of the flow dissipates, much like water sloshing back and forth in a moving bowl.

The effect of a seiche on fish behavior can be similar to the effect of tidal movement. Anglers may find that fish will feed during a certain direction of the seiche, or during slack movement periods. The seiche may also pull enough water out of an area to strand boats and cause fish to move out.

If the fishing in Chequamegon Bay sounds too good to be true, to a certain extent it is. The shoreline along all of these areas is part of the Bad River Band of the Lake Superior Tribe of Chippewa Indians Reservation, and there is virtually no access except by boat. The ramp at Second Landing off Reykdal Road gives motorized boats ready access to this area, but the location is a long way off for self-propelled craft.

If you are looking for a guide for the area, Capt. Roger Lapenter, of Anglers All in Ashland, has been fly fishing the bay for over 20 years and welcomes the chance to introduce first-timers to Chequamegon Bay. He is also a great source of information. Lapenter will make arrangements to ferry kayaks into the back areas of the bay; he will also provide drop-off and pick-up service for anglers interested in wading.

By July, the majority of smallmouth have departed the east bay shallows and have spread out into the main bay. Shoreline activity near Ashland picks up, with fish congregating around shoreline rocks, piers, and a variety of timber. Mid-bay humps and rock piles also hold fish. Angler will find pike, walleye, and panfish all year. A variety of sinking-tip lines will be useful to present flies in these areas. Crayfish patterns may be a good choice, because these crustaceans will be active across the bottom of the bay at this time.

A technique I have found productive in summer is to fish a Rabbit Strip Diver on a sinking line. The fly will be pulled under the surface when stripped, but will

Catching big smallmouth bass on topwater flies draws fly anglers to Lake Superior's Chequamegon Bay. Special regulations have allowed bass to reach large size in substantial numbers, creating a unique trophy fishery.

suspend and even rise slightly between strips. This stationary presentation is particularly effective when fish are in a tentative mood and not chasing actively. It has accounted for countless smallmouth, plus walleye and other species around the Great Lakes.

There are a number of launch areas along the main bay around Ashland, including the city power plant. The plant also offers shore access to its warmwater discharge, which attracts a variety of fish year-round and becomes, literally and figuratively, a "hot spot" for fishing during the colder months. When baitfish are in the discharge, predators are sure to follow, and the action can be fast and furious.

Exciting early season action may also be found at the extreme west end of the bay in the Fish Creek recreation area. Part of the South Shore of Lake Superior Fish and Wildlife Area, this location is accessible where U.S. Route 2 crosses the river. Both boat and wading anglers can fish here for northern pike, bass, and a variety of panfish, and in the fall, trout and salmon. The setting includes a large slough area as well as the creek mouth where the stream enters Chequamegon Bay.

Whittlesey Creek National Wildlife Refuge, the site of an ongoing effort to reestablish a population of coaster brook trout, is also at the west end of Chequamegon Bay. Brown trout and salmon can be found at the mouth of Whittlesey Creek in the fall, and both browns and steelhead frequent the area at ice-out in the spring.

Along the bay to the north, the topography changes, with higher bluffs appearing along the lake shore. The city of Washburn, with its New England–like setting, offers a number of launch areas but little in the way of shoreline access. Species in this area include smallmouth bass, pike, and brown trout. Look for the bass and pike around downed timber and weedy areas, and expect to encounter trout early and late in the season.

From Washburn it is possible to cross the bay and fish the east end, always remembering that the open waters of the bay can quickly become treacherous. Don't make the crossing in anything less than a 16-foot deep-V boat with adequate power. A wind change can turn a pleasant trip across Chequamegon Bay into a white-knuckle return trip. Always check the marine forecast before heading out.

From late August through September, and into early October, interesting things begin to happen here from an angling perspective. The mouth of the bay around Chequamegon Point and Long Island will have plenty of smallmouth already ganged up around structure. In addition, salmon and trout will begin to move toward the shallower areas of the bay. Capt. Roger Lapenter notes that these fish will be gorging on baitfish, sometimes pushing bait to the surface in a full-blown blitz.

This is one of the few times and places where a fly angler can encounter a full assortment of both coldwater and warmwater species on a single day. Baitfish patterns are good choices, and the line may vary from floating to fast-sinking, depending on the level where the fish are holding in the water column. The multi-tip line system I describe in the "Gearing Up" section is perfectly suited to this situation, allowing the angler to quickly adjust to conditions without having to carry a suitcase full of reels and lines.

North of Washburn on Highway 13 are the mouths of the Sioux and Onion Rivers. Both attract good numbers of steelhead and some brown trout in the spring. In the fall, salmon and some browns will be found here. This is a good area to launch kayaks, canoes, and float tubes to explore the visible drop-off to deeper water. Early in the morning and just before dark, fish may be seen rolling and chasing bait in the shallows.

Pikes Creek, a bit farther north along Highway 13, has a mouth area worth exploring. Good numbers of both chinook and coho salmon, along with brown trout, can be found here in early fall. Lake trout also show up from time to time, and this may be one of the better locations around the lakes to encounter splake, the lake trout–brook trout hybrid. Again, low-light periods promise the highest success rates.

Chequamegon Bay, which ranks as one of the most diverse fisheries in the Great Lakes, provides fly fishers with a variety of opportunities from ice-out to ice-up. Many areas are quite accessible, although others require bringing your own boat or hiring a guide. Regardless of how the angler decides to approach it, anyone interested in fly fishing in the Great Lakes should plan to visit Wisconsin's Chequamegon Bay.

Minnesota's North Shore, North Shorelines of Wisconsin and Michigan

To those living in the Great Lakes area, the North Shore refers to the Lake Superior shoreline from Duluth, Minnesota, to Grand Portage on the Canadian border, a region of cobblestone beaches, granite cliffs, and spruce-covered hills periodically bisected by rivers rushing to join Lake Superior. Highway 61 from Duluth is the main route through this near-wilderness.

The St. Louis River, the largest of Lake Superior's tributaries, empties into the lake between Duluth, Minnesota, and Superior, Wisconsin. Primarily a warmwater fishery, this area provides fly-fishing opportunities for smallmouth bass, pike, muskie, and walleye, along with a good population of white bass. Although the St. Louis is technically a tributary and outside the scope of this book, the lower estuary area deserves a mention. Fly anglers may also want to consider the Duluth–Superior Harbor.

Capt. Ouitdee Carson, an Arrowhead Fly Angler guide on the river, provides a map (http://files.dnr.state.mn.us/maps/canoe_routes/stlouislower.pdf) of the estuary/harbor showing various launch areas. The estuary has a variety of riprap, weedlines, and back bays. Near the main harbor, the St. Louis has a more industrial character, with docks, boat slips, riprap, and other structure. Smallmouth are the main fly-rod quarry here, although pike are abundant, and there are enough muskie to keep things interesting.

From a rocky perch, Capt. Leo Wright pushes out a cast into Lake Superior. Being able to throw for distance and cover water can be an asset when blind-casting areas in search of fish. Being elevated above the surface is also an advantage for increased casting distance and visibility.

Sunrise hits a coaster brook trout from the Michigan waters of Lake Superior. Remnant populations of these fish still exist. BRAD PETZKE

You have to stick with an 8-weight outfit here as a minimum: there is always the chance to hook up with a big pike or a muskie, and the lower river is wide enough that you may be dealing with windy conditions. Also, most fishing here involves larger, air-resistant patterns, and the heavier gear makes casting easier.

Adding a short bite-tippet of the new knottable titanium wire is a plus to help keep toothy critters attached, and doesn't seem to have a significant negative effect on smallmouth's interest. Pike fishing is generally better early in the season; at that time, they are eager to hit a variety of bright, flashy streamers.

Muskie can show up at nearly any time, but the best time to target them is early fall, when they are on the prowl for food. Look for muskies in isolated weed beds, where they wait to ambush the smaller fish that swim by. Big flies are the norm in the fall, so a 10-weight outfit with a 350- to 400-grain integrated sink-head line is the best choice to make casting as easy as possible.

Numerous streams of various sizes enter Lake Superior between Duluth and the Canadian border. The smaller river mouths are more likely to attract fish during high-water periods. Spring will attract steelhead, while good rains in the fall will bring

Superior steel. This fish hit a baitfish pattern worked just off a creek mouth.

some steelhead, coho, and chinook. The region also has a hatchery-based put-and-grow program for Kamloops rainbow. The best time to find these is often late winter: February and March. Cold stuff for sure!

The Kamloops—or "loopers," as they are known locally—are generally caught with a nymph and a slow retrieve on either a floating or intermediate line. Prince nymphs, stoneflies, beadhead caddis, and small Buggers work, but the favorite fly is the Superior X-Legs. Anglers also may discover they've caught a steelhead while chasing loopers.

There is a small group of anglers who chase steelhead at the river mouths exclusively from small craft, including float tubes. Jeff Hinz, a veteran North Shore fly fisher, uses a Hobie Float Cat with fins and oars to target both staging and drop-back steelhead. Hinz uses an intermediate line most of the time, but he also brings Type II and Type III sinkers into the mix as needed.

Hinz will fish any time of day, but he prefers a slight chop on the surface and overcast conditions. His favorite fly is a Woolly Bugger in black or brown—sometimes with a bead, sometimes with-

A mature Lake Superior coho. Most will weigh 3 to 5 pounds due to a limited food supply and slow growth rate in the lake's cold waters. Even in midsummer, average surface temperature is in the mid-50s.

out. His back-up pattern is an Egg Sucking Leech in black or purple, with a red or pink egg. There can be a lot of fishless time, Hinz says, but when you hook up, "it's worth it." He fishes for steelhead into late May; he also reports encounters with lake trout and the occasional coaster brookie.

Other locations for Kamloops include the Lester, French, Knife, and Sucker Rivers, all crossed by Route 61 between Duluth and the town of Two Harbors, and the Stewart and Split Rock Rivers further north. These streams also see migratory steelhead and salmon, as well as brown and lake trout from time to time. "A Fishing Guide to Lake Superior and North Shore Trout Streams," an excellent map available online from the Minnesota Department of Natural Resources (http://files .dnr.state.mn.us/maps/trout_streams/ns_fishing_guide02.pdf), gives detailed information on stream location, access areas, and boat launches for a good portion of this area.

Minnesota North Shore, North Shorelines of Wisconsin and Michigan Essentials

Primary Species and Peak Times

Steelhead and brown trout: May, October, November
Salmon: mid-August–mid-October
Coaster brook trout: May
Lake trout: May, September
Kamloops rainbows: February, March
Northern pike: May, June
Smallmouth bass: May, June
Muskellunge: June, September, October

Useful Fly Patterns

Steelhead and Brown Trout
Superior X-Legs #8-12
Woolly Buggers #6-10; brown and black
Egg Sucking Leech #6-8; black and purple
Black Lake Leech
Bait Bugger
Ice-Out Alewife

Coho and Pink Salmon
Deep Minnows #4-8; all-pink, pink-white, chartreuse-white, chartreuse-pink

Chinook Salmon
Half and Half #1/0-4; gray-white and glo
Chartreuse and White Glow
Flashtail Deceiver
Ice-Out Alewife

Coaster Brook Trout
Black Lake Leech
Bait Bugger

Lake Trout
Half and Half #1/0; all-white
Meatwagon #1/0; all-white
Great Lakes Deceiver; all-white, olive-white, gray-white

Kamloops Rainbow
Superior X-Legs #8-12; regular and beadhead
Beadhead Prince
Stonefly and caddis nymphs #8-12
Egg patterns #8-12

Northern Pike
Double Bunny #3/0; red-white, chartreuse-orange
Meatwagon Max; fire tiger
Great Lakes Deceiver; red-white, fire tiger, chartreuse-black

Smallmouth Bass
Deep Minnow and Half and Half #1/0-4; chartreuse-white, olive-white, olive-orange
Mike's Murdich; all colors
Meatwagon #1; olive and fire tiger
SF Crawfish
Crazi Craw
Blockhead
Baby Blockhead
Zudbubbler
Diver and popper #1; frog-colored

There are still more interesting opportunities along the 150-mile stretch from Duluth to the Canadian border. Shallow reef areas close to shore attract plenty of fish, including lake trout in the fall, coming in to spawn. Lakers can also be caught in harbor areas off piers and breakwalls. The month of May into June is also a great time to target lake trout from river mouths, because the water coming from the rivers then is warmer than the lake water. The warmer waters host active insects, which attracts baitfish—and the lake trout will follow. To get their attention, throw a white flashy streamer on an integrated sinking-head line.

The Arrowhead River north of Grand Marais, Minnesota, provides a little-known opportunity for smallmouth bass at its mouth and estuary. It is a real mystery as to exactly where these fish are from, but it is believed they may drop back to the

Muskellunge

Swaptail Streamer
CAT 5; fire tiger, black-
   orange, black-chartreuse
Super 8; brown-orange, gray-
   orange
Muskie Meth
Muskie Marauder
Natural Born Killer

Fly Shops, Guides, Information

Anglers All
Ashland, WI
anglersallwisconsin.com
715-682-5754

Bow-Fly
Ashland, WI
bowfly.net
715-682-3277

Great Lakes Fly
Duluth, MN
greatlakesflys.com
218-740-3040

The Superior Fly Angler
Superior, WI
superiorflyangler.com
715-395-9520

Capt. Ouitdee Carson
arrowheadflyfishers.com
218-590-1712

Damien Wilmot
Fly By Night Guide Service
fbnguideservice.com
218-390-0629

Tim Pearson
River Blend Studio
riverblendstudio.com
218-220-9371

Capt. Brad Petzke
Rivers North Fly Fishing
   Guide Service
riversnorth.net
906-458-8125

Scott Thorpe
Scott Thorpe Fly Fishing
scottthorpeflyfishing.com
612-669-9601

Books & Publications

Fishing Lake Superior by
   Shawn Perich
Flyfisher's Guide to Michigan
   by Jim Bedford
*Flyfisher's Guide to Min-
   nesota* by Mickey Johnson
*Flyfisher's Guide to Wiscon-
   sin and Iowa* by John
   Motoviloff
*Fly-Fishing the North Coun-
   try* by Shawn Perich
Michigan Atlas and Gazetteer
   by DeLorme Publishing
*Minnesota Atlas and
   Gazetteer* by DeLorme
   Publishing
*Wisconsin Atlas and
   Gazetteer* by DeLorme
   Publishing

mouth from a lake upriver. Anglers fishing the Arrowhead have the rare possibility of catching brook trout and smallmouth from the same river on the same day.

The real jewel catch for North Shore anglers is the coaster brook trout. Research indicates their numbers have increased over the last few years, perhaps owing to a slowly increasing population in Ontario waters, or maybe the result of restrictive limits put into place on the North Shore a number of years ago. Regardless of the cause, the prospects of catching a coaster in Minnesota are better than they have been for a long time.

Except during spawning season, coasters are elusive and hard to locate. As their name implies, they move around constantly. When they are found, it is generally in a very narrow band of habitat along the shoreline. Coasters are more common

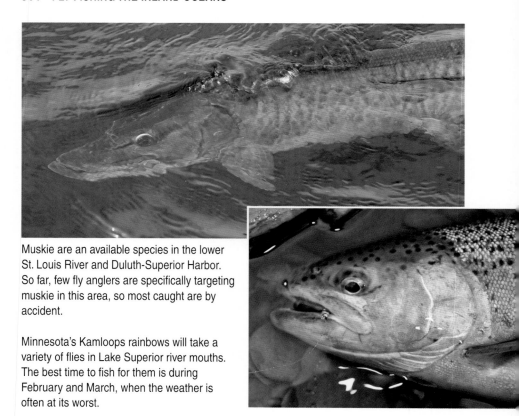

Muskie are an available species in the lower St. Louis River and Duluth-Superior Harbor. So far, few fly anglers are specifically targeting muskie in this area, so most caught are by accident.

Minnesota's Kamloops rainbows will take a variety of flies in Lake Superior river mouths. The best time to fish for them is during February and March, when the weather is often at its worst.

toward the Canadian border, which would seem to support the idea that they are moving south in increasing numbers into Minnesota waters.

Tim Pearson, a North Shore fly-fishing guide from Silver Bay, searches for coasters in sheltered bays and along shallow reef areas. He has caught them at the mouths of rivers, including the Arrowhead, Devil Track, and Poplar. Pearson tries for coasters mainly in the spring, when steelhead and sucker eggs are available. This food source seems to attract coasters. However, Pearson finds them to be opportunistic feeders and reports that he has caught more on a black strip leech than anything else. He prefers not to fish for them in the fall when they come into spawn. Despite his experience, "most coasters," Pearson says, "are still caught by accident."

Heading east from Duluth to Sault Ste. Marie, Michigan, there are countless areas worth exploring; an angler could spend several lifetimes just on this stretch of water alone. Chequamegon Bay has been deservedly discussed as a separate entity, but I want to highlight several other areas that are easy to get to and that provide a variety of angling opportunities.

The Bois Brule River is one of the best known of Lake Superior's steelhead streams. To most anglers it is known as simply "the Brule." Its fish are pure, wild, and known for their fighting ability. There are no supplement steelhead stockings here. The population is self-sustaining. The Brule gets a good run of steelhead in the fall—trailing behind the salmon entering the river—and another run in the spring.

Kings and pinks stage here in late August, entering the river in September. Coho stage and enter the river later in the fall, normally from late September into October.

Anglers can get to the river mouth and estuary by following Brule River Road off WI Route 13. There is no formal boat launch here, but smaller craft can be carried to the water and launched. The few anglers who fly-fish the river mouth generally throw black Woolly Buggers. They are successful with these, but this area is totally open to exploration with respect to technique and patterns. Damian Wilmot, of Fly By Night Guide Service and Arrowhead Fly Angler, guides here for fly anglers.

The mouth of the Ontonagon River, in Michigan waters, also deserves highlighting. One of the largest rivers on the South Shore of Lake Superior, the Ontonagon empties into a small harbor with a marina and launch area. Two parallel piers extend out into the lake, where anglers can take advantage of seasonal opportunities for salmon, steelhead, browns, lakers, and pike. The Ontonagon Lighthouse is a popular attraction. This is also the gateway to the Porcupine Mountains Wilderness area, which includes 60,000 acres of the last stand of virgin hardwood forest left in Michigan.

The Keweenaw Peninsula is another area that could sustain a lifetime of exploration. There are dozens of small streams along the shoreline, and any trickle emptying into Lake Superior has the potential of drawing fish to its mouth during high water. The Keweenaw Waterway and the Portage River connect to cut across the peninsula. Anglers can establish a base in the town of Houghton and fish the peninsula for trout, salmon, pike, smallmouth, walleye, and panfish.

Eagle River, Eagle Harbor, Copper Harbor, Lac La Belle, Traverse Bay, and Jacobsville are towns and villages on the peninsula with boat launches. Much of this area is virtually unexplored, especially from a fly-fishing standpoint. Consult a gazetteer and take a look at Google Earth to help select fishing areas. The web site http://www.keweenaw.info/activities/fishing gives an excellent overview of fishing opportunities on the peninsula.

There are several rivers named Huron in Michigan. The one cited here enters Lake Superior between L'Anse and Marquette. It is considered one of the best steelhead rivers on the Upper Peninsula. The mouth is best reached from the west via the town of L'Anse. This Huron River has a steep gradient and runs clearer than most other waters in the area, lacking the characteristic tannin color.

In the spring and fall, fish streamers at the mouth of the Huron for steelhead and salmon. Lake trout are another potential target. This is even a spot where an angler might encounter a coaster brook trout.

Marquette, the largest city on Michigan's Upper Peninsula, is within easy distance of a variety of fly-fishing destinations, but there are also opportunities right at its doorstep. There are two harbor areas, each with public launch ramps, and piers that have plenty of room for casting. The lower harbor seems to be the most popular with anglers; it has resident populations of both northern pike and smallmouth bass, and it attracts a full range of migratory fish as well. Splake also are caught here regularly.

Throwing baitfish patterns is the easiest way to locate fish in the lower harbor. Once again, the 250- to 300-grain integrated sinking, shooting-taper line is the tool for this work. If you are using watercraft, you can fish old ore docks and other structure. The period of ice-out through May offers the best change for a variety of species. Capt. Brian Petzke, of Rivers North Fly Fishing Guide Service, has fished the Marquette area for many years.

The Two Hearted River may be the most recognized name among Upper Peninsula streams thanks to the short story by Ernest Hemingway—"Big Two-Hearted River"—inspired by a Michigan fishing trip. Today, this river mouth area experiences a fair amount of fishing pressure, at least by Lake Superior standards, when Pacific salmon stage for their spawning runs. Chinook, pinks, and coho all enter this stream, along with brown and steelhead in the fall. In the spring, lake trout cruise the mouth and adjacent shoreline in search of prey. Coho and browns are also part of the mix, along with drop-back steelhead.

This has been just a small sampling of the area. The amount of water here is mind-boggling, and simply trying to pick a place to fish is a challenge in itself. There is some fly-fishing history in this region, but countless areas remain to be explored and tested. In this near-wilderness, with wonderful scenery, any fish caught becomes an extra bonus.

Thunder Bay, Nipigon Bay, and Ontario's North Shore

A drive around the top of the Lake Superior on Ontario's Highway 17 goes over the backbone of the earth, the Canadian Shield. This is the oldest rock on the planet, formed during the Precambrian era. Highway 17, a necessary link between small outposts of civilization, follows lakeside cliffs and cuts across forested hills. This road travels through some of the most spectacular scenery in North America, as endless stands of conifers give way to vistas of Lake Superior's brilliant blue waters to the south.

Thunder Bay is the largest city in northwest Ontario and the starting point for travel around the top of Lake Superior. From Duluth, Route 61 continues north across the border and ends at Route 17, the Trans-Canada Highway. To give an idea of the size of Lake Superior, the distance from Sault Ste. Marie to Thunder Bay is nearly 440 miles. The distance from Duluth to Thunder Bay is 191 miles. That's a lot of area for exploration.

There is excellent fly fishing in and around Thunder Bay. Several accessible river mouths offer a variety of species. The mouth of the Kaministiquia ("Kam") River, reachable from Mission Island, holds large pike, smallmouth, and walleye. A dam on the Current River forms Boulevard Lake. Below the dam, anglers encounter pike, walleye, and all the migratory trout and salmon species, according to their season. Successful fishing strategies here include streamers on a sinking-tip or even swinging flies on a two-hander, depending on flows. The site www.thunderbay fishing.com gives good general information.

There are other excellent resources here as well. At River's Edge Fly Shop, located inside D&R Sporting Goods, owner Bill Boote can advise about fishing the area and can help connect anglers with a local guide. Scott Earl Smith, a well-known Canadian fly-fishing writer based in Thunder Bay, can also help direct visiting anglers (www.scottearlsmith.com). Smith wrote the *Ontario Blue-Ribbon Fly Fishing Guide*, which is available through his web site and at many shops in the area.

A tannic-colored river meets clear water on the North Shore of Lake Superior. JIM LINEHAN

Nipigon Bay is the northernmost point in the Great Lakes. The township of Red Rock is at the mouth of the bay, while the town of Nipigon is bit upstream. The Red Rock Inn caters to anglers and a host of other outdoor folk. The stretch of the Nipigon River from Lake Superior to Alexander's Dam is, in a sense, a lake fishery, because all the species found in Superior may be encountered here at any time of the year. This is big water—with an average flow of 12,000 cubic feet per second. The best access areas for walk and wade anglers are at Alexander's Dam off Highway 585 and at the Highway 17 bridge over the river.

Boats can be launched at both Alexander's Dam and in the town of Nipigon. Red Rock also has a full-service marina and launch ramp. Due to the Nipigon's size and flow, a boat with at least a 10-hp motor is needed to move anywhere up river. According to Scott Earl Smith, the best way to cover water from shore is to use large rabbit-strip patterns. Depending on flows, the use of a sinking-tip and even a longer sinking-head may be called for. Switch rods and even light two-hand rods are an effective tool for this purpose and are already being used by some anglers. This area is where the Muddler Minnow was created, and the pattern continues to produce well here.

June and July evenings on the Nipigon bring a variety of hatches, mostly caddis, but also giant stoneflies. Even though fishing pressure on the river is low, the fish can still be very selective, at times requiring an extra-long leader and a downstream presentation to catch their interest. Use as heavy a tippet as possible, since there is a chance for rainbows, brook trout, and whitefish up to five pounds.

Steelhead spawning occurs in April, May, and June, but this species can be found year-round in the lower river. Scott Earl Smith prefers the post-spawn period when steelhead are recovering and actively on the feed. A black Woolly Bugger swung on a sinking-tip is a favorite pattern. Anglers will encounter both bright-chrome fish and brightly colored rainbows here, which indicates there is probably continuous movement to the lake and back in this area.

Thunder Bay, Nipigon Bay, and Ontario's North Shore Essentials

Primary Species and Peak Times

Steelhead: May to October
Salmon: August, September
Coaster brook trout: May through August
Lake trout: May, June, September
Northern pike: May, June

Useful Fly Patterns

Steelhead

Black Lake Leech
Nipigon River Leech #2-6; black and olive
Bait Bugger
Lion Bugger
Blue Belly Dancer #2

Chinook Salmon

Half and Half #1/0-2; all-white, olive-white,
    gray-white
Flashtail Deceiver
Blue Belly Dancer

Coho and Pink Salmon

Deep Minnow #4-8; all-pink or pink-chartreuse
Yellow-Butt Monkey #4

Coaster Brook Trout

Black Lake Leech
Zoo Cougar #2; olive and yellow
Crawpin #2; olive and brown
Green-Butt Monkey #2-4
Nipigon River Leech #2-6

Northern Pike

Wabigoon Rattler #3/0
Meatwagon Max; fire tiger
Great Lakes Deceiver; red-white, black-
    chartreuse

Lake Trout

Half and Half #1; gray-white, olive-white
Blue Belly Dancer #2
Great Lakes Deceiver; all-white, gray-white,
    fluorescent blue-white

Fly Shops, Guides, Information

Bowman Island Charters
bowmanislandcharters.com
807-886-2504

Caribou Charters
cariboucharters.com
807-825-3719

Nipigon River Adventures
nipigonriveradventures.com
807-621-6342

Slate Island Charters
807-825-9333

Red Rock Inn
redrockinn.ca
888-547-1402

Rivers Edge Fly Shop
(D&R Sporting Goods)
Thunder Bay, Ontario
riversedgeflyshop.com
807-983-2484

Misty Mountain Fly Shop
Haviland Bay, Ontario
705-649-5813

Soo North Fly Shop
Sault Ste. Marie, Ontario
soonorthflyshop.shawwebspace.ca
705-575-7739

Thunder Bay Fishing
thunderbayfishing.com

North Shore Steelhead Association
northshoresteelhead.com

Books & Publications

Fishing Lake Superior by Shawn Perich
Fly-Fishing the North Country
    by Shawn Perich
Ontario Blue-Ribbon Fly Fishing Guide
    by Scott E. Smith

Some areas on the hiking trail from Nipigon to the head of the bay at Red Rock border the water's edge, where anglers can step in and swing flies, or cast to rising fish during hatches. It's important to be cautious here, though. Depending on the outflow from Alexander's Dam, wading can be challenging. A wading staff and shoes with cleats or studs may be necessary to ensure safety.

Chinook salmon have been known to enter the river as early as July, but most fish start their spawning run in August. They often hit large, flashy streamers while they are still in the pre-spawn period. Coaster brook trout and lake trout also come into the river during this same period. Overall spawning activity is at a peak from late September into October.

In October, the abundance of eggs in the river attracts steelhead in significant numbers. Like all Lake Superior steelhead, Nipigon fish are tremendous fighters for their size, making sizzling runs and twisting jumps. October also brings salmon, brook trout, and lakers.

The area does have fish sanctuaries to protect spawning brook trout, so be sure to double-check regulations; closing dates vary according to species. Any fish caught out-of-season must be released immediately with a minimum of handling.

Nipigon Bay has a myriad of islands and channels with shallow reefs and rock piles in the western end. Although boats of any size can be launched at either Red Rock or Nipigon, extreme caution is advised, especially in the Red Rock area where it is extremely shallow.

The folks at Nipigon River Adventures near Red Rock offer fishing as well as a variety of outdoor adventures in the area. Their lodge is an old corporate retreat center; it belonged to a paper company that operated in Red Rock for a number of years. They also offer places to stay on the lower Nipigon below Alexander Dam.

This area is part of the Lake Superior Marine Conservation Area, which was designated in 2009 to prevents resource extraction or other activities that would damage aquatic or terrestrial ecosystems. It is the largest protected freshwater marine area in the world. Some commercial marine activity is excluded, but sport-fishing is permitted.

Bowman Island Charters in Nipigon provides rental boats and transportation around Nipigon Bay. In addition, they have a lodge and several cabins on Bowman Island, just off the south shore of St. Ignace Island, giving access to rarely fished waters.

The Nipigon River holds a very special place in fly-fishing history. Here in July 1915, Dr. J.W. Cook caught the largest brook trout ever officially recorded: 14 pounds, 8 ounces. Further, Dr. Cook was on a seven-day fishing trip, and the fish was not weighed until after he returned. Based on length and girth measurements, it is believed the fish may have weighed close to 20 pounds when it was first caught.

Past the Nipigon River, there are a variety of river-mouth fishing opportunities all the way to Sault Ste. Marie. The Jackpine River is considered one of the best of these. It is a spate river at the mercy of snowmelt and rainfall. It is often unfishable during the melt in April and early May and a heavy rain at any time may also raise the water level too high and discolor the water too much to fish. Luckily, it has an accessible river mouth that holds steelhead, lake trout, and coasters through the summer. As fall nears, coho and pink salmon come into the mix.

A small streamer swung on a switch rod tempted this coaster brook trout. JIM LINEHAN

A float tube, kayak, or similar craft is a help here to fish a sinking, shooting-taper line into the lake. Fish a flashy streamer pattern and hang on when you get a grab, because you never know what might be on the other end. This same scenario holds true on most of the accessible river-mouth areas. Other patterns to try would be strip leeches and Woolly Buggers in a variety of colors. Scott Earl Smith and Bill Boote also favor Butt Monkey–style streamers as well as Zoo Cougars.

Another interesting opportunity at all these locations is the chance to take lake whitefish on dry flies. Normally a deep-water fish, whitefish often come in when regular hatches occur. They can be found most calm evenings off the river mouths. Whitefish will also takes midges at the surface if no large bugs are available, and can be very selective under this situation. Often a small Adams dry with a midge pupa suspended below it will get strikes. Whitefish are exciting fighters when hooked under these conditions, so don't overlook them as potential targets.

Unfortunately, there is no longer public access to the mouth of the Cypress River. The location changed as a result of flooding, and the river now runs through private property. However, farther east on Highway 17, other spots worth checking include McLeans Creek at the town of Rossport and the Whitesand River just past there.

The Steel River is a sizable stream that enters Lake Superior near the village of Terrace Bay, Ontario. Santoy Lake feeds the river and helps to stabilize flow and temperature throughout the summer. Subsequently, the Steel attracts good numbers of fish all summer long: wandering Atlantic salmon and brown trout from Lake Huron in addition to steelhead, brook trout, and lakers. Good numbers of chinook, coho, and pink salmon also ascend this river.

Terrace Bay is the gateway to the Slate Islands, an archipelago located about eight miles off shore. Now a provincial park, the islands are unique for their herd of woodland caribou whose ancestors crossed from the mainland in the early 1900s. Lake trout are the main quarry for anglers, who also take coasters and the odd northern pike. For adventurous anglers, there are several operations, including Caribou Charters and Slate Island Charters, that shuttle canoeists and kayakers to the islands for day trips and camping.

Michipicoten Harbor near Wawa, Ontario, has an excellent marina and launch area. The river attracts good runs of both spring and fall steelhead, and the harbor is excellent for lake trout. A bit south of here, where Highway 17 crosses the Old Woman River, the bay often holds cruising lake trout, salmon, and steelhead that will chase baitfish patterns on a sinking-tip.

Closer to Sault Ste. Marie, anglers can fish the mouth of the Agawa River and Montreal River Harbour. As you continue east, the chances for brook trout decrease, but all other species stay in the mix. Batchawana Bay, at the mouth of the Chippewa River, holds some monster pike and has good fishing for smallmouth, walleye, and perch, plus seasonal opportunities for steelhead and salmon. Use caution here: this is big, deep water compared to other areas and can get rough quickly.

Goulais Bay holds an interesting assortment of species, including pike, small-mouth, walleye, and perch. There are also muskie, and this is one of the few areas in Lake Superior where carp can be found. The usual seasonal mix of migratory species also appears in the spring and fall. The lagoon in the town of Goulais is a great pike fishery right after ice-out.

Many streams enter the lake between Wawa and the Soo. Mica and Alona Bays hold lake trout that cruise near shore all season long. There are also small, unnamed tributaries—some just trickles—that hold fish. Expect to find salmon and steelhead as well.

There are a number of boat launch sites along this stretch of shoreline. Misty Mountain Fly Shop in Haviland Bay, Ontario, can provide gear, guiding, and infor-mation on fishing this area.

Other than the Nipigon and Steel Rivers, all of the rivers along this section are spate rivers, depending on rainfall and spring melt to draw in fish. Fish are likely to be found at their mouths most of the time, but it is high water that really draws the fish into the streams. When flow is minimal, fish tend to scatter along the shore and

This coaster brookie exhibits a unique coloration pattern. Like other trout and salmon, coasters color up for spawn-ing. BRAD PETZKE

Ontario's Nipigon Bay area is once again producing trophy coaster brookies. Restrictive limits and regulations are slowly increasing numbers and allowing them to reach large size. SCOTT EARL SMITH

out in to deeper water. When waters are low, having a float tube, pontoon boat, or other personal watercraft is a big advantage, allowing an angler to quickly cover a much larger area.

The Canadian North Shore offers a wide range of fly-fishing opportunities, including the best chance to catch one of the most treasured of Great Lakes fish, the coaster brook trout. Stricter regulations have been having a positive effect on their numbers, and populations are slowly increasing. Lake trout also appear here in shallow water, giving fly anglers the chance to catch a fish not normally on their radar screen.

Another word of caution: if you are fishing this area in June, take bug dope and have a headnet handy! The blackfly hatch occurs at this time, and, to quote Scott Earl Smith, "it can make a city-slicker put a gun to his own head." The earlier part of the month is usually the worst. Also, blackflies seem to love the color blue, so best have another scheme for clothing. With a little preparation, anglers can cope with these biting swarms.

The Ontario Provincial Parks as well as Canadian National Parks provide a variety of recreational activities for travelers. The scenery in places is so beautiful that it is nearly indescribable. For anglers, fishing this area involve a lot of "do-it-yourself" work, since detailed fly-fishing information is minimal. Sea kayaking is growing in popularity here, and more outfitters are focusing on this activity. These can be a great source of information for anglers. While not focused on fly fishing, kayak outfitters can identify access areas and launch points for anglers seeking to go beyond the shoreline to the many islands along this route.

Out-of-the-Way Places

Lake Superior's Isle Royale has the hardest-to-reach shoreline fishing in the Great Lakes. The island receives fewer visitors in an entire season than Yellowstone Park gets in a single day. Roughly 45 miles long and 9 miles wide, Isle Royale is the largest island in Lake Superior. While it lies within 15 miles of both Minnesota and Ontario—and more than 50 miles from Michigan's shoreline—Isle Royale is in fact part of the state of Michigan. The island is probably best known as the site of predator-prey studies of the interactions between moose and eastern timber wolves.

For anglers, there are numerous interior lakes with northern pike and walleye, and streams with brook trout. More importantly, Isle Royale is the final bastion of natural coaster brook trout in the US waters of the Great Lakes. The redfin subspecies of lake trout can also be found cruising the island's shoreline.

There is minimal information available on fly fishing here; note that only artificial lures may be used in park waters. For a starting point, fly anglers should throw attractor streamers around accessible creek mouths and points that drop into deeper water. The ferry docks can also be productive locations. Smelt and other baitfish patterns would work here, and intermediate- and sinking-head lines will be most useful. Park rangers and other personnel can provide information on specific fishing locations.

Ferries from both Michigan and Minnesota land at Rock Harbor on the eastern end of the island, where a lodge, campground, and information center are located. Ferries from Minnesota also land on the west end at Windigo, which has a

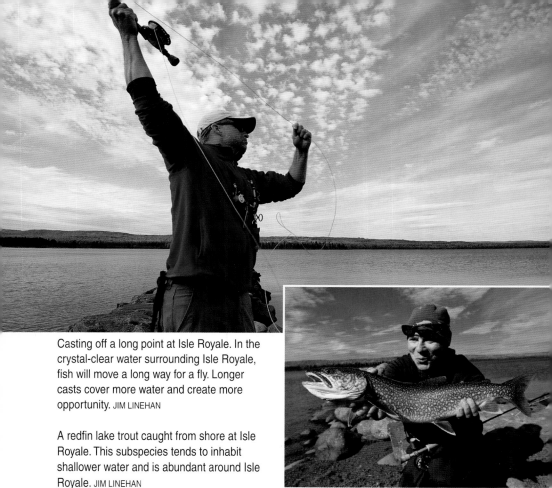

Casting off a long point at Isle Royale. In the crystal-clear water surrounding Isle Royale, fish will move a long way for a fly. Longer casts cover more water and create more opportunity. JIM LINEHAN

A redfin lake trout caught from shore at Isle Royale. This subspecies tends to inhabit shallower water and is abundant around Isle Royale. JIM LINEHAN

campground and visitor center. Float-plane service is also available, and there is a marina at Rock Harbor. Once on the island, walking is the only way to get around. Rock Harbor and Tobin Harbor provide excellent shore-fishing opportunities.

The island is crisscrossed with nearly 170 miles of hiking trails, providing access to a number of fishable shoreline locations. Anglers and other visitors can bring small boats, canoes, and kayaks across on the ferries to travel around the island. These may also be necessary to reach some of many campsites on Isle Royale; some can only be reached by boat.

For noncampers, Rock Harbor Lodge offers accommodations, a restaurant, and a store for supplies. Lodging reservations should be made well in advance. The Rock Harbor marina rents canoes, kayaks, and boats with motors for those wanting to explore farther-away areas. A water-taxi service from here will also take visitors to more remote areas so they can hike out.

Lake Superior contributes another "off-the-grid" location for fly anglers in the Stannard Rock Reef, a shoal area 44 miles off the shore of Marquette, Michigan. This underwater mountain range is nearly five miles long and a mile wide, with numerous peaks and pinnacles rising out of 700 feet of water. There are several areas where the reef stands completely out of the water.

Out-of-the-Way Places Essentials

Primary Species and Peak Times

Coaster brook trout: May–August
Lake trout: May–August

Useful Fly Patterns

Coaster Brook Trout

Black Lake Leech
Yellow-Butt Monkey #4
Zoo Cougar #2; olive
Crawpin #2; olive and brown
Nipigon River Leech

Lake Trout

Half and Half #1/0-2; gray-white and olive-
   white
Blue Belly Dancer
Great Lakes Deceiver; all-white, gray-white,
   fluorescent blue-white

Fly Shops, Guides, Information

Great Lakes Fly Shop
Duluth, MN
greatlakesflys.com
218-740-3040

Superior Fly Angler
Superior, WI
superiorflyangler.com
715-395-9520

Capt. Brad Petzke
riversnorth.net
906-458-8125

Capt. John Tomczyk
daybreakfish.com
906-250-1052

Books & Publications

Fishing Lake Superior by Shawn Perich
Fly-Fishing the North Country
   by Shawn Perich
Michigan Atlas and Gazetteer
   by DeLorme Publishing

Stannard Rock was long considered one of the most dangerous navigation hazards on Lake Superior. A lighthouse was first constructed there in 1883, and the crib supporting it is considered one of the top ten engineering feats in the United States. The lighthouse is 24 miles from the nearest land—the most distant from shore of any lighthouse in American coastal waters.

The draw of Stannard Rock is light-tackle sportfishing for lake trout. Normally a deepwater fish—except during short periods in spring and fall—lakers can be caught in the shallows around Stannard all summer long. Mid-May to mid-August is considered prime time. Both redfin (lean) and siscowet (fat) lake trout subspecies are available and—very occasionally—splake, steelhead, Atlantic, or Pacific salmon species are caught.

Fly fishing for lakers at Stannard Rock is a relatively recent occurrence. Capt. Brad Petzke, of Rivers North Fly Fishing Guide Service, has teamed up with Capt. John Tomczyk, of Daybreak Charters, Marquette, Michigan, to start throwing large streamers on sinking lines for Stannard Rock lakers. Fish of up to 60 pounds have been caught here in recent years, and populations are healthy. This out-of-the-way spot on Lake Superior provides an alternative to lengthy trips into the Arctic to catch trophy-sized lakers on flies.

chapter 13

Environmental
Issues

The environmental legacy of the Great Lakes could fill a number of volumes. So could the issues that still remain to be resolved. Much has already been written by others, but I would like to offer a short review of the past and present the current state of affairs.

Today's Great Lakes are certainly different from those seen by the first European explorers. As much of the world has changed between then and now, so have the lakes. Humans now have significant control over water levels in the Great Lakes Basin. The original forests have been replaced by farmland and housing tracts. Shorelines are populated with skyscrapers, office buildings, and industrial factories. Many tributary streams are warmer than they used to be, and carry more sediment. Fish populations have changed: some native species are extinct, while other invasives or nonnatives deliberately introduced into the lakes are thriving.

The lakes have been besieged by man's influence. Once abundant natural resources have been abused and, in some cases, nearly depleted. Toxic chemicals can be found in lake sediments and in the flesh of fish taken from the lakes. Acidic rain falls from the skies, and few of the original wetlands along the lakes shoreline still exist.

It is easy to trace the transformation of the region. Early explorers, eager to supply the European fur trade, pushed animals such as the beaver to near extinction. The massive forests surrounding the lakes were cut down in less than a century. Commercial fishing, once a major industry of the region, is nearly nonexistent. The earliest settlers thought that the resources of the lakes were inexhaustible, but now we know otherwise.

By the start of the twentieth century, the lakes were well on their way to tragic degradation. Streams full of raw sewage, and waste from meat processing and the growing steel and chemical industries were pouring directly into the lakes. As early as the late 1830s, sea lampreys were entering Lake Ontario through man-made canals and locks. Until 1919, Niagara Falls served as the barrier that prevented them from entering the upper lakes. After 1919, improvements in the Welland Canal allowed passage of the lampreys to Lake Erie and beyond.

By 1938, sea lampreys had reached Lake Michigan. In the 1940s and '50s, the double knockout-punch from the lampreys and pollution caused the collapse of native fish populations, in particular deep-water species such as lake trout.

Sea lampreys are still a threat to fish populations in the Great Lakes. They will attack both warm and coldwater species. An ongoing parade of invasive species continues to threaten Great Lakes sportfishing.

The canal also opened the entire Great Lakes system to other invasive species. Alewives, a herring species, arrived and, lacking a top-level predator, began to fill the lakes. In the 1960s, massive die-offs of alewives covered Great Lakes beaches by the millions. In Lake Erie, blooms of toxic blue-green algae caused oxygen depletion, killing fish and fouling beaches. The lakes were in big trouble, with little help in sight.

The infamous fire on Cleveland's Cuyahoga River in 1969 helped spur the passage of the Clean Water Act in 1972, legislation that led to controls on industrial and municipal discharge into the lakes. In the late 1970s, the discovery of toxins at Love Canal near Buffalo, New York, brought attention to hazardous waste dumps that were leaching dangerous chemicals into the lakes. Overall awareness of the problems of the Great Lakes increased significantly.

In 1966, coho salmon were stocked in Lake Michigan, and a year later chinook salmon were planted. It was hoped that these Pacific coast natives would prey on the nuisance alewives and bring their numbers under control. For better or worse, these salmon species took hold much better than expected. Now, nearly 50 years later there are naturally reproducing populations of both species in the lakes. Their presence has created a multibillion dollar sport fishery.

The alewife is an invasive species whose explosive populations and die-offs fouled beach and shoreline areas. This led to the stocking of predatory Pacific salmon in an attempt to bring alewife populations under control.

Pink salmon, introduced accidentally, are also now considered one of the regular species found in the Great Lakes. Migratory rainbow trout, called steelhead, have been present in the lakes for over 140 years. Brown trout imported from Europe are here. And there are current efforts to reestablish naturally reproducing populations of Atlantic salmon, the native salmon of Lake Ontario.

A variety of methods are used for lamprey control in Great Lakes tributaries. This barrier is on Wisconsin's Kewaunee River. In some locations, chemical lampricides are put into tributaries to kill lampreys.

Alewife numbers in Lake Huron have decreased to the point that the salmon that feed on them are struggling to survive. Populations of native lake trout are starting to rebound. Good news, some may say—but, then, it is the salmon that draw more interest and money from sport anglers. The sportfish industry drives much of the economy around the Great Lakes; this is of particular importance to areas that have lost their economic base of industry or shipping.

The parade of invasive species continues. White perch, ruffe, zebra mussels, spiny water fleas, round gobies, and quagga mussels have all entered the Great Lakes system through ballast water discharge from ocean-going vessels. Most have had initial population booms, which have then decreased to a level that the system could support. Quagga mussels are the latest of these invasives and their overall effect is yet to be felt. Both zebra and quagga mussels are filter-feeders that remove nutrients from the water. This can affect the entire food chain by reducing the amount of phytoplankton and zooplankton, the building blocks of the Great Lakes food web.

Other invasives causing concern are the bighead carp and silver carp. These species were brought to the southern United States for weed control in aquaculture, but escaped and became established across the Mississippi Basin. They are now at the doorstep of the Great Lakes.

These, too, are filter-feeders, and the fear is if they enter the Great Lakes in numbers, they will create further pressure on an ecosystem already under stress from the zebra and quagga mussels: further disruption at the base of the food chain supporting most Great Lakes fish species. The U.S. Army Corps of Engineers has erected an electric barrier on the Chicago Sanitary and Ship Canal to block passage

Despite great strides in improving water quality, much of the Great Lakes is still subject to industrial discharges as well as agricultural runoff. These will continue to require continuous monitoring to ensure that the waters of the lakes stay up-to-standard.

of these fish. So far this appears to be successful; however, genetic material from these fish has been detected in DNA testing of Lake Michigan and Lake Erie water samples.

It is interesting to note that the fall of 2011 saw one of the best returns of both coho and chinook salmon to Lake Michigan tributaries in several decades. Overall numbers and average size of both species were significantly larger than in the several previous years. Fishery managers are still analyzing information to determine why this occurred.

At the same time, reminiscent of the 1960s, the years 2010 and 2011 saw large summertime blooms of toxic blue-green algae in Lake St. Clair and the western basin of Lake Erie. The combined impact of several factors are believed to have caused this. First, increased water clarity (attributed to the filtering impact of the quagga mussel population) allowed radiant energy from the sun to reach deeper into the water, stimulating growth. Second, above-average summer temperatures also stimulated growth. The third, and perhaps most important, factor was an increase in spring rainfalls that washed freshly applied, phosphate-rich fertilizers into the water systems. (Research has shown that phosphates are a major cause of blue-green algae blooms.)

Another ongoing threat to the Great Lakes centers around their essence: water. There have been many proposals to export water from the lakes to arid areas throughout the United States and other parts of the world. In his book *The Great Lakes Water Wars*, author Peter Annin reviews this issue in depth. While oil may be necessary to maintain our way of life, water is necessary to maintain life itself.

The Great Lakes Water Pact—banning the commercial export of water from the lakes and pledging to continue its cleanup—was signed in 2005 by governors of eight states and two provinces. The pact became federal law in 2008. For now, the threat of out-of-basin diversions of water has been eliminated, but other provisions of the law—such as continued reduction of pollutants and increasing water-use efficiency—have been slow to take hold.

The Clean Water Act of 1974, which addressed point-source pollution, mainly from industrial sources and municipal water treatment facilities, has been extremely effective and has had a significant positive impact on the lakes. However, non-point-source pollutants, mainly farmland fertilizer run-off, has continued nearly unchecked. In addition, antiquated sewer systems in a number of municipalities can be overwhelmed during significant storms, allowing millions of gallons of untreated raw sewage to be discharged into Great Lakes Basin waters. The recent algae blooms should be a warning shot across our bow that significant problems still exist and need to be addressed.

Despite all of the abuse that has been heaped upon them, the Great Lakes have endured. They exhibit an amazing, almost human-like ability to adapt and survive. Granted, our intervention has played a large role. Still, given the chance, natural forces also will respond quickly to stabilize after sustaining a damaging blow.

In Lake Huron, for example, the loss of the alewife food base resulted in a crash of the chinook salmon fishery, which has been introduced by humans. At the same time, the native lake trout and naturalized steelhead populations are rebounding without our help, simply because these species are more opportunistic in their feeding and able to adapt to other food sources, such as the invasive round goby.

I grew up on the shores of Lake Erie and in the 1960s and '70s, witnessed first-hand the mats of stinking, rotting blue-green algae that robbed the lake of much-needed oxygen to sustain life. I was there when gas and oil slicks on Cleveland's Cuyahoga River caught fire, and I listened to the jokes made about the lake and river. I heard the pronouncements that "Lake Erie is dead," and that the rest of the Great Lakes were not far behind.

I also witnessed, in the 1980s, the rebirth of this lake, as the regulations set forth in the Clean Water Act took effect, and Lake Erie emerged as a nationally known sportfishing destination. Through the 1990s and into the twenty-first century, Lake Erie's tributaries became known as "Steelhead Alley," attracting fly anglers from all over the world. Even then, however, the ongoing parade of invasive species continued—and still continues today. The fish are still here, we thought, so no problem.

A new alarm bell rang in the summer of 2011, as algae blooms again began to choke the life out of western Lake Erie, creating a giant "dead zone" where no fish could live. This was the second summer in a row this had occurred. I listened as Capt. Brian Meszaros canceled trips on his beloved Lake St. Clair, where farmland sediment and runoff had turned the normally crystal-clear waters to the consistency of pea soup. Much of St. Clair remained in that condition until fall.

In 1987, a book titled *The Late, Great Lakes* was published. Written by William Ashworth, it predicts the death-knell of the lakes. Although a number of the threats he outlines have been addressed or averted, we can see that there still many potential threats and issues to contend with. Perhaps the most dangerous is the continuing trend of self-serving politicians to focus on local special interests rather than the good of the entire system.

A number of studies have called for the construction of a permanent barrier to block the passage of Asian carp into Lake Michigan. Yet we continue to rely on a suspect electronic barrier to hold back this potential invader. Farm lobbies resist changes in the use and type of fertilizers on farmlands in Great Lakes drainage areas. Money-starved municipal governments do not have the funding for improving infrastructure to deal with storm-event problems.

It would be folly to think that the Great Lakes are in great shape and everything is fine. Early explorers thought the resources of the region were "inexhaustible," but we know otherwise. The blue pike, a popular Lake Erie food and sport fish became extinct in the 1950s because of pollution, overharvesting, and lack of proper management. Millions of people depend on the lakes for water, work, and recreation. The total value of the region is impossible to calculate.

In spite of this, there are positive signs that show awareness of the Great Lakes and their value is increasing. Although frustratingly slow at times, this is happening. I remain very cautiously optimistic that common sense will prevail and that the positive legacy of the lakes will continue. I hope that this work will help provide a step in that direction.

Bibliography

Bedford, Jim. *Flyfisher's Guide to Michigan*. Belgrade, MT: Wilderness Adventures Press, 2010.

Hauptmann, Cliff. *The Fly Fisher's Guide to Warmwater Lakes*. New York: Lyons and Burford, 1995.

Holschlag, Tim. *Smallmouth Fly Fishing: The Best Techniques, Flies, and Destinations*. Minneapolis: Smallmouth Angler Press, 2005.

Johnson, Mickey. *Flyfisher's Guide to Minnesota*. Belgrade, MT: Wilderness Adventure Press, 2001.

Kustich, Rick, and Jerry Kustich. *Fly Fishing for Great Lakes Steelhead: An Advanced Look at an Emerging Fishery*. Grand Island, NY: West River Publishing, 1999.

Linsenman, Bob. *Best Streams for Great Lakes Steelhead: A Complete Guide to the Fish, the Tactics, and the Places to Catch Them*. Woodstock, VT: Countryman Press, 2005.

———. *Michigan Blue-Ribbon Fly-Fishing Guide*. Portland, OR: Frank Amato Publications, 2002.

Linsenman, Bob, and Steve Nevala. *Great Lakes Steelhead: A Guided Tour for Fly-Anglers*. Woodstock, VT: Back Country Publications, 1995.

Mitchell, Ed. *Fly Rodding Estuaries: How to Fish Salt Ponds, Coastal Waters, Tidal Creeks, and Backwaters*. Harrisburg, PA: Stackpole Books, 2003.

Motoviloff, John. *Flyfisher's Guide to Wisconsin and Iowa*. Belgrade, MT: Wilderness Adventures Press, 2006.

Nagy, John. *Steelhead Guide: Fly Fishing Techniques and Strategies for Lake Erie Steelhead*. Pittsburgh: Great Lakes Publishing, 1998.

Newman, Eric. *Flyfisher's Guide to New York*. Belgrade, MT: Wilderness Adventures Press, 2003.

Perich, Shawn. *Fishing Lake Superior: A Complete Guide to Stream, Shoreline, and Open-water Angling*. Minneapolis: University of Minnesota Press, 2002.

———. *Fly-Fishing the North Country*. Duluth, MN: Pfeifer-Hamilton, 1995.

Roosevelt, Robert Barnwell. *Superior Fishing*. New York: Carleton, 1865. Digitized, Memphis: General Books, 2009.

Rybaak, Spider. *Fishing Western New York*. Guilford, CT: Globe Pequot Press, 2004.

Sander, John M. *Sander's Fishing Guide: Western New York Edition*. Amherst, NY: Sander's Fishing Guides, 1992.

Smith, Scott E. *Ontario Blue-Ribbon Fly Fishing Guide*. Portland, OR: Frank Amato Publications, 1999.

Streeter, Robert W. *New York Fly Fishing Guide*. Portland, OR: Frank Amato Publications, 2000.

Tabory, Lou. *Inshore Fly Fishing, 2nd Edition: A Pioneering Guide to Fly Fishing Along Cold-Water Seacoasts*. Guilford, CT: Lyons Press, 2011.

Tomes, Robert S. *Muskie on the Fly*. Mill Creek, WA: Wild River Press, 2008.

Von Schrader, George. *Carp Are Gamefish*. Mountain Home, AR: Gil Finn Books, 1990.

Weixlmann, Karl. *Great Lakes Steelhead, Salmon & Trout: Essential Techniques for Fly Fishing the Tribuataries*. Harrisburg, PA: Stackpole Books, 2009.

Wolfe, Dave. *Flyfisher's Guide to Pennsylvania*. Belgrade, MT: Wilderness Adventures Press, 1999.

Acknowledgments

I n a work such as this, there are certainly a large number of people to thank for making my vision become a reality. First of all, I was lucky enough to have two outstanding writers, D'arcy Egan and Bob Linsensman, serve as mentors. Thank you, D'arcy, for encouraging me to write "way back when." Bob, thank you for your advice in helping me pitch this idea to a publisher and for writing the foreword.

My long-time friend Jeff Liskay spent countless hours and miles helping me explore and experiment at a variety of locations around the lakes. Thanks for being there whenever I asked. The following folks selflessly gave time on the water; shared information, fly patterns, photos; or gave any kind of help I asked for. Some of you I have never met face-to-face; some of you are now good friends. All of you helped make this book possible: Capt. Austin Adduci, Ian Anderson, Dave Barkman, Eli Berant, Graham Bristow, Ouitdee Carson, Paul Castellano, Graham Coombs, Scott Currie, Wael Dardir, Matt Erny, Capt. Kevin Feenstra, Glen Hales, Paul Hansen, Dustan Harley, Chris Helm, Jeff Hinz, Ady Hoke, Neil Houlding, Pat Kelly, Geoff Kowalczyk, Ted Kraimer, Rick Kustich, Bart Landwehr, Capt. Roger Lapenter, Jim Linehan, Russ Maddin, Capt. Brian Meszaros, Brett McCrae, Capt. Kevin Morlock, Kelly Neuman, Jim Oates, Tim Pearson, Capt. Brad Petzke, Charlie Piette, Dave Pinczkowski, Nick Pionessa, Capt. Jon Ray, Mike Schmidt, Mike Schultz, Greg Senyo, Capt. Jim Sharpe, Bill Sherer, Jim Simonelli, Nate Sipple, Scott Earl Smith, Scott Thorpe, Robert Tomes, Jon Uhlenhop, John Valk, April Vokey, Steve Wascher, Karl Weixlmann, Capt. Leo Wright, Matt Zudweg. If I have forgtten to name someone, please forgive me. Thanks so much, everyone, for your help.

Thanks also to my editor, Jay Nichols, who organized my random words and sentences into a readable, understandable form. To Amy Lerner and all the folks at Stackpole Books—thank you for your help.

To my wife, Lori, and daughters, Leah and Christy—thanks for accepting me as I am and putting up with me. I love you dearly.

Finally, I would like to dedicate this book in memory of my parents, Mark and Helen Darkes, who always encouraged me to go fishing, and to Michael Bennett and Tom Helgeson, two Great Lakes fly fishers who left us way too soon.

Index

Page numbers in italics indicate illustrations and sidebars.